ERASURE OF THE EURO-ASIAN

ERASURE OF THE EURO-ASIAN

recovering early radicalism and feminism in South Asia

Kumari Jayawardena

women UNLIMITED
an associate of
kali for women

Erasure of the Euro-Asian
was first published in 2007
by
Social Scientists' Association
No. 12, Sulaiman Terrace, Colombo 5
Sri Lanka

This edition published in 2009
by
Women Unlimited
(an associate of Kali for Women)
K-36, Hauz Khas Enclave
New Delhi-110016

ISBN: 81-88965-40-5

Cover design: Neelima Rao

Printed at Raj Press, R-3, Inderpuri, New Delhi-110012

"The youthful band of reformers who had been educated at the Hindoo College, like the tops of the Kanchenjunga, *were the first to catch and reflect the dawn.*"

Kishorichand Mitra, writing in 1866, on the Derozians of the Young Bengal group (quoted in Susobhan Sarkar, 1979, p.111, emphasis added)

"He had no mother, no father, no country, no nationality, no lineage, no God even."

Rabindranath Tagore, on Gora, who discovered that he was not a Bengali Brahmin, but an orphan of Irish parentage (from *Gora* [1910], 2002, p.562)

"The cry is *forward.* Every man now labours for future good… Whatever Folly had established, and Imbecility has… sanctioned, is passing away; and all things are about to be… more in accordance with the design of Nature and the necessities of Man… *We live not for the past… our physical… and mental powers are directed to higher objects which are yet before us — to other times which are yet to come — to generations yet unborn.*"

Charles Lorenz, essay in *Young Ceylon,* c.1850, quoted in B.R. Blazé, *The Life of Lorenz* (1948, p.11, emphasis added)

In memory of Lal

and for Rohan & Suriya

Contents

Preface i

Introduction: The Utopian Vision of Euro-Asians 1

Part I: CREATING EURO-ASIAN COMMUNITIES

1. Portuguese and Dutch Colonialism and the *Mestiços* **19**

The Portuguese Confrontation 19

Casados and the Mixing of Races 21

Racism of the Portuguese 27

Race and Gender during Dutch Rule 29

Euro-Asians of the Dutch Indies 35

2. Racial Mixing during British Rule **37**

Mixed Reactions to Mixed-race Liaisons 37

Defining Burghers 41

The New Community of Eurasians 45

Singapore Eurasians 45

What's in a Name? 46

Appearance and the 'Colour Chart' 49

Patriarchy and Mixed-race Descent 52

3. Class, 'Caste' and Taking 'Stock' **55**

Stratification among Euro-Asians 55

Liaisons in the Planter Raj 62

The Paynter Homes for Euro-Asians 70

'Tommy Conquests' 73

'Railway Stock' 78

Part II: EURO-ASIAN RADICALISM AND MODERNISM

4. Fears of Euro-Asian Subversion **85**

The 'Subversive' Hybrid 85

Enlightenment, Revolution and Early Anti-Colonialism 87

Fearsome '*Mulattos*' 90

The Baptist 'Menace' 91

The Age of Reason and Secularism 94

The Utopian Socialist Vision 95

"Claptrap about liberty of the press" 97

Colonial Intelligentsia – 'not quite white' 98

5. Henry Derozio and Young Bengal 'Catching the Dawn' **100**

Kolkata Euro-Asians 100

The Derozio Phenomenon 103

The "Root of all Evils" 107

Young Bengal 109

The Rights of Women 112

The 'Other England' and Byronic Transcendent Nationalism 113

"Mad, Bad and Dangerous to Know" 115

Derozio and Euro-Asian Politics 117

Erasure of the Kolkata Euro-Asians 120

John Ricketts and the Rights of Euro-Asians 121

6. 'Turbulence' among Euro-Asians and Europeans **127**

Euro-Asian Lawyers 127

Political Struggles in Europe 129

Radicalism in Sri Lanka in the 1840s 132

Dr Christopher Elliot and Local Dissidents 134

Richard Morgan's Early Radicalism 140

7. 'Riotous Independence' of the Lorenzians 145

The Magic Aura and *Young Ceylon* 145
Charles Lorenz in Politics 147
Frederick Nell and "discordant notes" 152
The *Examiner* – Promoting Pluralism 153
Lorenz's Secularism 155
Nascent Oppositional Politics 159
Leopold Ludovici and the *Examiner* 163
John L.K. van Dort – Artist of Social Satire 165

8. Radicalism and Workers' Rights 167

The Tradition of Charles Lorenz 167
A.E. Buultjens Follows Lorenz 169
Secular and Socialist Influences 172
From Agnosticism to Buddhism 173
Striking at Capital 175
Lisboa Pinto and the Indo-Portuguese Connection 177

Part III: GENDER, PATRIARCHY AND NATION

9. Myths of the 'Oriental' and Euro-Asian Woman 185

The 'Orient' in Western Culture 185
Fantasies of the 'Half-Caste' Woman 195
The Euro-Asian Image 198
Leonard Woolf and Pablo Neruda among Euro-Asians 203
Euro-Asian Self-portrayals 205
The Asian Gaze on Euro-Asians 207

10. The Euro-Asian 'New Woman' 212

Feminist Consciousness among Euro-Asians 212
The Sri Lankan Debate on Women 213
The Euro-Asian Headstart in Education 218

Breaking into the Medical Patriarchy 222
Anglo-Indian Pioneers 225
Modernism in Education 227
Pioneers of the Nell Clan: Eleanor Lorenz, Winifred Nell, Agnes, Anil & Minnette de Silva 228

11. Revivalism and Gender **239**

Eurasians as *Mischmaschvolk* 239
The 'Pure' and the 'Hybrid' 243
The Aryan Myth in Asia 247
Creating Tradition 251
Gender and Nation 252
"They Be All Whores" 255

12. 'Correctly' Reproducing the Nation **258**

Laissez-faire and Mixed Marriage 258
Mudaliyars, Capitalists and Professionals Marrying 'out' 261
Local Bourgeois Women defying Tradition 266
Buddhists against Mixed Marriages 268
Statistics of Admixture 272
Mixed Marriages in India, Pakistan and Bangladesh 275

13. Conclusion: Euro-Asians As Public Intellectuals **281**

Bibliography **289**

Index **303**

Illustrations

Amrita Shergil — opposite title page
Charles Lorenz – cartoon of himself — *15*

Part I

- 'Mestice woman going to church in state,' 1808, — preceeding Chapter 1
- A Portuguese Mechanic. — end of Chapter 3
- 'Mestice woman,' 1711.
- Arthur Paynter, his wife and her brother.
  Paynter Homes' children and teachers and Allan, Fannie and James.
- British Officer of the 73rd Regiment and Bombardier Alexander. A. J. van der Poorten & family

Part II

- George Keyt's "Woman with Sarangi", 1945. — preceeding Chapter 4
- The *Examiner* editorial group, *1862.* — end of Chapter 8
- The Pretender of 1848 and Sketches by Charles Lorenz .
- Charles Lorenz, Dr Christopher Elliot, Richard Morgan, Frederick Nell.
- Henry Derozio, John Ricketts, David Hare.
- The Derozians of 'Young Bengal'.
- A.E. Buultjens, his wife Sylvia and family.
- Dr Pedro Manuel Lisboa Pinto.

Part III

- Anil de Silva, circa 1955, photographed by Henri Cartier-Bresson. — preceeding Chapter 9
- Agnes de Silva driving a Ford car — 238
- Vivien Leigh, Merle Oberon, Marlon Brando and Anna Kashfi. — end of Chapter 12
- Sri Lankan medical students, 1911.
- Dr Alice de Boer and Dr James Loos.

- Constance Blacker, Cora Abraham, Bertha Rodgers, Emily van der Poorten and Julia Hermon.
- Three generations of the Nells, 1909.
- Jawaharlal Nehru, Agnes and George de Silva. Minnette de Silva with Pablo Piccaso and Mulk Raj Anand.
- Kewal Motwani and Clara Heath. Walter de Soysa and first wife. Charles Don Carolis and Lillian Gregory. Henry Engelbrecht's granddaughter Lily Nona.
- Patrick Kularatne and Hilda Westbrook; Dr G.P. Malalasekera and Margaret Russell.
- Dr S.A. Wickremasinghe and Doreen Young; Eleanor Hutton and Dr A.P. de Zoysa.

Portrait of Agnes de Silva by David Paynter. 288
Portuguese Kaffiringha dancers by J.L.K. van Dort. last page

Tables

1 The Nell family tree. end of Chapter 8
2 The Lorenz family tree. end of Chapter 8
3 Literates of each Sex and Race. 219
4 Statistics of Mixed Marriages. 273

Preface

While writing this book, I wondered why I had chosen the topic. Was it because I belonged to an ethnic category that intrigued me – being 'officially' Sinhala but biologically Euro-Asian with a Sinhala Buddhist father and an English agnostic mother? So if I was Euro-Asian (a term I have coined), why did local Burghers and Eurasians argue that I did not belong to their communities since my father was Sinhala? The answer was that ethnicity has always been determined by paternal descent under the patriarchal laws of the country during and after colonial rule. This meant not only that my mother was 'erased,' but also that there were many like me, who 'passed' for Sinhala, Tamil or Muslim but whose real mixed ethnic identity was ignored.

Since some of my research in the past has been on feminist and ethnic issues, it interested me that two persons of the same admixture (Asian/European) could be classed on the basis of *paternal* origin, as belonging to two different *ethnic* groups – namely the local group which prided itself on its 'purity,' and the group of Euro-Asian origin, considered 'hybrid.' Another reason that made me curious was that critics of my views on the ethnic issue or on feminism often labelled me '*sankara*' – a derogatory Sinhala word connoting a person of mixed ethnic origin.

I also noticed that there were many Euro-Asians of *paternal* European descent such as Charles Lorenz and A.E. Buultjens whose pioneering contributions to political and social change in the 19th century were 'erased,' while illustrious Euro-Asians of *maternal* European descent such as Ananda Coomaraswamy were revered and commemorated. I decided to pursue some issues concerning hybridity and find out about the origins, politics and ideology of the mixed community during colonial rule. In doing so, I came across some forgotten Euro-Asians – namely the Burgher, Anglo-Indian and Eurasian radicals who, in both India and Sri Lanka, were inspired by the Enlightenment, the French Revolution, as well as by their association with dissident radicals in the West and western radicals in the colonies.

These Euro-Asians who were, in modern parlance, 'public intellectuals,' questioned both foreign domination and oppressive local social structures, and played an important part in modernizing society. Rather than being 'marginal' to society they were utopian-like visionaries and agitators, active on important political and social issues long before the time was ripe for major reforms or social change. Their support was for nascent nationalism, feminism, pluralism, secularism, and the rights of workers and peasants. They also opposed those South Asian hierarchical formations based on caste, ethnicity, patriarchy and semi-feudal class structures. If these Euro-Asian men and women, so many decades ahead of their time, were in the vanguard of democratic struggles and of reform and resistance to Church and State – why were they 'hidden from history'? If much was written about women of mixed origin who were represented and fantasized about in western culture as the exotic 'Other,' why was the role of Euro-Asian women as early South Asian feminists forgotten? What is more, why were all these pioneering Euro-Asians not celebrated as national heroes? This book attempts to answer these questions. It inquires into issues of 'purity' and 'pollution,' and the critique of the 'hybrid' as a source of contamination and cultural subversion, resulting not only in the erasure of the Euro-Asians from South Asian history, but also a failure to recognize their contributions to radical politics and feminism in the region.

This book does not, however, claim to be a history of the Euro-Asians, although some data about their origins, as well as the attitudes of Europeans and other local communities to those of European-Asian origin, is discussed. It is rather an attempt to highlight the radical achievements of the Euro-Asians and the reasons why these have not been recognized. I am also aware that the topic of my research is a sensitive one. There are people of all communities who claim 'purity' and deny that they are of 'mixed' origin, and disclaim European or 'native' ancestors as the case may be. Others are concerned with nomenclature and resent being referred to as 'Eurasians.' I hope I have not caused offence, but I refer in this book to *all* of European and Asian origin through maternal or paternal ancestry as 'Euro-Asian,' including Burghers, Anglo-Indians and communities calling themselves 'Eurasian.'

In researching this book, I used the Sri Lanka National Archives and the libraries of universities and civil society organizations in Sri Lanka, including the Dutch Burgher Union and the Tulana Library, Kelaniya. I also obtained material from the British Library in London and the library of the National University in Singapore. I consulted many secondary sources and interviewed scholars in India, Sri Lanka and Singapore, who had written on Euro-Asians, as well as individuals of mixed origin who narrated their own histories. Invaluable sources of material were the writings of Michael Roberts, and the work of B.R. Blazé, Deloraine Brohier, Neloufer de Mel, C.R. de Silva, Ann Stoler, Jean Arasanayagam, Dennis McGilvray, Donovan Moldrich and Carl Muller. I thank Robert Crusz, Malathi de Alwis, Neloufer de Mel, S.B.D. de Silva, Ram Manikkalingam, Judith Waters Pasqualge, Vyvette Uyangoda, Suriya Wickremasinghe and May Yee for reading the manuscript, and making valuable suggestions. For substantive editing, advice on content and help with secondary sources my sincere thanks to May Yee. For permission to use the Ivan Peries watercolour on the cover I thank Veronica Peries, and for designing the cover I am grateful to Albert Dharmasiri.

Many thanks also to those who were generous with their ideas and comments on my research, and helped in tracing material for this book. They are: Patricia Alailima, Mano Anandappa, S. Anandasivam, Jean Arasanayagam, Parvati Arasanayagam, Jasodhara Bagchi, Susie Beling, Kamla Bhasin, Shobana Bhattacharji, Clifton Bocks, Myrna Braga-Blake, Deloraine Brohier, Andrew Buultjens, Ardil Cader, Paul Caspersz, Radhika Coomaraswamy, Malathi de Alwis, Ranjani de Mel, C.R. de Silva, R.K. de Silva, Shehara de Silva, Peter Ronald deSouza, Christopher Don Carolis, Manel Fonseka, Lakmali Gunawardena, Goolbai Gunasekara, Elizabeth Harris, Ameena Hussein, Laksiri Jayasuriya, Pradeep

Jeganathan, Rosanna Favero-Karunaratne, Rehan Kularatne, Rachel Kurian, Farida Macan Markar, I. S. Madanayake, Sucheta Mazumdar, Nivedita Menon, Ritu Menon, Jennifer Moragoda, Carl Muller, J.B. Müller, Ramani Muttetuwegama, Vasuki Nesiah, Nimanthi Rajasingham-Perera, Ranjith Perera, Sam Perera, Sonali Perera, Amali Philips, L.S.D. Pieris, Ismeth Raheem, Delini Raheem, Anne Ranasinghe, V.K. Ramachandran, Chitra Ranawake, Michael Roberts, Gerard Robouchon, Aurele Samuel, Shyam Selvadurai, Maya Senanayake, Vivan Sundaram, Gayani Sylva, Sithie Tiruchelvam, P. Thambirajah, Tula Tuominen, Jayadeva Uyangoda, Menika van der Poorten, Ananda Wakkumbura, Neville Weereratne and Lorna Wright.

I thank Rasika Chandrasekera for formatting the book and am grateful for her support at all times. Many thanks to Quintus Fernando for preparing the manuscript and compiling the Index. I thank Prarthana Gamaaratchige for checking the Index and Chandrika Withanapathirana, Aruna Prasanna Enderage, Sultan Shahul Hameed, Rohana Wasantha, Anil Jayath and Ajith de Silva of the Social Scientists' Association for their assistance in many ways. Thanks also to Ajith Kumarasiri who helped in archival searches and to Amanda Kumarasiri, A.L. Hajireen, Vidya Abhayagunawardena, H.G. Dilan, S. K. Harischandra and R. Yogarajah for their support; as well as to Chatura Jayankitha, Gayani Sudasingha, Ajanta Kumara and others at the Karunaratne Press for their help in this publication.

Kumari Jayawardena
Colombo, 2007

INTRODUCTION

THE UTOPIAN VISION OF EURO-ASIANS

> The utopian ideas of the early 19th century can be said to have emerged from the contradiction between the possibilities of creating a better life for all and the [prevailing] backward and inhuman social relations and institutions.
>
> Maria Mies, "Utopian Socialism and Women's Emancipation," in Maria Mies and Kumari Jayawardena, *Feminism in Europe*, 1981, p.37

The poet of imperialism, Rudyard Kipling in 1889 wrote the famous lines "East is East and West is West / and never the twain shall meet." But the twain did meet with European conquests in Asia. Along with the heavy imprint of foreign rule in terms of the political economy, legal system, education, lifestyle and culture, was the dramatic emergence of Euro-Asian Christian communities in the colonial territories including India, Sri Lanka, Myanmar, Indonesia, Philippines, Vietnam, Macau, East Timor, Malaysia, Singapore and Hong Kong. These communities were the descendants of European men and local women, and although small in number relative to the total populations of the colonized lands, had a lasting impact on colonial society. They were known by many names.

Persons of mixed European and Asian origin have had problems in nomenclature and have been sensitive about the terms used to denote their particular community. During Portuguese occupation, the words officially used for those of mixed origin were *mestiços* (male), *mestiças* (female); the Spanish used *mestizo* and *mestiza;* the French, *métis, métisse* and the British word was '*mixed*'. The derogatory but often-used terms were, however, *mulatto, half-blood* or *half-caste* (English) and *mulâtre/ mulâtresse* (French) and *halfbloed* in Dutch. In India, other terms such as 'Eurasian' and 'East Indian' were used and discarded; finally, 'Anglo-Indian' came into official and popular usage, although it was also used for Europeans resident in India. In Sri Lanka, the Dutch descendants were called 'Dutch Burghers' but the term 'Burgher' was also applied to designate people of Portuguese descent, while those of British/Asian descent were referred to as 'Eurasians.' In all these cases, the European ancestor had to be in the paternal line. In South Asia, the term 'Eurasian' unfortunately acquired a pejorative connotation. It is, however, an accurate term, but in this book I refer to *all of mixed Asian/European origin* as 'Euro-Asian' whatever the European land of origin or the extent of admixture, and irrespective of whether the European ancestry was in the paternal or maternal line.

In numbers, the Euro-Asian community in Asia remained small. But what is often forgotten and unrecorded is that in urban and rural areas and plantations, liaisons between local women and European planters, traders, soldiers, skilled workers and officials produced numbers of Euro-Asian children who were not enumerated as such in the censuses. They merged with the local population, and were usually categorized as belonging to their mothers' ethnic group. In Asian colonies, as Ann Stoler has claimed, there were many more Euro-Asian children "than official statistics often revealed" (1991: 78).

In politics, many Euro-Asians of South Asia collaborated with the foreign rulers and took a cautious, conservative stance on issues. However, others were radical, with a Utopian-like vision of a democratic, plural society of the future. They emerged as catalysts for modernization and social change, and were, on occasion, proto-nationalist and feminist, participating in the vanguard of the early anti-colonial challenge. In Sri Lanka, they were, what Michael Roberts (1989) called, 'the people in between,' who liaised in two languages between the rulers and the ruled. Many performed intermediate functions (especially in government service). Others included intellectuals and independent professionals (lawyers, doctors, writers and politicians) who had the freedom to simultaneously take a critical look at both the colonial rulers and indigenous social structures and practices. The Euro-Asian community was also composed of the earliest trade-union leaders, and of craftspersons and members of the petty bourgeoisie and working class, who in many instances were the first to be conscious of their rights as workers (Jayawardena 1972).

Recently, more attention has been focused – especially by feminists – on persons, groups and movements that have been "hidden from history," to use the title of Sheila Rowbotham's book (1973). One such group has been the Euro-Asian community, the visible byproducts of European colonial conquest who were not only hidden, but often also erased from the historical record. While the existence of Euro-Asians had been a challenge in terms of race to both the European rulers and 'native' ruled, the services of the Euro-Asians were also much needed. They have been in consequence both praised and reviled by the 'pure' Europeans and 'pure' Asians, whose attitudes to Euro-Asians have ranged from admiration for their role as interlocutors and modernizers, to ambivalence and bigotry towards the 'hybrid.'

In this context, what did the mixing of peoples (*métissage*) entail, politically and socially? According to Stoler, "*métissage* represented, not the dangers of foreign enemies at national borders" but its "interior frontiers." which the German philosopher Fichte called "the essence of the nation." She adds that this meant that "*the purity of a community* was prone to penetration on its *interior and exterior borders*" (1997: 199, emphasis added). The imperialist expansion of the 19th century and the growth of racist theories in Europe increased concern and anxiety about a country's internal borders. In Germany, for example, obsessiveness with racial purity and supremacy led to lines being drawn between the 'pure' and 'impure,' the latter being defined as inferior or *untermensch* (sub-human) and a threat to the majority.

While such concerns influenced German political life, a similar fear persisted in South Asia, where, on occasion, the internal 'enemy' became more immediate than the external. Indian and Sri Lankan nationalists of the late 19th century, while resenting the 'external' invasion and colonization by foreigners, were alert to perceived 'interior' threats to the dominant local culture from minority ethnic and religious groups. In Sri Lanka, from the 1880s onwards, the preoccupation of the early nationalists with 'Aryanness' meant a demonizing of the 'lower races' of other ethnic and religious origins, the valorizing of Sinhala Buddhism, and a demeaning of the 'impure' Christian Euro-Asian.

The mixing of the races presented a problem to both the white rulers and the non-white ruled in terms of 'purity of race.' Hybridity, as Robert Young remarks, was threatening as it implies the "impossibility of essentialism" (1995: 27), challenging the claims of 'purity of race' which had been a 'sacred cow' in both the Eastern and Western traditions. The nation state with its boundaries and borders highlighted ethnic purity to justify the concept of 'nation.' In doing so, racism often became a strong component of nationalism and of the ideology of the nation-state, thereby resulting in the marginalization of minorities. In the 19th century when European Orientalists were writing on the Indo-Aryan language group, some Indian and Sri Lankan nationalists constructed myths of racial purity and 'Aryan' origin. To both Europeans and Asians, the Euro-Asians or *mischmaschvolk* (bastard people), as the Germans termed the 'others,' were subverters of the 'pure' race.

Obsession with racial purity gave rise consequently to issues of racial mixing. In the absence of European women in the colonies, policies about mixed marriages and liaisons had to be formulated. The Portuguese in the 16th century, although reputedly non-racist, had placed importance on *pureza de sangue* (purity of blood) and officially resorted to abusive phrases such as *raças infectas,* namely 'impure' or 'contaminated' races (Boxer 1973a: 251). According to the anthropologist Mary Douglas, concepts of 'dirt' and 'disorder' in a society, were linked to "certain moral values... and social rules defined by beliefs in dangerous contagion" (1989: 3). A French traveller in the 1650s commented on the *mestiços* of Goa, claiming that "the stigma of having an Indian woman ancestor" lasted to the hundredth generation (Yale and Burnell 1986: 604). Ironically, however, this did not prevent the Portuguese administration in the colonies from encouraging their army personnel to marry local women – hoping thereby to create a mixed community supportive of Portuguese colonialism. The Dutch also had bigoted attitudes on 'purity' and 'pollution' based on the "innate conviction of white superiority" (Boxer 1973b: 261).

Colonial ideology was not only based on asserting racial superiority and purity, but was also an upholder of male hegemony. Sarojini Jayawickrema's re-reading of Robert Knox's 17th century account of the Kandyan kingdom stresses that "the most salient threat to the blurring of the defining markers of identity that separated colonizer and colonized" was the female 'Other.' She claims that the "intersecting discourses of gender and race" gave rise to fears of "sexual contamination, cultural decline and moral breakdown," and suggests that the realities of colonial life provided an insight into "the inordinate anxiety about the loss of racial purity" (Jayawickrema 2004: 125-26).

At the time of the advent of British imperialism there were mixed communities already in existence, and in the early decades of British rule, liaisons and marriages between Europeans and Asians were tolerated. But racist attitudes prevailed among diehards, who believed that the 'pollution' of mixed blood also had dangerous political implications. At certain periods of time, European rulers warned of the Euro-Asian potential not only for revolutionary or anti-colonial political activity, but also for reformist agitation led by the more intellectual members of the mixed community, who were considered a threat and a political liability. Viscount Valentia, in the early 1800s, sounded the alarm that the growth in the numbers of 'half-caste' children was "the most rapidly increasing evil of Bengal" and predicted that their links with 'the natives' was politically subversive (Stark 1934: 19).

The *Calcutta Review* in 1870 alleged that "the worst points of both the European and native character are not infrequently combined in the hybrid" (quoted in Sen 2002: 47). But these "worst points" were undefined, and they may have included the subversive potential of Euro-Asians and their links with radical Europeans resident in the colonies who were considered 'disorderly' and 'turbulent.' As Indrani Sen has suggested, there were also other reasons why Euro-Asians were "a colonial embarrassment":

> Racial hybridity… [was] viewed with anxiety as potentially subversive of race hierarchies in the colony, *bridging that vital social distance between the ruler and the ruled* and eventually threatening the stability of colonial identities. (Sen 2002: 48, emphasis added)

The community of Euro-Asians – which allegedly faced both ways – inevitably caused concern, especially as the mixing of races in all the colonies also created specific political and legal problems. It disturbed, for example, "the very criteria by which Europeans could be identified, citizenship … recorded, and nationality assigned" (Stoler 1997: 199). Where there were two sets of laws, European law for resident Europeans and local customary law for the 'natives,' the question was which of them should apply to the *mixed population?* This issue became problematic for Euro-Asians in early 19th century India. In the French and Dutch colonies too, jurists found the question of citizenship of Euro-Asians a vexing problem. A Dutch lawyer, J.A. Nederburgh, quoting a statement that "in the civilized world, no one may be without a relationship to the state," drafted colonial laws in 1898 to cover the new category of Euro-Asians whom he called the "wavering classes." Colonialism had, he argued, destroyed 'racial purity' and made obsolete the old criteria of nationality, namely place of birth (*jus soli*) and blood-descent (*jus sanguinus*). On these two counts, the Euro-Asians "questioned the earlier criteria" (ibid: 215).

Since Euro-Asians had access to reformist and revolutionary European thinking, and were in contact with both radical politicians in Europe and European radicals in the colonies, the dangers that such ideas would be transmitted to other sections of the local population also seemed to be ever-present. In many colonies (including Dutch-ruled Indonesia), the question facing the ruling group (as summarized by Stoler) was:

> What could be done with this mixed population, whose ambiguous positioning and identifications could make them either dangerous adversaries or effective partisans of the colonial state?
> (Stoler 1997: 208-9)

The multi-class nature of the Eurasians caused their basic ideologies to vary and shift with the times. In 19th century India and Sri Lanka, for example, there were significant reformist and radical trends among the Euro-Asians, and their challenges to colonial authority made them "dangerous adversaries." But the trend weakened by the early 20th century, to be replaced by a conservative conformism and loyalty to British rule. The earlier proto-nationalist radicalism of Eurasians was erased from history, while the loyal and collaborationist image of Eurasians as "partisans of the colonial state" was reinforced.

In South Asia, Europeans, Euro-Asians and the 'natives' had their stereotypes about each other. Nationalists, who were anti-European, generally despised and distrusted the Euro-Asians as supporters of foreign rule, while the Europeans were varied in their assessment. At certain moments, the Euro-Asians were seen as subversive and potentially seditious, and at other times as allies. Carl Muller, a Burgher, writing about his community, claims that the British saw "something vaguely off-white" about them, and since Burghers were "rooted in the west," the British could relate to them with greater ease, while not trusting the other locals and believing that "black skins were the receptacles of black hearts" (1994: 11). In turn the Euro-Asians, while being ideologically "rooted in the west" and clinging to a European lifestyle, deplored the arrogance and racism of the colonial Europeans which often affected them. To the Europeans, the Euro-Asians had the 'taint of the tar brush,' and to the 'natives,' the Euro-Asians were not only coated in 'whitewash,' but were also a source of pollution and therefore of social disorder. The Euro-Asians themselves had a hierarchical system involving (as in caste society) the observance of social distance – the 'Brahmins' among Euro-Asians often not consorting with those at lower levels on the socio-economic ladder.

The attitudes of the colonial powers towards the mixed groups were also tinged with a sense of guilt and shame. There was the Christian guilt about liaisons with local women and shame about their illegitimate children. Racial 'purity' was deemed to be morally correct, and 'hybridity' was seen by both Europeans and Asians as a moral flaw (Pereira 1995: 5). The Euro-Asian was said to "live in two worlds, in both of which he is more or less a stranger" (R.E. Park 1950, quoted in Pereira 1995: 9). In the Netherlands Indies (Indonesia) and French Indochina (Vietnam, Laos and Cambodia), *métissage* or interracial unions, according to Stoler, were seen as "a dangerous source of subversion ... a threat to white prestige, and an embodiment of European degeneration and moral decay" (Stoler 1997: 199). The Dutch in the Indies viewed the poorer elements of the mixed population as "déraciné, rootless, and therefore dangerous" (ibid: 224); and a Dutch Governor of Sri Lanka referred to the island's Portuguese *mestiços* as "*canaille*" (rabble) (Reimers 1932: 18). Hawes (1996) called Anglo-Indians the *Poor Relations*, who could, however, cause various types of problems.

Euro-Asian identity was often fragmented, and sometimes even hidden. Where there was achievement, there was often denial; the celebrated film stars Merle Oberon and Vivien Leigh were careful not to acknowledge their mixed Indian origin, regarded as a stigma that might affect their careers. For Euro-Asians, there was no geographic location, no plausible historic myth of ethnic origin based on purity or high status, and there was no caste identity based on occupation. Nor did they have folk heroes who defended the land and died for the 'race,' and there was no literature extolling their early glories. One important aspect of Euro-Asian identity was their alienation from the local caste system which dominated the lives of Hindus in India and Sinhala and Tamil society in Sri Lanka. In fact, Euro-Asians led the way in denouncing caste. In Kolkata in the 1820s, the Hindu followers of the reformist Euro-Asian, Henry Derozio, "broke asunder the shackles of caste and ate with their Eurasian friend" (Sastri 1907: 66). In Sri Lanka Eurasians spoke out against caste. For example, Richard Morgan opposed the caste system especially in the selection of juries, and Frederick Nell, in the 1850s expressed revulsion about the "leprosy of caste" (Roberts et al 1989: 83).

The situation was complex and complicated, as Euro-Asians did not identify totally with either or both of their "parent races or cultures" (Stonequiest, quoted in Pereira 1995: 3). In the colonies, some of them who associated with the European colonialists tried to 'pass' for white.

Or as Kenneth E. Wallace said, "The lighter-hued Eurasian is often tempted to pass as a domiciled European" (quoted in Cox 1948: 385). Such persons were politically pro-colonial, spoke of Britain as 'Home' and held conservative political views while being modern in their lifestyles. With the mixing of the races it was not just the complexion that changed. Euro-Asians, who were more attuned to the West and its world outlook and social practices, were inevitably more receptive to western ideologies, culture and other influences. Moreover, the Euro-Asians represented themselves as 'western,' as they were immersed in the history, political ideology and lifestyles of the West.

But the western heritage that Euro-Asians valorized also had a tradition of dissent and protest against injustices of many kinds, including the arrogance of colonial rulers. The thinkers of the Enlightenment in the 18th century and the events of the French Revolution influenced Euro-Asians in their opposition to racism, feudal structures, hereditary privilege, aristocratic hauteur, tyrannical monarchs, the caste system, inequality and oppression. Revolutionary upheavals in Europe – especially France – in the late 18th and first half of the 19th centuries, reverberated in the colonies and these events were keenly followed through newspaper reports, especially by the Euro-Asian intelligentsia in India and Sri Lanka, who also idolized the poets of protest, notably Byron, Keats and Shelley.

Euro-Asians could be the subverters of both the colonialists' hegemony and local traditions and structures. To the British, it was difficult to dismiss them as 'mongrels' and 'hybrids' since they were also composed of leading professionals and public intellectuals, who could speak out fearlessly. In addition, educated Euro-Asians, being part European and westernized, could challenge and take on the British at their own game, using European radical thought as a weapon against colonial oppression as well as feudal and autocratic local systems. Euro-Asians thus often opposed the misdeeds of colonial rulers while being simultaneously critical of local customs, traditions, taboos and values. The problem was that the mixture of races had created an indeterminate social identity which did not fall into earlier accepted categories.

Significantly, Piyadasa Sirisena, who in 1916 wrote a cautionary tale on the dangers of mixed liaisons, called it *Maha Viyavula (The Great Disorder).*

Apart from the fact of 'hybridity' raising problematic issues of class, racial origin, skin colour, language, culture, history and politics, there was also the question of patriarchy. For Euro-Asians, there could only be a fairly recent genealogy that began when a male European trader, official, soldier, settler or adventurer in a colony founded a family. Patriarchy was the dominant ideology and European descent in the father's line ensured recognition and acceptance as a Euro-Asian. Mothers were thereby 'erased', and the European name was officially recognized, however dark the skin colour of the offspring of intermarriage. Obsession with genealogy and colour was common among the mixed population who were concerned about their claims to European ancestry. Racial pride and class bias were also seen in the aphorism understood in South Asia that 'the poor are dark and the rich are fair.' Ironically, however, the preferred skin colour for a European was to be tanned as a Euro-Asian, but not as dark as a 'native'; and to locals it was to be fair-skinned like a Euro-Asian, but not as fair as a European.

It was on the issue of western lifestyle and culture that Euro-Asians were ostracized and reviled by those nationalists who were concerned about 'purity'. The stereotype Burgher in Sri Lanka lived for the day, in Carl Muller's words, always "putting a party," drinking, dancing and eating beef and pork – all anathema to the traditionalists who used numerous abusive epithets for these 'impure' ones. A Burgher himself, Muller's popular novels are hilarious farces, based on the alleged loose lifestyles of the poorer Burghers who spoke a distinct English (almost a *patois*) that was neither 'pure' English nor Sinhala, but often a literal English rendering of Sinhala words and phrases.

But class issues predominated, and those educated Euro-Asians of India and Sri Lanka, whose earliest ancestors were high officials and army personnel, and who had wealth and economic security, were proud of their connection to upper-class Europeans. They drew a boundary between themselves and the poorer Euro-Asians, descended from subalterns in the British army, or from other colonial 'poor whites' such as shop assistants and railwaymen. Country of origin and religion was also linked to class. The lighter-skinned, upper-class Euro-Asians constructed for themselves an 'imagined community' that was white, Protestant and of Dutch or British origin, distinguishable from the darker-skinned of Portuguese origin who were Catholics. Class was also a sensitive issue, especially since in colonial times mixed liaisons and marriages had often taken place between men of a higher social standing than the local women. The children's future was unpredictable – some were assimilated to the mother's community, while others including those from orphanages often succeeded in professions, in trade and in the plantation sector.

Since the words 'hybrid' or half-caste' often implied 'bastard,' those of mixed origin were keen to establish legitimacy and therefore respectability. The focus was on education, wealth and western lifestyles, including dress and behaviour patterns, and an ability to speak 'correct' English, as well as concern about skin colour that offered visible proof of foreign origin. Among the 'top' Euro-Asians however, there were further divisions – the most important being political – between radicals and conservatives. Some were supportive of British rule, but a minority developed into radical critics of colonial policies as well as local customs and practices.

In both European and Asian culture and society, one common factor was the importance attributed to class and social identity. The categories of class, caste and ethnicity determined high or low status and became distinct markers of social identity. In the case of Europe, with the development of the nation state, the 'nation' came to be associated with the rule of the majority. And with the accumulation of capital, class in Europe took on a new dimension, clear hierarchical social divisions emerging between the bourgeoisie, petty bourgeoisie and working peoples. In South Asia, where the vertical division of society on caste lines prevailed and was at the core of social practice, there was an additional dimension of a 'high/low' hierarchy based on caste occupation. Among the Euro-Asians, however, there was no caste but only those few who could climb the class ladder could divest themselves of the 'stigma' of mixed origin.

Many Euro-Asians had a sense of *angst* about not being fully accepted by either the colonial power or local society. This feeling was occasionally directed to a dislike of 'whites' in the colonies – for their racist attitudes to those of mixed origin; this was seen in the latter's exclusion from both political power and white society, as well as the personal insults and sometimes discrimination in daily life. Some of mixed origin channelled such resentment into radical and dissenting movements. They also used their energies to enter the educational system and excel in the professions. Where radicalism coincided with brilliance in intellectual achievement, Euro-Asians became catalysts for change, often gaining national prominence, and sometimes notoriety. Moreover, since Euro-Asians belonged neither to the European ruling-class nor to local semi-feudal families, they were well - positioned to take up causes of oppressed groups in society, whether peasants, women, urban workers or the petty bourgeoisie. In their role as public intellecuals, Euro-Asians were regarded with suspicion and reviled by the colonial authorities.

The real asset of the Euro-Asians was their ability in the 19th century to be part of a 'double critique' of West and East while valorizing the best of both these worlds. Euro-Asians had contacts with the more radical members of the British parliament and other western radicals and their writings. They were inspired by the poetry of Byron, a man considered by the British 'establishment' to be "mad, bad and dangerous to know." In Sri Lanka, erudite Burghers were also members of the Royal Asiatic Society and were involved in scholarship on Sri Lankan themes and colonial history – among them Charles Lorenz, Eleanor Lorenz, Leopold Ludovici, Dr Andreas Nell and A.E. Buultjens. They were also, in the 20th century, pioneers of avant-garde trends in art, architecture and design.

The story of the Euro-Asians in the colonies was also linked to struggles for women's rights. The portrayal in western culture of Euro-Asian women, as exotic créoles, totally ignored the fact that capitalist development in the colonies, and the advances in education, had given a headstart to Euro-Asian women. In the 19th century these *women* were significantly more literate and educated than *men* of other local communities. The forgotten reality was that Euro-Asian women were the pioneers of feminist emancipation and made inroads, with notable success, into the male-dominated fields of education and employment, and achieved success in the medical profession. They also had more freedom to socialize with men – many Euro-Asian women marrying into other local communities.

Such marriages led to concern among nationalists about 'purity' of lineage and vigilance about 'correctly reproducing the nation'– namely the next generation. This meant marrying within one's own class, ethnic and religious group, and producing children who would be socialized into their ethnic and religious roles. Hence the growth of a strong critique of mixed marriages and liaisons between European men and 'native' women and between 'native' men and European and Euro-Asian women. This sentiment against racial mixing arose during the period of ethnic-cum-religious revival and early nationalism in the late 19th century, and survived into the 20th century. It sometimes prevails even today.

* * * * *

Using the case of Sri Lanka, and to some extent India and elsewhere, this book deals with issues resulting from European conquest and domination, and the growth of Euro-Asian communities from the time of Portuguese colonialism. In Part I, "Creating Euro-Asian Communities," the policies of Portugal, the Netherlands and Britain – in terms of the emergence of Euro-Asian communities – is discussed. The class stratification within these groups, was primarily based on occupation, along with distinctions based on religion, skin colour, legitimacy and country of original ancestry. Class, however, dominated, and social status within the mixed community was based on access to wealth, property and professional achievement. This resulted in some status anxiety in the community, and interest in racial 'stock,' genealogy and the occupation of the male ancestors. Euro-Asians were descendants of persons of many classes – officials, planters, soldiers, shop-assistants or railway and other workers. This stratification replicated the existing class system of the European rulers, resulting in divisions among Euro-

Asians, similar to caste, as to who was 'high' or 'low' among the mixed community.

Part II, "Euro-Asian Radicalism and Modernism" considers the important development of a political consciousness among sections of well-educated Euro-Asians causing some concern among the colonial rulers. Influenced by the ideologies of the French Revolution and the various revolutionary struggles in Europe, the Caribbean, and by the writings and literature of 'Enlightenment' and rebellion, the Euro-Asians were among the first to propound proto-nationalist ideas in India and Sri Lanka. They were thus many decades ahead of the late 19th and early 20th century 'national heroes' and social reformers who are celebrated today. The radicalism and modernism of the Euro-Asians covered many areas: a critique of British rule, concern for the rights of workers and peasants, speaking out on the rights of women, and promoting secularism, pluralism and democracy, as well as avant garde culture.

In Part III, "Gender, Patriarchy and Nation," this study focuses on gender and the patriarchal and chauvinist aspects of nationalism. It examines the influence of European racist ideologies in South Asia, including the myth of Aryan origin, and the emergence of imagined 'chosen people,' resulting in an obsessive concern with purity and pollution. The Euro-Asian woman also became the object of 'colonial desire.' While in western art, literature, music and dance, Euro-Asian women were represented as 'available' for European men, the rules of the colonial game abhorred the idea of European women consorting with Euro-Asian or other local men, who were depicted in an unflattering way. And to the local nationalists, the 'danger' of contamination came from marriages with Euro-Asian or European women, seen as a threat to the nationalist project of preserving the 'purity' of the nation.

The Euro-Asians have been considered 'marginal,' but some of the leading members of the community took on the most central issues of the 19th and 20th centuries. This book attempts to bring some of this lost story of Euro-Asian radicalism and feminism to the main text of history. It highlights the dissident, visionary Euro-Asians of Asia – among them Henry Derozio and John Ricketts in India, and Charles Lorenz,

A.E. Buultjens and Agnes Nell de Silva in Sri Lanka – who were advocates of the rights of women and workers, and championed freedom of the press, in a repressive colonial situation where religious conformism, patriarchy and undemocratic structures prevailed. It was such political ideologies, creative skills and modernist tendencies of the Euro-Asian population that propelled them into action in the movements of political reform and dissent in the colonies. And they were certainly well ahead of their time in espousing pluralism, secularism, trade unionism, gender equity and nascent anti-colonialism. Although these movements only materialized more fully in later decades, Euro-Asian utopianism served to inspire others into visualizing and campaigning for a democratic, liberated society of the future.

Cartoon of himself by Charles Lorenz.
From B.R. Blazé, *The Life of Lorenz*.

Part I

CREATING EURO-ASIAN COMMUNITIES

'Mestice woman going to church in state', 1808.
Engraving by Jacob Haafner. From *Illustrations & Views of Dutch Ceylon.*
Courtesy R.K. de Silva & W.G.M. Beumer.

1

PORTUGUESE and DUTCH COLONIALISM and the *MESTIÇOS*

> Individuals of mixed race… taken all round, resemble white men, but… betray their coloured descent by some striking feature or other, and on that account are excluded from society and enjoy none of the privileges of white people.
>
> Sigmund Freud, "The Unconscious" (1915), 1986, p.163

The Portuguese Confrontation

At the onset of European colonialism, Sri Lanka was already a 'Hybrid Island' where for centuries, migrations and invasions from all parts of southern, eastern and western India, with additions also from the Arab, African and Malay world, had mingled to form communities of Sinhalese, Tamils and Muslims. In this ethnic mosaic, Buddhism, Hinduism and Islam increased the diversity of beliefs and made the island a plural society, but one where differences based on caste and class also existed. When the sailing ships of Portuguese colonial invaders arrived, the island was already a multi-ethnic, multi-religious group of communities, each having its kinship patterns and customary laws. But there was also some fluidity of boundaries, resulting over the years in cross-cultural assimilation and mutual adaptions of social practices, religious beliefs and rituals.

With Portuguese colonial conquest and the spread of what Wallerstein called "the discovery business" (1974: 51), distinct Euro-Asian communities emerged in Asia which developed their separate identities and cultures, differing from both their European and Asian lineages. The Portuguese had invaded societies which were already stratified by ethnicity, religion, caste and social class. Moreover, in the case of the Sinhalese and Tamils, marriages were determined by caste and were preferably between cross-cousins. In such a society, the intrusion and influence of the Portuguese was somewhat convulsive. There occurred a sharp breach in the ethnic and religious order with the creation not only of local Christian converts but also of a community of Christian Euro-Asians, that cut across class, but did not belong to the local social formations based on caste, ethnic or religious divisions. The Portuguese impact was thus as sudden as it was far-reaching. But how did Portugal, a small country "on the Western rim of Christendom," develop a far-flung empire stretching from Brazil to the African coast and to ports and regions of Asia? (Boxer 1973a: 1). This has been a matter for much speculation.[1]

In the 15th century, Portugal had the advantage over Spain, France and England of being a united country, politically relatively stable and free of civil strife and feudal conflicts. Portugal also had experience in long-distance trade with northern Europe and was geographically closest for exploring West Africa. The economic climate favoured entrepreneurs venturing abroad and the Portuguese furthermore had access to capital, being part of the "relatively monetized" Islamic Mediterranean zone. Portugal had also an interest in an "expansion of revenue and accumulation of glory" (Wallerstein 1974: 49-51). While the "gunned ship" gave Portugal technological superiority, the country also had material reasons and an ideological fervour combined with religious commitment in finding the "route to the Indies" (ibid: 326).

The historian John H. Plumb describes the Portuguese ships "armed with the best artillery" which bombarded "on the slightest pretext the rich and prosperous ports of Africa and India, firing the houses, plundering the warehouses, slaughtering the inhabitants" (quoted in Boxer 1973a: xxii-iii). He also remarks that the Portuguese "demonstrated ...the effectiveness of a sailing ship armed with cannon." It was a "murderous Western onslaught on India and the East," and Portuguese ships "piled high with loot – pepper, cinnamon, silks, pearls, rubies – aroused the lust of Europe." The Portuguese had "made the breach," through which other European states, most notably Holland and Britain (whom he calls "jackals"), "raced to get their fill" (ibid: xxiv-v). [2]

By the 16th century, Portugal had set up trading posts along coastal Africa, and in Asia it controlled several ports – Goa, Cochin (Kochi), Colombo, Malacca, Timor and Macao. In a few areas, the Portuguese exercised sovereignty or controlled the local ruler, but in others, trade was the main concern – especially the trade in pepper and other spices. As Wallerstein notes, Portugal also had a lead over others in colonial conquest: "for the state, for the nobility, for the commercial bourgeoisie (indigenous and foreign) even for the semiproletariat of the towns," there were advantages in colonial conquest (Wallerstein 1974: 51). For groups such as Jews, moving to the colonies was an escape from persecution.[3]

Casados and the Mixing of Races

Vasco da Gama, the Portuguese navigator, and his fleet had landed in 1498 in Calicut (Kozhikode) on the Malabar coast of south India (Kerala). The exploratory voyage around Africa to India was followed by other adventurers in pursuit of the trade networks of Asia controlled by the Arabs, Indians and Chinese. The early policy of the Portuguese was to establish trading centres and to make alliances with local rulers in India, as they did in Kochi from 1501. The Portuguese also were the first Europeans to invade and occupy parts of Sri Lanka. The navigator Don Lourenco de Almeida and his fleet had anchored in Colombo briefly in 1506,[4] and subsequently the Portuguese intruded into the kingdoms of Sitavaka, Kotte and Jaffna, but failed to capture the Kandyan kingdom. By the mid-16th century the Portuguese controlled the south-western maritime areas of Sri Lanka, until they were ousted by the more powerful forces of Dutch imperialism in 1656.

In the absence of European women in the colonies, a persistent problem of colonial rule was that of marriages for Europeans stationed as colonial officials and soldiers. As C.J. Hawes writes, the dilemma was finding "suitable women to make the journey out to Asia," leading the Portuguese to recognize that "a policy of local marriage, particularly for their soldiers was inevitable" (Hawes 1996: 1). This, however, created problems for the colonial rulers, who, in tolerating marriages or alliances between European men and Asian women, had to face cultural and religious obstacles, especially in the attempt to impose Christian marriage on non-Christian women. If the children were illegitimate, this raised a further problem of whether their "welfare was a matter of private or public responsibility" (ibid: 2).

The question of wives for Portuguese soldiers and others employed in India was resolved in favour of intermarriage and the assimilation of locals through conversion. As Gaikwad remarks: "A native girl had to be baptized before she could be married to a Portuguese man. … marriages with native girls thus meant a greater number of Christians" (1967: 15). The children of these mixed marriages, termed Luso-Indians, formed a new community. When the Dutch replaced the Portuguese, the Luso-Indians were allowed to remain, and when the Dutch surrendered to the British, there was special provision for those of mixed race (ibid: 16). Michael Roberts asserts that Portuguese policy actually discouraged Portuguese women from going to the colonies, in order to "encourage miscegenation as a bulwark of colonial control" (1989: 35). There was also the question of labour. The Portuguese Governor "advocated a solution to the manpower question by the evolution of a half-breed population" (E.E. Rich, quoted in Wallerstein 1974: 327n121). Thus with state backing and the force of circumstance, liaisons took place in the colonies between Portuguese men and local women. The children of these mixed alliances (*mestiços* and *mestiças)* spoke a créole Portuguese which persisted during Dutch and British rule in Sri Lanka as the 'home language' of the mixed population and of the slaves in their households – who included persons of African and south Indian origin. The *mestiça* wives and slave women perpetuated an "Indo-Portuguese culture" reinforced by the Roman Catholic priests who preached in Portuguese (Karl Goonewardena, quoted in Roberts, et al. 1989: 37).

The Portuguese in their colonies consisted of *soldados* (unmarried soldiers), *casados* (householders) and *padres* (Catholic priests). A Portuguese scholar commented that "the Portuguese encrust themselves into the worlds of the Orient, installing themselves everywhere as *casados* (and) fit themselves into local or regional interests" (V.M. Godinho, quoted in Wallerstein 1974: 343). There were also issues of status among Portuguese in the colonies; those of humble origin often 'passed' for high-born *fidalgos* in the colonies, the word originating in *filho d'algo* — a 'son of somebody' (Boxer 1954: 273). In Portugal during the 14th and 15th centuries, *fidalgos* of real or imagined noble blood lived in style, with "servants, weapons and horses" (Boxer 1973a: 6). In Malacca by 1511, there were 300 families composed of Portuguese soldiers and local women and children, but after the Dutch conquest in 1641 their descendants were treated as "a pariah group" because of their Catholicism and poverty (Alexius Pereira 1995: 28-30).

In India, following the capture of Goa in 1510, the Viceroy Alfonso Albuquerque encouraged a class of settlers or *casados* through marriages of Portuguese and local women. The intention was not only to combat labour shortages but also to create a mixed population owing allegiance to the Portuguese.The *casados* were rewarded with land, houses, horses, cattle and cash, and used the chance to become farmers, artisans and traders. In villages they became landlords – while those in the towns were traders and master craftsmen, as well as tailors, cobblers, carpenters blacksmiths, bakers and tavern-keepers (Azevedo 1993:105 & 111). In Chennai (Madras) there were Portuguese settlements from the early 16th century, and by 1675 there were 3,000 Portuguese residents (Caplan 2001: 22).

In Sri Lanka, Portuguese *casados* were found in several parts of the island including Colombo, Jaffna, Trincomalee, Kotte and Madampe. These settlers, who were retired soldiers, were not part of the army, but were called up during battles (de Silva 1972: 187). The income of the *casados* came from trade and revenues from villages (ibid: 138). Those Portuguese settlers who were allies of the Sri Lankan puppet-king, Don Juan Dharmapala, were also exempt from customs charges in 1584. Subsequently this privilege was revoked, but in 1643, when Dutch occupation was imminent, the *casados* had to be kept content and the exemption was allowed (ibid: 183). Also disputed were the garden lands of the *casados* near Colombo which were rent free, but a one-tenth tax on produce was levied in the 1630s. Many *casados* also plied the coastal trade of the island (ibid: 184-85).

A class division existed among rich and poor *casados*. C. R. de Silva has described the case of Lancarote de Seixas, a *casado* trader and soldier, who had left Portugal for Asia never to return, and who "wandered about in search of riches." In India, he married the daughter of a *casado* of Kochi. His services to the Portuguese in Malacca were rewarded by the grant for three generations of land in Madampe, in western Sri Lanka. Madampe was a "prized possession" yielding paddy, coconut, cinnamon and pepper, some of which was traded for cloth and salt from Kandy. Thus from being "a relatively little-known soldier," de Seixas became within two decades "one of the wealthiest and most influential *casados* in Ceylon" (de Silva 1971: 33).

Paul Pieris has observed that the Portuguese themselves were of mixed origin – "the product of a heterogeneous agglomeration" and were therefore willing "to contemplate with equanimity, the introduction of another race within their social circle." (Pieris 1983, Vol 2: 118). A Franciscan priest, Fr Miguel, noted in the 1630s that there were dark-skinned Portuguese in India who were part African (*mulattos* and *quadroons*), "contaminated by Negro blood… although they allege that they got sunburnt during the voyage" (Boxer 1973a: 253). According to Cordiner (1804), the Portuguese descendants in Sri Lanka were darker than "any of the original natives," but "yet they retain a considerable portion of the pride of their ancestors." They gave expression to this by wearing European dress and professing Catholicism, thinking themselves "far superior to the lower classes of the Sinhalese" (quoted in Digby 1879: 15). Pieris also argues that intermarriage was "not specially repellant to the Sinhalese, whose liberal trend of mind enabled them to absorb within themselves so many and diverse settlers from South India" (Pieris 1983, Vol. 2: 118).

Political expediency was also the aim of the Portuguese policy of mixing the races, and the authorities "encouraged intermarriage so that in a few generations" there would arise a new class which would help "to bridge the gulf between the races" (ibid: 118). Soldiers, tavern-keepers, butchers, bakers and shopkeepers contracted marriages or had liaisons with local women. In time, many of the minor officials and traders in the fortress towns were "Porto-Sinhalese, the offspring of the mixed marriages which the Government vigorously encouraged" (Brohier 2000: 13). The British sea-captain Robert Knox (around the 1680s) wrote of a Portuguese-Sinhalese marriage and a *crime passionelle* involving a Portuguese whom he knew, who not only caught "a Chingulay with his wife" but also "killed them boath the same time and was Justified and took another Chingulay woman for his wife" (Knox 1989: 263).

Intermarriages were made occasionally for political reasons. Paul Pieris refers to the experiment that was "tried by a few of the highest and a large number of the lowest among the people" with disappointing results.Four Sinhala Mudaliyars, "from whose Portuguese connections great hopes had been entertained," defected from the Portuguese in 1630 (Pieris 1983, Vol. 2: 118-19). There are records of a Portuguese woman with a Sinhala husband (ibid: 119),and reference to a Sinhala man, Don Theodosio,"who married a honourable *mestiça* from Colombo," dressing himself up for the occasion in Portuguese fashion "with a gilt sword and rich trappings" (Perniola Vol III, 1991: 161). Gaspar Figueira de Serpa, a *mestiço* whose father was Portuguese and mother Sinhala, was considered an "outstanding" soldier and in 1655-58 was given "the Chief command in the field against the Dutch and Sinhalese" (Boxer 1973a: 305-6).

The new community of *mestiços* of *casado* origin in Sri Lanka, created by the Portuguese settlements, took different paths. Some kept the 'European' traditions alive and married Dutch and later British residents, forming by the 19th century a community of Euro-Asians (Burghers and Eurasians). Other *casado* descendants maintained their local identity by marrying Sinhalese, but kept Portuguese names, and over time were 'deemed' to be Sinhalese. This may partially account for the large number of Sinhalese with Portuguese names, even today. Contrary to the belief that all Sinhalese who took on Portuguese names did so in order to be baptized, and therafter get jobs or to avoid taxes, many Sinhalese were, more likely, the descendants of *casados*.

Intermarriage between Portuguese men and locals in the colonies provided the rulers with a cadre of *mestiço* soldiers, clerks, artisans and shipbuilders. The racial admixture that took place – especially in urban areas – led to what McGilvray calls the "multi-ethnic confusion of port cities" (1982: 235). In the 16th century in the Portuguese enclave of Malacca, for example, a distinct class of *mestiços* emerged, many of them settling in Singapore during early British rule. Their families bore such names as de Almeida, Noronhas, da Silva, de Souza, Pereira and de Oliveira (Braga-Blake & Ebert-Oehlers 1992: 26-28).

In the mixed population of Sri Lanka and elsewhere, there was both hierarchy and fluidity. Roberts notes that terms used to describe the mixed community "changed over time in meaning, with a certain vagueness and multivalence... reflective of the proportion of mixture" (Roberts et al. 1989: 39). While the children were called *mestiça (*female*)* or *mestiço (*male*),* there were also persons known as *castizo* (or *casties*), who were three-quarter European (*mestiça* mother and European father). Another word, *pusties* was used to describe the descendants of *casties* (ibid: 41). In European writings of the 17th century, the mixed population was referred to as "mixties, mestice and toepassie" (Goonewardena, quoted in Roberts et al. 1989: 42). The category called *tupasses* (topass) were converts to Christianity of European-Asian origin. R. L. Brohier describes the *tupasses* as "a term loosely applied to the descendants of Portuguese and Sinhalese by mixed marriages" (2000: 31), while *Hobson Jobson,* the Anglo-Indian dictionary, says the term was "used in the 17th and 18th centuries for dark-skinned or half-caste claimants of Portuguese descent and Christian profession." The etymology of the word is unclear. Other suggestions were *top-chi* (gunner), *topeewala* (wearer of a hat), *dabash* (*do-bhashiya* – 'two tongued' or those speaking two languages). (Yule and Burnell 1986: 933). In Sinhalese, *thuppahi* (from *tupasses*) was, and even today, is used perjoratively for persons considered of 'low' class, mixed origin and supposedly lacking in culture.

Racism of the Portuguese

Many have viewed Portuguese colonialism as being free of racial prejudice, in contrast to the Dutch and British. "It is to the credit of Portugal," Edgar Prestage wrote in 1923, "that slaves and Jews apart, she made no distinction of race and colour and that once they had become Catholics, were eligible for official posts" (quoted in Boxer 1973a: 251). Gilberto Treyne, a Brazilian sociologist, argued that eight centuries of Moorish domination of Portugal and Spain led Christians of that region to ignore the colour bar, regard Moors as social superiors and be tolerant of persons of 'mixed blood' (quoted in ibid: 2). But Boxer rejects these views since discrimination existed against African slaves and Jews, who were part of Portuguese colonial society, this itself undermining the claim "about the absence of race and colour prejudice" (ibid: 251). There was also a myth that Iberians were of Gothic Germanic descent, and the word 'gothic' (*godo*) came to be associated with 'noble.' Christianized Spain and Portugal also looked down on Muslims and Jews, and it was in these regions that "an institutional form of racism made its first appearance in European history" (Poliakov 1977: 12-13). What is evident, however, is that encouragement and tolerance of mixed marriages could co-exist with racist policies of the State and Church in the colonies.

The Portuguese for centuries laid much emphasis on 'purity of blood' (*pureza de sangue*), and terms such as 'contaminated races' (*raças infectas*) were encountered in official documents and private correspondence until the last quarter of the 18th century (Boxer 1973a: 251). But the Catholic Church was ambiguous. In Goa, the Jesuits ran the Seminary of the Holy Faith (Santa Fé) as a multi-racial venture, but entry into the Jesuit Order itself was prohibited for Asians, including Euro-Asians. Throughout the 16th and 17th centuries, no Sri Lankans were accepted into the Catholic priesthood. A Jesuit, Fr Alexandre Valignano, had harsh words about "these dusky races" whom he labelled "very stupid and vicious, and of the basest spirits":

> As for the *mestiços* and *castiços*, we should receive either very few or none at all; especially ...the *mestiços*, since the more native blood

> they have, the more they resemble the Indians and the less they are esteemed by the Portuguese. (ibid: 254)

There were, however, others like Fr Ardizone Spinola who in 1680 condemned the 'colour bar' in Church and State matters and accused the Portuguese of regarding "all coloured races... as intrinsically inferior to the white" (ibid: 255). Writing in 1653 about Goa, a French commentator stated: "The *Mestiços* are of various types, strongly despised... because of a drop of black blood in the generation of their ancestor – the stigma of having an Indian woman ancestor lasts up to the hundredth generation" (Yule & Burnell 1986: 604, translation). C.L.R. James also writes of the "elaborate tom-foolery" of colour in the West Indies, where the descendants of white and black parents were divided into 128 groups based on skin colour, and a person with 127 white parts and one black part "was still a man of colour" (1980: 38). A character in Patricia Dunker's novel refers to a "litany of prejudice:"

> The offspring of a white man and a black woman is a *mulatto*; the *mulatto* and the black produce a *sambo*, from the *mulatto* and the white comes the *quadroon*, from the *quadroon* and the white the *mustee*, the child of a *mustee* by a white man is called a *musteefino* and the children of a *musteefino* will be free by law and will count as whites. (Duncker 2000:293)

While a 'drop of black blood' was thus crucial, if it was not evident in a person's physiognomy, it was possible to 'pass for white' and become assimilated with European society. Where mixed ancestry was visible, some 'compensated' for the problem by claims of high status and class. The Portuguese were far from being non-racist. While permitting mixed marriages, they followed distinct racist policies associated with colonial conquest. In the words of Benedict Anderson, European expansion to Asia and Africa "led inevitably to the appearance of Eurasians (and) Eurafricans, ...not as occasional curiosities but as visible social groups." And the significance of this, he claimed, was the flourishing of "a style of thinking ... which foreshadows modern racism" (1983: 60).

Race and Gender during Dutch Rule

The emergence of Dutch colonialism as a rival to the Portuguese led to the further Europeanization of Asia and gave racial mixing a new dimension. By the 16th century, Holland had expelled its Spanish rulers, united the Northern and Southern Provinces and established a Dutch Republic, as "a confederation of states and towns, jealously guarding their rights and liberties," and characterized by aggressive commercialism. Dutch power grew between 1580 and 1640 with its "great navies and armies" paid for by taxation, achieved mainly by the Calvinist oligarchies with their "strong and viable sense of their own destiny as a class and as a nation." The Dutch dominated the Baltic trade, and had a stake in the commerce of Western Europe along "the great rivers that the Dutch controlled" and became the world's leading sea-faring nation in the 17th century (Plumb xxii-xxiii & xxvii, in Boxer 1973b). The Dutch had traded in Asia through commercial companies, which were eventually brought together in the Dutch East India Company (Vereenidge Oost-Indische Campagnie, VOC) in 1602. The Company had a trade monopoly with wide powers "to make war and peace with the indigenous powers, to maintain naval and military forces, and to exercise judicial and administrative functions in those regions" (Boxer 1973b: 27). Poets like Joost van den Vondel romanticized the trade "to distant and exotic lands, as far as shines the sun" (ibid: 31), but the reality was less romantic. It was a story of plunder and exploitation by a colonial power.

In Sri Lanka the king of Kandy, Rajasinha II, in 1636 bargained with the Dutch to oust the Portuguese from the island, tempting the Dutch with trade monopolies. But the Dutch, who used the occasion to outwit the king, increased their physical presence and expanded their governance over the littoral regions. The wars of conquest with the Portuguese ended with the capture of Colombo in 1656 after a siege of six months, and the Dutch-occupied parts of the country were administrated by officials of the Dutch East India Company up to 1796.

The highly patriarchal East India Company allowed no role for women in the colonies. It even prohibited the transport of women in its ships, but some of them stowed away to be with their menfolk or seek their fortune in the colonies. A common belief was that "white women of lowly origin had a good chance of making a rich marriage in the East" (Boxer 1973b: 254), and that "even an unmarried woman could have a prosperous and easy life," especially since "the lowest white woman was considerably exalted above native women" (Dekker & van der Pol 1989: 27-28, 34). Moreover, in an era when there were few opportunities for women, there were cases of Dutch women who disguised themselves as sailors and went to sea as a means of escape from the constraints imposed on them by patriarchy and by Calvinist dogmatism. Not surprisingly, women cross-dressers who sailed to Asia were denounced as 'transvestites' or 'prostitutes.' In 1629 the Governor-General, Jaques Specx, complained about the presence on his ship going East of "so many filthy strumpets and street-walkers who have been found on all ships" (Boxer 1973b: 254). In the 17th century Nicholas de Graff, a Dutch surgeon, was outraged by Dutch women in Asia, who were merely "prison whores, drunken street pigs and thieves who no longer dare to remain in Holland," but who, in the Indies, are "ostentatious, haughty, (and) wanton" (Dekker & van der Pol 1989: 34). These strong words, reflected the misogyny aroused by 'deviant' women, or women of the poor who defied traditional social and religious codes.

As Boxer's studies show, the Dutch were faced with a problem of keeping "the white man, whether merchant, mariner or settler… 'above and apart' from the coloured races among whom he lived." Yet neither the East India Company nor the state were involved in organizing the migration of Dutch women. European rulers have always been sensitive about the social behaviour of fellow Europeans in the colonies. The Dutch believed that 'respectable' women were unlikely to migrate to the colonies, and those who did were called "light women" who created scandal "to the great shame of our nation"(Boxer 1973b: 241-42). But the Dutch made allowance for their men to make marriages with Portuguese *mestiças* or with Christian Asians. However, these 'coloured wives' were banned from going to Europe with their Dutch husbands (ibid: 243). William Digby claimed that, in any case, a Dutchman with a local wife would not have "dared to take her to his friends in Holland," and gave an example from a family of six, from which five went to the

Dutch-occupied Batavia (Jakarta) after the Dutch defeat in Sri Lanka, but the sixth "having married beneath him," and whose wife was considered "tainted," remained in Sri Lanka and later became the chief lawyer to the British government (1879: 14-15).

Dutch policy thus aimed to create – in Batavia, Malacca, the Molucas and Sri Lanka – a class comparable to the Portuguese *casados*. These were the Dutch free-burghers (*vrij burgher*) subject to the Company's rules who were former merchants, soldiers, sailors and clerks. Many were reviled by Governor-General Reynst in 1615 as "the scum of our land" who had married "the scum of the East Indies." The view was also that free-burghers were "dissolute drunkards, to whom no respectable Asian father would give his daughter in marriage" (Boxer 1973b: 244).Notwithstanding these censures, the Dutch Governor, Johan Maetsuyker, attempted to promote mixed marriages. After the Dutch captured Colombo and Jaffna, around two hundred Dutchmen married women of Indo-Portuguese origin (ibid: 248). McGilvray refers to"considerable intercultural creativity and vitality" as reflected in "interesting multi-ethnic domestic arrangements."He writes about Christopher Schweitzer, a German in the Dutch East India Company in 1680, who kept the company of a widow, Branco de Costa whose father was Portuguese and mother Sinhalese. He would not marry her, "not for her being black," but because she had elongated earlobes and used "Oyl made of coconuts" on her hair. Another such case was a baptized Jew named Moritz who married his Sinhala mistress only after she had her elongated earlobes clipped (Raven-Hart, quoted in McGilvray 1982: 241-42).

Another Dutch Governor, Rijkloff van Goens, did not oppose Dutch marriages with Sinhalese, Tamil or *mestiça* women. Yet attempts to establish a Dutch middle class of traders failed, leading van Goens to observe "gloomily … (that) tavern keeping was the only occupation for which they showed any great enthusiasm" (Boxer 1973b: 248). However, as Boxer writes, the Dutch in the East, like the Portuguese, Spaniards, British and French, believed in white superiority and were "convinced that all Europeans were superior to any other race." This view was particularly strong among Protestant Calvinists, who also believed "they were the Elect of the Lord and the salt of the earth" (ibid: 261).

The Portuguese empire in decline had been challenged by the Dutch with their superior technology and naval power. After the Portuguese defeat, some of their officials and soldiers returned home but many remained (Brohier 2000: 24). Wallerstein writes that even earlier: "Portuguese citizens… began to cut themselves off from the home country and adjust to survival in Asia. They became… Asians of European extraction" (1974: 343). After the ousting of the Portuguese, the Dutch regarded the *mestiços* and *tupasses* as 'natives.' Some years after the Dutch occupied the maritime areas of Sri Lanka and south India, Governor van Goens estimated that there were "not less than 13 to 14 hundred children… by Dutch fathers …and also the children of Dutch parents." He expressed concern that these children "should not be reduced to the necessity of marrying native women," and added that "the boys should be brought up with care and… (not) allowed to follow the habits of the natives or their mothers" (Reimers 1932: 33).

R. L. Brohier describes the variety of Westerners present in the country during Dutch rule; they included officials of the Dutch East India Company (VOC) recruited not only in the Netherlands but also from the German states, Denmark, Sweden, France, Italy and Britain. All these were classed as *Hollandsche Natie* (Hollanders) or Burghers (Brohier 2000: 31). The VOC in addition used European mercenaries of the Swiss Regiment of Neuchatel, led by Colonel Charles Daniel de Meuron. The recruits were from Switzerland, which itself was multilingual, and also included Dutch, French, German and British persons whose descendants became a part of the Burgher community. The French names included Toussaint, Mortier, Thorne(t), Grenier, Rode(t) and Andree; the German names were Wolf, Saar; Schneider, Potger, Redlich and Dornhorst (Roberts et al. 1989: 212, Brohier 2000). There were also British names such as Smith, Fisher, Gilbert, Wigan, Elders and Anderson. Many Burghers claimed ancestry to the de Meuron regiment, and this myth of origin became as strong as the claim by Americans to be descendants of the Pilgrim Fathers. But as Max Weber, in defining an 'ethnic group,' wrote, "its members entertain a subjective belief in their common descent... and it does not matter whether or not an objective blood relationship exists" (1968, quoted in Pereira 1995: 14).

The de Meuron Regiment, in Brohier's words, was composed of "soldiers of fortune whom the Powers employed to fight their battles." Consisting of 1,200 men it was "well officered and disciplined... the chief European force of the Dutch, and one on which they primarily relied for defending their possessions in Ceylon" (Brohier 2000: 43). Some of this multi-national group were sensitive about their national origins. Charles Lorenz's father, Johan Friedrich Wilhelm Lorenz from Prussia, who had arrived in Galle in 1793, was fussy about his name and reminded his son that it was Lorenz – not Lourensz. "The latter is Dutch but the former is a German name and for the whole Island of Ceylon I would not be mistaken for a Dutchman" (quoted in Roberts et al. 1989: 39).

Definitions of 'race' were also not easy to sustain, since many *mestiças* had married Dutch men despite being forbidden to travel to Holland. The Dutch, "thin on the ground," also relied on Topass men as a support to sustain colonial rule (ibid: 42). William Digby claims that, "every respectable Portuguese or Mestiço family had been absorbed into the clan of 'Dutch' and 'burghers' who had been left behind when the European Dutch left the island *en masse*" after the British occupation of the island (1879, Vol. 1: 8n). In 1832 an anonymous letter complained that those calling themselves 'Burgher' included "natives in European costume... Fishers, Chandos, Half-Castes, Chitties, Parawas, Slave-descendants, foundlings etc. etc. passing for genuine Burghers of High Blood and admitted into their societies." In addition, many Sinhala Christians ("natives in European dress") 'passed' into the Burgher community, and slaves after emancipation "merged with the poorer strata of the Créole population" (quoted in Roberts et al. 1989: 44). McGilvray claims that "a strict division between Dutch and Portuguese Burghers was impossible to sustain" because these identities "were totally mixed and intertwined" (1982: 237).

While many Burghers kept up the illusion of being pure European, others were more realistic. Percy Colin-Thomé, a retired judge whose ancestor was in the de Meuron regiment, wrote:

> The Burghers are the descendants of intermarriages between the Portuguese and the Dutch with Sinhalese and Tamils. The Dutch also married the progeny of the unions between the Portuguese and local races. (quoted in Ludowyk 1989: xii)

E.F.C. Ludowyk, a Burgher from Galle, reminiscing about his childhood in 'colonial Ceylon,' referred to class differences in the community, remarking that the Burghers were "an ethnic group of European descent, whose forebears, culled from every class in their original homeland, had settled in the island." This added, he said, "a new social grouping to the mixture of races produced by conquest and immigration" (ibid: 1).

The race policies of the Dutch reflected the contempt and prejudice of northern Europe against southern Europeans such as the Portuguese – prejudices reinforced by Calvinist hostility to Catholics. Governor Rijkloff van Goens – who had, through necessity, not opposed mixed marriages – in a Memoir to his successor in 1663, nevertheless gave expression to bigotry about mixed persons. Using the French word *canaille* (scoundrels) to describe the Portuguese *mestiços*, he writes:

> Your Excellency should… proceed against and drive away from the country the Portuguese canaille, such as toepasses and similar folk… [T]he chief reasons… are that they do nothing but continually pursue the native women who are married to Netherlanders in order to debauch them. (Reimers 1932: 18)

The offences listed by van Goens were not merely sexual, but also included other general allegations of sloth, theft, papism and espionage. These "scoundrels live without toil, seduce the slaves to thieving, correspond with the papists on the opposite coast (India), and spy on all our activities" (ibid: 18).

During Dutch rule, there was also a French interest in the island, and Laisne de Nanclair de la Nerolle, an emissary from the French in Trincomalee, was sent to the king of Kandy to obtain trade concessions (Jayawickrama 2004: 113-14). He was imprisoned for insulting the king, and stayed on to marry locally, and founded the de Lanerolle family of Sri Lanka, who are considered to be Sinhalese.

Euro-Asians of the Dutch Indies

In spite of prejudiced views, the Dutch in their colonies had married or cohabited with both local and Portuguese *mestiça* women. In Malacca, for example, there are records of marriages between Dutch settlers and Euro-Asian women of Portuguese origin (Braga-Blake & Ebert-Oehlers 1992: 29). And in the Dutch East Indies (Indonesia), the Euro-Asians (called 'Indos') were regarded by both locals and the Dutch with some disdain. This is reflected in the Dutch writer Louis Couperus' famous 'colonial' novel, *The Hidden Force*, on the futility of Dutch colonial rule, written at the turn of the 20th century. Couperus, born in the East, had what Ian Buruma calls "an insight into the tragedy of European colonialism," as well as "sympathy for the hybrid, the impure, the ambiguous" which gave him a "peculiarly modern voice" (Buruma 2000b: 72). A character in Couperus' novel, van Oudijck, the Dutch bureaucrat (whose wife was part Javanese) was described as having:

> a patronizing view of natives and contempt for half-castes, so typical of Dutch colonial administrators... It is the *idea* of the 'Indo' that van Oudijck cannot abide – the idea of something less than pure. (ibid: 66)

Buruma also notes that the Dutch in the Indies "enjoyed the *droit de seigneur* in the Kampong," and believed that "anyway, native women and half-castes were supposed to be unusually highly sexed" (ibid: 70).

> The Indos were commonly regarded by the Dutch as lazy and stupid, as well as over-sexed... The Indos overcompensated by disdaining the natives, as though this would make the Dutch accept them as equals. (ibid: 72)

In Couperus' book, both the 'pure' Dutch and 'pure' Javanese are portrayed unfavourably, and the characters "entirely at ease with themselves... are the Indos...They appear to have the best of both worlds" (ibid: 71). But Buruma disagrees and says that in reality the Euro-Asians "probably had the worst of both worlds." Even those who were "acknowledged by their western fathers" and were legally Europeans, were "subject to subtle forms of discrimination in a society obsessed by race and colour" (ibid : 72).

Dutch colonialism thus added to the nucleus of communities of mixed origin resident in Asia, often intermarying with locals and Portuguese descendants. In the wake of Dutch rule was the introduction to local society of a Dutch 'reformed' version of Protestantism, Roman-Dutch laws and Dutch culture. The British were to follow in the 18th century, and further add to the community of mixed origin, as discussed in the next chapter.

Notes

1. Adam Smith made the comment that the 'discovery' of America and the passage to the East Indies by the Cape of Good Hope "were the two greatest and most important events recorded in the history of mankind" (quoted in Boxer, 1973a: 1). The eminent historian of Portuguese and Dutch colonial rule, C.R. Boxer asserted that prior to the 'discoveries,' human society in its different branches was dispersed. The voyages linked up '*for the better and for worse* the widely sundered branches of the great human family" (ibid: 1-2, emphasis added). However, Chinese and Arab merchants had earlier traded along many of these sea routes.
2. John H. Plumb has called Portugal's empire "one of the great enigmas of history" and posed the question: "why was this small, rather poor, culturally backward nation... so dramatically successful in that great century of enterprise?" (quoted in Boxer 1973a: xx-xxi). He partially answers the question: Portugal was heir to the "long accumulation" of technical shipbuilding and cartography skills of Europe and the Arab world (ibid: xxii-iii).
3. According to J.B. Müller, many Portuguese and Dutch in Sri Lanka were of Jewish origin (see Müller, 2006).
4. Scholars fix the date as 1506, and not 1505 as hitherto believed. I am grateful to Professor C.R. de Silva for this and other references.

2

RACIAL MIXING DURING BRITISH RULE

> Many persons, who do not possess the necessary qualifications, describe themselves as Burghers in preference to the more correct term 'Eurasians' ...it is *difficult to make the distinction clear without undue inquisition.*
>
> L.J.B. Turner, in *Report on the Census of Ceylon*, 1921, Vol. 1, 1923, p. 281, emphasis added

Mixed Reactions to Mixed-race Liaisons

Britain's advances as an industrial and commercial nation and the expansion of British colonialism led to the decline of Dutch and French influence in South Asia. The British intrusion into India had begun in the early 17th century, when the East India Company made inroads into Bengal, monopolized trade and established trading posts in Calcutta (now Kolkata), Madras (Chennai) and Bombay (Mumbai). Under the leadership of Robert Clive, who defeated the French, the East India Company acquired territory and waged war against the French and local rulers. This resulted in the need for political rule and the appointment of a Governor-General to establish efficient administration, the first being Warren Hastings who between 1774 and 1785 consolidated imperial rule. In 1784 Prime Minister William Pitt passed the India Act, setting up dual control of the Indian territories between the Company and the British government. After British authority had extended, following on successful wars against local rulers, a Viceroy replaced the Governor-General and became the direct representative of the Crown.

In Sri Lanka the transfer of power in the coastal regions from the Dutch to the British took place in the late 18th century amidst the conflicts between France and Britain. French troops had occupied Holland, whose ruler fled to Britain and ceded the Dutch-ruled regions of Sri Lanka to the British, the transfer being later confirmed in the Peace of Amiens of 1802. By 1815 the king of Kandy was deposed and the whole island came under British rule.

From the earliest days of East India Company rule in India, the issue of wives for the Company's officials arose. Since the men had come to India without wives, many British company officials and military personnel of all ranks had Indian women partners. There were numerous mixed marriages of high-up administrators and officers.

A scale of preference existed based on class and race; the more "suitable local women" were upper-class Hindus or Euro-Asians. There were also many Muslim-British alliances; for example, in the late 18th century, the British Resident in Delhi, General Sir David Ochterlony lived in Mughal style with his senior *bibi* (consort) Mubarak Begum and a harem of women; and General William Palmer, the British Resident at the Maratha Court in Pune, married Begum Fyze Baksh of Delhi, the daughter of an Iranian-born captain of cavalry in India (Dalrymple 2002: 182-83). Their granddaughter, Mary Palmer married Philip Meadows Taylor, who wrote novels on Indian social reform (Sen 2002: 107). Major Hugh Sutherland married a Muslim, as did his cousin, Lieutenant Colonel John Sutherland who married Usrat Hussaini; Lt Colonel William Gardner married Begum Mah Munzel ul-Nissa, daughter of the Nawab of Cambay (Dalrymple 2002: 382-83, 120); and her sister Zuhur-ul-Nissa married the son of Lt Colonel Andrew Hearsey (Hawes 1996: 163).

According to Dalrymple, the rich East India Company officials sent their Anglo-Indian children to Britain for education and "many mixed-blood children were successfully absorbed into the British upper classes"; among them several attained high office, including Lord Liverpool, prime minister of Britain from 1812 to 1827, who had an Indian grandmother. (Dalrymple 2002:51) In this context, contemporary novelist Hari Kunzru (of mixed Indian-British origin himself) in his novel *The Illusionist*, describes the plight of Harry Begg, the Anglo-Indian, who endures all kinds of insults, and feels that everything is "so bloody unfair":

> It isn't as though things weren't different once. Skinner... who founded the Bengal Lancers, was one of Harry's type. So was Lord Roberts, who commanded during the Boer war. Even Lord Liverpool, yes the Liverpool who was PM – he was one. His grandmother on his mother's side was a Calcutta woman. (Kunzru 2002: 38)

Euro-Asians born to upper-class British men in India in the late 18 century were generally socially accepted, often well educated, and given employment "as a support for English activities" (Ballhatchet 1980: 96). Lower down the social scale, marriages of British soldiers were also encouraged; and a directive issued in 1687 to officials in Chennai (by the Court of Directors) stated: "the marriage of our soldiers to the native women (was)... a matter of such consequence to posterity that we shall encourage it." The suggestion was even made to make payments to the mother of a child by a British soldier (ibid: 96-97). By the late 18th century, as Hawes writes, there was much mixing of the races and more British men "lived with Indian women than were married whether to Europeans, Eurasians or Indians" (Hawes 1996: 4). It was flippantly said that 'necessity was the mother of invention, and the father of the Eurasian.'

In the period 1780 to 1785, of the wills of British persons in Bengal, 83 of 217 contained "bequests to Indian companions or their natural children." In Kolkata between 1767 and 1782, 54% of the children baptized at St John's Church were "Eurasian and illegitimate ...the children of high and low in British society ...from attorneys and surgeons to ships' mates, doctors and soldiers" (Hawes 1996: 4). Even by the years 1830 to 1832, when such liaisons had declined, 28% of British military officers and 12% of British civilian men in Bengal had "Indian companions" (ibid: 175: n78). Many reasons were adduced for this trend; one was that £600 a year was needed to support a British wife, but only £50 a year for a local wife. Another was that the "claims to gentility of many British women were tenuous at best"; a British surgeon from Kanpur (Cawnpore) wrote with disapproval in 1785 that many of the women, who possessed neither "sentiment nor education... are mere adventuresses from the Milliners' shops on Ludgate Hill... some even from Covent Garden and Old Drury" – areas of prostitution in London at that time (ibid: 6).

In the earlier period, Euro-Asian children often obtained prestigious jobs in the army and bureaucracy, but by the late 18th century, this policy changed. Euro-Asians became suspect, their loyalty was questioned, and they were excluded from higher posts and only allowed in clerical grades (Ballhatchet 1980: 97). By the early 1800s the *bibis* were not so frequently mentioned in wills, and by the 1850s, they had almost disappeared (Dalrymple 2002: 52). There was also some self-censorship. In the second edition of Thomas Williamson's *East India Vade Mecum* of 1825, references to *bibis* were deleted, and other books and biographies of important British officials were also revised to exclude the Indian wives (ibid: 52). 'Going native' went out of fashion, and consequently "wearing Indian costume, marrying Indian wives and living a hybrid Anglo-Mughal lifestyle" went into abeyance (ibid: 53). As a character in Kunzru's novel (2002: 38) says: "once upon a time you could say intermarriage was almost the done thing: back in the Company days, before all those biologists and evangelists made everyone scared of black blood" – a reference to racist views of scientists and missionaries in the 19th century. Dalrymple also observes that: "All sides seemed, for different reasons to be slightly embarrassed by this moment of crossover, which they preferred, to pretend had never happened" (Dalrymple 2002: xli). Hyam also noted that: "Miscegenation was frowned on... and Anglo-Indians repudiated... in the belief that all half-castes inherited the worst characteristics of both races *and were potentially subversive*" (Hyam 1990: 213, emphasis added).

In Sri Lanka, even before Britain ousted the Dutch, there had been mixed marriages between British seamen and Kandyan women which occurred after 1660, when Captain Robert Knox and his crew of 16 were taken captive by the Kandyan forces on landing on the island. For 20 years, Knox was not allowed to leave. Fifteen of the crew married local women and earned a living through agriculture, peddling and crafts. Robert Knox, a Scots Calvinist, and one of his crew did not marry locals.

Marriage, Knox wrote, led to many "sundry disputes" about "the lawfulness of matching with Heathens and Idolaters, and whether the Chingulays Marriages were any better than living in Whoredome" (Knox 1989: 382-83). Later Knox noted with some disapproval that those Englishmen who married "did frequently change their wives according to the Country Custome, when they disagree or liked other women better" (ibid: 383). One of Knox's crew, William Hubbard, born in 1637, who escaped to the Dutch-held maritime areas, gave a statement that he had married a Kandyan and had five sons and five daughters. These Euro-Asian daughters married into several ethnic communities. Knox enumerated the husbands: 1. the Disava of Sabaragamuwa; 2. Ratgeyava Appuhamy of Uva, "in service at the Court"; 3. Alverinho, the son of a Portuguese former storekeeper to King Rajasinha; 4. a Chetty; and 5. "a certain Payagala Appuhamy" (ibid: 370-1). Knox refers to Hubbard's wife as "Old Mother Hubbard" who "is alive, staying in Kandy," noting that Hubbard "did not dare mention his intended flight either to his wife or the children he left behind," as he had been severely punished by the king earlier for trying to escape (ibid: 37).

With the Dutch capitulation to the British, the future of those who had served the Dutch as soldiers, officials and in other capacities became an issue. These persons included the existing mixed population, the European-born former 'servants' of the Company and their descendants, the *vrij burghers* (free Burghers) who had special privileges during Dutch rule – based on occupations and trade, all tightly controlled by the mercantilist Dutch East India Company. With British rule, the Dutch and some v*rij burghers* either went to Batavia or to Holland. Those who remained were referred to as 'Burghers'– a convenient name used for those linked to the Dutch who stayed on after British occupation.

Defining Burghers

The British benefited from the services of the educated mixed population, now all considered Burghers. Many rose to high positions in government and dominated the medical, legal and teaching professions in the 19th century. The class-cum-ethnic distinction, however, between Portuguese and Dutch Burghers was kept alive. The Dutch Burghers–more prosperous and more educated were socially distinct from the Portuguese, who were "poorer,... more numerous, and less European" (McGilvray 1982: 236) and had lived in the island for a longer period. Portuguese descendants who were part of the skilled working class, following "a range of petty trades and crafts" including carpentry, tailoring and shoemaking, were designated 'mechanics' or *thuppahi* (tupass) which acquired a derogatory connotation (Roberts et al. 1989: 243; McGilvray 1982: 236). "The abuse heaped upon the Mechanics in most of the published sources of the period was quite intemperate," according to McGilvray, and such criticism reflecting "a prevailing repugnance towards racial or cultural hybridization" (1982: 244). E.F.C. Ludowyk describes the divisions among Burghers of the early 20th century:

> There were Dutch Burghers of august pre-eminence... (and) Burghers of various styles and colour. ...those classified by their place of origin such as Jaffna or Batticaloa, and... those dismissed as 'Micks' or 'mechanics' because they worked with their hands at some trade. (1989: 15)

Inevitably such debates on "styles and colour," about who were 'Burghers' and who were not, became fairly acrimonious during British rule. As McGilvray notes:

> British colonial writers of the nineteenth century and the Dutch Burgher partisans of the early twentieth century emphasized a wide social cultural, even racial division between these two categories of Burghers and to a considerable extent this remains the conventional view of the Burghers today. (1982: 236-37)

An eminent Burgher, R.L. Brohier, however, had an answer to the vexed issue of "Who is a Burgher?":

> Burgher is not an ethnographic name, and has nothing to do with race. The term is of historic origin and refers to a political community which had a distinctive character when it entered under the sway of the British government. (2000: 47)

But some Burghers claimed they were more than a 'political' category; they were an 'ethnic' category – a community of white Dutch Protestants that jealously guarded its boundaries and distinguished itself from the Portuguese Catholic or other mixed groups in colonial society. The ever-present question of how this imagined white community were darker-skinned than Europeans was evaded. However, by the time of British rule there were many categories of such persons, descendants of the Portuguese and Dutch and other Europeans, also including mixed descendants of former slaves and Africans of the 'Kaffir' regiment of soldiers recruited by the Portuguese. Roberts states that from the 1820s to the 1830s, the word 'Burgher' was used in a general way to mean "European descendants domiciled in Ceylon," appearing to apply to "the upper strata of the Burgher population" (1989: 212). With the British replacing the Dutch in 1796, a new British input was added to the pool of mixed people. The British, who were not concerned with the various refinements and shades of colour, consisting of *mestiços, casties, mixties, tupasses* and free Burghers, began to group them all together for census purposes as 'Burghers and Eurasians.'

The 1871 Census allowed people to classify themselves and "the resulting statistical data was bewildering and bizarre," as far as the Burghers, Eurasians and similar categories were concerned (Moldrich: n.d. 4). The Census recorded 5,771 Burghers, 2,256 Dutch and 783 Dutch descendants, along with 1,229 Portuguese and 3,431 Eurasians. But the list included many other variations including 'half-caste' (22), 'Indo-Briton' (57), 'East Indian' (65), and people who described themselves as being of French, German, Irish and Portuguese descent. This Census, as Moldrich observed, produced "chaotic statistics" (ibid: 9). In later decades (1881 and 1891), further reductions in classification were made. The Superintendent of the Census in 1891, Lionel Lee, admitted that:

> Some, perhaps, have been excluded... who might properly have been included, for it was not uncommon to find different members of the same family claiming different nationalities. Thus, one brother wrote... 'Burgher;' another 'Eurasian' and a third described himself as of... European nationality. (*Report on the Census of 1891*: 12, quoted in Roberts et al. 1989: 285 n84)

Among the upper-class Burghers who claimed Dutch descent there was much opposition about their classification with Eurasians. In the 1901 Census, Ponnambalam Arunachalam wrote of the problem of differentiating between the various groups of European origin; he quotes a 'Burgher gentleman' who said:

> It is not an uncommon experience for every nondescript who affects a pair of trousers and cannot with any right be classed under any particular category, to call himself a Burgher and take refuge under that very common term. (Arunachalam 1902: 83)

Arunachalam further described the class realities among the groups claiming European descent:

> The Dutch descendants… are among the most educated and most useful members of the Island's population and form the upper stratum of the Burgher community… the lower stratum consisting of those of Portuguese descent and Eurasians. (ibid)

In the 1911 Census, E.B. Denham made the point that differentiating between Eurasians and Burghers posed a dilemma since many called themselves Burghers "without any claim to the description"; and that the term Burgher "is now frequently incorrectly used to describe all persons of mixed descent." He also made the class distinction between Dutch Burghers who had produced not only many judges, lawyers and literary men, but also held leading posts in the clerical service, with the Portuguese descendants who "form an entirely different class known as the mechanic class" (Denham 1912: 239). But these distinctions between Burgher and Eurasian were invidious; and the Superintendent of 1921, L.J.B. Turner observed that since many Eurasians 'passed' for Burgher, the Census avoided probing further since it would mean "undue inquisition" (Turner 1923: 281).

The practice of lumping the two groups together was continued, and when the issue came up again at the 1946 Census, there was differentiation between Burghers and Eurasians, who were enumerated as separate 'races' the latter being referred to as Euro-Ceylonese; enumerators were instructed to follow "the statement of the persons themselves" (Ranasinghe 1950: 160). The total of Burghers and Euro-Ceylonese was 42,000 in 1946, the figure rising to 45,000 in 1953 and declining to 39,000 by 1981, due to migration abroad.

The New Community of Eurasians

While the British in Sri Lanka were content to refer to Portuguese, Dutch and British descendants of mixed origin as 'Burghers and Eurasians,' thereby erasing the diversity of the earlier groups, new feelings of difference grew between Burghers and Eurasians that paralleled the increased concern for 'racial purity' in the 19th century. Similar to the experience of the Portuguese and Dutch colonizers, in the early years of British rule, when few British women travelled to the colonies, partnerships occurred between British men and local women. British of all classes – government officials, planters, soldiers, policemen, railway workers and shop assistants – married or had liaisons with Burgher and other local women. Some of their children could 'pass' for British or Burgher, but the others, usually referred to as 'Eurasian,' were distinct from the mixed population of Dutch and Portuguese origin. Many British descendants (English, Irish and Scots) 'deemed' themselves to be Burgher, especially after they married Burghers. Roberts notes that they included the families of Austin, Beven, Crowe, Cooke, Eaton, Garth, Garvin, Keith, Morgan, Sproule, Steward and Wright; and possibly also the Armstrong, Ball, Davidson, Dick, Gray, Jennings, Mcleod, Nelson, Taylor and Gibson families (Roberts et al. 1989: 212). But the richer Eurasians – planters or professionals – kept a separate identity as 'Eurasians,' thereby distinguishing themselves from Burghers.[1] In Singapore, however, the term 'Eurasian' was used.

Singapore Eurasians

After the 'founding' of Singapore by the British in 1819, Eurasians – as they were called – from Malacca and India were early migrants, their numbers increasing by "the arrival or creation of new Eurasians," and by 1832 they formed 2.2% of the population (Braga-Blake 1992: 13).

In early 19th century Singapore, there was a "casualness" in ethnic classification for Census purposes, and categories of "native Christian" and "Indo-Britons" included those who were officially called "Eurasian" by the time of the 1849 Census (ibid: 12). Myrna Braga-Blake (herself a Eurasian) notes that the Eurasian community, being Christian, took advantage of missionary schools established in Singapore between 1834 and 1879, and made impressive gains in literacy and education. From 1885 to 1910, out of 45 government scholarships, 24 went to Eurasians, who were also among the first Asians to study abroad and become lawyers, doctors and engineers in Singapore and Malaya. Moreover, Eurasian women in Singapore (as in South Asia) were among the pioneer teachers, nurses and clerks (ibid: 14-15). Socially, however, by the 1850s racial barriers became more pronounced: "Eurasians were held in contempt and excluded from the social circles of the European ruling class." Thus Eurasians began to get together as a community to further their own interests and to regard themselves as true Singaporeans whose only 'motherland' was Singapore (ibid: 17). In contrast to India and Sri Lanka, the term 'Eurasian' was accepted and is still in use today.

What's in a Name?

For the Euro-Asians of Asia there was a great deal in a name. Over the decades they had difficulties in describing and defining themselves and in adopting an acceptable name for the community. In both India and Sri Lanka, the self-image and self-worth of the mixed groups were strongly linked to the name by which they were known. Gaikwad remarks on the heterogeneity in the Anglo-Indian community, which was composed of "persons belonging to many European countries and... to different parts of India." The Anglo-Indians, known by different appellations, searched "from the very beginning... for a *good respectable name*" for themselves. Several were considered: 'East Indian,' 'Indo-European,' 'Indo-Britain' and 'Eurasian' (1967: 42-43, emphasis added). Laura Roychowdhury has also comments on: "Anglo-Indians' multiple names... Eurasians, Firinghees, East Indians, Britasians, Indo-British." The way these names "constantly shifted" was suggestive of the "mixed parentage" of those in question and their "multiple cultural affiliations" which defied "easy definition" (2001:30).

In India, naming the mixed community was an old problem. Up to the end of the 18th century one popular usage was 'country born.' Special documents such as those of the East India Company of 1791 had references to "the sons of Native India," who unofficially were called 'half-castes.' By the mid-1820s, the community preferred the term 'East Indian.' A Kolkata Euro-Asian, John Ricketts, in evidence before the House of Commons in 1830, spoke of:

> The descendants of European British subjects and European foreigners by Native mothers, legitimate and illegitimate... have been called by various names... Eurasians, Anglo-Indians, Indo-Britons etc. but they have lately selected for themselves the name East Indians. (Stark 1934: 2)

Another Indian Euro-Asian, G.S. Dick, considered: "East Indian to be an excellent designation that approximates closest to the name of our country, the East Indies" (ibid: 4). According to Hawes (1996: 90), this name had connotations with the East India Company. As Caplan states the "colonial sin of mésalliance gave rise to a plethora of pejorative terms for Anglo-Indians, among them 'half and half' and 'chee-chee' (2001: 61). The popular but disparaging term, however, was 'half-caste,' which Hawes felt was not only "meaningless," but also "deeply resented." In Kolkata in 1818, the Euro-Asians petitioned the Governor-General asking him "to abrogate the degrading term of 'half-caste' from the Public Record of Government" and use the term Eurasian instead (Hawes 1996: 89). And in 1827, 200 Euro-Asians of Madras petitioned the government to abolish the official use of 'half-caste.' Even in early 20th century Sri Lanka, invective in reports against nationalist politicians by British officials included the phrase "unscrupulous half-castes" (Jayawardena 1972: 200). But in spite of all protests, says Hawes (1996: 90), "the abhorred term *half caste*" has continued in popular usage to this day.

In the 1860s, when the term 'Eurasian' was widely used, distinctions were made between those of mixed origin and 'domiciled Europeans,' the latter being those of unmixed British origin who had settled in India and were referred to as Anglo-Indian. In western literature and popular parlance, derogatory references to 'half-castes' and 'Eurasians' persisted. Caplan notes that Kipling was "repelled by the 'half-caste', the Eurasian who is 'neither flesh nor fowl', those disturbing 'rem(a)inders of the sexual traffic across the racial divide" (2001: 62). The famous crime writer of the 1930s, Edgar Wallace depicted 'Eurasians' in his novels as "cowardly… cunning and treacherous"—and such prejudice was cited as another reason for Anglo-Indians rejecting the name (Gaikwad 1967: 43). In a novel of the 1950s, John Masters' *Bhowani Junction*, an Anglo-Indian bitterly comments:

> We didn't look like English people, we looked like what we were – Anglo-Indians, Eurasians, cheechees, half-castes, eight annas, black-whites. I've heard all the names they call us, but I don't think about them unless I'm angry. (Masters 1960: 14)

The term 'Anglo-Indian' instead of 'Eurasian' was used in the Indian Census of 1911, and by the time of the 1919 electoral reforms it became an accepted category (Roychowdhury 2001: 327-30). Although 'Ango-Indian' also referred to domiciled British, the term was preferred and accepted by the mixed community and was recognized by the India Act of 1935 which defined an Anglo-Indian as: "A person whose father or other male progenitor… was of European descent but who is a native of India." This definition was accepted in the 1949 Constitution of India, and Anglo-Indians were represented by nominated members of the legislature (Gaikwad 1967: 42-43). Since travel between India and Sri Lanka in colonial times was relatively easy, it is not surprising that many 'Burghers' were actually Anglo-Indians, the Census of 1901 recording 322 'India-born' Burghers in Sri Lanka.[2]

In Sri Lanka too, there was continuous discussion about the 'correct naming' of the Euro-Asian community. In the 19th century, British-Asian descendants were known as 'Eurasians' and, as noted for census purposes, Burghers and Eurasians were classified together. But the question was a tricky one, and by the 1930s the debate on Eurasians was still on. At a meeting held in Kandy in November 1931, 87 Eurasians formed an association and launched a Bulletin.[3] The key question was whether the body should be termed 'Eurasian,' 'Euro-Ceylonese' or 'Anglo-Ceylonese. After discussion finally the term 'Anglo-Ceylonese' was narrowly accepted over 'Euro-Ceylonese.' This avoided the derogatory connotations and usage of the word 'Eurasian' and corresponded with the term 'Anglo-Indian.' Soon after in 1932, however, the they had second thoughts and the next Bulletin of the Anglo-Ceylonese Association challenged the name of the organization – especially its 'Anglo' connotation:

> There are many who still feel that the name of the Association should be altered to suit every individual in the fold... How can Anglo-Ceylonese refer to the descendants of Scottish, Irish or Belgians who settled down here in Ceylon? (Moldrich n.d.: 16, 25)

The name was changed to "Euro-Ceylonese Association," which figures from 1938 to 1950 in the *Ferguson's Directory.*[4] But since census categories continued to refer to 'Eurasians,' the use of the word 'Anglo-Ceylonese' lapsed, and the Census Report of 1946 referred to "Eurasians or Euro-Ceylonese."

Appearance and the 'Colour Chart'

Much diversity in appearance also existed within the communities of Burghers, Eurasians and Anglo-Indians, especially in the colour of skin, hair and eyes, as well as height and build. There being both dark and fair-skinned Euro-Asians in Asia, skin colour was prominent in the community's self-awareness. As the visible sign of European origin, the fairer the skin, the more dominant or recent was considered the European factor in ancestry; while the darker the skin, the more remote was the European connection. Fairer skin also corresponded to local concepts of beauty in South Asian cultures in general in colonial and post-colonial times. As Amali Philips has pointed out, in South Asia, dark skin is "considered an undesirable physical feature for a woman" and the words 'fair' and 'beautiful' are "often used synonymously, in female beauty descriptions and feminine gender identity constructions." Skin colour is also "symbolic capital for marriage and dowry negotiations" (Philips 2004: 253).

As noted earlier, such prejudices also applied to the mixed community, the Portuguese descendants in Sri Lanka being depicted not only as poor, but also dark-skinned "and less European" (McGilvray 1982: 236). The Dutch in Colombo were described by a British traveller in 1819 in terms of their virtue as well as "patience, thrift and care," whereas the Portuguese were called "mongrel" and reviled as "degenerate" (ibid: 246, quoting Thomas Ajax Anderson). The Dutch descendants prided themselves on being of "a distinctive northern European racial identity," with a Calvinist emphasis on correct living (ibid: 246). Race, colour and good conduct went together. One strong emphasis was on correct dress and a good command of the English language with a proper accent. All this was bound up with class hierarchies among the mixed communities (Caplan 2001: 64-5).

The consciousness of colour was a crucial element to those of the Euro-Asian community anxious to be seen as European in descent and lifestyle. In India there was also, as Caplan notes, a "collective amnesia concerning female ancestors among so many Anglo-Indian families" (2001: 23). According to an Anglo-Indian writer, Cedric Dover, this was "an urge for purity among the impure" (quoted in Caplan 2001: 72). Digby, writing on Burghers of Sri Lanka in 1879, spoke of "the desire for a fair complexion," which they all have "in greater or less degree." On the birth of a child, visitors desiring to compliment the parents would say, 'I think it will be a fair child' (Digby 1879: 31). An anxiety over skin colour was seen in the unsuccessful request by Indian Euro-Asians in 1886 for new racial classifications: the term 'Anglo-Indian' to be used for the "nearly white," 'Eurasian' for "evenly balanced" admixture, and 'East Indian' for "remote European ancestry," whose colour was nearer to that of 'natives' (quoted from *The Anglo Indian*, 9 Jan. 1886, in Sen 2002: 49n). Although with time the community as a whole became darker-skinned, the concern for skin colour persisted. Gaikwad reports: "Their greatest pride is that they are descended from Europeans…and there is nothing an Anglo-Indian deplores more than his dark skin …he would rather see his daughter married to a low, vulgar European… than marry one of her own kind" (1967: 44). In India, Gaikwad added, references to colour were "found more often in… abusive talk of women than in… men" (1967: 174).

Michelle de Kretser's novel *The Hamilton Case* also reveals derogatory references to skin colour in 'Burgher' conversation to vilify each other. Referring to a Burgher as being of a lower-class railway family, another Burgher says: "The cheek of that woman… black as the ace of spades and always passing herself off as one of us" (2003: 19). The theme of skin colour among Anglo-Indians and their reference to England as 'Home' was also highlighted and ridiculed in *Bhowani Junction,* in which Victoria Jones' father is ambitious for her to marry 'correctly': "You could… marry a British officer and then… go home… You can say you are partly Spanish" (Masters 1960: 191-92). But Victoria despises such attitudes. When her Anglo-Indian friend says, "My God, if they [the British] leave I will go home with them," Victoria replies in anger: "Home? Where is your home, man? England? Then you fell into the Black Sea on your way out?" (ibid: 26). The British in India also consistently mocked Anglo-Indian fantasies about 'Home' and their obsession with skin colour. In Kunzru's novel, the British discuss:

> the absurd way they talk of Home all the time… everyone knows none of them has ever been anywhere near England… They wear hats and read all they can of Home and avoid the sun like the plague. (2002: 37)

In Singapore, too, as Braga-Blake writes: "fairness was associated with the closeness of a European ancestor …it helped to be able to identify a white ancestor within living memory." In contrast to those of Dutch or British ancestry, "the Portuguese-Eurasian from Malacca is dark …the original Portuguese blood, if any, is extremely remote and lost in distant history" (1992: 119-20). Burghers from Sri Lanka and Anglo-Indians from India who had migrated to Singapore "felt uncomfortable about sharing a label with local Eurasians, particularly those from Malacca":

> Because of their fair skins, their Dutch and Anglo-Saxon surnames, their levels of education, the Queen's English they spoke and their way of life, it was conceivable for them to pass off as white. (Braga-Blake 1992: 122)

Obsession with colour among Singapore Eurasians was linked to "denial of Asian roots" and also with an attempt "to pass off as white." Some Eurasians would refer to 'black' or 'white' branches of the family and keep their distance accordingly. Distinctions were made between those who were white and those who had a 'touch of the tar brush.' But as in other colonies, the Eurasians of Singapore were humiliated by the British. They were regarded as Asians and were "at the receiving end of colonial arrogance," excluded from private clubs, some hotels and from the first-class wards in hospitals that were exclusively for Europeans (ibid: 123).

Patriarchy and Mixed-race Descent

Strong European patriarchal biases were reflected in the labelling, enumerating and classifying of the mixed (Euro-Asian) communities in the colonies. The European father – from Portuguese rule onwards – was the key player, while the local mother was 'erased' from the chronicle. In many genealogies of Burghers of Sri Lanka (as seen in the journals of the Dutch Burgher Union) there were blank spaces for the female ancestor's name if she happened to be 'coloured.' Since descendants took on the father's patronym, and European laws of the time were heavily patriarchal, descent was calculated in the father's line. The Dutch Burgher Union, formed in 1908, was only open to persons of "Dutch descent," defined as "descendants *in the male line* of all those of European nationality who were in the service …of the Dutch East India Company in Ceylon, and children of such descendants *in the female line* by marriage with Europeans" (Moldrich n.d.: 15, emphasis added). This bit of racism and sexism meant that a Burgher man marrying a local non-Burgher would qualify for membership, but a Burgher woman making such a marriage was disqualified. As mentioned earlier, the position in India was similar, where an Anglo-Indian was defined as a person whose *male* ancestors were of European descent.

In Singapore, however, there were two trends. One was to insist on descent in the male line, as for example in the constitution of the Eurasian Association (1990) which defines Eurasian as a person "whose father or... male progenitors in the male line is or was of European descent and whose name is etymologically European" (Braga-Blake 1992: 11). But other organizations of Eurasians, such as the Girls Sports Club, were more relaxed and allowed for European descent of either parent or ancestor (ibid: 11). According to Braga-Blake, Singapore Eurasians are "aware of distinctions related to European origins" and "placing a person on a social grid is an important part of Eurasian culture." When Eurasians first meet they:

> speedily ask questions about parentage and other blood links. [T]he questions are usually asked in varying degrees of subtlety. [T]he most undisguised questions would be 'Who's your mother?' or 'Who's your father?' (Braga-Blake 1992: 20)

Status also included important class distinctions. In Eurasian terminology in Singapore, there are references to "the upper ten," the "half-past six," "lower ten" and "first-second and third-class" Eurasians – distinctions based on "skin colour, wealth, education, occupation, religion... place of residence and lifestyle" (ibid: 119). Among Burgher and Eurasian families in Sri Lanka too, there was a distinct class division, the richer who were landowners, planters and professionals, being in a category separate from the orphans and the poor. The word 'stock' was frequently used by Burghers and Eurasians themselves to denote class, social origin and status. Some categorization was occupational in origin (similar to the caste system) and included 'loaded' words such as 'Railway Stock,' 'Tommy Stock,' and 'Planter Stock' – discussed in the next chapter.

Notes

1. Jean Arasanayagam née Solomons of Kandy recalls some other Eurasian families – Emersley, Murray, Thompson, Harvey, Cockburn, Clements, Forrest, Thorpe and Le Marchant (personal communication, 20 June 2005). She also refers to some Euro-Asian families, and marriages and liaisons of British planters with local women, in her book, *A Nice Burgher Girl* (2006).
2. Anglo-Indians who came to Sri Lanka as government servants and teachers, or as wives of Sri Lankans often called themselves 'Burghers.' One notable Anglo-Indian who settled in Sri Lanka ,was the lawyer Richard Morgan's father (see Chapter 6). Examples in the 20th century include Evelyn Cooke, a matron in the Civil Hospital, Chennai, who in 1926 married Gerard Ernest de Silva, a Sri Lankan studying engineering in Chennai. (I thank their daughter Barbara Seneviratne for these details). The principal of Mahamaya, Kandy, and later Museaus College was Bertha Rodgers, an Anglo-Indian (see Chapter 10). Another Anglo-Indian was William McClean Lawrence, from Kolkata, who joined the Sri Lankan police. He married a Sinhalese and his son, Harry McClean Lawrence, an insurance agent, also married a Sinhalese. The family still use the surname Lawrence, and talk freely about their British connection. (I thank their daughter Ranjani Lawrence for this information).
3. The office bearers elected were C. Robinson, C.G. Reith, J. Duff Tyler, A.T. Thomas, J. Barnet, C. Bolling, E. Boulton, H.S. Hudson, R.L. Jones, J. Jackson-Smale, Ms G. Hermon and Ms J. van der Poorten (Moldrich n.d.: 16).
4. C.G. Reith was President, and C. Robinson, Vice-President (1938-43). The secretary was R. Tennant (1941-50), and C. Bolling was Treasurer (1938-45) (Moldrich n.d.: 26).

3

CLASS, 'CASTE' and TAKING 'STOCK'

> Everyone was vaguely related and had Sinhalese, Tamil, Dutch, British and Burgher blood in them going back many generations… Emil Daniels summed up the situation for most of them when he was asked by one of the British governors what his nationality was – 'God alone knows, your excellency.'
>
> Michael Ondaatje, *Running in the Family,* 1984, p.41

> The Indos (Eurasians) were commonly regarded by the Dutch as lazy and stupid as well as oversexed… [T]he Indos overcompensated by disdaining the natives… Our tropical paradise was a madhouse, whose people looked on one another in ways that no outsider could ever fathom. It was a factory of inferiority complexes, which produced all manner of contorted behaviour that still has not entirely disappeared.
>
> Rudy Kousbroek, in *Het Oostindisch Kampsyndroom,* 1992, on his birthplace, the Dutch East Indies (quoted in Ian Buruma 2002b, p.72)

Stratification among Euro-Asians

South Asian preoccupation with hierachical formations also extended to the Euro-Asians, who like other communities jealously guarded their 'internal borders.' They had their own stratification and policies of exclusion based mainly on class, legitimacy and what was called 'stock' – a code word for class-cum-occupation. Included in these boundary markers were social status and cultural capital based on education. In Sri Lanka, the Burghers with Dutch family names and claims of Dutch or northern European origin were an exclusive group, often highly qualified, who on occasion adopted an almost apartheid-type ideology. Others who were not of Dutch origin, but of mixed European descent, also called themselves 'Burghers,' thereby poaching on the preserves of the Dutch and clashing with Dutch Burghers who strictly 'patrolled' their boundaries. In an interesting discussion on this issue in the *Madras Mail* in 1875, Anglo-Indians were said to be of lower status than the Burghers of Sri Lanka where, it was claimed, there was no 'poor white' question as in India, since three fifths of the mixed population were "offspring of lawful marriages," and two fifths were "absorbed by marriage into the Burgher class."

> The English, Scotch or German mechanical engineer, road officer, locomotive foreman or platelayer generally *marries* the native, or burgher female with whom he 'amalgamates.' The civil servant, the merchant, the planter and the army officer only *keeps* her. (quoted in Digby 1879: 38n1)

One notable example of the civil servant 'keeping' women was H.C.P. Bell, the eminent Archaeological Commissioner of the island from 1890 to 1912, who, in spite of an English wife and five children, had liaisons and children by local women. In Bell's biography, written by his two granddaughters Bethia and Heather Bell in 1993, some of his secrets are revealed, for by then frankness about such issues was the fashion. Bell, they remark, was "not a man to do without women," living in a period "when extra-marital relations were both utterly accepted and utterly ignored" (Bell & Bell 1993: 202). H.C.P. Bell's reputation "was and is legendary in the Island," they wrote, and "it was common knowledge that one of the comfortable bullock-carts which accompanied Bell on his circuits was specially fitted out for the accommodation of his female companion" (ibid: 202). This seems to have been a common practice. For as Leonard Woolf the assistant government agent of Hambantota – from 1908 to 1911 recalled: "a Prince, a Duke, and a Count… one a Bourbon, one an Orleans, and one a Napoleon," came to his office for licenses to hunt big game. Their expedition of four bullock carts contained "boxes, tents and furniture":

> The fourth contained a bevy of ladies who seemed to me most unsuitable for the jungles of Magampattu; their normal place of domicile was, I guessed, a Colombo brothel.(Woolf 1961a: 218-19)

In contrast, H.C.P. Bell's 'companions' were Sinhala and Tamil women from nearby villages or plantations or from among the many women who worked as wage labour on archaeological sites. An old villager recalled that "Bell chose a beauteous Sinhala belle as his mistress from his own Bathgama clan in the village" (Vesak Nanayakkara, quoted in Bell & Bell 1993: 202). Another mistress was Saveri Amma, whose daughter, Lourdette born in 1908, was placed in a Kandy convent, at the age of five. Lourdette's son by her marriage to a Burgher, Benedict Lambert, in 1936, recalls that "she was supposed to be an orphan, but her needs were provided for by her father, H.C.P. Bell." Lourdette became a teacher and telephone operator, living in the Kandy convent up to the time of her marriage. Bell continued to send her money each month, but they kept the relationship impersonal and secretive and never met. Similarly, Bell supported his son John, born in 1916 to Perumal Akka. He was sent to the Boys' Industrial Home and Orphanage in Colombo, spending his holidays in Nuwara Eliya. He joined the police force, but did not use the name Bell until after his father's death in 1937. John Bell only met his sister Lourdette by chance around 1944, when he was in his late twenties. In later years he met H.C.P. Bell's English daughter Zoe, his half-sister, but she "did not encourage the acquaintance" (ibid: 203). The Bell granddaughters finally met their Euro-Asian cousins in 1987, 50 years after their grandfather's death (ibid: 203-4).

Such examples based on illegitimacy and the existence of working-class mothers among 'Eurasians' caused continuous problems for the Burghers, who were obsessively preoccupied with class and status. E.B. Wright admitted that "some Burghers may be called Eurasians in an ethnological sense... (having) intermarried in the past, with Sinhalese and Tamils in their own station in life" (*The Searchlight*, 11 Aug. 1934). But there were others, he said, who were "no more Burgher than the man in the moon," and "took refuge in the term," as they found it advantageous "to pass off for a Burgher" (ibid, 8 Sept. 1934).

Similarly in 1934, B.R. Blazé – who highlighted the exclusiveness, high moral values and virtues of the Dutch Burghers – also admitted that the community was ethnically mixed. But being obsessed with class, Burghers such as Blazé stressed that such 'natives' whom they had married were highborn. The forefathers of the Dutch Burghers he says:

> did sometimes marry even Orientals, but these were naturally the pick and the flower of Ceylonese womanhood. The Burghers must therefore inherit all the best traits of the East together with their own ancestral qualities. There is possibly no Burgher family that has not by now acquired at least a slight strain of Eastern blood; and these inter-marriages… are nevertheless an important bond that inevitably links the Burghers in close friendship with the pristine inhabitants of the land (A. Ohnimesz [B.R. Blazé] 1934:10 & Roberts et al. 1989: 124-5)

While those of mixed descent in Sri Lanka were called 'Burghers,' some Dutch Burghers objected to such indiscriminate labelling. E.B. Wright wrote on "The Term Burgher," explaining that it was "a Dutch word meaning citizen," applicable to a person of "legitimate descent in the male line." He claimed that the Dutch Burghers were "a distinct and honorable community… many of (whom) trace their descent back to the nobility of various European countries":

> They are not a race of accidents, bastards or nondescripts. They… have never been confused with Eurasians, Anglo-Indians, domiciled Europeans, or the lowly and hybrid class of Portuguese known as Mesticos and Tupasses or mechanics. *(The Searchlight*, 6 Oct. 1934)

Those of mixed origin encountered a problem of legitimacy – an issue of crucial importance in 'respectable' society, governed by patriarchal Roman-Dutch and British laws. Legitimacy conferred various legal and social advantages, whereas illegitimacy incurred many disadvantages, the word 'illegitimacy' itself signifying 'bastard' – an abusive word. Illegitimate descendants of Europeans or Burghers took *the nationality of the local mother*, but if a Burgher or European woman married a local Asian man, the children took *the father's nationality.*

This was a clear case of 'palming off' mixed-origin children on to the Asian parent. F.H. de Vos, a Dutch Burgher Union (DBU) genealogist, firmly invoking the rule of patriarchy, proclaimed:

> The test of a man's race is that of his earliest known ancestor in the direct male line of legitimate descent... A wife or child follows the racial status of her husband or father, a bastard that of his mother. (McGilvray 1982: 248)

At a Commission in 1910 to prepare for electorates on ethnic lines, the issue of Burgher identity caused some confusion and concern. Roberts writes that under interrogation, many eminent Burghers were "forced to indulge in fancy footwork, to twist and turn and end up quite convoluted" (1989: 123). Giving evidence at this Commission, a Dutch Burgher professional, Dr W.G. van Dort (famed for clashing with British planters on his critical report condemning the high mortality rates among plantation workers), was very obstinate about his identity. He expressed the deep prejudices among some Burghers on the definition of 'Burgher,' an issue fraught with class and race overtones. Van Dort insisted that:

> There is the Burgher community proper, and then there is a large admixture – a number of different shades and sorts of people, composing the bulk... partly European descendants, partly Indo-Portuguese, partly "Portuguese" of the lower classes (including) the children of emancipated slaves inter-married into descendants of Portuguese who have married native women. (ibid: 245)

While the problem of self-definition remained to torment the mixed population, patriarchal intolerance persisted. The DBU in 1939 ruled that a woman member who had married a man who did not qualify for membership would be expelled. McGilvray described this as a:

> caste-like solicitude for the endogamy of Dutch Burgher women (which) was chiefly focussed on the threat of low-status out-marriage, whereas the prospect of producing... new members through hypergamous unions with European men had always been warmly applauded. (McGilvray 1982: 248)

But discrimination by Dutch Burghers against Eurasians also existed and tensions flared up during the First World War over the question of a Volunteer Force in Kandy. Burghers had earlier been part of the Ceylon Light Infantry Volunteer Movement (1881), where they outnumbered all "the other indigenous communities combined,"[1] some Burghers and Eurasians serving in the British army in Europe.[2] During the late 19th century, Burghers and Eurasians were together in the Volunteers, but by the early 20th century – when concern about ethnic identities became more pronounced among all communities—hostility also mounted between the two groups. The British who acceded to ethnic feelings had established five platoons of volunteers: European, Dutch Burgher, Sinhalese, Tamil and Muslim, and Eurasian. The Dutch Burgher Union had raised a volunteer Colombo Town Guard and proposed to form a Town Guard in Kandy, composed exclusively of Dutch Burghers. When the British authorities, however, tried to streamline the platoons, combining the Burgher and Eurasian ones, the Burghers protested and "ceased to attend drill." In addition to excluding Eurasians, they also refused C.L. Jansz entry to the Burgher platoon on the grounds that he was not a Dutch Burgher (Moldrich n.d: 48-51).

The Kandy Burghers even vented their class consciousness about the possibility of 'lower-class' Englishmen being in charge of their platoon. A Burgher, J.D. Jonklaas was prepared to join the platoon "on condition that he did not have to take orders from 'any damn shoppie'" – a reference to British salesmen in large shops who had a low social position in the colonial hierarchy of the resident British (Moldrich n.d.: 59). But both Burghers and Eurasians in prestigious professions were also class conscious. Dr Peterson, a Eurasian, records the indignant response of a Burgher doctor (Noel Spittel) to a complaint about their noisy motorcycles at night outside the doctors' and nurses' quarters. He claimed that his own motorcycle and that of Dr Peterson were of the "latest silent models," unlike those of the "shopees" who come to take the nurses out (Fonseka 2001: 34). This reference to British salesmen reflected the hostility of some Burghers and Eurasians to British in the island of lower social status.

But there was also resentment at British in positions of authority who used derogatory language – such as 'half-caste' – and often discriminated against those of mixed origin. In the early years the planters' clubs in the tea-growing areas did not admit Eurasians – a practice the latter bitterly resented. The Catholic Church also, for a period, refused to accept Eurasian clergy on the grounds of their illegitimacy. But rich Eurasians who owned plantations were socially accepted and often married into Burgher families. Some Burghers, however, had 'hang-ups' about Eurasians based on legal status and class, namely their illegitimacy and relative poverty. Although marriages between Burghers and Eurasians took place, this was not the first option of status-conscious Burghers as a whole, while the top Eurasian families of the plantation areas preferred to marry fellow Eurasians of direct British origin, to marrying Burghers who were of Dutch and Portuguese descent. It was, in practice, a type of class-caste system, based on what was called 'stock.'

Of the wealthy Eurasian families, the richest was that of Antoine Joseph van der Poorten (1849-1936), a Belgian who had arrived in Sri Lanka in the 1860s. During a coffee blight he bought 'Greenwood,' a 1,000-acre coffee plantation in Galagedera (near Kandy) from the former owner who had been bankrupted. Van der Poorten planted the estate with cocoa seeds acquired in the Belgian Congo where he had spent two years. He also expanded his landholdings and branched out into dealing in French cars and wine, and lending money. He owned the Hotel Suisse in Kandy and developed estates – tea, rubber and coconut – stretching up to the east coast, making him one of the largest owners of cultivated and uncultivated land in the country. Van der Poorten married a Kandyan Sinhalese, Ranasinghe Mudiyanselage Menika (called Ran Menika), and had seven children. Two of their sons, Henry and Benjamin, continued the acquisition of land, but disputes over property split the family into warring factions. Henry married several times, his wives being Sinhalese, while Benjamin married a Eurasian, Nellie Winter of Baddegama. Their two sons, Antoine (Tony) and Michael were Marxists, active in the Lanka Sama Samaja Party (LSSP). Moving to Britain in the 1950s they joined the Socialist Labour League (a Trotskyist group) – Michael changing his name to Mike Banda. He married Kamini Meedeniya (now Vitharne), a granddaughter of Kandyan chief Meedeniya Adigar, who had been a friend and debtor of A.J. van der Poorten.

Liaisons in the 'Planter Raj'

White women were rare in the colonies not only during Portuguese and Dutch rule, but also in the early decades of British occupation. At that time in Sri Lanka, there were some wives of top officials and businessmen in the cities, but hardly any on plantations, or among the lower ranks of the army or railway employees. On the coffee plantations of the mid-19th century, the rare sight of a British woman was compared to an "apparition." The pioneer coffee planter in Sri Lanka, James Taylor wrote to a friend – which Forrest paraphrases:

> Ah well, if only he had a wife! But he was never trained for ladies' society, and indeed a white woman with petticoats and talking his own language would frighten him out of his wits. (1967: 75-76)

Similarly William Boyd in his *Autobiography of a Periya Durai* (1889) describes his first sight of an English woman in Kundasale, "so unexpected was this apparition that my heartbeat thumped as… never… before" (quoted in Moldrich n.d.). Since British women were at best ephemeral and unattainable in those early days of coffee planting, bachelor planters often resorted to liaisons with local women. The British writer William Digby observed (in 1879), that Europeans of all classes in Sri Lanka "employed on railways and elsewhere, and even those in higher destinations marry Burghers or native women" (1979 Vol. 1: 51-52). Some of these relationships were temporary, with their children being given to orphanages or being absorbed into the mothers' communities.

There was a clear class difference among the Eurasian descendants of European planters, based on land-ownership, wealth, and professional skills. Some planters looked after their Eurasian offspring – by educating them to be professionals or to take up jobs in the plantation sector. They occasionally bequeathed plantation property to them, as well as shares in companies, land and houses. These rich Eurasians developed a strong sense of being of British descent (rather than Dutch or Portuguese). They kept the Union Jack flying, and followed a British upper-class lifestyle.[3] Such families were careful not to be mistaken for Burghers, and tended to marry within the Eurasian community. Some of the wealthy plantation Eurasians in colonial Sri Lanka included the families Barnet, Bolling, Duff, Tyler, Hermon, Johnson, Nichol, Reith, Tindall, Wilson and Winter.

The origins of the Eurasian community in Sri Lanka remains an untold, hidden part of history, not discussed in the standard British works on colonial society of the time nor in any of the local historical writings. Eurasians themselves hardly ever spoke about the alliances their European ancestors had with local women. One occasionally sees the issue raised in fiction – in recent novels and short stories written by Burghers. One such author, Jean Arasanayagam (née Solomons) fictionalizes the cohabitation of British planters with estate or village women. In one story, a Eurasian woman reminisces about "the women who bedded with our grandfathers – Jesupulle, Shanthi, Saraswathi, Meenambal and the women from nearby villages" (2001:117). About the grandmother, Jesupulle, she surmises:

> my grandfather had seen her on that upcountry estate as he rode the winding tracks on horseback and summoned her to his trimmed lawns and flowerbeds. Were her parents ordered to bring her to the big bungalow? Perhaps it was her father who took her there… (ibid: 123)

The protagonist also muses about the way Eurasians were over determined by their male ancestry: "In our lives so strong had patriarchy been that we had only the names of our English and European forefathers…my father, his brothers, created their own country in their manner and style of living." In contrast, the Tamil grandmother and her family were 'erased' out of existence, about which the narrator feels great regret. "I never heard her legends, their myths, their epics, unwritten sagas, journeys" (ibid: 119). She adds: "I see only the portraits of my grandfather and my own father. There is an empty space where Jess's

(Jesupulle) portrait should have been" (ibid: 124). The class divide between the rich tea planters and the poor tea-pluckers is described in terms of the English grandfather with his planting enterprises and the grandmother who had toiled on the estate. We were, she says, "unique in being mixed" with the community of Jessupulle, who:

> no longer picking tea but sitting in the Suisse Hotel and sipping the finest Broken Orange Pekoe from China cups in the dining hall would no doubt have appreciated the ironies. (Arasanayagam 2001: 125)

At the end of the story, the narrator accepts her mixed identity. There were two portraits in her room – of her father and grandfather. She perceives the lacuna, which she then decides to fill:

> I will search out Jesupulle's photograph from the family album, get it enlarged… and placed between those of the two men. Fill in the gaps. Retrace the routes her forefathers took. Acknowledge the part that women like Jesupulle played in creating our kind. Celebrate her birth. And that of her children. (ibid: 132)

Another Burgher, Lorna Wright (née Jansz), in her novel *Just Another Shade of Brown* (1976), fictionalizes some true stories of life on the tea plantations. She describes the connivance of planters with local men to procure girls from the estates and villages, and the plight of the children of these unions. Wright explains the modalities:

> Procedures were simple and accepted. A woman he fancied, and there would be instructions for the tea-maker. An appropriate day, and the appropriate hour was always at night… Nameless women. Often nameless progeny, muddied lives. A muddied minority problem for the distant future. (1976: 4-5)

The prospects in life for these illegitimate children varied. A famous Burgher doctor of the early 20th century, Lucien de Zilwa recalled family life on the plantation in Pussellawa, where his father worked in the 1880s. A British planter from a nearby estate had two children by a Tamil worker, who was later sent away with the children to the "cooly lines." The planter, who did not like to see his children "running about almost naked, like the children of the coolies," wished to have the son Percy educated. He arranged to pay Rs. 25 monthly to the de Zilwas to house the boy, and gave the child's mother an additional allowance for not only "surrendering the child" but also agreeing not to visit him. Lucien de Zilwa's mother proceeded to cut Percy's "Robinson Crusoe hair, (and) deloused and washed him" and also intervened successfully with her husband for Percy's mother to visit him monthly (de Zilwa 1967: 11). Percy was brought up as one of the de Zilwa family; after Lucien was admitted to the prestigious St Thomas' College, Colombo, two younger de Zilwa brothers and Percy were admitted to the school in 1892 at a concessional charge (ibid: 27-28). There is no further mention of Percy in Dr de Zilwa's memoirs, and hardly any of Percy's sister who lived in the de Zilwa home in 1888, on the same terms as her brother had done. She received more than a clean-up; for as de Zilwa writes:

> She needed… an operation for the repair of her ears. The lobes had been pierced, and heavy metal earings had enlarged the hole to a diameter of three inches. A few years later she was sent to a convent. (ibid: 14)

Ronald Hyam has referred to the persistence of sexual exploitation on plantations, "whether worked by slaves or indentured labourers" (1990: 93). In Sri Lanka, this was sometimes officially deplored. In 1848, for example, Governor Lord Torrington in a private letter to Earl Grey, the Secretary of State for the Colonies, put some of the blame for the insurrection of that year on the behaviour of the planters:

> The mass of the coffee planters, many of them the very worst class of Englishmen, has very much tended to lower and degrade our caste and character in the eyes of the natives. The habits of the planters particularly with the women has been most objectionable and in the eyes of a Kandian a *coffee planter* is a term of reproach. (de Silva 1965: 98)

An account of violence, rape and exploitation is also given in William Knighton's memoir, *Forest-life in Ceylon,* published in 1854. It describes a coffee plantation where the 'good' planter (Hofer), married to a British woman, is contrasted with the violent bachelor planter (Siggins), who when acused of giving a Sinhala worker a "frightful flogging," said:

> I honoured the rascal's daughter with a little attention – she was a fair, neatly-formed Kandian girl – and he sulked about it... grew... so insolent... demanded her out of the bungalow, where she was living infinitely more decently and respectably than... before. The servants had particular orders... that she should not leave. (Knighton 1854 Vol.1: 284-85)

While such attitudes, similar to the *droit de seigneur* in Europe persisted in the 'planter raj,' the prerogative was obviously that of the male. In both India and Sri Lanka, the big taboo and constant fear was of sexual contact between resident European women and local men. In India, a servant was the victim of a trumped-up charge of assault that he had molested an official's wife (see Chapter 12). In Sri Lanka, a horsekeeper on an estate, who had been severely beaten up by a planter named J. Tyndal, took the latter to court, whereupon Tyndal fabricated a story that the worker was watching his wife undressing, "his lascivious eyes glued to the keyhole." The result was that Tyndal was acquitted and the worker fined for frivolous litigation (Lewis 1926: 71).

Many well-known British planters had local liaisons. Recently it was revealed that a planter and reputed writer, John Still (1880-1941), author of *Jungle Tide*, who arrived in Sri Lanka in 1897 and first worked on a tea plantation in Dickoya (and later in H.C.P. Bell's archaeological survey), had a Kandyan Sinhalese, Joslin Hamine, as his mistress. Their daughter Laura – who did better than many of the children of such unions– married a Burgher, J.C. Christiansz, in 1934. John Still secured her financially by creating a trust which gave her the income from 200 shares in the Mylanda Rubber Company (*Sunday Observer*, 30 Sept. 2001). The Eurasian Cameron family of Sri Lanka were the descendants of two distinguished ancestors – Charles Hay Cameron, the civil servant who was co-author of the Colebrooke-Cameron reforms of 1833, and his more famous wife, the pioneer photographer Julia Margaret Cameron. After C.H. Cameron's retirement, they continued to live in Sri Lanka, acquiring coffee plantations. Their third son Evan Wellesley Cameron (1843-83) a coffee planter, had Eurasian descendants who moved to Galle and married into some well-known Sinhalese families.

Another glimpse into the Eurasian community is seen in a letter by George E. Leitch, a Eurasian former government servant. He raised the issue of citizenship (in 1988), and spoke openly about the origins of Eurasians:

> When English planters were running our plantations, some decided to marry Asians, either Sinhalese, or Indian Tamil, and their off-spring were called Eurasians... Today there are many in Sri Lanka ...the McShanes, Taylors, Barnes, Bowles, Leitches... having names of their English ancestors. (Moldrich n.d. 27)

In contrast to the privileged Eurasians were those who were in 'orphanages' or remained with their mothers and lived in the villages or plantations. K.P.S. Menon, Agent of the Government of India in Kandy, records: "from Nuwara Eliya you descend into Welimada which the rest-house keeper would tell you with a twinkle in his eye is called 'Little England' because of the number of blue-eyed babies there" (Menon 1981: 105). Many other villages were also known as 'Little England' for the same reason. In many cases, Eurasian children were sent to 'Homes' or 'orphanages.' There is also record of a planter, Edward Theodosius Gerlitz of Badulla, who died in 1879 leaving his estate worth Rs 42,194 and property in the town for the education of poor Burgher women and children (*Ceylon Daily News Weekly*, 24 Dec. 1928, "Free Schools for Burghers"). This bequest was probably mainly for Eurasian children. Also in Badulla, was a 'Girls' Home' for Eurasians started by a Methodist missionary, Fanny Cooke, who lived in Sri Lanka from 1888 to 1926 and was affectionately remembered as a 'surrogate mother' to the children. The best-known 'orphanage' was run by the Irish nuns of the Good Shepherd Convent in Kandy (founded in 1867), where Eurasian girls received some basic education at the convent school before having their marriages arranged.

The situation in India was similar for Euro-Asian girls in convents. Roychowdhury refers to "the excitement and humiliation when convent girls of marriageable age were lined up by the nuns in front of potential husbands, all Anglo-Indian or enlisted British men" (2001: 128). She also describes a specific case, where an Anglo-Indian says: "Maureen, over there, I rescued her from one of those orphanages. The nuns were just keeping her locked up until they could marry her off to any old fellow who would have her" (ibid: 235).

As Stoler has noted, orphanages for European and Euro-Asian children, supported by state and private charities, were features of Dutch, French and British colonial rule. In India, there were such institutions in "almost every town, cantonment and hill station" (Stoler 1991: 80, quoting David Arnold 1979). One motivation was to "keep fair-skinned children from running barefoot in native villages." Moreover, Euro-Asians could not only shame the colonial rulers (by running barefoot, etc.), but more seriously might also become "anti-colonial revolutionaries" or prostitutes – two recurrent colonial nightmares. As Stoler writes: "the gender breakdown was clear: moral instruction would avert sexual promiscuity among métisse girls and political precocity among métis boys who might otherwise become militant men" (Stoler 1991: 79).

While some educated Eurasian girls in Sri Lanka found employment, usually as nurses, nannies, secretaries and teachers, many were less fortunate and were subject (like their mothers before them) to sexual exploitation. Arthur Paynter, who ran an orphanage in Sri Lanka for Eurasians, gave a grim picture of the fate of many such children:

> The worst village in Ceylon is commonly known by the name 'Little England' because of the number of fair children and adults… every girl without exception as she grows up, becomes the mistress of a white, or other man, or becomes a public prostitute. (Darling 1991: 262-63)

There was some anxiety among Europeans about 'half-caste' children living in orphanages. Indira Ghosh cites a "revealing example of a disruption of the smooth surface of the colonial textualization of the Eurasian" in the writings of Viscountess Amelia Falkland, wife of the

Governor of Bombay. She made an official visit (in the 1850s) to a school for Euro-Asian 'orphans' and wrote of a "ridiculous incident" to which her response was nervous laughter and escape:

> One of the gentlemen of the party... just arrived from England, found himself in a very unforseen position. A very little child ... with large black eyes, a flattish nose, and a complexion shading off ... into yellow ochre clung round his legs, ...and cried out 'Pa-pa! Pa-pa!' ... I hastened to escape from a scene which was much too laughable. (Ghosh 1998: 150)

The *Madras Mail* of 1875 discussed the question of the mixed child of planters and remarked on a gender difference. The male child of a planter by "his illicit connection with Muniamma of the ...cooly-lines or Menicka of the next village... is allowed to grow like a weed on the estate, picks up a smattering of the three R's" and becomes a conductor (supervisor) described as a "class of people only one step removed from... the cooly lines." The female offspring might be luckier, "(the planter) cares for her, has her educated, and sometimes ships her home to his friends and provides for her in his will" (Digby 1879: 38 n1). But the prospects of Eurasian boys could vary. Some did well and attended the prestigious Colombo Academy (begun in 1836), their fees being paid by their fathers. During the years 1836 to 1840, of the boys at the Academy, 60 per cent were Burgher and Eurasians (Roberts 1989: 56); some of the latter coming from an orphanage for Eurasian children. Confirmation of the existence in the mid-19th century of such an orphanage (probably state- run) was made by a well-known Sinhalese arrack-renter and merchant, Jeronis Pieris, who was at the Academy in the 1840s. He refers in the 1850s to his Eurasian schoolmates:

> A great many of our schoolfellows... are now in this District; they are chiefly those of the orphan asylum. I have seen Atwell, Scofield and some others. They often call in at the (Arrack) Godowns to pay me a visit when they come down from the coffee estates. Atwell is Assistant Superintendent of Veddihille Kadulla Estate. (Roberts 1975: 79)

The Paynter Homes for Eurasians

Many aspects of intermarriage, hybridity and concern for Eurasian children are seen in the story of the Paynter family. Arthur Paynter (1862-1933), originally of Cornwall, England, joined the Salvation Army as a young man and first worked in India. He dressed in local garb, lived close to the people and took on an Indian name (Jai Bhai). There in 1893 he married a Sinhalese, Agnes Weerasooriya from a prominent Buddhist family of Dodanduva, who had studied in a missionary school in Kotte. She was in Britain in 1885 with her brother, Arnolis Weerasooriya, who had joined the Salvation Army. While attached to the Clapham training centre of the Salvation Army, they did social work in the slums of Paris (Darling 1991: 11-18). They returned to work among the poor in India, but Major Arnolis (as he was known) died of cholera at the age of 33 in 1888. Agnes, known as Lieutenant Anagi, continued to live and work in India, even after the death in India of her cousin Lucy during a plague epidemic.

The problems that Arthur Paynter had with the Salvation Army reveal the racial tensions that could prevail even among those trying to alleviate the suffering of the poor. He was criticized for 'nativism' because of his belief that "India could only be evangelised by the Indians." With Agnes and some other Englishmen who had similar views he left the Salvation Army in 1897 to form the India Mission which would work "on Indian lines" (ibid: 42). His unconventional views continued in later years. He was an admirer of Gandhi and the Indian freedom movement, and also spoke out against racism. As the parent of four Euro-Asian children himself, he was conscious of the problems faced by those of mixed origin and, settling in Sri Lanka, devoted himself to their cause.

In 1924 Arthur and Agnes Paynter started the Paynter Homes and Schools in the Sri Lankan plantation district of Nuwara Eliya. Their aim was to educate Eurasian children and later settle them on farmlands in a colony started in Champawa at the Himalayan foothills. Paynter's work was supported by his own children. The eldest, Arnold, was, in his father's words, "able to understand intimately the needs of a particular class of children, more than any ...other man," (ibid: 265). Arnold with his brother David Paynter (a famous Sri Lankan artist) also helped in the Himalayan farm, while their sister Evangeline supervised the Homes in Sri Lanka. The project became well known, and the children also achieved some fame for their excellent public singing performances in Colombo.

Those involved in the Paynter Homes were always on the look-out for Eurasian children. Arnold Paynter tried to persuade village mothers, to place their Eurasian children in the Home, and many "children ... of mixed parentage" were enrolled. Arthur Paynter records the case of a planter named Plumridge who wanted the school to take charge of three of his five children, with the sixth child "due next month" (Darling 1991: 187). Among those brought to the Homes in 1929 were Mary, speaking only Tamil, and Leo, who only spoke Sinhalese (ibid: 193); a girl aged 6, named Merle de la Pole, arrived from Ratnapura (ibid: 221), and two years later "a beautiful little girl of 9 years" named Mary Linnel who came to the orphanage (ibid: 245). By 1929 there were 60 Eurasian children in the Paynter Homes, the figure rising to 77 in 1931 (ibid: 248). But the Homes had many problems, including the perennial one of funding. Efforts had to be made to collect donations locally and from abroad. Lorna Wright has highlighted the issue in her novel: "Every planter knew of the orphanage in the hills... but to pay it a visit was to have an interest." Donations were therefore sent by cheque, and the "contributions were from those who had a guilty conscience" (Wright 1976: 272-73).

Another thorny problem was that of the older Eurasian girls at the Homes whose mothers wanted them to return to the village, occasionally even taking Paynter to court on this issue. For instance, Mary and Julia Horsfall's mother Dingiri unsuccessfully petitioned the courts in 1929 for their return (ibid: 215). Paynter was convinced they were to be used for prostitution and cited the cases of Ruani, Mabel and Ada (Eurasian girls) who were part of "the business of the village" named Malpotha which had a bad reputation. "It cannot be God's will for us to train and educate girls to be superior prostitutes," Paynter wrote (ibid: 217). He also "earnestly begged" a leading planter and Legislative

Councillor, Sir Thomas Villiers, to make all efforts "to protect girls under 16 from their guardians and parents who introduce them to a life of prostitution or batten on their vice" (ibid: 218).

One case reported in the Paynter Homes' newsletter was that of Fannie and her brothers Alan and James, children of a Eurasian woman of Mahagama, "a notorious haunt of Eurasian prostitutes." She had been "for years the mistress of a white man." The three children were "rescued' in 1925 and were referred to as "among the brightest of our family of over 115 Eurasian children." The allegation was made that in some villages "every such Eurasian girl is sold when she is 12 or 13, for Rs 200 or Rs 300" (*India Christian Mission Document*, c. 1930).

Jean Arasanayagam has described the other side of the picture, through the pain felt by two Eurasian sisters, brought up on their father's plantation, but separated from both parents and sent to an orphanage:

> It was more than a physical pain. It's a growing feeling of hurt that has haunted me from childhood beginning with that violent break from the two human beings with whom I had shared my early years. (Arasanayagam, *Dragons in the Wilderness*, forthcoming)

The Paynter Homes survived the economic depression years of the 1930s. After Arthur Paynter's death in 1933, the family continued its work for the project. From 1947 to 1983, his daughter Evangeline Darling (1905-92) worked in the school, and his granddaughter Averil Greet was active from 1953 onwards, becoming the Homes' Superintendent for nine years from 1983, and was succeeded by Suzette Boulton.

The Eurasian population was not confined to the plantation sector but included an important component of employees of the railways and the armed forces. These groups had some of the features of the caste system. They were preoccupied with status and hierarchies of 'high' and 'low' sustained by myths of origin, and aware of their ambiguous relationship to the 'Brahmins' – namely the Dutch Burghers.

'Tommy Conquests'

While occupation was the strongest determinant of status in Euro-Asian society in India and Sri Lanka, hierarchy within the mixed community was also intertwined with country of origin. Among the Anglo-Indians, there was the broad regional divide between those of south and east India of Portuguese descent (known as *feringhis*) – and the north Indian Anglo-Indians of mainly British origin. Among the latter were those referred to as being of 'Tommy stock.' Gaikwad has revealed that some diehard upper-class Anglo-Indians excluded those with Portuguese surnames from the community, and Anglo-Indians from south India in turn looked with disdain at those from north India. He quotes a rich Anglo-Indian woman from Kerala dismissing the north Indian Anglo-Indians as "descendants of soldiers," labelling them 'Tommy Atkins' or 'Tommies' (a slang word for soldiers):

> They are uneducated and rude people… [W]e people of Portuguese descent are better than these from 'Tommy' stock. Our forefathers were rich businessmen so we are also in business and not in railways. (quoted in Gaikwad 1967: 166)

In South Asia, the term 'Tommy stock' was thus used derisively for the mixed descendants of British soldiers of the lower ranks of the army stationed in the region. During British rule, a strict class distinction was observed between the higher echelons of the armed forces and the subalterns recruited from the British working-class including destitutes and orphans. Geoffrey Powell writes of the "perennial recruiting problem." The 65th Regiment in Sri Lanka in the early 19th century – along with five other regiments – had been filled with boys less than 16 years of age. They were often orphans who relieved the parishes in Britain "of the expense of maintaining… young paupers," or were farm workers given over to the army. And although conditions in the army were "deplorable," the recruits had already been conditioned to "a harsh existence" (Powell 1973: 81). The unmarried subalterns abroad lived in barracks, often forming liaisons with local women. In India, as Hawes writes, the practice of the lower ranks of the army consorting with "native women" was "tacitly condoned" but never "officially countenanced":

> In Royal regiments a 'policy of attaching soldiers to native women' was in operation by 1810. If regiments left for Europe, as the 66th and 78th did in 1817, their women were taken on by soldiers in other units....many other soldiers, found female company in casual relationships. (1996: 14)

Moreover, there was the issue of rape of local women by European soldiers, always a controversial problem in a colonial situation, but hardly ever acknowledged. Powell says that Bombardier Alexander wrote of his regiment's exploits in Sri Lanka (in 1804), and describes a punitive expedition, painting "a lurid canvas with a looting of an arrack store, a broad hint of rape, and a mob of hysterically unnerved soldiers" (1973: 164).

Although the Euro-Asians in India were descendants of British of all classes, most were from the armed forces – the result of the expansion of the military from a few hundred in mid-18th century India to 18,000 by 1790. Hawes refers to these Euro-Asians as the "poor relations of the larger British community in India" (1996: 9). While both the officers and the rank and file had local women consorts, there was a marked difference in the fate of their Eurasian children. The top brass usually made efforts to look after their children, had them educated (in Britain or India), and found employment for the males and arranged marriages for the females.

In India, the class barriers were sharply demarcated, even among the orphans. The military orphans, so-called despite the mothers and sometimes fathers of the 'orphans' being alive, were stratified according to the fathers' class and position. Admission to the Upper Military Orphan School in Kolkata depended on the father's high rank and bequests to the orphanage. Some of the girls of this school who married British officers moved into a higher level of society and avoided sinking "into the working classes in India." Their origins had made them very status-conscious and "vulnerable to the obsessive preoccupation with ancestry and pigmentation" (Chatterjee 1999: 93-94). In contrast, the Lower

Military Orphan School in Kolkata was for the children of subalterns. Some of the girls became domestic servants in the houses of East India Company officials and Army officers. Many orphans were displayed like slaves and 'married off.' The case of the 'half-caste' *ayah* in the house of Fanny Eden, sister of Governor-General Aukland, is documented. She had been "married at twelve years old to a man forty years older... who came and *chose* her from the school as was then the custom" (Dunbar, quoted in Chatterjee 1999: 91).

Hawes has described the class system of the Euro-Asians in India, noting the difference between army bandsmen at the lower levels, the senior grades of government service, and "the few wealthy Eurasians" who themselves had "little in common" with them except except their racial origin (1996: 74). An upper-class origin on the paternal side enabled some Euro-Asians to socially distance themselves from those doubly disadvantaged by working-class or poor origins on both the British and Indian sides of their families.

In Sri Lanka, some women of Dutch descent married British officers. As Powell notes, "a few fathers of marriageable girls did entertain bachelor British officers with some notable successes" (1973: 192). In India, public dances were held for the Euro-Asian women of the Upper Military Orphanage in Kolkata, to enable them to meet prospective British husbands. Several marriages to British officers took place and by the late 18th century, many "Eurasian military daughters" with inherited wealth were "a marked marital attraction" (Hawes 1996: 11). Even if some Euro-Asian women married into the upper levels of British society, Euro-Asian males could hardly do likewise. They were not welcome at the public dances, since the women were aiming at marrying British 'gentlemen.' But the dances were discontinued by the 1830s, when there was "growing disapproval ... of marriages amongst the British elite to Eurasian women," and the view prevailed against "*any*... relationships" of British men which "sullied their racial purity" (ibid: 17). But in 1832 a contemporary writer noted that nearly every high officer of the East India Company in Kolkata was "married to a female of Indian descent" (quoted in Hawes 1996: 19). There thus arose a group of Euro-Asians in India at the top level who either 'passed' for white or staked a claim to social superiority over the rest of the community. The mixed children of the 'poor whites' of the army, in contrast, had little support from their fathers. If they did not enter orphanages, they were brought up by their mothers and merged into Indian society.

As in India, the term 'Tommy stock' was current in Sri Lanka where upper-class Burghers and Eurasians consciously distanced themselves from the Eurasian poor. British soldiers and village women had liaisons during British colonial rule, which Elizabeth Harris describes as "basic sexual exploitation" (1994: 13). In the higher ranks, too, there were such unions. The famous British official John D'Oyly had paid "monthly bounties to 115 indigenous Ceylonese, among them the natural son of Major Adam Davie," after Davie and his troops were ambushed and killed in Kandy in 1803 (Powell 1973: 273). Accounts of the Army's lower ranks and their Sri Lankan mistresses was given in the writings of Bombardier Alexander of the Royal Artillery, and in the memoirs of Private George Calladine of the 19th Foot Regiment. Their well-written accounts, according to Powell, reflected the spread of literacy in late 18th century Britain, with "a few better taught men finding their way into the ranks" who were able "to record their experiences" (ibid: 186).

Alexander, the illegitimate son of a wealthy Scots merchant, was raised in a workers' family and had received some education; he described the harsh lives and living conditions of the British subalterns – bad food and severe punishments, including flogging. According to Powell, a liaison with a local woman in the colonies afforded a release from the rigours of the barrack-room; Alexander found "an attractive Sinhalese, who cooked his food properly" and "bore him a fine son" (Powell 1973:190). George Calladine, son of a gardener in Leicestershire, joined the army and served in Sri Lanka from 1814 to 1820 in the 19th Foot Regiment (ibid: 13, n21; Ferrar 1922). He too recorded liaisons between soldiers and local women. "We had several women of the 73rd," he candidly wrote, who were "sent away on account of their bad behaviour." He described the scene in the port of Galle:

> as the men came down the country there was a great deal of drinking... To keep myself from doing worse, I made up my mind to take a black girl, and it was not long before I got one. (Ferrar 1922: 72)

He also commented on his departure to England at the port:

> I turned away from my black girl as soon as possible... my poor little Dingy... cried bitterly... [T]he next day one of our men who had volunteered into the 73rd Regiment took up with her, and she went off with him... to Trincomalee. (ibid: 75)

Calladine also writes of "a number of black women coming alongside" the ship who were "left behind, some with three and four children, and although they were only blacks... they felt as keen a sorrow as if they had been white" (ibid: 77). In this context, Kabbani, however, suggests that the black woman, mourning her loss was a myth:

> The Western male could possess the native woman by force of his domination over her native land; she was subjugated by his wealth, his military might... [S]he was his colonial acquisition, but one that he pretended enjoyed his domination and would mourn his departure. (1986: 81)

Apart from the 73rd, Calladine also claimed that the 19th Regiment, which had been nearly 25 years in the country, "left more children than any regiment." The children's fate, he claimed, varied: "Girls were married, while the boys... brought up at the Government School at Colombo were filling respectable places as clerks or... had entered the army" (quoted in Ferrar: 77).

Racial mixing also occurred among soldiers stationed in plantation and other areas. The Boer prisoners of war from South Africa, who were in a camp in Diyatalawa in 1899, were allowed to mix socially with villagers in nearby Hingurugamuwa, Malpotha and Galedanda and this area between Welimada and Diyatalawa was referred to as 'Little England.'[4] Their liaisons led to a visible Eurasian presence in such villages. Similarly in the north of Sri Lanka, the island of Delft also became known for some of its blue-eyed inhabitants. It is said that

Lieutenant Nolan "found such favour with the ladies of Delft," that after his retirement in 1824, he "left behind a legacy of Irish features and blue eyes." According to W.T. Keble, writing in 1940, such traits were still visible (2001: 110).

'Railway Stock'

In India and Sri Lanka, the railways were vital both for the growth of the export economy and in administering and militarily controlling the territories. In India, the railway network was run by British officers with Anglo-Indian and Indian subordinates. The British concern about 'race and morality' led to the creation of separate railway colonies for the Anglo-Indians and British respectively. These colonies, which began in the 1860s and spread around the country, were 'total institutions' with their own recreation facilities, schools, churches, police stations and health centres (Roychowdhury 2001: 110-11). In Sri Lanka, the railway enclaves were less elaborate, and consisted mainly of living quarters and separate clubs for the British and Burghers.

The club was an important centre of Euro-Asian social life in India and Sri Lanka. Members could relax in an atmosphere free of both British and local prejudice and members could "be themselves," according to Hari Kunzru who fictionalized the typical, exclusive Anglo-Indian Post and Telegraph Club, similar to the Railway Clubs:

> They can dance and play housie-housie without having to endure the hostile eyes of the natives and the whispered jibes of the junior officials [of] the Civil Service Club, which will never admit an Anglo-Indian through its doors. (Kunzru 2002: 37-38)

This segregation resulted in an Anglo-Indian 'railway subculture' and the use of the term 'railway stock' to designate a group of persons of mixed British origin employed on the railways. In India, according to Gaikwad, Anglo-Indians not linked to the railways often spoke disparagingly of "railway people," calling them, 'roving stock,' 'rowdy' and 'flirts.' The railway Anglo-Indians in turn regarded the others as snobs who were trying to "separate themselves from us, as if it will bring them nearer to Europeans"(Gaikwad 1967: 166).

In Sri Lanka the railways, which were constructed from 1867 onwards, gave employment to lower-middle-class Euro-Asians as drivers, guards and skilled mechanics. The first drivers, foremen, platelayers, inspectors and guards had been recruited from Britain on a contractual basis ('covenanted workers'). When some of these covenanted engine drivers in 1915 successfully petitioned for better wages, hours of work and leave, it was feared that the the militancy of the organized railway workers in Britain at the time might spread to Sri Lankan railway workers. The Colonial Secretary derided the local British engine drivers as "low-grade Europeans" and advocated their deportation. Recruitment from Britain was phased out, and Burghers and Eurasians replaced the British (Jayawardena 1972: 215-17).

Even as early as 1879, Digby had commented on the relations of "Europeans employed on the railways" with the local community in Sri Lanka. "They marry burgher or native women," giving rise to the mixed community which in later times also became associated with the railways (Digby 1879: 51-52). As the railway community expanded, 'railway stock' came to have a class connotation. Linked as it was to occupation, it acquired some of the features of caste with its various gradations – the managers at the top, below them the more skilled drivers, guards and mechanics, and at the lowest level the lesser-skilled workers. These class hierarchies were reflected within the railway community, based on differences in wages, and in privileges in the form of housing, allowances and holiday travel.

In his hilarious novel *Yakada Yaka* (1994), Carl Muller, a Sri Lankan Burgher whose father worked on the railways, gives us a glimpse of life on the railways in the mid-20th century. The story focuses on Burgher and Eurasian railwaymen and their families. Muller describes them as being "tied in blood to the west, although diluted in varying degrees… English-speaking, fair-skinned relicts of colonial trespass, eminently usable by the British." (Muller 1994: 11). The novel pours scorn on those who put on airs about their 'Britishness.' Several characters are Eurasians with British names – Kirby, Jackson, Tucker, Dickson, Gibbs, and Dickie Byrd – the latter an engine driver who "fancied himself a cut above the rest." He boasted, much to the amusement of the other railwaymen, that his great-uncle was Admiral Byrd: "We are Byrds... my grandfather fought with the British at Ypres," claiming that "being born in Ceylon was a pure accident of geography." When over his glass of gin, Byrd declared, "I'm English... real English," another Burgher driver, referring to Byrd's local accent, said, "You're a bloody crow... just see how the bugger is talking" (ibid: 91). And Muller embellishes the portrait, observing that "Byrd had no real objections to arrack but felt a mite superior with his gin and ale" (ibid: 93).

At the top of the railway pyramid were the British managers and divisional inspectors, "the Pukka Sahibs who wore natty uniforms with brass buttons" (ibid: 8). Muller's book reveals the Burgher engine drivers' attitude to the British: "The British Railway nabobs who were a bunch of stuffed ducks had no business coming to this country to tell him what to do" (ibid: 20). The Burghers were also contemptuous of the 'whites-only' clubs, especially the Swimming Club in Colombo, which bordered the coastal railway line. It was common knowledge that the engine drivers, on passing the club, used to send out clouds of smoke. Muller wrote:

> British Club is having a party... all the white buggers are going to get together on the lawn and stand and hold their drinks... and the ladies will come like bloody sailing ships, all la-di-da. Governor will come also. ... and the police band will play. (ibid: 21)

Muller fictionalized the scene where the party ended in a huge uproar caused by the dare-devil railway drivers who had sent out a stream of black smoke and fired logs and coal into the club's premises.

Such confrontation between Euro-Asians and the British even led to occasional violence between the covenanted drivers and the others. The issue was the privileged salaries and facilities of "a clutch of whites" who also took "the plums" in the form of driving the prestigious "long-haul mail trains." A Burgher driver, Edema, asks, "Who are these buggers?" and replies "some bloody convent drivers" (ibid: 52). Another

English covenanted driver named Shakespeare was called a "china pig" by a Burgher driver, who explained that "Chinese pigs were white with big ears and liked to frequent station latrines…never met a China pig before with a name like Shakespeare. He was a poet or something no?" A fight ensued and Shakespeare asked to be hospitalized. On this occasion another Burgher railwayman, using a pejorative term for white men, said: "not like our people these *suddha* drivers. Slightest thing asking to go to the hospital" (ibid: 97).

Muller's fiction reflected the attitudes of the Euro-Asians working on the railways towards their British counterparts. But the prejudices against 'railway stock' by those who were 'good' Dutch Burghers also prevailed, even in the post-colonial period. In 1997 Linda van Schagen, a Burgher, complained about the deterioration of a Colombo club where the President ("who is from 'railway stock,' but denies it vehemently") had proposed an increase in entrance fees "to get 'quality' members." Van Schagen scoffed at this, saying that 'quality' cannot be got for money "because the riff-raff of the community are the ones with cash"; and she condemned the members of "dubious background" who keep "snaking their way in and out of committees" adding, for effect, that "most club managers are crooks" (*Daily News*, 4 Oct. 1997). Another aspect of club life is seen in van Schagen's comments on the Burgher Recreation Club, nostalgically recalling the past when "Burgher ladies could relax over a drink and a cigarette without being molested or gaped at." The entry of non-Burghers to the club, she writes, had destroyed the elegance and refinement of the club's atmosphere. The snobbery against those on the railways is also revealed in Michelle de Kretser's novel, where one Burgher comments on another's social pretensions: "As if everyone doesn't know she was of the railway Rosairos before she married" (2003: 19).

The novel *The Year Before Sunset* (2005) by two Anglo-Indians, Hugh and Colleen Gantzer has perceptively raised issues of class between 'railway Anglo-Indians,' and those in the military or bureaucracy. In the year before independence, an Anglo-Indian from a civil and military family, who decides to stay on in India, tells a young woman from a railway family about the class barrier between them:

> We have different customs and traditions, we have different values … we even speak differently. Frankly my people feel more at home with, we're more at ease with, people of other communities and religions who share our background. (Gantzer & Gantzer 2005: 111)

There is a recognition of difference between what Ranjana Kaul describes as "the genteel upper-class Anglo-Indians" and those without social and economic advantages, the barriers being based on "protocol, manners and economic standing." As the narrator in the novel admits "we were not only as class conscious as the British *but we were also very caste-conscious*" (quoted in Kaul 2005: 37 emphasis added).

This chapter, in probing the terms 'Burgher' and 'Eurasian,' has tried to unravel some features of the class and 'caste' consciousness that prevailed among the mixed communities – which were as diverse and complex as their origins. They asserted superiority over each other, reflective of the hierarchical societies from which they originated in Europe, with their long-entrenched and continuing class divisions. Euro-Asians were also born into societies where the caste system prevailed. But many of them were able to critique such structures and become the vanguard of social and political change – as discussed in Part II of this book.

Notes

1. The Infantry Volunteers included 440 Burgher volunteers, 97 Malays, 80 Sinhalese, 68 Tamils, and 23 Indians (Moldrich n.d.: 51).
2. A Eurasian, Captain Edward Stork received the DSO award; and a Burgher, E.C. Weinman was in the Cold Stream Guards (Moldrich n.d.: 48).
3. A Eurasian engineer of Badulla, popularly known as 'Joy' Ryde, used to fly the Union Jack on his car (communication of Clifton Bocks, November 2004).
4. I am grateful to J.B. Müller for this information.

"The Musical Mechanic (Portuguese) with his Bandrinha" by John L.K. van Dort in A. M. Ferguson, *Souvenirs of Ceylon*, 1868.

'Mestice woman' 1711. Engraving by de Bruyn. From *Illustrations & Views of Dutch Ceylon*. Courtesy R.K. de Silva & W.G.M. Beumer.

Arthur Paynter (standing), his wife Agnes Weerasooriya and her brother William Weerasooriya. Courtesy Ranjani de Mel.

Eurasian children, Allan, Fannie and James. From *India Christian Mission Report*, 1930. Courtesy Ranjani de Mel.

Children and teachers from the Paynter Homes, from *India Christian Mission Report*, 1930. Courtesy Ranjani de Mel.

British Officer of the 73rd Regiment.
From Geoffrey Powell,
The Kandyan Wars

Bombardier Alexander. From
Geoffrey Powell,
The Kandyan Wars

A. J. van der Poorten, his wife Ran Menika
and some family members at the
Hotel Suisse, Kandy (circa 1948). Courtesy, Menika van der Poorten.

Part II

EURO-ASIAN RADICALISM & MODERNISM

"Woman with Sarangi," George Keyt, 1945

4

FEARS OF EURO-ASIAN SUBVERSION

> [The Eurasians are] a heterogeneous set – some by Hindu, others by Mahomedan and Malay mothers at the will or caprice of the father – what is not in time to be apprehended from the union of so large and discontented a body? Why may we not expect the scenes of South America to be displayed in India? *A body who have neither riches, honour, nor any advantage to sacrifice, must ever pant for revolution.*
>
> *Sketches of India,* 1816, quoted in Stark 1934, p.20, emphasis added

The Subversive 'Hybrid'

Given some of the anxieties and concerns about class exclusiveness and boundaries – characteristic of those of mixed European and Asian descent – and the ambivalence in attitudes towards Euro-Asians by both races from which they originated, it was only to be expected that the mixed community resisted discrimination by Europeans, and asserted their own rights and liberties as colonial citizens. Moreover, the Euro-Asians being neither fully European nor Asian gave some of them the ability to challenge authority and orthodoxy, to face unpopularity and to take risks by championing democratic rights. What might have been called "rootlessness," far from being a source of weakness, was often a liberating factor and a source of strength. The colonial governments were quite conscious of the Euro-Asian potential for subversion and the dangerous reality of their dissenting opinions. Even in the 18th century, a Dutch official in northern Sri Lanka protested about the "perverse race" of petition writers including those of mixed origin, "the Topasses and Mestices," who wrote complaints "under the name of petitions, often so *full of impertinent and seditious expressions* that they more resemble libels than petitions"(Denham1912: 483,quoting Hendrick Zwaardecroon, emphasis added).

Up to the mid-19th century, colonial rulers had several major concerns linked to possible insurrection. In the backdrop of world events such as the French Revolution, the Euro-Asian intelligentsia was suspected of political disloyalty and alleged even to be "panting for revolution." Having stereotyped Euro-Asians as 'two-faced', devious and subversive, the rulers in both India and Sri Lanka were ill-at-ease with the educated elements of the community, suspecting that they would be the first – given their educational advantages – to question authority and give leadership to movements of revolt. In a period of expanding imperial conquest, there was always concern about the possible influence in the colonies of revolutions, insurrections and other forms of dissent elsewhere in the world.

Events that inevitably caused anxiety to colonial governments were the war of independence in North America; the upheavals in France; the Latin American struggles for independence – achieved in Argentina 1816, Chile 1818, Colombia 1819, and Mexico 1821; the revolts in the West Indies, especially in San Domingo (Haiti) and Jamaica; resistance to colonial conquest in parts of India; unrest in Ireland; and political and economic reform movements in Britain – including chartism, franchise rights, the struggle for a free press, for free trade and laissez-faire policies. The influence in the colonies of non-conformist Christian dissenters (such as Baptists) was also one such source of concern. In addition, the alternative ideologies challenging Christian orthodoxy, such as secularism, Darwinism, theosophy and freethought, shook the ideological foundations of traditional society. Influences of Utopian Socialists and Marxists – with their trenchant critiques of capitalist society, as well as the labour agitation and trade unionism of 19th century Europe, were considered subversive by the ever-vigilant colonial rulers who monitored the influence of such movements on colonial society.

The great fear was that revolutions and radical movements in Europe along with revolts in some colonies, which were extensively reported in the local press, would promote revolts among other colonial peoples. Linked to this was the belief that leadership for such challenges would come first from Euro-Asians and radical British professionals living in the colonies, who would inspire the 'seditious' elements of the local population. The fear, however, was not unfounded.

Enlightenment, Revolution and Early Anti-Colonialism

One factor common to all the revolts, revolutions and subversive ideologies of the late 18th and 19th centuries in the Americas, the Caribbean, Europe and elsewhere was the continuous impact and inspiration of the French Revolution of 1789 and the influence of the ideologues of the Enlightenment – most notably Thomas Hobbes, John Locke, David Hume, Mary Wollstonecraft and Thomas Paine in Britain, and Rousseau, Voltaire and Montesquieu in France. They had played a subversive role in mercilessly critiquing and satirizing the doctrine of the divine right of kings, and the despotic, feudal, ecclesiastical and patriarchal institutions and ideologies of the *ancien regime*. They wrote of universal rights and a social contract between ruler and ruled, and the need for a separation of powers to counteract tyranny and ensure liberty. Friedrich Engels praised "the great men" of France who "prepared men's minds for the coming revolution," and were themselves revolutionaries who subjected "religion, natural science, society, [and] political institutions" to the most unsparing criticism:

> Reason became the sole measure of everything. Every form of society and government then existing, every old traditional notion was thrown into the lumber room as irrational... henceforth superstition, injustice, privilege, oppression were to be superceded by... equality... and the inalienable rights of man. (Engels [1880] 1969: 109-10)

Events that had a global impact were the revolutions in France of the period 1789 to 1848, which in Eric Hobsbawm's words "transformed... the entire world." It was, he said, also the triumph of capitalism and liberal democracy which had emerged in France and Great Britain. He argues that the dual revolution – the political in France, and the industrial revolution in Britain – fostered imperial expansion (1962:13-14). But as Hobsbawm noted: "The dual revolution – to make European expansion irresistible, was also to provide the non-European world with the conditions and equipment *for its eventual counter-attack*" (ibid: 40, emphasis added).

It was the French Revolution of 1789 that provoked the most intense political and emotional responses around the world. This revolution, along with the American War of Independence, also influenced the uprisings and liberation of Latin America from Spanish rule, slave revolts in the West Indies, and had an impact on the Asian reformist intelligentsia. "Bliss was it in that dawn to be alive, and to be young was very heaven," wrote Wordsworth. Subsequent radical poets, Byron and Keats among others, wrote movingly against prevailing tyranny in Europe and elsewhere, and their works became popular among the 19th century intelligentsia of the colonies.

In the colonial world, the great awakening of the French Revolution of 1789, as well as the subsequent revolutions of 1830 and 1848, reverberated throughout the following decades, much to the chagrin of the colonial rulers. The emergent colonial bourgeoisie and intelligentsia eagerly grasped the ideas of liberty, equality and fraternity, and were quick to use these slogans to challenge colonial rule. They focused on liberty from tyranny (and thus colonial domination), the equality of black and white races in both theory and practice, non-discriminatory access to judicial and administrative structures, and equal entry to public office, schools and other institutions. Reformist slogans on the freedom of the press, greater political representation and cries for 'careers open to talent' were also current. These ideas were popular among the leading Euro-Asian proto-nationalists of Asia: most notably Henry Derozio and the Young Bengal group in India; radical Burghers in Sri Lanka, especially Charles Lorenz and the Young Ceylon circle, as well as Euro-Asian nationalists such as José Rizal, Philippine's nationalist martyr, and Eduard Douwes Dekker of Indonesia, who in 1912, along with others, formed the country's first political party, the *Indische Partij*.

In the Caribbean, too, slaves and sections of the mixed population (known as '*mulattos*') joined the revolts for independence, the earliest anti-colonial uprising occurring in San Domingo (Haiti and the Dominican Republic), inspired by the French Revolution and Napoleon. The struggle against French rule and British intervention in San Domingo was also an early event that gripped the minds of both rulers and ruled in other colonies. In 1791 a slave insurrection led by Toussaint L'Ouverture (the 'Black Napoleon') ended French rule, but wars continued and an independent state was finally proclaimed in 1804, after the defeat of Napoleon's expedition in 1803. L'Ouverture was captured, imprisoned and died in France. A succession of black and *mulatto* presidents continued to rule Haiti, and in 1818 Jean Pierre Boyer, a *mulatto,* was declared President. This early defeat of a colonial power and the proclamation of independence became a spectre that haunted colonial rulers. As Hyam has written of this event: "the shock waves generated by the unprecedented explosion against white rule… reverberated around the world" (Hyam 1990: 117). Wordsworth wrote a poem, "To Toussaint L'Ouverture," after his capture, which exhorted him to:

> Live, and take comfort. Thou hast left behind
> Powers that will work for thee; air, earth, and skies;
> There's not a breathing of the common wind
> That will forget thee; thou hast great allies;
> Thy friends are exultations, agonies,
> And Love, and Man's unconquerable mind.

C.L.R. James, the Caribbean writer, also records the excitement caused by "the only successful slave revolt in history," claiming that "the odds it had to overcome is evidence of the magnitude of the interests that were involved":

> The transformation of slaves, trembling in hundreds before a single white man, into a people able to organize themselves and defeat the most powerful European nations of their day, is one of the great epics of revolutionary struggle and achievement. (James, quoted in Lamming 1984: 119)

James also discusses the impact of the French Revolution in the Caribbean, where people believed that in France "the white slaves" had revolted, decimated the oppressors, and were now "enjoying the fruits of the earth." It was "greatly inaccurate in fact," noted James, but the Caribbean people "caught the spirit of the thing. Liberty, Equality, Fraternity."

> Before the end of 1789 there were risings in Guadeloupe and Martinique... [and] in Fort Dauphin, one of the future centres of the San Domingo insurrection, the slaves were... holding mass meetings in the forests at night. (James 1980: 81-82)

Britain which had its own interests in the Caribbean also suffered militarily in San Domingo, which made a deep impression on the British administrators, for as the military historian Sir John Fortescue wrote (in 1906), "the secret of England's impotence in the early stages of the war against Napoleon lay in two fatal words, St Domingo" (quoted in James 1980: 214).

Fearsome *Mulattos*

These "fatal words" spread to the British colonial world. In India, suspicion about those of mixed race was fuelled by the rebellions against foreign rule in South America and the Caribbean. *The Calcutta Chronicle* in May 1792 (referring to Euro-Asians as 'East Indians') predicted that:

> If forthwith drastic measures are not put into operation to keep down the East Indian race, they will do to the British in India what the mulattoes have done ... in San Domingo. (quoted in Stark 1934: 18)

The press continued to ring alarm bells and there was speculation about revolutionary tendencies among Euro-Asians. Such panic was further fostered by British travellers in India such as Viscount Valentia, who after visiting the East from 1802 to 1806 warned the East India Company: "The most rapidly increasing evil of Bengal is the increase of half-caste children. They are forming the first link of union between the English and the natives"(ibid 19). Valentia's warning was strongly worded: "with numbers in their favour, with a close relationship to the natives, what may not in future time be dreaded, from them?"– suggesting that "the evil ought to be stopped" (ibid: 19-20).

Another traveller, Bishop Heber, whose infamous opinion of Ceylon was "only man is vile[1]," felt similarly about the Indian Euro-Asians. "I never met with any public man connected with India," he wrote, "who did not lament the increase of the half-caste population as a great source of the present mischief and future danger to the tranquility of the Colony" (Hawes 1996: 20). An additional factor was that Lord Cornwallis, the Governor-General of India, had earlier, during the American War of Independence, suffered a historic defeat by George Washington in Yorktown in 1781 (ibid: 64). As Dalrymple remarks, Cornwallis was determined "to make sure that a settled colonial class never emerged in India to undermine British rule as it had done, to his own humiliation in America" (2000: 50). In India, Cornwallis excluded Euro-Asians from the army in 1789 and warned of:

> The injuries which would accrue to the Discipline and Reputation of H.M's troops … from the admission of Persons as officers, or even as soldiers, who are born of Black women, natives of the Country. (Hawes 1996: 64)

As fears of resistance to colonialism grew in the late 18th century, the Euro-Asians were not only excluded from the military (where they had access to arms), but were also barred from civilian posts in government for reasons of "internal security." By the 1830s, as Hawes notes, further turmoil in Spanish America and colonies of other powers "ensured that doubt over Eurasian political reliability was never quite dispelled" (ibid: 72).

The Baptist 'Menace'

In the 17th and 18th centuries in Europe and the USA, periods of political upheaval and religious dissent coincided with revivalism. Many radical sects challenged the Church, the clergy and traditional religious rituals, believing that the individual could relate directly to God. Such groups often had heretical views on ownership of private property, on sexual relations and women's role in society. Some of these heterodox dissident religious groups had utopian visions of a millennium of heaven on earth. Others such as the Baptists, Methodists, Diggers, Ranters, Quakers and Shakers put forward views on democracy, common ownership and gender that went against prevailing religious, social and political orthodoxy. The oppression of women was strongly challenged. The Quakers have been called the 'Mothers of Feminism,' and the Shakers in the USA, believing that the 'Second Coming' would be a woman, not only chose a British former factory-worker, Mother Ann Lee, as their leader, but also abolished marriage and private property in their communes. Basically all these movements were 'subversive,' questioning and fighting the authority of the repressive Church and State. The heretics and non-conformists had a base among the poor, the Baptists taking on many radical issues concerning peoples' rights – thereby giving the British government cause for concern both at home and abroad.

In the colonies, officials had reason to distrust the dissident Christians. As the Church of England was the official religion, colonial administrators looked with disfavour on those non-conformists who clashed with the 'High Church' on matters of faith, education and ritual. They were regarded as suspect, and were also subject to civic disabilities in Britain. Among the 'Low Church' groups, such as Baptists and Methodists, whose support base in Britain was mainly working class, there were strong currents of political radicalism.

The Baptists were very active in the campaign for the abolition of slavery and spoke out on the 'rights of man,' and against the oppression of women. They were a thorn in the side of British rulers in India, Sri Lanka and the Caribbean. Baptists firmly believed in eradicating social evils in the colonies and publicly condemned 'heathen' religions and practices, also attacking the colonial government for evading issues of social reform. The government was, however, wary of the dangers of tampering with local customs, especially since a committee of the House of Commons had warned in 1781 that "any interference with the religion of the native would eventually insure total destruction of British power" (Pathak 1967: 16).

The Baptists had pioneered English education in Bengal, and Euro-Asians especially benefited from their schools. Moreover, many Euro-Asians, such as John Ricketts, who participated in protest movements, were active Baptists; and some prominent Euro-Asians reformers and agitators of Kolkata, including William Benjamin Kirkpatrick, Charles Fenwick, John Fink and John Thompson, were all Baptist ministers. Other active Euro-Asian Baptists were Willoughby Da Costa, William Buckingham and John Doveton (Hawes 1996: 158-69). Many of them made donations to the Baptist cause, most notably Michael Derozio, a benefactor of the Serampore Mission (ibid: 160), whose grandson was Henry Derozio, the writer, reformer and inspirer of the Young Bengal movement (see Chapter 5).

British Baptists in the Serempore mission in Bengal, including their leader William Carey, drew attention in 1796 to "certain Dreadful Practices" prevalent in India, especially *sati* and infanticide (Potts 1967: 140-46). An activist Baptist, Rev. James Pegg, had been prominent in the protest against the East India Company's 'association' with Hinduism, and on this topic wrote *India's Cries to British Humanity* (1832), a book which influenced public opinion in Britain. In 1843 Pegg denounced the British connection with 'idolatry' in Sri Lanka, and the protection given by the British to the tooth relic of the Buddha in Kandy, leading the Governor to call Pegg's interference "unfortunate" (de Silva 1965: 46 n19).

In the Caribbean, the Baptists had been active in Jamaica from 1814 and had worked among the slaves, championing their emancipation, thereby, according to Ken Post, arousing "the white plantation owners to paroxysms of rage" (Post 1978: 32). In Jamaica, there were also many revolts in the 1830s; most notably in 1831-32, a rebellion linked to the 'native' Baptist movement and local revivalism, led by Sam Sharpe, was the culmination of a series of uprisings (ibid: 30). By 1848, when there was a rebellion in Sri Lanka (see Chapter 6), and an Irish Baptist, Dr Christopher Elliot, was accused of involvement in the events, the Governor resorted to the Baptist bogey; "Dr Elliot is a Baptist and in Colonies this sect always takes part in disturbances – his agents are Baptists," wrote Lord Torrington privately in December 1848, to Earl

Grey (Secretary of State for the Colonies), also reminding him that that "the Baptists got up an insurrection at Jamaica some years ago" (de Silva 1965: 123).

The Age of Reason and Secularism

Apart from dissenting non-conformists, a strong challenge to orthodox Christianity came from anti-religious, secular trends. Many enlightenment thinkers, including David Hume, Voltaire and Thomas Paine, had earlier fired shots against religion and religious fanaticism. Hume believed (according to Denby 2004) that "religion is a portrait not of how the cosmos works but how the human mind works"; Voltaire was known for his diatribes, "God is dead" and *"écraser l'infâme"* (crush the infamy), directed at the Catholic Church; Thomas Paine (1737-1809) created a sensation around the world with his books *Rights of Man* (1791) and *The Age of Reason* (1794). In the former, Paine, replying to Burke's attack on the French Revolution, defended the revolution, advocated republicanism, and claimed that Burke's apology for the French court showed that "he pities the plume but forgets the dying bird" (Rudé 1964: 183). *The Age of Reason* created a great scandal, Paine was branded an atheist, and as a result his fame spread.

In the USA, American founding father Thomas Jefferson was influenced by *The Age of Reason,* and in the colonial world, the book was hailed as a critique of Christian orthodoxy. Paine, who also attacked the British monarchy and the Church of England, was "eagerly read by reformers, Protestant dissenters, democrats, London craftsmen and the skilled factory-hands of the new industrial order." His book sold one million copies (ibid: 183). Paine's books were influential among the intelligentsia in India and Sri Lanka. In Bengal in the 1820s Henry Derozio (the Euro-Asian radical) introduced *The Age of Reason* to his students, and in the 1830s, the book had brisk sales in Kolkata (see Chapter 5). In *Young Ceylon,* a journal of the 1850s Charles Ferdinands refers to *Rights of Man* (Vol. 1, No. 1, 1850: 18). And many decades later, the book was similarly much-quoted. Sri Lanka's labour leader of the 1920s, A.E. Goonesinha, recalling his youth said he was inspired by "that stirring book, *Rights of Man* by Thomas Paine" (Jayawardena 1972: 235).

There were further sharp challenges to Christianity. The Utopian and Marxist socialists were highly critical of religion in general, and Christianity in particular. But the real fuel to the fire came with Charles Darwin's *On the Origin of Species* (1859) and *The Descent of Man,* (1871), which undermined the basis of biblical accounts of the world's creation. Many members of the western intelligentsia were convinced by scientific theories of evolution and natural selection, and the 'Age of Disbelief' was given new scientific backing. All over the world, freethinkers, agnostics and atheists rejected religious orthodoxy, and even the clergy were affected. In South Africa, Bishop Colenso of Natal created a scandal in 1862 by publishing a criticism of the Old Testament from a scientific point of view, thereby challenging the literal interpretation of the Bible (Jayawardena 1972: 51-52). In Britain Annie Besant published a *Gospel of Atheism* claiming "the grand title of Atheist" for Copernicus, Spinoza, Voltaire, and Paine. Charles Bradlaugh and Annie Besant published *The Free-Thinkers Textbook.* Also popular was G.W. Foote's journal *The Free-Thinker,* started in 1881, and his pamphlets "Bible and Beer," "Blasphemy No Crime," and "Bible Romancings"– the latter making fun of Bibilical stories (ibid: 51-53). All such iconoclastic material was circulated among Hindus and Buddhists in India and Sri Lanka and used by them against missionaries and the Church.

The Utopian Socialist Vision

The emergence of an intelligentsia among the Euro-Asian communities in Asia occurred during a period of profound economic change in Europe, where in the late 18th and early 19th centuries the capitalist onslaught on the old oppressive feudal institutions of Church and State took place. These were also years of revolution, political upheavals, social turbulence and religious dissent – defying the ideologies of the 'Old Order.' Inspired by the philosophers of the Enlightenment and by revolutionary movements, new ideas flourished about future society. Many protests occurred against the dogmatism of the Church, its harsh control over peoples' lives and the remnant feudal laws and undemocratic structures, including archaic marriage laws. While agitating on contemporary problems, some ideologues not only conceptualized a future 'new' society, but also actually experimented in communal living. One daring trend was the challenge to all the institutions of capitalist society by the Utopian Socialists, notably Robert Owen,[2] Charles Fourier[3] and Saint - Simon,[4] with their plans and dreams for communally organized societies, free not only from Church and State, but also from patriarchal constraints on women. Such visions of a better future were a reaction to the horrors of early unregulated capitalism, the inhuman exploitative conditions of workers and the subordination of women.

These Utopian Socialists, with their blueprints for the ideal society, caused much controversy. Their impact was considerable on other streams of thought – based on a critique of capitalist society and its institutions – especially the status of women under capitalism. Utopian Socialists were acknowledged in the *Manifesto of the Communist Party* (1848), where Marx and Engels argued that "such fantastic pictures of future society" were "painted at a time when the proletariat is still in a very underdeveloped state." But they argued that the Utopians were nevertheless revolutionaries, and praised their publications which attacked "every principle of existing society" and were full of the "most valuable material for the enlightenment of the working class." But they also warned that such writing was "of a purely Utopian character" and in the context of the time amounted merely to "castles in the air."

Many of the ideas propagated by Utopian Socialists, which were regarded as scandalous by bourgeois society, were certainly known to the British ruling class – and its officials in the colonies. For example, Sir Edward Barnes, the Governor of Sri Lanka in the 1820s, opposing constitutional and other reforms proposed by the Colebrooke-Cameron Commission in 1832, condemned them as 'utopian.' He attacked Levellers, Utopians and those who not only preached popular government but also believed that "black and white people" could be "amalgamated":

> ...whatever Utopian ideas Theorists may cherish of universal fraternity without regard to Colour, Religion or Civilization... I am ...of the opinion that this people cannot nor ought to have... any greater share in the Government. (Mendis 1956, Vol. II, 25-26)

"Claptrap about Liberty of the Press"

The value of a free press and freedom of expression, which were vigorously advocated and defended in Britain in the early 19th century, also aroused controversy in the colonies. This was often sparked off by the liberal attitudes and radical opinions of some British editors of newspapers in India and Sri Lanka, who questioned and critiqued the colonial government. The 'dangerous' link between the politically conscious Euro-Asians and their involvement in the free-press issue was also voiced as early as 1824 by Sir John Malcolm, a former Governor of Bombay who warned that "among that increasing part of the population called half-castes... a free press would do infinite harm":

> There are many of this class... who are prone to impatience and discontent at their condition; and these, who naturally seek to make converts to their opinion, will be found among the *loudest advocates for a free press.* (Stark 1934: 44-45, emphasis added)

A controversy flared up in Kolkata in 1823 around the case of James Silk Buckingham, a liberal British editor of *The Calcutta Journal* whose articles critical of the colonial authorities led to a deportation order being issued against him. Some Europeans of Kolkata organized a meeting in support of the government decision, where the only opposition expressed came from a Euro-Asian, John Ricketts (ibid: 44) (see Chapter 5). In Sri Lanka the Governor Lord Torrington, warned in 1848 that "a seditious press" was "the most ruinous thing" that could influence "a native Eastern population," and queried the outcome if "a seditious press" was allowed to inflame "the minds of the people":

> You stop it in Ireland, it *can do much more harm here.* ...if you allow things to go on... you may have a Rebellion which will not be easily put down and the destruction of the whole Kandian and even

> Maritime Provinces, and all for *a bit of that claptrap about liberty of the Press.* (Torrington quoted in de Silva 1965: 180, emphasis added)

The Colonial Intelligentsia – 'not quite white'

In this context one may observe that imperialism paradoxically created its own grave-diggers in the form of a local educated group – called *évolués* (evolved) in French and *illustrados* in Spanish – who had been schooled in the language of the colonizer and been taught European history, with its rebellions, revolutions and radical ideologies – a history they were to turn against the colonial rulers. But as Homi Bhabha argues: "colonial mimicry is the desire for a reformed recognizable Other, as a subject of difference *that is almost the same, but not quite*" (1997: 153, emphasis added). Benedict Anderson describes the way "European 'national histories' entered the consciousness of the colonized... through reading rooms and class rooms." The reach of European history, however, into the far-flung colonial schools, had unintended consequences:

> Vietnamese youngsters could not avoid learning about the philosophes and the Revolution... Magna Carta, the Mother of Parliaments and the Glorious Revolution, glossed as English national history, entered schools all over the British Empire. Belgium's independence struggle against Holland was not erasable from school-books Congolese children would one day read. (Anderson 1983: 108)

The same was eminently true of Sri Lanka, where those children taught in English-medium schools were drilled in British history and the struggles of the British for democratic rights. Even though the accounts of the French Revolution and conflicts in Ireland in school textbooks were biased, local students certainly would have learnt their own 'lessons of history.'

The other influence on nationalists in the colonies was the emphasis in Europe on youth in revolt, as seen in movements such as Young Italy and Young Ireland. There were similar trends in the colonies – Young Bengal, Young Ceylon and Young Java, among others led by the educated, modernized local intelligentsia, who as Anderson notes "attached a complex political significance to their youth." For in Europe and the colonies, 'youth' signified "dynamism, progress, self-sacrificing idealism and revolutionary will" (ibid: 109). Where the supporters of these organizations were liberal and radical Euro-Asians, a close watch was kept on such movements. The following chapters record instances of the involvement of the Euro-Asian intelligentsia in pioneering democratic movements for political and social change in South Asia.

Notes

1. What though the spicy breezes
   Blow soft o'er Ceylon's isle
   Though every prospect pleases
   And only man is vile!
   (Verse of a hymn composed by Heber in 1811 for the Society for the Propagation of the Gospel)
2. In Britain, Robert Owen (1771-1858), a Utopian Socialist cotton-mill owner, believed in applying 'reason' to society. The main evils of society were the profit motive in capitalism, private property, organized religion, and monogamous marriage. He experimented in the USA with a model of co-operative and communal living called 'New Harmony,' where incomes were to be shared equally. But such ideas were unsuccessful at a moment of expanding capitalism and intense competition, and were ridiculed as 'utopian' and unrealistic (see Mies 1981: 36-40).
3. In France, the Utopian Socialist Charles Fourier (1772-1837) spoke of harmonious living in communities. He linked the evils of the capitalist system with women's enslavement, and his most famous theme was the liberation of women (which influenced Marx). As Fourier wrote: "Social progress is in proportion to the progress in the liberation of women, and the decline of the social order is in proportion to the reduction of the freedom of women" (quoted in Mies 1981: 40-47).
4. The best-known French Utopian Socialist, Count Henri Saint - Simon (1760-1825), criticized capitalist society, orthodox religion and the prevalent marriage system. The 'Community' he envisaged was based on common ownership of the means of production and on equal income distribution. Not surprisingly, the ideas of Utopian Socialists were considered outrageous by bourgeois society, which denounced their views on religion, communal property and 'free love' (see Mies 1981: 47-59).

5

DEROZIO and YOUNG BENGAL – "CATCHING the DAWN"

> [The Derozians] sowed a seed of secular and radical nationalism... in sharp contrast to the reactionary obscurantism that was to play such a large part in the subsequent history of the sub-continent.
>
> Premen Addy and Ibne Azad, 1973, "Politics and Culture in Bengal," p.82

> [Henry Derozio was] modern India's first patriot to give expression to that patriotism in verse, the first to sing of freedom... the first to contemplate an intellectual renaissance for an ancient civilization through 'new perceptions,' the first to exalt reason as an instrument of progress.
>
> R.K. Das Gupta, in Bradley-Birt 1980, *Poems of Henry Derozio,* Foreword

Kolkata Euro-Asians

Westernization in India took place earliest in the 18th and 19th centuries in Bengal and especially in the city of Kolkata (Calcutta), which for a time was the commercial and political capital of India. The city, with its flourishing trade, banking system, export and import firms, had the necessary infrastructure of a colonial economy. Economic development led to an expanding secondary education and college system in English, producing a middle-class Bengali intelligentsia. These changes led to a debate on tradition and modernity in education, between those who advocated traditional Indian practices and those who favoured a western education. The intellectual and political life of Kolkata, with its western influences and pioneer reformist and modernizing trends, flourished from the early 19th century onwards, making Bengal a forerunner in India of movements of social reform and anti-colonial activities.

The best known of the early Bengali reformers, Rammohun Roy (1772-1833), a scholar influenced by British liberal thinkers and the philosophers of the Enlightenment, was in contact with British radicals in Kolkata and Britain. Roy was a theist who advocated a reformist interpretation of Hindu texts and an abolition of social evils such as *sati* and other forms of women's oppression. Along with reformist Bengalis in 1828 he started the Brahmo Samaj that challenged certain debased practices of Hinduism and spoke out for female education and social emancipation. Although Roy advocated western-type education, his campaign was within the framework of a reformed Hinduism.

More politically and socially radical, however, was Henry Louis Vivian Derozio (1809-31) who lent his name to a group, the 'Derozians.' They inspired the Young Bengal reformist movement, which lasted up to the mid-19th century and paved the way for social and political reform. The Derozian challenge confronted Hindu religious rituals, patriarchal and caste structures, female subordination and social evils affecting women, and also, significantly, the political conservatism of the period. Fired by the French Revolution, and the movements for freedom in Italy and Greece, Derozio himself not only expressed patriotic and secular views many decades ahead of the time, but also strongly influenced a generation of Bengali reformers with a Utopian vision of the future. He was, as Pallab Sengupta says, "one of the stalwarts of modernism in the history of our nation" (2001: 1).

The most important Euro-Asian community in India was based in Bengal. They were the descendants of Indian mothers and European fathers from all sections of colonial society. But these mixed marriages and liasions were never without dilemmas and posed thorny problems for the rulers. As noted earlier, some conventions were followed on this issue, but these too were fluid and changed with time. By the late 17th century, Britishers of the upper levels of the administration "were expected to marry suitable local women"– namely Euro-Asians of Portuguese ancestry – but "irregular unions with Indian women were frowned upon," one example being the liaison of the 'founder' of Kolkata, Job Charnock, with a Hindu woman, which "brought censure" from his superior in 1682 that it was "to ye great scandal of our nation" (Hawes 1996: 2-3). In the absence of British women in India in these years, marriages or alliances occurred with women of Portuguese mixed descent, producing an Indo-Portuguese-British community (Gaikwad 1967). One such marriage in 1808 was that of the British official Henry Russell to Jane Casamajor, an Anglo-Portuguese with a Malay great-grandmother (Dalrymple 2002: 458-59). But it was also common in the late 18th century for the East India Company's officials and for military personnel to have liaisons with Indian women, Hawes remarking that the majority of unmarried British men in Kolkata at that time reportedly had mistresses of Indian or mixed origin (1996: 18).

According to Dalrymple, this early period of British life in India was "about intermixing and impurity, a succession of unexpected and unplanned minglings of peoples and cultures and ideas" (2002: xl). He also observes that both in India and Britain, "illegitimate children born to lower-class mistresses were treated in a very different way to children of aristocratic women, whether born in or out of wedlock" (2002: 383n). From the early days of the Euro-Asian community, there thus arose a strong class division. Up to 1785, educated Euro-Asians occupied high positions in the army and bureaucracy, but discriminatory rules were introduced from 1786 onwards. In that year, Euro-Asian boys from the Military Orphanages were prevented from going to Britain for education. In 1791 all mixed-race persons were banned from military and marine services and the civil service, and in 1795 they were further disqualified from "the combatant ranks" except as "pipers, drummers, bandsmen and farriers," even in the regiments in which their fathers had served (Stark 1934: 10). More setbacks occurred, and in 1821 the courts in Murshidabad (in the case of a Euro-Asian, Charles Reed vs Baijnath Singh) ruled that Euro-Asians were not British subjects under the law. On appeal, the Supreme Court declared that children of "British-born subjects" and "native women," if "born in wedlock" were British subjects, but illegitimate children were held to be Indian, and therefore not subject to laws governing the British (ibid: 37). This caused much bitterness among Euro-Asians, who began to agitate for changes in their legal status.

Deprived of prestigious jobs, Euro-Asians went in for other types of occupations, especially with the development of the railways, post and telegraph services and teaching professions, where their knowledge of English gave them an advantage. But discrimination persisted. Euro-Asians could not sit on juries until this law was changed in 1827. A shift took place, however, in 1832 with a decree that no one should be excluded from service in the East India Company on grounds of creed or colour (Edwards 1884: 253-54). It was in the context of these trends that a strand of radical thought emerged among Kolkata Euro-Asians, pioneered by Henry Derozio, a young member of the community.

The Derozio Phenomenon

Henry Derozio, born in Kolkata in 1809, belonged to the Euro-Asian community who were sometimes referred to as 'East Indians' or Anglo-Indians. His mother, Sophia Johnson was of British origin, and his father Francis Derozio was a Protestant Portuguese-Indian (born in 1779), who worked for the mercantile firm J. Scott & Co. He was a man of some means, described as a "Portuguese merchant and agent in Kolkata" (Madge 1982: 2). Francis Derozio's father Michael Derozio (1742-1809) had also been a merchant (Hawes 1996: 160). Such well-off, educated Portuguese Euro-Asians, who distinguished themselves from British Euro-Asians of the orphanages, made a point of further advancing through education.

The 'Scottish Enlightenment' of the 18th century had a direct impact on Bengal through several inspiring and influential teachers from Scotland. From the age of six to fourteen, Henry Derozio was educated at Drummond's Academy, a school run by a Scot, David Drummond (1785-1843). Drummond was a "scholar... equally versed ...in the classics, mathematics and metaphysics of his day... and trained in the power of independent thinking" (Edwards 1884: 4-5). He was part of the flowering of knowledge in Scotland in the 18th century and the political and economic challenge to the old order associated with the names of David Hume, Adam Smith and James Boswell.[1]

Drummond was described as a poet and "notorious freethinker," from whom Derozio "derived… his taste in literature and philosophy, his love of Burns, his faith in the French Revolution and English radicalism" (Sarkar 1979: 102). Drummond was a disciple of the Scots philosopher and freethinker David Hume, who "revered the new science, believed in the experimental method and loathed superstition" (Denby 2004). Drummond's Academy has been described by Bhattacharya as India's "first modern educational institution" (1968: 3). There, Derozio became well versed in "the thought of England… as …embodied in the poets, novelists dramatists, and philosophers of that country" (Edwards 1884: 7). Drummond admitted Europeans, Euro-Asians and Indians into the school, and "infused the revolutionary ideas of the time into his students," especially 18th century rationalist philosophy, which turned Derozio into "a full-blooded rationalist in thought and action" (Bhattacharya 1968: 2). Leaving school, Derozio worked as a clerk in his father's firm, but being dissatisfied with routine work he left and spent two years with his mother's brother, Arthur Johnson, an indigo planter of Bengal. There he wrote poems and essays and read the work of philosophers. Returning in 1826, Derozio joined the Hindu College (later Presidency College) as a teacher of history and literature, and gathered a group of loyal students around him.

Another Scot who had an important influence on Derozio was David Hare (1775-1842), who was one of the founders of the Hindu College, Kolkata, in 1817. Hare, also in the rationalist trend, had lost faith "in the tenets of religion" and had become "completely secular in words and deeds" (Bhattacharya 1968: 12). Sarkar writes that Hare and Derozio had a "passionate conviction" that India needed to be exposed to European thought and scientific developments. Both were also "godless, secularists with little faith in denominations or religious instruction, yet staunch idealists" (1979: 101). To Bhattacharya, Derozio was "the first man of Indian Enlightenment," who became the *enfant terrible* of Hindu society (1968: 8 & 10). He was a popular teacher, described by his disciple Pearychand Mitra as one who "gave the greatest impetus to free discussion on all subjects, social, moral and religious," encouraging students to speak openly, exchange ideas and read relevant books (ibid: 15). It was a case of mutual respect, admiration and commitment to the cause of social change. Derozio's "Sonnet to the Pupils of the Hindu College" revealed his deep feelings for his students:

> Expanding, like the petals of young flowers;
> I watch the gentle opening of your minds,
> And the sweet loosening of the spell that binds
> Your intellectual energies and powers,
> That stretch (like young birds in soft summer hours)
> Their wings, to try their strength. O how the winds
> Of circumstances, and freshening April showers
> Of early knowledge, and unnumbered kinds
> Of new perceptions shed their influence;
> And how you worship truth's omnipotence
> What joyance rains upon me, when I see
> Fame, in the mirror of futurity,
> Weaving the chaplets you have yet to gain,
> Ah then I feel I have not lived in vain.
> (quoted in Bradley-Birt 1980: 43)

Derozio taught in the Hindu College where he promoted a questioning of Hindu traditionalism. In Bhattacharya's view, Derozio "sowed the seeds of revolt" and his teachings "subverted the ideological bases on which the orthodoxy stood" (1968: 16). Several magazines, including *Hesperus* and the *Calcutta Literary Gazette,* were edited by Derozio, who also politically assisted the *India Gazette* which was "ultra radical" (Sarkar 1979: 102). Derozio's writings and poetry expressed patriotic sentiments, which Sarkar calls "unusual" for Euro-Asians (ibid: 102). One of Derozio's poems, "To India – My Native Land," included the following lines:

> My country! In thy day of glory past
> A beauteous halo circled round thy brow,
> And worshipped as a deity thou wast.
> Where is that glory where that reverence now?
> Thy eagle pinion is chained down at last,

And groveling in the lowly dust art thou:
Thy minstrel hath no wreath to weave for thee
Save the sad story of thy misery!
(quoted in Bradley-Birt 1980: 2)

The message to fellow Indians in another poem, entitled "Sonnet," was also one of resistance to tyrants and priests:

Your hand is on the helm – guide on young men
The bark that's freighted with your country's doom.
Your glories are but budding; they shall bloom
Like fabled amaranths Elysian, when
The shore is won, even now within your ken,
And when your torch shall dissipate the gloom
That long has made your country but a tomb,
Or worse than tomb, the priest's, the tyrant's den.
Guide on, young men: your course is well begun.
(ibid: 120)

In "The Harp of India" (1827), Derozio shows a consciousness of his own role in India's rejuvenation, "taking into his youthful hands the Harp of India which had so long been silent, and whose music he awoke again to such wonderful effect" (Bradley-Birt 1980: iii)[2]:

O! many a hand more worthy far than mine
Once thy harmonious chords to sweetness gave,
And many a wreath for them did fame entwine
Of flowers still blooming on the minstrel's grave:
Those hands are cold – but if thy notes divine
May be by mortal wakened once again,
Harp of my country, let me strike the strain!
(ibid: i)

While retaining his patriotism and feelings for India, Derozio's aim was to introduce his pupils to European philosophers (Bacon, Locke, Hume, Kant), to the events of the French Revolution and thinkers of the Enlightenment (Rousseau, Voltaire and Thomas Paine). Sengupta claims that Derozio's "social and moral attitudes" were influenced by Paine's *The Age of Reason* and that he introduced the book to his students (2000:

6 & 17). The Bengali intelligentsia were also inspired by the literature and poetry of the British 'Romantics' – Wordsworth, Burns, Shelley, and especially Byron.

The "Root of all Evils"

The Academic Association, begun in 1828 by Derozio and his pupils, debated topics such as "free-will, virtue and vice, ...patriotism, ...the existence of God, the shame of idolatry and priestcraft." These meetings attracted "the elite of Calcutta to the exciting sessions" (Sarkar 1979: 104). Bhattacharya claims that "Derozio's intellectual scepticism was based on Cartesian rationalism," and that this rationalistic philosophy made him an exemplary man of his time "who created a tradition of moral conduct and enlightened social consciousness for the first time in the social life of Bengal" (1968: 23).

The 'scandal' created by the Derozians was mainly linked to their secularism, defiance of Hindu religious practice, and espousal of free-thinking. The common assumption among orthodox Hindus, as expressed by the *Oriental Magazine* (1843), was that the Derozians were "cutting their way through ham and beef, and wading to liberalism through tumblers of beer" (quoted in Sarkar 1985: 18). Derozio's pupils met at his home, where they indulged in "forbidden food and drink." Many of the group were defiant; one of them, Madhab Chandra Mallik, wrote: "If there is anything we hate from the bottom of our hearts, it is Hinduism"; while another, Rasikkrishna Mallik, refused to swear in court on the holy water, saying, "I do not believe in the sacredness of the Ganges" (Sarkar 1979: 103). Not surprisingly, orthodox caste-conscious Hindus were "deeply alarmed," and rumours and gossip about the group abounded. It was said that:

> Some Hindu College boys, when required to utter mantras at prayers, would repeat lines from the Illiad instead; that one student, asked to bow before the goddess Kali, greeted the image with 'good morning, madam.' (ibid: 104)

The students inevitably aroused opposition for breaking food and alcohol prohibitions, and revolting against caste and Hindu traditions which they labelled 'superstition.' Moreover, the "surge of radical opinion" was evident from some other unusual events in Kolkata. On 10 December 1830, two hundred persons attended the celebrations of the July Revolution in France, and on December 25th that year, the French tricolour flag was hoisted in the Indian city. In 1830 this group also started a paper, the *Parthenon*, advocating female education, and denouncing the "curse of superstition" (Sarkar 1979: 104). As Sivanath Sastri, biographer of Ramtanu Lahiri (Derozio's disciple), wrote, Derozio had "a mighty influence" on Hindu society and "sent out a band of harbingers of light to their benighted countrymen" (Sastri 1907: 182 & 68). Sastri also elaborated on the "great attraction" Derozio's home had "for these young lads":

> There they learned much and enjoyed much... the Hindu lads brought up in the belief that the society of a Christian is contaminating, and that food... prepared in his house is so defiling as to hurl him who ate it to the lowest depths of hell, *broke asunder the shackles of caste and ate with their Eurasian friend.* (ibid: 66, emphasis added)

Once established as a poet, Derozio was in demand as a guest at the Kolkata homes of others, such as the English poet Henry Meredith Parker. Chaudhuri describes the scene: "Henry Derozio and Parker, regardless of race, were clearly friends," and both were not only friends of Emma Roberts, an English poet and writer living in Kolkata, but also kept company with another Bengali, Kasiprasad Ghosh, who wrote poetry in English (Chaudhuri 2000: 436). Emma Roberts was sensitive to Indian society, and in 1835 published three volumes of *Scenes and Characteristics of Hindostan, with Sketches of Anglo-Indian Society*. Derozio thus belonged to "a distinguished part of an elite literary circle," whose mixed race and gender ambiance was "a testament to the cosmopolitan, entrepreneurial quality of East India Company rule in early nineteenth-century Calcutta" (ibid: 437).

Not surprisingly, the orthodox reacted sharply, and vilified the students. Religion was said to be in danger from "atheist beasts" led by "vagabond *firingis*" (those of foreign origin) – a reference to Derozio. He was denounced as "the *root of all evils* and the cause of public alarm," who should be "discharged from the college" (Sarkar 1979: 105, emphasis added). Such protests by orthodox Hindus finally led to Derozio's dismissal, and he was accused by the Hindu College authorities of denying the existence of God and being guilty of incest.[3] His defiant reply to the charges reflected the spirit of the times – especially among dissidents in Europe:

> That I should be called a sceptic and an infidel is not surprising, as these names are always given to persons who think for themselves in religion. Vague reports and unfounded rumors went abroad concerning me... in their rage they have forgotten what was due even to common decency. (Bhattacharya 1968: 22-23)

Young Bengal

After his dismissal, Derozio continued to write, compose poetry, edit journals and to organize discussions at his home. This group, known as Derozians, developed into the Young Bengal movement. The 'Derozio phenomenon' was indeed a historical breakthrough in India. Sumit Sarkar calls it an "interesting though short-lived, *atheistic phase all but unique in our (Indian) nineteenth century intellectual history*" (1985: 25, emphasis added). In 1861 Kishorichand Mitra evaluated the Young Bengal group as "a youthful band of reformers who... like the tops of the Kanchenjunga, *were the first to catch and reflect the dawn*" (quoted in Sarkar 1979: 111, emphasis added). Yet as Rosinka Chaudhuri writes, postcolonial narratives have "strangely bypassed" Young Bengal, although it was a "historical and epistemological movement that defined the shape of modern India." It was both "radical" and "imitative," incorporating "paradoxes that continue to inhabit Indian public life" (2000: 424).

A common criticism of the Young Bengal movement was that it was 'denationalized' and 'westernized' and too critical of Indian society. Dinesh Chandra Sen in 1896 argued that they had forgotten their own literature and were "thoroughly anglicanised in spirit."

> They exalted in Shakespeare's dramas and Milton's poetry; they read Schiller's *Robbers* and Goethe's *Faust*; they could name all the English dramatists of the Elizabethan age... and reproduce from memory lines from still earlier dramatists... [T]hey grew mad after Shelley's *Epipsychidion*, Keats' *Hyperion*... and Chatterton's *Death of Charles Bodwin.* (Chaudhuri, 2000: 433, quoting Sen 1911: 883)

The Derozians of Young Bengal contributed generally to issues of social reform from the 1830s onwards. Their paper *Jnananveshana* campaigned on women's emancipation and education, widow remarriage, and against polygamy. Although Derozio was forced to leave Hindu College, as Sarkar noted, "the spell he had cast on the youth persisted," and even after his early death in 1831, "his impact continued to be manifested" (1979: 106-7). His immediate students continued to agitate in the 1830s and 1840s on a series of reform issues, but their iconoclastic zeal did not last; and the Young Bengal movement that had such promise, and for a time blazed a trail of dissent, petered out by the 1850s. But the Derozians and the Young Bengal group had started the process which inspired and heralded other Indian nationalist and reform movements of the late 19th century. Sumit Sarkar, in a critical assessment of Derozio and Young Bengal, states that the Derozians "thrilled to the ideals of European radicalism," which, he says, is "exciting and interesting news." But he queries the "applicability of such ideas by an intelligentsia reared in a colonial environment and as yet largely identified with it" (1985: 19). They were, claims Sarkar, "followers of the British liberal model" (ibid: 34). However, even this had revolutionary implications in a colonial context where few democratic rights prevailed.

Radical and liberal political attitudes and secular views persisted among Bengali youth and Thomas Paine's *The Age of Reason* had brisk sales among students in 1832 (Sarkar 1985: 25). Alexander Duff, a well-known missionary, complained that "college students were avid readers of Thomas Paine." He blamed a "wretched American bookseller" for taking advantage of the "infidel leanings of a new race of men in the East" and sending to Kolkata a thousand copies of *The Age of Reason*, "that most malignant and pestiferous of all anti-Christian publications" (Chaudhuri 2000: 428). There was also the Whig lobby in India, and the journal *Englishman* observed in 1836 that the Hindu College students, being all radicals, "the very word 'tory' is a sort of ignominy" among them. The Derozians branched out along several reformist paths: Rasikkrishna Mallik condemned police corruption, the condition of the peasantry and "the political power of the merchant company" (Sarkar 1979: 107); Ramgopal Ghose joined George Thompson (a leading British campaigner against slavery) when he visited India and spoke along with him on public platforms in Kolkata; Dhakshinaranjan Mukherji in 1843 condemned the "ambitious and domineering" Hindu priests; and in 1846 Pearychand Mitra claimed "it is private property which gives rise to government... the opulent and powerful do not require so much of its constant care... as the poor and helpless" (ibid: 107-8).

The Derozians also launched several periodicals: the *Enquirer* run by Krishnamohan Bannerji combatted obscurantism among the Hindus; a bilingual journal *Jnananveshana* was started by Rasikkrishna Mallik to promote the "science of government and jurisprudence"; the *Hindu Pioneer* in the late 1830s complained about the exclusion of Indians from government; Tarachand Chakrabarti edited the *Quill,* also critical of the government; and the *Bengal Spectator,* begun in 1842, not only advocated the right of Indians to compete for the civil service, but also raised the issue of forced labour and urged the right of widow remarriage (ibid: 108).

"The opening up, by Derozians of wider horizons," became a feature of Bengali culture and this tradition was "perpetuated through the newspapers and associations they founded" (Addy & Azad, 1973: 82). There was also what Susobhan Sarkar calls the "Derozian penchant for societies"; apart from the Academic Association started earlier by Derozio himself, the Derozian group (Chakrabarti, Ghose, Pearychand Mitra and Ramtanu Lahiri) founded the "Society for the Acquisition of General Knowledge" in 1838, where papers were read and the proceedings published (Sarkar 1979: 108). Inspired partly by the advice of George Thompson, that Bengalis should organize politically, more associations emerged. The Bengal British India Society was formed in 1843, composed of the "aristocracy of intelligence"; and by the early

1850s (when the Young Bengal group had declined), the society merged with the British Indian Association, described as "the first united front of the politically minded educated Indians" (ibid: 109).

Sumit Sarkar (1985), writing on the challenge to established religion by the Young Bengal members, stressed their patriotism and contributions to Bengali prose. They had also made a great leap in terms of rationalism, secularism and acceptance of revolutionary thinking from the West. But the old attitudes still prevailed in India. In contrast to the Derozian ideologies of an earlier phase, there was, by the late 19th century, an emergence of a nationalism linked to cultural and religious revival. The early radicalism in Bengal, however, did not die out, but was visible in social reform movements and various expressions of secular nationalism and anti-colonialism, keeping alive the Derozian spirit of a secular, radical – albeit utopian – challenge to patriarchy, orthodoxy and obscurantism. What was the most daring campaign, perhaps, of Derozio and his followers was their advanced attitudes on social evils affecting women, and their pioneering writings on women's rights.

The Rights of Women

Derozio had the advantage as a 'Christianized' Euro-Asian of being an 'outsider' to Hindu caste-based society, which was reflected in his ability to ignore orthodoxy and face controversy. But yet he was also a part of Bengali society, expressing patriotic views and showing a keen concern and sympathy for the plight of Indian women. These emotions were reflected in his poetry. During the time he spent with his uncle (Arthur Johnson) in Bhagalpur, a town on the Ganges, he wrote poetry, including *The Fakir of Jungheera* (1827), a poem of two cantos (inspired by Byron) about a young widow about to perform *sati* who is rescued by a former lover (a robber chief) and taken to the rock of Jungheera, only to die there in a subsequent raid. What is revealing is that Derozio, at a young age, was not only conscious of women's oppression in India, but was also among the first (along with Rammohun Roy) to publicly denounce the practice of *sati*, long before other more famous Indian social reformers. Derozio, explaining his poem, makes an important point; his mission was to "break illusions" in the "cause of truth," and he perceptively refers to:

> a mistaken opinion, somewhat general in Europe, that the Hindu widow's burning herself with the corpse of her husband is an act of unparalleled magnanimity and devotion. To break those illusions that are pleasing to the mind, seems to be a task that no one is thanked for performing; nevertheless he who does so serves the cause of truth. (quoted in Das Gupta 1973: 22)

In another remarkable poem, "On the Abolition of Sattee," Derozio has a verse, that covers a range of issues affecting women (ibid: 21):

> Nurtured in darkness, born to many woes,
> Words, the mind's instruments, but ill supplied,
> Delight, even as a name she scarcely knows,
> And while an infant sold to be a bride,
> To be a mother, her exalted pride,
> And yet not hers a mother's sigh or smile;
> Oft doomed in youth, to stern the icy tide
> Of rude neglect, caused by some wanton's wile,
> And forced at last to grace her lord's funeral pile.

The 'Other England' and Byronic Transcendent Nationalism

Sumit Sarkar has critiqued the Young Bengal group for its "bourgeois liberalism," which although "a progressive and even revolutionary force" in Britain, "turned into their opposites wherever attempts to apply them were made by foreign administrators ...or indigenous [Indian] intellectuals." Yet, as he admits, there were echoes of the 'Other England' in Kolkata. Sarkar cites an important example, from the *India Gazette* of July 1831 (with Derozio on the editorial staff), which attacked a book subtitled "An address to the working men of the United Kingdom," as reflecting the "odious plague-spot of Whig perfidy," whose author was "an advocate for the people's submission to misery." It quoted from Thomas More's *Utopia,* and denounced the Reform Bill as a product of

"Whig treachery" (1965: 34-35). The 'Other England' also included the Chartist movement and the continuous class struggles in Britain as well as Robert Owen's Utopian Socialist vision and experiments in communal living. Alternative ideologies had been taken up by the revolutionary poets and writers of the day in Britain, of whom Byron was important, in terms of his influence on the Derozians and other radicals of South Asia.

Lord Byron (1788-1824) used his privileged class position to shock the British establishment through his politics, poetry and lifestyle. It was a turbulent period in Europe – Napoleonic wars, the struggles for emancipation of the Irish and Catholics in Britain, Italy's revolt against Austrian rule, and the Greek battles for independence from Turkey. André Maurois claimed that Byron was part of the "restless age" of the period after the French Revolution, with its "great hopes" and disappointments: "Millions… had experienced as Byron did, the feeling of injustice and madness of the universe" (1984: 13).

Byron's political rebellion consisted of a critique of British politics, and opposition to tyranny abroad. He supported the reformist Whigs and championed the Irish peasants, whose condition he said was worse than that of "black slaves" (Eisler 1999: 348). He also advocated the removal of discriminatory laws against Catholics, and fiercely opposed Lord Elgin's removal of the 'Elgin marbles' from Greece to Britain. Defiantly, he praised Napoleon, going against the prevailing political climate in Britain, and also supported Italy's liberation and Greek independence. Byron's poetry highlighted "national independence" in Europe, but the implication, according to Marilyn Butler, was that "liberty itself is a universal ideal… the enemy is not Napoleon, who is England's enemy: it is tyranny" (1981: 118). While in 1870 John Morley named Byron the "poet of the Revolution" (ibid: 85), among the British establishment Byron caused great offence by his libertine ways, his "scorn of convention and hypocrisy, his idealism, his cynicism," transcending his class and country of origin (Calder 1977: 11 & 17). He was "the Whig aristocrat in exile, self-assured, responsible to nobody, reckless, voluble, exuberant, wickedly ironical, and deceptively informal" (J.D. Jump, quoted in Ford 1962: 257).[4]

To rebels in the colonies, he became the ideal heroic figure and, according to Jenni Calder, the word 'Byron' was a symbol all over the world, to "a selfless commitment to the freedom of a country not one's own, a kind of *transcendent nationalism, at a time when nationalism was a moving force*" (1977: 10, emphasis added). The spectacle of a defiant British lord, subverting the politics, ideologies and hypocritical sexual morality of the British, was certainly startling and exciting to patriots, nationalists and reformers in Asia and the Middle - East. The poet Wilfrid Scawen Blunt claimed that Ahmed Orabi, the Egyptian nationalist leader of the 1890s, had been inspired by Byron (Foot 1988: 379).

Byron's poetry reverberated among subject peoples in Europe and elsewhere; his revolutionary stances, and especially the tragic manner of his early death in Greece in 1824, at the age of 36, heightened his romantic heroism and charisma. His death was mourned all around the world. Joseph Mazzini, leader of the Italian *Risorgimento* who wrote a hymn to Byron, also predicted that "the day will come when Democracy will remember all that it owes to Byron" (Foot 1988: 375-76). As Michael Foot writes:

> Byron was in marvelous accord with the spirit and the cravings of the age… [It] was the spirit of rebellion… which through his voice made the young generation in all lands one cosmopolitan society. [Byron] let loose all the passions… he aimed at revolutionizing men's minds, at awakening them to a sense of tyranny. (ibid: 381)

"Mad, Bad and Dangerous to Know"

Byron became famous worldwide – including India and Sri Lanka – as the poet of rebellion. Many of his characters, as Marilyn Butler notes, were: "moody outcasts with the mark of Cain upon them, mad, bad and dangerous to know," projecting the stereotype of the "passionate, rebellious, Romantic Poet" (Butler 1981: 2-3). Since the British ruling – class thought him 'dangerous,' he became immediately attractive to the dissidents and radicals in the colonies, most notably to the Derozians and Young Bengal in India, and in the 1850s to the Young Ceylon group led by Charles Lorenz, Louis Nell and Frederick Nell (see Chapter 7).

The latter went around with a copy of Byron's poems in his pocket (Roberts et al. 1989: 7). According to Arabinda Poddar, a literary critic, Henry Derozio was the first in Bengal to be dubbed 'Byron,' and his poem *Fakeer of Jungheera* was "in imitation of Byron" (Bhattacharji 1999: 5-6).

In 1850 Derozio was called a "Young poet of considerable genius, ...styled the Byron of the East" (Madge 1905: 24, quoting Commander Elliot's *Illustrated Hindustan*, 1850). The Academic Association formed by Derozio, and inspired by Byron's outbursts against tyrants, debated issues such as the "the fallen state of India" (Bhattacharji 1999: 6, citing Poddar). The cause of Greek independence, the political commitment of Byron, and later his death, fired Derozio's many 'Greek' poems. In one of them, *Phyle*, while citing Byron's line "And Freedom's fame finds wings in every wind," Derozio wrote:

> There is a sacred halo round thy brow;
> 'Tis sanctified by ages and by fame,
> For here the glory of the Grecian name
> Received another dazzling ray – and thou,
> Immortal Phyle, smiling in the light
> That heaven shed o'er thee, didst behold the deed,
> The generous patriot rushing to the fight,
> The tyrants conquered, and the people freed:
>
> (quoted in Bradley-Birt 1980: 71)

Derozio's 'Greek' phase included the poems "The Greeks at Marathon," in 1825; "Hellenic Chronicle of Missolonghi," in 1827; as well as a poem "Sappho," which quoted from Byron's *Don Juan*, Canto 4: "and love too much, and yet cannot love less" (ibid: 76). Derozio's Byronic influence was openly acknowledged and was reflected in his poems. Byron, in one of his famous verses of resistance, had written:

> But I have lived and have not lived in vain,
> My mind may lose its force, my blood its fire,
> And my frame perish even in conquering pain,
> But there is that within me which shall tire
> Torture and Time, and breath when I expire...

Derozio used the famous first line of this poem as the last line of his own sonnet to his students (quoted earlier). The political impact of Byron's "passionate love of freedom... and strong resentment of wrong" was also felt by the Derozians (Bhattacharji 1999: 6, quoting Poddar). Even in later decades, Byron inspired nationalist Indians including Rabindranath Tagore who described Byron's impact on the Bengali "well-behaved social world":

> Our literary gods were Shakespeare, Milton and Byron and the quality of their work which stirred us most was strength of passion. This bacchanalian revelry of Europe woke us up, and made us lively. We were dazzled by the glow of unfettered life which fell upon our custom-smothered heart pining for an opportunity to disclose itself. (ibid:7)

Derozio and Euro-Asian Politics

While Derozio was a patriotic Indian with strong universalistic feelings on social reform, he also fought for the rights of the small Euro-Asian community to which he belonged. While at Hindu College, he had started the *Hesperus,* a paper which aired some of the grievances of the Euro-Asians, and in 1831 Derozio with his own money turned the *Hesperus* into the *East Indian.* It was "the first newspaper that was the recognized organ of Eurasians and which advocated their claims... with an eloquence and ability and power of argument" (Edwards 1884: 142). The Indian Euro-Asians had many grievances, especially disabilities under the law. They rejected Hindu or Muslim customary and religious law, and protested that British law covering Europeans in India was not extended to Euro-Asians (the British fearing that claims of other Indians would surface). A petition to the British parliament bearing "the touch of Derozio's hand" was drawn up in June 1831. It was a "most damning indictment of British racialism in India" (1973:5). The Euro-Asians bitterly complained that discriminatory practices were "degrading, invidious, and proscriptive," and that they were:

> systematically and as a class, excluded from all superior and covenanted offices in the Civil and Military Services... the Marine Service of the East India Company, ...and subordinate employments in the Judicial, Revenue and Police Departments, which are open without reserve to Hindu and Mahummudan natives of the country. (Edwards 1884: 150-51)

The protest by Euro-Asians caused a stir, and an article by Derozio succeeded in provoking the editor of *John Bull* (a paper run by Britishers in Kolkata) to storm into Derozio's office with a cane to assault him, but changing his mind, indulged in a "war of words." The incident was highlighted in the Bengal press, but Derozio took it lightly: "Having fixed upon my assailant the infamy which his conduct deserves, I abandon him to his own reflections and the charity of the public" (ibid: 154-57).

The petition was successfully presented to both houses of parliament in London by another Euro-Asian, John Ricketts, who gave evidence on the issue; and as a result, by 1833 discrimination "on grounds of creed or colour" was forbidden in the Charter of the East India Company. In March 1831, on the occasion of a reception for John Ricketts on his return. Derozio (of Portuguese origin) allied with those of British descent, stressing their common identity as East Indians.

> Why... am I here this day?... I am an East Indian... I am interested in the welfare of my countrymen... I am anxious to know what measures have been taken to promote that welfare... I love my country and I love justice, and therefore I ought to be here. (quoted in Das Gupta 1973: 6)

Derozio also deplored the attitude of the more conservative Euro-Asians. In the *East Indian*, he praised those Hindus and Christian Euro-Asians who studied together at the Dharrumtollah Academy, and referred to the prejudices of those Euro-Asians who "declined to have their sons educated side by side with the native lads of India for moral and religious reasons" (Edwards 1884: 164). Urging harmony between Hindus and Euro-Asians, he quoted Burns:

> Man to man the world o'er,
> Shall brothers be and a' that.

Derozio was appointed to examine the pupils of the Academy, and his report reflects his liberal stances. He was also ahead of others in combating religious bigotry. As Derozio wrote:

> It is quite delightful to witness the exertions of Hindu and Christian youths, striving together for academic honours; this will do much towards softening asperities which always arise in hostile sects. ...Hindu and Christians have learned from mutual intercourse how much there is to be admired in the human character, without reference to differences of opinion in religious matters. (Edwards 1884: 162–63)

Derozio argued that it would be "suicidal" for Euro-Asians to object to their children studying "among native youths," also commenting that "they cannot withhold knowledge from Hindu youths, and if they manifest illiberal feeling towards those youths, are they not afraid of a reaction?" Predicting that "in a few years the Hindus will take their stand by the best and the proudest Christians," he stated that it was undesirable "to excite the feelings of the former against the latter." Euro-Asian grievances, he argued, should "teach us not to make others suffer"; he urged that it was in the best interests of Euro-Asians that they "unite and cooperate with other native inhabitants of India" (ibid: 163). These were his last writings; for soon after, Derozio, aged 24, died of cholera in December 1831. Thomas Edwards in 1884 refers to "these, the last public words of the greatest Eurasian... that shed lustre on his race," whose charity and toleration made him "not only *much in advance of the men of his own day, but also far ahead in wide sympathy and true liberality even of the men of today*." Referring to Derozio's warning to his community, Edwards said this advice was not followed and "the Eurasians of today are reaping the folly of their fathers' sowing" (1884: 165, emphasis added).

Erasure of the Kolkata Euro-Asians

> There are murals, tablets, portraits and busts in the various educational institutions of Calcutta, commemorating the worth and work of men who have laboured for... the people of India... The visitor looks in vain for any memorial to Derozio.

This was the conclusion of Thomas Edwards, Henry Derozio's biographer, who in the 1880s berated fellow Euro-Asians for having "shamefully neglected" his memory (1884: 118 & 189). R.K. Das Gupta claims that the most famous Bengalis – Rammohun Roy, Vidyasagar, Tagore, Vivekananda and Aurobindo – ignored Derozio, either because he "preached a dangerous gospel," was "too young to be taken seriously," or because of his "spirit of non-conformity." He added, "some due fate denied Derozio the tribute he deserved as the first evangelist of free thought in the traditional society of early nineteenth century Bengal" (Das Gupta 1980: Foreword: E–F). The Anglo-Indian member of the West Bengal Legislative Assembly in 1973 referred to Derozio as "a national figure... the first Indian nationalist, the first patriot," alleging that "conservative upper-class landlords, and the British ruling classes, conspired in vain to consign him to oblivion" (G.A.W. de Roze, quoted in Das Gupta 1973: 6).

But in retrospect it is evident that Derozio could never qualify as part of the *bhadralok* (Bengali elite) and that his Euro-Asian origin was his "due fate," putting him 'beyond the pale' to the Indian intelligentsia. The latter denied that Euro-Asians could have any nationalist sentiments, accusing them of forgetting their Indian origins and being pro-imperialist imitators of the British. And Susobhan Sarkar, commenting on Derozio's patriotic verse, said it was "*unusual in one from his community*" (1979: 102, emphasis added).

Many have ignored Derozio and the Young Bengal movement. A.R. Desai's book on the social background of Indian nationalism makes no mention of Derozio and his disciples by name, but claims that the first contact Indians had with "modern western culture was electrifying," but that some Indians used the occasion to regard "freedom as license to drink or to indulge in unhealthy modes of sex life" (1966: 143). Addy and Azad claim that the "tragedy of the Derozians was that their Enlightenment aspirations carried them far beyond the pre-occupations of their own class without allowing them to establish an organic link with the majority of the exploited and oppressed." They also argue that although the Derozians were "disinherited or run out of respectable Hindu society," their movement pioneered "secular and radical nationalism," which contrasted to the obscurantist and reactionary trends of later decades (Addy & Azad 1973: 82).

Pallab Sengupta, however, argues that while in the 19th century the "bogey of being Eurasian" was partly responsible for the "reserved attitude towards Derozio's contribution," the underlying reason was that "what Derozio wanted to establish, was not at all congenial to the interests of the overlords of society," claiming that India's social conservatism "deprived Derozio of the honour he deserved" (Sengupta 2000: 55-56). What is clear, is that unlike later nationalists, who were politically militant but socially reactionary, Derozio was the earliest proponent of radical thinking in both the political and social spheres.

John Ricketts and the Rights of Euro-Asians

By the 19th century, when Bengal was the centre of British rule in India and Kolkata was intellectually and culturally the most advanced city, the Euro-Asians of Bengal led the way in championing movements of reform, and espousing radical views. Henry Derozio, however, was not the sole Kolkata Euro-Asian to speak up for social change. While his student group was composed of Bengali Hindus, Derozio did have another link to a small coterie of reformist Kolkata Euro-Asians. We are fortunate that while in later years several Anglo-Indian writers, including Thomas Edwards, H.A. Stark and E.W. Madge, recorded the life of Derozio, Stark also wrote the biography of John Ricketts, another reformist member of the community. Ricketts and other politically conscious Euro-Asians, educated in English, were aware of liberal ideologies and reformist currents in the West, and were inspired to champion a free press and more democratic rights in India. They had grievances specific to the community of Euro-Asians and resented the discrimination they experienced. These Euro-Asians were also in contact with radicals in Britain and British dissidents resident in India.

Of this Euro-Asian group, John Ricketts (1791-1835) stood out as a spokesperson for the rights of the community. He was the son of an Indian mother (Bibi Zenut) and Ensign John Ricketts (whose father was a British surgeon), and was the nephew of Vice-Admiral Sir Robert Ricketts (Hawes 1996: 167). On his father's death in battle, John was placed in the Upper Military Orphanage in Kolkata. In the late 18th century, British policy in respect of 'military orphans' was that only those few who were British and legitimate were sent back to England for education. The others were divided according to class, with the Upper Military Orphanage taking on the Euro-Asian or British (illegitimate) children of army officers and the Lower Military Orphanage being established for similar children of the rank and file (ibid: 24). Euro-Asians after the 1790s were prohibited from travelling to Britain for studies and were also disqualified from the armed forces. Ricketts estimated there were 800 Euro-Asian boys and girls in the Military Orphan Schools, while there were around 140 of them in the Parental Academy (founded by Ricketts in 1823 in Kolkata on the lines of an English public school) and 50 in the Grammar School (Stark 1934: 20).

In the Orphan School, Ricketts was taught English, arithmetic, geography, reading and writing, but not, as he himself noted, Latin and Greek (Hawes 1996: 42-43). Stark commented that it spoke "volumes for the quality of instruction imparted" at that "humble institution," that Ricketts "grew up to be a man of culture and literary taste"; the pages of Thomas Addison being "his delight in youth," and in later life, Ricketts contributed "thoughtful and elegant articles to the magazines and journals of the day" (Stark 1934: 117-18). Hawes also notes that Ricketts was "well-educated and widely read" and had an "extensive library" (1996: 92).

Ricketts and the Euro-Asian boys of the orphanage bitterly resented their lack of future prospects due to government policies. "They felt they belonged to a race – cruelly and undeservedly reduced to moral and material beggary" (Stark 1934: 9). Ricketts on leaving the orphanage became a clerk at the East India Company, and in 1810 was sent to its office in Amboina, previously a Dutch colony in the Malay Archipelago. He rose to become secretary to the English Resident. Ricketts "could not avoid making comparisons" between his own experience in India and Dutch policy to those of mixed origin, who enjoyed "every privilege of citizenship" including the right to join the army and the public service (ibid: 25). Ricketts during this period was a friend of the Superintendent of Education, Jabez Carey, son of William Carey the famous Baptist missionary of Serampore, Bengal. Jabez Carey and Ricketts worked together in the Bible Society, and Ricketts, thus inspired, returned to Murshidabad in Bengal as an itinerate catechist but then moved to Kolkata due to ill health. He continued his links with the Baptists while working at the Board of Customs, rising to be the deputy-registrar of the Board of Revenue.

While Ricketts and the reformist Euro-Asians were supportive of freedom of the press in India, the British were wary of any talk of a free press and feared the Euro-Asian enthusiasm for such reforms. In 1824 warnings of such dangers had been made by a former Governor of Bombay, Sir John Malcolm, who deplored the fact that the 'half-castes' were the greatest supporters of a free press. A notable stir occured in 1823 when James Silk Buckingham, the British editor of *The Calcutta Journal* – the first liberal English paper in India, started in 1818 – was ordered to be deported for articles critical of the government. At a meeting of Europeans to support the deportation, John Ricketts dissented and spoke for freedom of expression and the need of a free press. As Stark commented, Ricketts:

> courageously stood up, and in manly spirit maintained that... it was iniquitous to deny any people under the British flag, freedom of speech in criticizing Government officials and measures merely because at times that freedom may be betrayed. (Stark 1934: 45)

Ricketts was not alone and had "a band of earnest workers... pledged to do their very utmost to uplift their community through concerted action" (ibid: 47). Among them was James Kyd, a wealthy trader, who published his "Thoughts, How to Better the Condition of Indo-Britons," urging the community to enter a variety of professions and "cease staking their all upon government and mercantile offices" (ibid).

This group of concerned Euro-Asians – many of them Baptists – also organized the "East Indians' Petition to Parliament" enumerating their grievances. In 1829-30, Ricketts was sent to London to lobby British politicians on the petition. Lord Carlyle presented the petition in the House of Lords, and Ricketts was examined by a Select Committee of the Lords. The petition was presented in the House of Commons by C.W. Wynn, a British MP. Several liberal British sympathetically received Ricketts, among them the former Chief Justice of Ceylon, Sir Alexander Johnston, an advanced liberal and reformist of his age who had campaigned for the abolition of slavery in the colonies. Ricketts, in his evidence before the House of Commons, referred to the treatment of Burghers in Sri Lanka, whom Sir Alexander Johnston had found to be "the most efficient instruments in the public service," with whose assistance he was able to carry out "slave emancipation, and bring into operation trial by jury" (ibid: 43).

When Ricketts returned, he was enthusiastically received by his community with receptions and public meetings. The *Government Gazette* described the banquet given to Ricketts by the Euro-Asian community of Chennai, which spared "neither expense, nor trouble" to make the occasion a success. "The repeated plaudits" that interrupted Ricketts' address amounted to "spontaneous recognition of the unselfish and patriotic work he had done for his people by his deputation to England" (ibid: 110-11). In Kolkata another meeting and public dinner were held to honour him, where among the speakers was Henry Derozio. The results of Ricketts' mission were not long in coming. In 1833, when the reform movement in Britain was in full swing, the East India Company was subject to administrative reforms and the former restrictive provisions regarding the civil and military services were changed.

It was certainly a victory for the struggle of the Euro-Asian for equality and for Ricketts' efforts personally to publicize the East Indians'

Petition. In 1835 the Euro-Asians further benefited from the rule that English would be the official language of government, enabling them to find a "ready market for their knowledge of English" (Stark 1934: 16). John Ricketts' career flourished, and he was given a government post in Gaya. But in July 1835, aged 43, Ricketts died of a fever, depriving the Euro-Asian community of a reformer and champion. Commenting on his death, Stark claims that "he died universally loved and deeply lamented by persons of all stations in life, of all shades of opinion, and all classes and races in Bengal" (ibid: 118-19). In another tribute, a judge (J.S. Cuthbert) of Bihar, wrote that "the whole native community of this place, amounting to some thousands, evinced their respect for his public character by following his remains to the grave" (ibid: 116-17).

With the deaths of both Derozio and Ricketts in the early 1830s, the phase of Euro-Asian agitation based on radical political ideologies and opposition to social backwardness faded. In subsequent decades, the banner of political reform was taken up by Hindu and Muslim nationalists. Many of them spoke out for political change and Home Rule, but hesitated to espouse secularism or to critique local social practice. The few who were social reformers did not become nationalist leaders. Only a small minority of ideologues were able to combine secularism, nationalism *and* social change – among the pioneers being the Derozians.

Susobhan Sarkar, the eminent historian, while commenting on the failure of the Young Bengal group to build an ideology and "a sustained movement," says its "most memorable positive aspects" included "a fearless rationalism and a candid appreciation of the regenerating new thought from the West." He laments that "much of this was drowned in the current of traditionalism, mysticism, religiosity and revivalism fashionable in the later part of the century." Sarkar significantly adds that "it is permissible to doubt whether the change has been a gain in our national life" (1979: 111).

But if the contribution of the Euro-Asians of India to radical thought diminished by the mid-19th century, the Euro-Asians of Sri Lanka in this period lit the torch of reform, based (as in India) on revolutionary ideas from Europe, combined with concern about local social and political injustices. In these efforts they too, like the Euro-Asians of India, were many decades ahead of other communities of the region, and can be classed among the utopian visionaries of Asia, who were able to "catch the dawn" long before the rise of fully fledged nationalist and reform movements.

Notes

1. In the article "Northern Lights," David Denby discusses the drastic "intellectual break with the past" that had occurred in Scotland, where "the rudiments of modern psychology, anthropology, the earth sciences, and theories of civil society and liberal education" had their origin in the 18th century. One profound influence was that of David Hume, whom he calls "perhaps the most thorough going skeptic in the history of philosophy" (*The New Yorker*, 11 Oct. 2004, p.91).

2. This poem figures today in some Indian school texts (personal communication from a student, Aftab Lall of Delhi).

3. This may have been 'inspired' by similar accusations of blasphemy, adultery and incest made against Byron (see Eisler 1999). Regi Siriwardena's novel on Euro-Asians, *The Lost Lenore*, is based on this theme.

4. Byron also had his admirers among the socialists. In 1845 Friedrich Engels remarked that: "It is the workers who are most familiar with the poetry of Shelley and Byron. ...Byron attracts their sympathy by his sensuous fire and by the virulence of his satire against the existing social order," noting in contrast that the British middle classes "ruthlessly expurgated" Byron and Shelley "to suit the hypocritical moral standards of the bourgeoisie" (quoted in Foot 1988: 383).

6

'TURBULENT' EURO-ASIANS AND EUROPEANS

> Efforts were made by one or two turbulent Europeans, supported and assisted by many of the peculiar class of people called burghers, to kindle dissatisfaction in the minds of the Singhalese natives.
>
> Lord Torrington, quoted in William Digby, 1879, Vol. I, p.24

Euro-Asian Lawyers

When the Dutch left Sri Lanka in 1796, the Burghers who remained behind swiftly learnt English, anglicized themselves and allied with Britain culturally, intellectually and sometimes politically. While sections of the Burghers 'played safe' with government posts and cautious politics, there were Burgher radicals who did not hesitate to 'take on' the colonial government on a variety of issues, and also show their support for slave emancipation, the free press and more representative government. One of the most important but neglected aspects of the 19th century political history of Sri Lanka has been the radicalism in theory and practice, sometimes amounting to early expressions of nascent nationalism, that surfaced among sections of the Burghers and the new community of Eurasians. Digby, writing of such Burgher dissidents, remarked that a generation after British occupation, they felt that:

> they had the rights of free-born citizens, *but once it was understood that the rights and privileges were theirs, none were more tenacious than they to maintain them inviolate.* In doing so they had to encounter much obloquy and scorn. (Digby 1879: 24, emphasis added)

During British rule some educated Burghers worked in government service, mainly as clerks, showing preference for 'safe' and 'genteel' jobs, which according to Digby carried an "aroma of undefined respectability" (ibid: 34). Others entered the legal and medical fields where they succeeded at all levels of these prestigious professions. The legal profession was divided into proctors (solicitors) and advocates, and some of the wealthier, who had travelled to England, became barristers.[1] In Colombo and the main towns in the 19th century, a large number of proctors were Euro-Asian (Burghers and Eurasians). Their knowledge of English and local languages gave them a privileged position in legally representing clients, and their role as intermediaries in a litigous local society was an important one. Moreover, in a colonial situation, practicing the law had added attractions, as it was one of the few independent professions. Lawyers were 'free' citizens, able to express their opinions and act in ways which were not possible for government servants. They had the space to criticize the authorities and bring grievances to the notice of British members of parliament and other radicals in Britain, and even to publicly welcome revolutionary movements in Europe.

In the forefront of campaigns for democracy and peoples' rights in Sri Lanka were several Euro-Asian proctors and advocates. They were bold in their challenges to the policies of the colonial government, denounced expressions of racism among resident Europeans and officials, and even attracted the hostile attention of the authorities, including the Governor, during times of political trouble. James de Alwis (1848) praised the proctors as "a class of men… who stood aloof without joining the Governor's party" and who exposed the "servile hypocrisy" of those who "fawned on the government." The Burgher lawyers, according to Digby, were part of the struggle for citizen rights and were capable of "being entrusted with yet further and fuller liberty" (1879: 23). A "Burgher gentleman" (whom Digby quotes) praised the Burgher lawyers in provincial towns, who kept those places from becoming "sleepy hollows," stressing also that "*every social movement, if it is not initiated, is materially helped by the burgher lawyer*" (ibid: 40, emphasis added). Digby also remarked that: "At the very time when the most supreme contempt was being expressed for the mixed population, some of the Dutch burghers were displaying a degree of public spirit not far behind that... in England by the Corn Law repealers" (ibid: 24). Thus in Sri Lanka a new phenomenon arose of the lawyer as 'public intellectual,' which is detailed in the following chapters.

Political Struggles in Europe

In the 1830s and 1840s, serious political upheavals in Europe resulted in revolutionary and reformist changes – which were keenly noted by both rulers and ruled in the colonies. In France in 1830, the king was replaced by King Louis Philippe who promised to rule as a constitutional monarch. In other parts of Europe, including Belgium and Italy, there were revolts in favour of constitutional government, and Mazzini's Young Italy group, with its call for Italian unity and independence (*Risorgimento),* received worldwide publicity, inspiring nationalists in the colonies for many decades.

In Britain, the struggles for the repeal of the Corn Laws and for constitutional change were led by the bourgeoisie. The issue of Free Trade and the Corn Laws were a source of bitter controversy between the landowners and the industrial interests in the 1830s and 1840s. The Corn Laws, which were duties on imported food items, especially corn, protected local producers from foreign competition. The repeal of these laws meant that food would be cheaper; hence the issue had mass appeal and the support of industrialists who had a vested interest in cheap food, and therefore lower wages for the working class. In 1846 mounting agitation from the anti-Corn Law League led by the radicals, especially Richard Cobden and John Bright (the Quaker businessman), together with the prevalence of industrial unrest and the outbreak of famine in Ireland, led to the repeal of the Corn Laws.

The Reform Bill in Britain in 1832 had allowed for more middle-class political representation, but had only benefited one class, resulting in a clamour for further democratization led by workers and middle-class radicals, and expressed in the militant Chartist movement. The agitation took place around the People's Charter of 1838, with its demands for full male suffrage, voting by ballot, annual parliaments, abolition of property qualifications for members of parliament, and equal electoral districts. These demands were accompanied by an economic struggle for better wages and conditions, an improved Factory Act providing for factory inspectors, and the regulation of child labour. The Chartist attempt at widespread insurrection failed in 1839, but the agitation continued in the form of a mass signature campaign. In 1848, the year of revolution in Europe, the Chartists unsuccessfully tried to stage a mammoth demonstration in London, but instead, presented a mass petition to parliament.

Radicalism among the middle classes in England also prevailed at a time when there was tension between the Conservative (Tory) and Liberal (Whig) parties in Britain. The Conservative party represented the traditional, land-owning interests ; while the Liberal party, dominated by the new industrialists and middle-class professionals, was more concerned with liberalized trade, representative government and social reform. The Liberals had a radical wing, that by the 1840s had become a strong minority current within the party, supporting democratic rights and radical reforms led by Richard Cobden, John Bright and Joseph Hume. The great battles fought in Britain by the rising class of capitalists on issues of political representation and free trade, echoed in the colonies. These issues were debated in India and Sri Lanka. The *Times of Ceylon* claimed that the editor of the *Colombo Observer* advocated free trade because he "had parted with his interest in land"; while the *Colombo Observer*, stating that other Indian papers in English were also for free trade, ridiculed the *Times of Ceylon* and called its editor "a red hot Anti-Free Trader, the only one… among the brethren of the craft on this side of the Cape"(*Colombo Observer*, 4 May 1848).

In February 1848, the *Communist Manifesto* of Marx and Engels referred to the 'spectre of communism' said to be haunting Europe, and that same month it looked as if the worst fears of autocratic governments were being realized. King Louis Philippe of France was deposed in late February 1848, and by March, revolutions had triggered off the dramatic collapse of absolute monarchs, princes and governments in Austria, the

Hungarian Empire, and the German and Italian states. As Hobsbawm (1985: 22) has written:

> There have been plenty of greater revolutions in the history of the modern world... yet there has been none which spread more rapidly and widely, running like a bushfire across frontiers, countries and even oceans... Within a matter of weeks no government was left standing in an area of Europe which is today occupied by all or part of ten states.

The events of 1848 were also regarded as "the first potentially global revolution," which inspired revolts in Latin America, becoming "the paradigm of the kind of 'world revolution' of which rebels were henceforth to dream" (Hobsbawm 1985: 22). There were several examples of shared consciousness between revolutionary forces in Europe and dissenters in the colonies. In Java, as Stoler comments, "colonial authorities imagined a shrinking-world with global resonance, in which riots in Paris could unseat Dutch rule in Java" (2004: 5). The unprecedented occasion was in May 1848, when 500 to 600 people, referred to as "European, Creoles and colored," demonstrated in Batavia (Jakarta) on several issues, focusing on government policies of reserving places in the colonial civil service only for those who qualified in the Netherlands. This was discriminatory against Indo-Europeans (Euro-Asians) and those Europeans unable to send their sons abroad for education. The question that disturbed the authorities was whether the event was a "home-grown colonial liberalism" or "revolutionary fervour that traveled with the mailboat from Marseille" (Stoler: 2004).

Revolutions in 1848 in Europe also reverberated in Sri Lanka, where there was an economic depression and agitation against the government's taxes and other revenue-increasing policies. Part of the opposition came from the urban Euro-Asian intelligentsia, whose education and way of life were oriented to western models, and who were conversant with liberal ideas from Europe and in touch with British radicals. These Euro-Asians were consequently in opposition to arbitrary government and in the forefront of agitation against the conservative British bureaucracy in Sri Lanka.

Radicalism in Sri Lanka in the 1840s

There were important contradictions among British residents in Sri Lanka over the administration's policies. Radically minded British professionals in the colony, who spoke out for representative government, democracy and a free press, joined forces with the dissident Euro-Asian lawyers. Also critical of the government were British merchants, coffee planters and urban professionals who had their own grievances. Up to 1833, trading interests had constantly protested against the East India Company's mercantilist-type restrictions on the freedom of trade. The merchants and planters also continuously clashed with the colonial bureaucrats in the Legislative Council, where mercantile representation was limited to three members with restricted powers, appointed by the Governor. The dominance of bureaucrats in the Legislative and Executive Councils irked the merchants and planters, and constant protests were made that the important merchant class, which produced the wealth, had little control over the finances of the country.

During the 1840s the free trade issue was keenly debated in the English newspapers of Sri Lanka; the *Colombo Observer* supporting the free traders and the *Times of Ceylon* advocating protectionism. These newspapers, which represented two interest groups – merchant capital and the colonial bureaucracy – made sharp attacks on each other. The issue of government intervention in economic affairs in the form of customs duties, taxation and restrictions on trade was linked with the question of representative government. This resulted in an alliance between the merchants who championed free trade and the urban professionals with radical views who seized on every opportunity to expose the undemocratic and arbitrary acts of the colonial government.

Events in Europe strongly influenced the radicals in the colony. In all the controversies and agitation that took place in Sri Lanka in the 1840s, local radicals were strengthened in their criticisms of government policies by their links, not only with British radical members of parliament, notably John Bright and Joseph Hume,[2] but also with British dissidents resident in Sri Lanka, such as John Selby, T.Y. McChristie, Lawrence Oliphant, and especially Dr Christopher Elliot, editor of the

Colombo Observer. Commenting on those Burghers who had links to British radicals, the Governor, Lord Torrington, complained privately to Lord Grey in May 1848 that there was "in this island no *middle class* independent in mind or [spirit]."

> The Burgher class which exists here, is perhaps ... not to be found in any other British Colony – they are the half-caste or white-brown descendants... of the old Dutch and Portuguese rulers. They have neither European or Ceylonese feelings, no principle of nationality whatever; ...and the peculiarity of their position engenders an uneasiness of feeling which is not traceable in their minds to any distinct appreciable cause – but the establishment of newspapers. The *(Colombo) Observer,* gives food for their querulousness.
>
> (Torrington, quoted in de Silva 1965: 81-82)

Such harsh comments by Torrington of Euro-Asian radicals reflected the extent of their involvement in controversial political causes. The Governor, while complaining bitterly of "low blackguard" lawyers in general (ibid: 173), alleged that:

> Their object was clear, the game they played was representative government... and thus for the future the Colony would have been ruled by Dr Elliot and a few half-caste proctors. (ibid: 97)

The late 1840s was a period of depression in the coffee economy and measures to raise revenue included the imposition of taxes, such as a gun tax of 2 shillings 6 pence, a dog tax of 1 shilling and a tax of £ 1 on carts, carriages, boats and shops, as well as an unpopular Road Ordinance which could enforce compulsory labour for 6 days a year in lieu of a tax of 3 shillings for males between 18 and 55 years. All this led to political disatisfaction and the growth of unrest resulting in an armed rebellion in July 1848. This was the year of turbulence and revolution in Europe, which the dissenters in the island enthusiastically publicized. The protests in the 1840s in the maritime areas and in the Kandyan provinces were different in intent, in leadership and in methods of struggle (see Jayawardena forthcoming). In the western regions and Colombo, the protests were for the most part confined to constitutional agitation and were led by radical professionals and by interests whose aim was a certain measure of representative government. In the Kandyan regions, the struggles were militant, taking the form of armed revolt, led by peoples' leaders Puran Appu and Gongalegoda Banda. While the main protagonists were the peasantry, the leadership was composed of an alliance of monks, chiefs, and a pretender to the throne of the last King of Kandy, all of whom aimed to expel the British from Sri Lanka. The revolt, however, was crushed and the main leaders hanged.

Dr Christopher Elliot and Local Dissidents

The radical challenges to the colonial government before and after the events of 1848 had been led by several Europeans, Burghers and Eurasians who formed the more enlightened intelligentsia of the colony. The revolutions in Europe, the English Chartist movement and the Irish revolt had aroused to action 'turbulent Europeans' of the colony and especially the Irish doctor Christopher Elliot (1809-59). Born in County Kilkenny, he came to the island in 1834 as assistant colonial surgeon soon after the great reform agitation in Britain. Leaving government service, Dr Elliot started a private practice in Colombo and became the proprietor and editor of the *Colombo Observer.* As a journalist and fighter against arbitrary government, Elliot became the most influential radical leader of Colombo in the 1840s, his popularity and stature being augmented by his practice among the poor of the city. "My long advocacy of what are called liberal opinions... often places me in strenuous opposition to Government measures," he wrote in 1848.[3]

Elliot was the main spokesman for dissident anti-government opinion in the 1840s, articulating liberal and radical viewpoints in his newspaper. He criticized the rulers as men who, knowing nothing of "the native character or circumstances," had tried to impose direct money taxation "upon an unrepresented people," thereby creating "universal discontent." Referring to the people's hatred of direct taxation, he wrote, "But my Lord Torrington will never... carry out these taxes, though he were to make a military post of every village in the country."[4] Elliot's distaste was for the typical conservative colonial bureaucrats, who were often both 'feudal' in birth and ideology. He referred to the "narrow minded colonial Tory" mentality of certain officials and wrote, "Who is to speak for the natives?... I see no hope for the country but from a representative assembly," adding that "the merchants, planters, proctors and burghers, whom he (the Governor) has so grossly slandered, would gladly subscribe for a rope to hang Lord Torrington."[5]

The *Colombo Observer* ridiculed and even parodied the Governor and the Colonial Secretary. A satirical note, purporting to be from the latter (Emerson Tennant) to Torrington, stated that Torrington had the 'admirable' idea of closing the leading boys' school (the Colombo Academy):

> more youngsters will come out with crazy notions about rights and freedom of the press... The moment they begin to know something, they render themselves dangerous enemies of the government.[6]

To government officials (and especially to Governor Torrington), Elliot and other radical Britishers were a source of acute annoyance and embarrassment, since they were breaking the unwritten law that British nationals in the colonies should not 'let the side down' by criticizing colonial policy. Their contacts and constant communication with radicals in Britain made them even more obnoxious. Their anger can be gauged in the Governor's references to Elliot as "a creature, as low and base as anything that lived on earth" (de Silva 1965: 190), and to another British radical, John Selby, who practised law in Colombo, as a "low blackguard," and "infamous character" (ibid: 121 & 210). In contrast was the praise Elliot received from another liberal Britisher, William Digby, who (in later years) claimed that Elliot's "efforts for the people of Ceylon... have never been surpassed," comparing him to Mazzini, the hero of Italian liberation (1879: 150).

What also disturbed the authorities was that Dr Elliot and the *Colombo Observer* were the means through which news of the revolutionary movements in Europe were transmitted to the Sri Lankan people. According to Torrington, Dr Elliot with the assistance of a "few ruined men, bankrupts in fortune and questionable in character" had publicized the events of 1848 in France and introduced ideas of political rights and representative government to the "ignorant minds" of the local inhabitants (de Silva 1965: 97). "The unsettled state of the public mind throughout Europe has extended its influence in some degree to a few excitable spirits in this island," wrote the Governor, accusing the Colombo agitators very specifically of conveying the news from France to the Kandyan areas. He spoke of "discontented Europeans who nourished the discontent of the Kandyans, related for their amusement some of the stories of the French Revolution and expounded to them the pernicious language of the *Observer*."[7]

Revolution and unrest in Europe in 1848 coincided with reverses for the British in India, and the *Colombo Observer* had continuous news reports and comments on these upheavals. It publicized the temporarily successful Sikh revolts of 1848, which occurred before the Punjab, the last independent state of India, was finally annexed in 1849 by the British. The *Colombo Observer* gave detailed dispatches of the fighting and quoted the *Madras Spectator* reporting that the Punjab was "thoroughly disaffected" (*Colombo Observer,* 8 June 1848). The news from Europe was also extensively covered; the *Colombo Observer* published accounts of the "Abdication of the King of Bavaria, Revolt in Lombardy, Riots in South Germany" (*Colombo Observer*, 1 May 1848). Comments from other sympathetic foreign papers were also quoted, including the *Madras Spectator,* which wrote:

> Europe exhibits a wondrous spectacle of its governments called to account by its peoples. East and West, North and South, with the oldest of existing governments and the newest, there is the same exhibition of authority rendering account to its subjects… more than one German potentate is peremptorily called forth, like the manager of a theatre, to bow frightened apologies and promises before an enraged audience. (quoted in *Colombo Observer*, 29 May 1848)

The *Colombo Observer* also quoted the *Madras Atheneum*'s comment:

> Lord Torrington... is likely to end his career, by alienating in heart, one of the finest colonies of the Crown... *There is a mode of arousing the hostility of people, which is equally efficacious when adopted in Paris and in the Kandian jungles.* It is to interfere with their common and ordinary privileges, to harass them with petty exactions. (*Colombo Observer*, 3 Aug. 1848, emphasis added)

Politically charged poetry was published in the *Colombo Observer,* (8 June 1848) in which a 'subversive' anonymous poem called *The Spirit of the Times* exclaimed, "Vive la France, all Europe wakes, oppression fires their blood"; it also had stirring references to "Prince and Peer passing away," the "mighty banner of the free press" and the "advancing sway of liberty":

The Spirit of the Times
Vive la France, the Marseillaise
Is ringing in the air
Mid sabres glance and musquets
Dark death is revelling there
The throne the Charter-King had raised
Has perished in its might
Lo! Prince and Peer have passed away
As stars at morning's light
Vive la France!

Vive la France, the tambour stirs
The hearts of high and low
Dark forms are pouring rank on rank
As waves that ebb and flow
The sovereign people, once again
Have risen in their might
And freedom's rays, with meteor
Have struggled into light
Vive la France!

Vive la France, all Europe wakes
Oppression fires their blood

The memory of a thousand years
Streams o'er them, as a flood
The Austrian Eagle droops its wings
The Prussians pride has flown
And Metternich – the soul of Kings
Falls, friendless and alone
Vive la France!

Vive la France, the enfranchised press
Its mighty banner rears
Hark! stronger than the trumpets blast
It rules man's hopes and fears
The Age has past – then Tyrants strove
Nature's fair form to blight
No power may stay the advancing sway
Of liberty and light.
Vive la France!

One of the most immediate consequences in Sri Lanka of the 1848 events in Europe was the famous letter in the *Colombo Observer* (attributed to Elliot) in which the right of representative government was emphasized and the allegation was made that "the government of Ceylon is as much despotic as that of Russia." In an allusion to the 1848 events in Europe, the letter said: "Millions in Europe have lately acquired these rights, and *enlightened Ceylonese who have heard of the onward movement were in hopes of sharing in the boon*" (*Colombo Observer,* 3 July 1848, emphasis added). It was predicted that the masses would not submit without the use of "those extreme measures adopted to resist oppression of the European continent," and a call for action was made:

> Let petitions be written and sent to every part of the island for signature. Let there be a universal denunciation of oppression and a universal cry for just, equitable laws... let a Representative Assembly be asked for... let it be known in high quarters that the spirit of oppression driven from its former haunts will not be allowed to find a resting place in Ceylon. (ibid)

Dr Elliot was influenced by events in Britain – most notably the Irish question, the Chartist movement and the 'Young Ireland' revolt in

1848. Not only were the best-known Chartist leaders of Irish origin (Fergus O'Connor and Bronterre O'Brien), but Elliot's views on the need for representative government and democracy were also similar to the Chartist demands, and his methods of agitation were also comparable. This caused much anxiety in official circles, which were also disturbed by his links with India. The Governor alleged that one of Elliot's articles was "first printed in a Bombay paper with a gross attack" on the former Chief Justice of the island (de Silva 1965: 213). Elliot's role as a newspaper editor was vital in the agitation he conducted. The *Colombo Observer*, which was used to express radical opinion on a wide range of questions, was the means of conveying dissenting opinion to areas outside Colombo.

In August 1849, Torrington wrote to the Colonial Secretary, alleging that Dr Elliot was in contact with G.A. Hagh, a Burgher resident of Ratnapura, who was collecting signatures against the new taxes on Elliot's behalf: "People who came to the Cutchery to register their guns were requested to sign this"; adding that the government "put a stop to it."[8] The Governor accused Elliot not only of Chartist-type agitation, but also (rather remarkably) of "passive resistance" to the taxes and contact with British radical members of Parliament, notably Joseph Hume:

> (Elliot) is getting up an agitation all over the country and sheets of paper *blank* or merely (with) such words as may suit the *locality* (are) sent everywhere by agents to obtain signatures. In the true Chartist fashion, pens with ink, paper and a table are stuck about in various parts of Colombo, Galle, Kandy and the lowest class of people induced to sign they know not what for. I am informed no respectable person has signed it, and I understand the document is to go to Joe Hume... Dr Elliot's real object was to *encourage passive resistance to the road ordinance*. (de Silva 1965: 156-57, emphasis added)

Torrington also gave dire warnings of political dangers if the local population became 'unsettled'. "No one can foresee the danger of tampering with an Eastern people; once unsettle their minds, you cannot tell where it will stop"(ibid: 156). The demands in the petition reflected the popular mood, namely the repeal of the Road Ordinance, pardon for the 1848 rebels in prison, and the removal of Governor Torrington and the Colonial Secretary, James Emerson Tennent.

The events of 1848 and the criticisms of the colonial authorities led to the appointment of a Select Committee on Ceylon, which resulted in the recall of both the Governor and Colonial Secretary from the island. Those radical Burghers who had participated in the many protests of the late 1840, continued to express their dissident views, and started a reformist journal, *Young Ceylon,* in 1850. They also challenged colonial policies in the Legislative Council, whose members included the leading Euro-Asian figure of the time – Richard Morgan.

Richard Morgan's Early Radicalism

Another Euro-Asian who publicly took a prominent role in oppositional politics in Sri Lanka was Richard Morgan (1821-76), whose grandfather was Welsh and grandmother Indian. His Anglo-Indian father Richard Morgan Sr came to Sri Lanka from India and married Behrana Lucretia, the daughter of a Burgher doctor, Jan Lourens. Their son Richard Morgan, in spite of his Anglo-Indian paternity, was accepted as Burgher. Politically the family environment was a liberal one; Morgan's father had been part of the campaign, sponsored in 1816 by British official Alexander Johnston, to abolish slavery in Sri Lanka (Digby 1879: 67). Johnston (who later became Chief Justice of the island) was described by William Digby as "an Englishman very far in advance of his age" who also "did much for the Burghers" (ibid: 19).

Many Burgher radicals, educated on British public school lines and conversant with ideas from Europe, aspired to a legal career which afforded some independence and freedom from subservience to the authorities. Richard Morgan was no exception. He obtained a classical education at the Colombo Academy and became a lawyer. The Morgan family was not rich, and Digby refers to "the plain fare of the daily life" of Morgan's boyhood in the Pettah (ibid: 70). The family raised funds for him to study law in England, but he returned soon after his arrival in London because of mounting financial problems. On his voyage to

England in 1839, however, Richard Morgan wrote "a few reflections on the legal profession," which also reveal his early social consciousness. A good lawyer, he stated, should be a person in whom "the oppressed find... a ready friend," and who, on his death, will be praised by "the poor whom he befriended, the oppressed whom he succoured, and the weak whom he defended" (Digby 1879: 350-51). Morgan's career in Colombo began in December 1840. He was (in his own words) "a proctor with a few books, wondering if he would ever get on, if he would live to have a fair practice and acquire property, if he would achieve success in a field where competition is keen" (ibid: 312).

The young Morgan was active in reformist movements. He spoke openly against the local caste system and supported the abolition of caste considerations in jury selection. He led a delegation to the Governor to protest on the 'Verandah Question' in 1846, which included other well-known Burgher professionals – Dr J.B. Misso, George Schneider and Philip Vanderstraaten. The issue was the attempt by the authorities to demolish the verandahs (of houses) encroaching on roads in the Pettah, the residential quarter of the Euro-Asians. Morgan also took this issue up with Joseph Hume, his radical contact in the British House of Commons (Digby 1879: 155).

Morgan belonged to the 'Friends of Ceylon' – an organization that promoted representative government. Dr Elliot was the prime mover in the formation in 1843 of this society for the "Native or European-born," whose main objectives were agitation for a more representative legislature and the achievement of self-government on the Australian and Canadian model. The focus was on public discussion, with petitions and appeals to the House of Commons and to sympathetic organizations in Britain. On issues such as 'taxation without representation,' government expenditure and the control of finance, the merchant capitalists could agree with the radicals, and there were several instances of joint action. A public meeting at the Chamber of Commerce in 1846, attended by "almost every British and native merchant in Colombo, together with other residents and planters," condemned the government's financial policy and the lack of expenditure on public works. At another meeting in 1846, Morgan denounced the Legislative Council and advocated a more representative assembly (Digby 1879: 137-38). Such activity, and Morgan's links with Dr Elliot, incurred the wrath of the Governor, to whom Elliot was the arch agitator and agent provocateur of unrest in 1848. As Digby wrote:

> Those who had agitated about verandahs and were active in other matters were held to be responsible for the (1848) disturbances. Particularly Dr Elliot and Mr A. Ferguson, as editors of the *Observer,* were considered to be enemies to good and peaceable government. (1879: 150)

When a call was made by Europeans in Kandy to boycott the *Colombo Observer,* "the Friends of Ceylon" held a meeting in Colombo, chaired by Richard Morgan, to protest this attempt and to show confidence in "that excellent Journal" for its "outspoken independence" (ibid: 151). After the 1848 rebellion, when the House of Commons appointed a Select Committee to inquire into the excesses and mistakes of government policies, Morgan campaigned for the recall of the highest officials in the island, noting that:

> Sir Emerson Tennent's cupidity in the verandah question and Lord Torrington's tyranny in keeping martial law in force... left me no alternative but to take a very prominent part in politics... I scarcely ate drank, or slept, until we had succeeded in getting both recalled. (ibid: 160-61)

Lord Torrington in turn expressed bitter feelings towards Richard Morgan, and denounced him sharply as "a man never seen in a respectable gentleman's house" (de Silva 1965: 180). At this time Morgan, along with Elliot and others, corresponded with Joseph Hume, "who wrote direct to Morgan and received much of his inspiration from the young burgher" (Digby 1879: 155). Morgan in later life used to speak of his link to Hume "as the brightest spot in his memory, and the event upon which he was disposed to dwell with greatest pleasure" (ibid: 155). Another friend, Lawrence Oliphant who had lived in Sri Lanka in the 1840s and was an opponent of the colonial government during the 1848 events, also kept in touch with Morgan, and wrote: "I am as great a radical as ever, and I hope you stick to your colours" (ibid: 185). But "sticking to colours" proved difficult. Morgan in 1850, aged 29, had quoted a verse which ended:

> But for the glorious privilege
> Of being independent. (ibid: 159)

But "being independent" was not so easy. Although in 1851 Morgan had been appointed to the Burgher seat in the Legislative Council, in order to counteract Morgan's radicalism, the colonial government co-opted him from the mid-1850s onwards by giving him tempting judicial posts. He was made district judge of Colombo in 1854, necessitating his resigning from the legislature. For Morgan, who had experienced financial problems since childhood, these were offers that could not be easily refused. Morgan, however, declined the post of acting Queen's Advocate (legal advisor to the government). This offer, according to Digby, "was doubtless meant as a bribe to stop the mouth of an able and determined opponent" (1879: 64). Subsequently, Morgan was promoted to the Supreme Court and was later appointed the Queen's Advocate, after which he came into conflict with his old radical friends – especially Charles Lorenz. Morgan, who had moved from the role of rebel in 1848 to a high judicial position, was rewarded with a knighthood in 1874.

Nostalgia for his heroic liberal phase remained with Morgan, and in 1865 during the British elections, he wished for a Liberal Party victory over the Tories, hoping that Gladstone, the Liberal leader, would be "at the head of affairs." He wrote to his son in London: "Mind you spend 7s 6d in illuminations when this takes place" (ibid: 298). Morgan also inspired many young men belonging to the Euro-Asian intelligentsia of the 1850s, most notably Charles Lorenz. Although Morgan in later life joined forces with the 'establishment' and clashed with local radicals, he was remembered as "a broad-minded man of most liberal views" (Weinman 1948: 12).

This dissident tradition, as expressed by the activities and agitation of Richard Morgan in his youth, was carried forward by his

Euro-Asian friends of the *Young Ceylon* group and the *Examiner* newspaper taking forward the popular demands of the earlier period.

Notes

1. For those who had already qualified as advocates in the colonies, the process involved 'keeping terms' by dining at one of the Inns of Court.
2. John Bright (1811-89) was a 19th century British radical of a Quaker family of mill owners. He was an activist of the Anti-Corn Law League. As a member of parliament he supported the move for parliamentary reform and the extension of the franchise, and was part of Gladstone's liberal governments in the 1860s and 1870s.

Joseph Hume (1777-1855), from Scotland, studied medicine in Edinburgh. In 1797 he lived in India and made a fortune there. Returning to Britain he entered politics, and became a member of parliament, noted for his radicalism. He was influenced by Bentham and James Mill, opposed archaic laws that were anti-working-class, also speaking out against flogging in the army and imprisonment for debt.
3. Elliot to Grey, 15 Aug. 1848, in *Second Report of the Select Committee on Ceylon*, p.430.
4. Ibid. The *Colombo Observer* of 4 Aug. 1848, refers to Torrington as "a young and inexperienced Nobleman."
5. Elliot to McChristie, 11 April 1849, *Second Report*, op.cit. p.339.
6. *Colombo Observer*, 10 Nov. 1848, "Contents of a Pocket Book found in Hospital Street."
7. Sri Lanka National Archives 5/35, Torrington to Grey, No. 141 of 9 Aug. 1848.
8. *Second Report*, op.cit., Torrington to Grey, Aug. 1849.

7

'RIOTOUS INDEPENDENCE' OF THE LORENZIANS

> Widened ideas have dropped among them (Burghers) as good seed in productive soil, bringing forth no insignificant crop of self-reliant, earnest men, who have in a struggle for citizens rights exhibited qualities which call for their being entrusted with yet further and fuller liberty.
>
> William Digby, *Forty Years of Official and Unofficial Life in a Crown Colony*, 1879, Vol. I, p.23

> Charles [Lorenz] was the most commanding personality in the Island. As a lawyer... scholar... literateur... journalist, he was unequalled. He had a magnetic personality, and was loved and revered equally by all communities...
>
> J.R. Weinman, *Our Legislature,* 1948, p.12

The Magic Aura and *Young Ceylon*

The Euro-Asians (Burghers and Eurasians) were the first locals in Sri Lanka to emerge as a distinct part of the bourgeoisie with a base in the professions rather than in capital accumulation in the mercantile and plantation sectors or in the lucrative liquor trade. Many of them had benefited from a secondary education in English, especially after the opening by the government in 1835 of the Colombo Academy (later Royal College), which was dominated by Burghers and Eurasians in its early years. Michael Roberts calculated that between 1836 and 1849, 60% of the Academy students were Burgher and Eurasian, and notes that "the content of this education – Latin, Greek, the works of the

Enlightenment, the English literary masters and British history – *acquired a magical aura of its own*" (1989: 56, emphasis added). This knowledge created what Roberts calls "the ideal of a Cultured Gentleman," the "well-read Man," the man of "Rounded Respectability" who was also a "Moral Man." But the "Cultured Gentleman" had also to have "character," an ability to stand up for himself "*or to express opinions on political matters*" (ibid: 65-67, emphasis added).

The Colombo Academy played a crucial role in forming the minds of the brightest of local students. Through its British principals and teachers, the school inevitably promoted an anglophile culture which included political loyalty to Britain, Anglican Christianity in religion, and gave students a British-type classical education similar to that imparted in elitist schools in Britain (Gooneratne 1968: 12-13). The intention was to produce educated Christianized locals to prop up the colonial economy and polity, and project an ideal of bourgeois respectability – a much-valued virtue in 19th century Britain. But paradoxically such an education had some unforeseen consequences. The Colombo Academy (and other such schools), which fostered loyalty to the government, the Church and the monarch, could hardly prevent its students from moving beyond such narrow ideals and questioning these 'hallowed' institutions. Some students of the Academy keenly followed the dissenting political movements of the West, showing enthusiasm about the slogans of liberty, equality and more representative government. They were inspired by the radical thinkers of the Enlightenment and the French revolutions – 1789, 1830 and 1848 – as well as British radical popular movements, currents of Darwinism, freethought and secularism. Thus the school was able to produce students with the ability to question orthodoxy, to disagree with their peers, and to have the courage to express their views even under conditions of colonial rule. Among such students of the Colombo Academy were James de Alwis, Muttu Coomaraswamy, Richard Morgan, and Charles Lorenz – all of whom were to make their mark in the Legislative Council.

Charles Lorenz in Politics

Nine years younger than Richard Morgan, who was his close associate, Charles Ambrose Lorenz (1829-71) was the son of Anna Smith (Euro-Asian) and Johan Lorenz (of Prussian origin) who had been a Magistrate in Matara. After spending his childhood in Matara, Charles Lorenz studied at the leading boys' school, the Colombo Academy. Like Morgan, Lorenz benefited from a rigorous education at this prestigious school. The curriculum in the lower school included English "with special attention to Shakespeare," Latin and Greek, Mathematics, European History, Geography, and Scripture. In the upper school, the subjects added were Theology, Natural Philosophy, Astronomy, Logic, and English law (Blazé 1948: 44-45). Lorenz entered the Academy in 1842, and in the words of Richard Morgan, "rapidly rose to the highest place, winning prize after prize" (ibid: 47). The principal of the Academy at the time, Rev. Barcroft Boake, and the teachers including two Cambridge graduates, provided the 'liberal education' for which the school became famous.

Lorenz, according to his biographer B.R. Blazé, had a "taste for current rather than classical literature." Although acquainted with Shakespeare, Milton, Bacon and Pope, "he would turn for light reading to *Fraser's Magazine* and *Blackwoods* ...the most popular... and the most distinguished of all the periodicals." Lorenz was also influenced by Dickens, Carlyle, Tennyson, Longfellow, Thackeray, Macaulay, and Professor John Wilson who:

> was to *Blackwood's Magazine* what Lorenz was to *Young Ceylon* in the early fifties and to the *Examiner* in the sixties. Each wielded a pervading influence... a fresh, exuberant style... *a kind of riotous independence, and an all-conquering enthusiasm.* (Blazé: 35, emphasis added)

Lorenz was the protégé of Dr Christopher Elliot, who "introduced him to other prominent men." Blazé says that Elliot was a man after Lorenz's own heart and Lorenz eagerly imbibed his "liberal-minded views... and broad-based philosophy and progressive ideas" (Blazé 1948: 56). On Elliot, Lorenz wrote:

> The many good works with which Dr Elliot was connected… have secured for him a place in the hearts of the multitude; and it will be many years before his virtues and kindnesses will be forgotten. (quoted in Blazé 1948: 133)

At the age of nineteen, Lorenz began his radical career by joining forces in 1848 with Dr Elliot in public protests against oppressive taxes, including participation in a mass meeting at Borella and collecting signatures against the taxes (ibid: 60). The events of 1848 in the Kandyan areas and Colombo were Lorenz's initial experience of dissent and agitation; he was also directly involved in radical journalism through the *Colombo Observer* and Dr Elliot. The inspiration of Elliott was crucial to Lorenz's radicalism. On Elliot's death in 1859, Lorenz wrote a poem about his friend "who hath done so much" in the cause of the people's welfare and their rights. Two verses from this poem are quoted below:

> And though among the living,
> There may be others such,
> As true, as noble-hearted,
> As the good man departed;
> Yet who hath done so much?
>
> In striving for our welfare,
> In battling for the right;
> In works of love, in acts of faith,
> In turning hearts from Sin and Death
> To realms of Life and Light?
> (Blazé 1948: 133)

There is also evidence that Lorenz was aware of the Chartist movement in Britain, for he referred in 1850 to Carlyle's "small pamphlet on Chartism" (*Young Ceylon*, Vol. 1, No. 1: 8). The other influence on Lorenz was Richard Morgan, who kept in touch with him at all times. In 1855 Lorenz, who was on a visit to Europe, wrote frequent letters to Morgan, full of political news and humorous comments:

> The King of Holland a nephew of the old villain (Czar) Nicholas... has committed a dreadful murder... I have made a note of it for future use against precocious Dutchmen... What a precious set they have... with the Czar, (and) his murderous majesty of the Netherlands. (quoted in Digby 1879: 181)

When Morgan visited England in 1858, Lorenz kept him informed and commented frankly on local politics, "forgetting for a moment that you are now a Government man" . Lorenz complained that what annoyed him most was "the self-conceited style (of) both Governor and Queen's Advocate" (ibid: 243-44).

Much of Lorenz's influence with people of all classes was based on his personal charisma. With his group of young friends – mainly products of the Colombo Academy – he started the literary journal *Young Ceylon* in 1850, which reflected the mood of the educated, sophisticated Burgher intellectuals of the time. Roberts comments that the main promoters of *Young Ceylon* – Charles Lorenz, Frederick Nell, Louis Nell, and Charles Ferdinands – were between 19 and 22 years, but notes that the title had "deeper implications," and was no doubt inspired by:

> Mazzini's Young Italy movement and the spirit of Romantic nationalism which had captured the interests of the intelligentsia... the implications were radical insofar as the Italian *Risorgimento* was enthused by the French revolution and republicanism. (Roberts et al. 1989: 59)

It is also possible that the Burgher radicals and those Burghers who had studied medicine in Kolkata were aware of the Euro-Asian poet, writer and agitator Henry Derozio, who had inspired a group of Kolkata reformers in the Young Bengal movement of the 1830s.[1] There is evidence that the other leading Euro-Asian reformer from Kolkata, John Ricketts was aware of events in Sri Lanka. In a petition he had compared the better status of Burghers to their Indian counterparts, and was in touch with the liberal Sir Alexander Johnston, the former Chief Justice of the island. Writing in 1879 on Richard Morgan, Digby referred to Ricketts' efforts "on behalf of Indian Eurasians" (1879: 20).

The *Young Ceylon* publication – which lasted two years – expressed its founders' interests in literary subjects, social and political reformism, and concern for the modernization of society. According to one of its young supporters, Leopold Ludovici, the *Young Ceylon* group of around twelve "was truly a typical array of talent… men of weight, giants in intellect" (Blazé 1948: 70). They tried to bring East and West together in ideological terms – a reflection of their own dual exposure to western education and their feelings, as Sri Lankans, for the rights of the local peoples. The Burgher liberals with their modernism were well placed to introduce radical and often avant-garde currents of opinion to the local intelligentsia, and at the same time to both criticize and sympathetically comment on facets of Sri Lankan society. As Frederick Nell wrote about *Young Ceylon*, its aim was to convey aspects of local society to European residents, and to "our countrymen," to present ideas "based on the premise that they had not only much to learn but also much to *un*learn" (Roberts, et al. 1989: 59).

The appearance of *Young Ceylon* was a watershed in the island's political history. The first issue in 1850 had an editorial by Frederick Nell which referred to "the Spirit of Enquiry which is our distinguishing feature of the present age" (*Young Ceylon* ,Vol. 1, No.1). "It was saturated with and permeated by a Ceylonese patriotism," notes Roberts (ibid: 156), who described the views of the *Young Ceylon* circle as consisting of a "patriotic Ceylonese consciousness which posed an opposition to colonial authoritarianism and to British racial prejudice" (ibid: 67). As Frederick Nell wrote with enthusiasm: "Our contributors are all Ceylonese, born in Ceylon, educated in Ceylon, and having at their hearts her welfare and her improvement" (ibid: 156). The contributors were not all Euro-Asians but included several Sinhalese such as Dandiris Gooneratne.

But the group always upheld the need for contact with Europe and especially with the currents of liberal and radical political thought. They urged the public to make a distinction between the ignorant and arrogant Britishers they encountered in the colony and the enlightened, radical British critics of their own society. Charles Ferdinands, for example, refers in the first issue of *Young Ceylon* to Thomas Paine and his book *Rights of Man* (*Young Ceylon*, Vol. 1, No. 1, 1850: 18). A *Young Ceylon* editorial on "A Day-Dream of the Future" claimed that Britain as the "Apostle of Freedom" promoted liberal ideas, freedom of speech and encouraged "independence and outspokenness," adding that "*Young Ceylon* had dreamed a prophetic dream" that "the meanest of (British) subjects, whatever his colour, caste or position, will be equal with her own (British) sons" (No. 1, Vol. 7: 143). Written in 1850, this was certainly a day-dream and wishful thinking, characteristic of the utopian optimism of the Burgher intelligentsia – and written many decades before such views gained currency among the educated of other ethnic groups. In fact, another editorial in *Young Ceylon* had contrasted the "European legacy of degrading vice" that coexisted with "high models of virtue and perseverence," and referring to Euro-Asians, noted that the mixture of races had "given birth to a race of men who are indefatigable in their efforts to enlighten" (Vol. 1, No. 6: 120).

The admiration of the *Young Ceylon* ideologues for things European, as Roberts writes, was not confined to technological progress; it also encompassed "elegant manners, refined ideas and gifted mental powers that could be found among Englishmen." However, Nell warned his readers not to expect this of every Englishman and noted that "England also had its quota of boors." Frederick Nell made this distinction forcefully (as did many other Euro-Asians) and, denouncing "that class of English whose manners and customs are not the most refined," he said:

> The few who have opportunities of mixing with some of the better classes of English society in Ceylon can alone have an idea of that superior state of civilization known in England, which has become the cradle of so many great minds. (Roberts et al. 1989: 60)

Roberts summarizes the ideology of *Young Ceylon* as:

> An expression of intellectual elitism and a celebration of excellence as framed within the discourse ...of the Christianized West, the legacy of the Enlightenment and the opposition to commercial rationality expressed within the Romantic movements of the eighteenth and nineteenth centuries. (ibid: 60)

In this context, the 'Grand Tour' of Europe also appealed to those professionals among Euro-Asians who could afford such a luxury and were keen to imbibe the European experience. Many made efforts to finance such tours; Lorenz aged 24, not yet established as a successful lawyer, with his wife Eleanor visited Europe from 1853 to 1855 The voyage enabled Lorenz, as a lawyer, to be called to the Bar at Lincoln's Inn, London. As Blazé notes: "To this end he had carefully saved, and ...supplemented from his wife's money, he was able ...to live there on £200 a year" (1948: 156). Many other Burghers travelled to Britain in the mid-19th century, among them Lorenz's relatives, Frederick Nell and Alfred Drieberg (Roberts et al. 1989: 267).

Frederick Nell and "discordant notes"

G. Frederick Nell (1828-67), who edited *Young Ceylon* (1850-52), was the son of George Michael Nell, an auctioneer, and Maria Elizabeth Conderlag; he was the grandson of Frederick August Nell, who left South Africa and joined de Meuron's regiment to Sri Lanka and in 1793 married a Sinhalese, Catherina Petronella de Fonseca (Bláze 1948: 90). Frederick Nell, who joined the judicial service, was thought of as one of the foremost intellectuals of the country. Educated at the Colombo Academy, Nell was called to the bar in Britain and also visited Holland (Roberts et al. 1989: 267). Inspired by the English romantic poets, he "went about with a book of Byron in his pocket" (ibid: 71). Nell's Byronic idealism was reflected in the political mood of the times – on liberty and resistance to oppression – popular among the young intellectuals of his own circle as well as the Derozians of the Young Bengal movement (see Chapter 5). Inspired by the ideal 'moral man' who resisted oppression and tyranny, he was unequivocal on issues of liberty. "Give me the patriot man, the freed, whose neck has known no tyrant's tread...", he wrote in *Young Ceylon* (quoted in Roberts et al. 1989: 76). Nell was also an early supporter of women's education (see Chapter 10).

Nell and his colleagues of *Young Ceylon* were influenced by the works of Thomas Carlyle, de Quincy, Wordsworth, Tennyson and Goethe (Roberts et al. 1989: 72). Roberts notes that, while "The *Young Ceylon* circle... drank deeply... at the well of Western civilization and imbibed its rational mode of discourse," it was also influenced by the Romantic counterculture in Europe with its "discordant notes" (ibid: 72). Nell, however, did not regard contemporary society as a "den of degeneration" but was also attuned to "liberal ideas of progress" (ibid: 77). He believed that Burghers, who had a "natural advantage" with their knowledge of English which they used both at home and in school, had an obligation, "a raison d'être ...to act as patrons and helpers of the Sinhalese" (ibid: 56). Frederick Nell also wrote a "seminal essay" on "The Social Improvement of the Ceylonese," in *Young Ceylon,* arguing that the Burghers should share the benefits they had with the Sinhalese (ibid: 179). Nell was also bold in his critique of local customs and social structures such as the caste system. He even found fault with the British for not eradicating "the leprosy of CASTE" in the Indian subcontinent, capitalizing the word 'caste' to show his strong feelings on the subject (ibid: 83).

The *Examiner:* Promoting Pluralism

The very mixed aspects of the origins and lifestyles of the Euro-Asians made them open to ideas of pluralism, which took an ideological form from the 1850s onwards. By the middle of the 19th century the Euro-Asians, who had lost touch with their European roots, opted for defining themselves as Ceylonese, and began to consciously use this appellation. As Roberts says, the majority of Burghers and Eurasians:

> eventually saw themselves as Ceylonese too, as one part of the Ceylonese peoples; ...a segment of the emerging Burgher community stepped out to argue for a cross-ethnic Ceylonese identity which should be made to subsume and dissolve the particularistic identities held by Burghers, Sinhalese, Colombo Chetties, Moors, Tamils, Malays and others. (1989: 178)

The *Examiner* from 1859 up to 1900 (when it ceased publication) consistently argued for a local, 'Ceylonese' identity, and the Euro-Asians associated with the paper thought of themselves as Ceylonese. As Lorenz wrote to Richard Morgan:

> I have purchased the *Examiner* from John Selby… If …we succeed … Fred, Louis (Nell) and myself being a sufficiently strong staff for the purpose, we shall prove after all that *Ceylon has arrived at a position when her children can speak out for themselves*. (in Hulugalle 1960: 90, emphasis added)

The *Examiner,* originally owned by John Selby, the radical British lawyer resident in Colombo, was bought and run by a group consisting mainly of Euro-Asians. It was thought of as a "Burgher newspaper," but its new owners had wider concerns, namely that the paper should be one to reflect the views of the "Ceylonese." The "dominant personality" in the venture was Lorenz; and this "first newspaper under Ceylonese management" was edited up to 1862 by Lorenz's wife's brother, Frederick Nell, and from that date by Lorenz, with Samuel Grenier as sub-editor (Blazé 1948: 175-77). They believed strongly in a free press. The first editorial noted that:

> The press generally as a vehicle of current information, as a medium of communication between ruler and the subject, as a theatre for discussion of public grievances, as a guide to popular feeling, has long since asserted its place and its rights in Ceylon. (in Blazé 1948: 175)

Until his illness in 1870, Lorenz inspired the *Examiner,* "guided and enlightened the public, fought their battles, entertained their spirits and educated their tastes through the medium of his ever more popular newspaper" (ibid: 177). His journalism was characterized by "a gentle if merry humour." But he could show "merciless sarcasm… for the perpetrators of any act of injustice or oppression," taking on the causes "of the weak and the underprivileged" (ibid: 178).

While the Burgher intelligentsia had indulged in youthful exuberance and idealism in the columns of *Young Ceylon,* the *Examiner,* in which they were later involved, became a serious critical journal with distinct political and social messages. Politically the *Young Ceylon* circle, writes Roberts, "were early heralds of a nationalist opposition that formed expression in the Ceylon League as well as the pages of the *Examiner.*" Such sentiments were inspired by a "search for self-respect," as seen in the writings of James de Alwis, and emerged from "colonial humiliations." The *Examiner* very pointedly and consciously argued for multi-ethnic rights in the island, and supported the fortnightly Sinhala paper *Lakminipahana,* begun in 1862 by a group of Sinhala-Buddhist laymen and monks. In the first issue, their indebtedness to the Nells and Lorenz was acknowledged (Roberts et al. 1989: 79).

Lorenz's Secularism

One important aspect of Lorenz's world view was his commitment to secularism and his lack of enthusiasm for organized religion. Born and brought up in a period when the 'Age of Reason' was discussed, when Christian dogmatism was being denounced, when Charles Darwin's *On the Origin of Species* caused a stir and when the great debates flourished in Europe about the separation of Church and State, it is not surprising that Lorenz was inclined to be secular. He was, also a "prominent Freemason" and Treasurer of the Sphinx Lodge founded in Colombo in 1861 (Blazé 1948: 199). Blazé also agrees that the Presbyterian Calvinism of his family "never suited" him, and that "even as a boy ... [he] felt himself to be out of tune with the severe code, self-denying discipline and rather negative virtues of Victorian nonconformity" (1948: 89). Lorenz's biographer B.R. Blazé, who tried to show that he had a "genuine spirituality," admitted that Lorenz "made no parade of his religion," and if he was unorthodox in his views, "he was merely a little ahead of his time" (ibid: 1948: 63).

But the evidence remains that Lorenz was a sceptic much ahead of his time. His earlier biographer Leopold Ludovici refers to the displeasure Lorenz incurred "from those who are accustomed to expect the outside trappings of religion more ostentatiously displayed"; and that many discovered "an entire absence of piety in his character," adding revealingly that Lorenz was also "beset with doubt on some points of dogmatic Theology" (quoted in ibid: 62). The devout Burgher Christians however, did 'protest too much,' persisting in their efforts to prove that their hero Lorenz was religious. In 1899 Francis Beven in a lecture said, "the stories of his (Lorenz's) doubtful religious views were not well founded." Blazé also adds that:

> His very doubts show that he was not one who merely adopted the conventional attitude as some may be tempted to assume from the circumstance that he changed over... from the Church of his parents [Presbyterian] to the Church of his bride [Episcopalian]. (ibid: 1948: 63)

Burgher orthodoxy may have invented a pious Lorenz, but his remarkably secular attitudes were evident from his writings. When the Roman Catholics opened the Good Shepherd Convent school in Jaffna, Lorenz protested and made fun of the proposal in an *Examiner* editorial (ibid: 188-89) :

> ... the bare statement of our opinion that such an establishment, however ably managed, however narrowly watched, however largely tinged with religion, is more likely to do mischief... and unsocialize the individual, than to refine the feelings or give a new tone to society...
> ... A *Convent*! – where young women are to be secluded from male society, – where religion is to be the sole study of life, – where the head is to be shaved, and the rosary to be the test of continuous prayer; – what do the people of Ceylon want with such an establishment?

Lorenz went into detail and joked about the harsh realities and torture of the Convent regime, with its renunciation of the 'good life':

> Are there to be processions of Nuns? Relics, Embroidery, Miracles and Candles? Horsehair Chemises and nightly flagellations? What are to be the rules regarding Diet? Are they, like Sir Ingoldsby Bray,

'Never to wash or comb or shave
Nor adorn their body
Nor drink gin toddy
Nor indulge in a pipe,
But dine upon tripe
And blackberries gathered before they are ripe;
And for ever abhor, renounce and abjure
Rum, hollands, and brandy, wine, punch and liqueur?'

In this same editorial, on a more serious note, Lorenz added:

> We are getting perhaps too merry on the subject; our remarks may perhaps be painful... but the subject is as suggestive of ridicule as of sorrow. In the interests of Sound Morality, in the interests of young Females destined to be useful to society as Sisters and Mothers, in the interests of Parents whose enthusiasm blinds their prudence, we protest against a Nunnery. (ibid)

Such a mocking protest inevitably led to a reply, and Archbishop Bonjean rejoined that it was not a 'Convent' but a 'Convent-school' that was proposed in Jaffna. Lorenz, conceding the point, wrote: "We distinguish between *Education* conferred by Religious Ladies and a *Convent* for the Segregation of Ladies" (Blazé 1948: 189). But in his tone and language on this issue, Lorenz reflected not only the spirit of cynicism about religion that had swept the western world, but also his self-confidence and courage that made him openly critical of Catholics.

Lorenz's critical attitude to religion was further expressed during the debate in the legislature on the General Cemeteries Bill, which included the allocation of portions of land for each religious community. Lorenz, who was on the Legislative Council subcommittee of six to consider the Bill, dissented – and was a minority of one. But he wrote an editorial on the subject:

> One result of these exclusive appropriations will be to prevent the possibility of an Episcopalian corpse being distracted by the close proximity of a Presbyterian corpse. The decaying churchman will thus be left to himself, undisturbed by the presence of a body which

> during life had never learnt the Church Catechism... the flowers which are to blossom over his grave will exhale purely Episcopalian odours.

Lorenz pleaded for a more enlightened approach on religion and deplored inequality:

> Let us avoid sectarianism, and discourage inequality and exclusiveness. Let us not endeavour by Ordinances, to make the flowers smell sweeter over the grave of an Episcopalian than over the grave of a Baptist; and let the grass be as green that grows on the one as on the other. (ibid: 190-1)

Lorenz also had a quarrel with Rev. O.S. Glenie, the Anglican Colonial Chaplain of Trincomalee. The issue was the marriage of Lorenz's cousin Andrew Roosmalecocq (District Judge at Trincomalee) to his deceased wife's sister. When Rev. Glenie denounced this marriage as "improper," Lorenz in the *Examiner* replied sharply, commenting that such marriages were not illegal. Replying to this, Glenie referred to "the advice which the Eurasian editor, who is said to be a lawyer, sneeringly bestows upon me," and reminded Lorenz that the (religious) law of the Church on this question differed from the civil law, adding that "it is the first so it will be the last time I shall notice any slanderous effusion proceeding from the Eurasian Editor of the Examiner" (Blazé 1948: 180-81). Blazé notes that the clergyman attempted to annoy Lorenz by "repeatedly applying to him the epithet 'Eurasian,' as though in contempt, thereby betraying a very unclerical race-prejudice which Lorenz was quick to note and chastize without the slightest bitterness" (ibid: 180).

No doubt, some of his religious-minded critics regarded Lorenz as a bit wild, not conforming to the high standards of propriety of the conservative Burgher families. While there was an impression that Burghers 'let the good times roll,' there was also among them a tradition of Calvinist puritanism. Blazé gives us an interesting picture of the contrasts in Burgher ways of life, "the chaste severity of taste in language, dress, diet and manners of the early Victorian Burghers" and their "self-indulgence" in later years (ibid: 224).

Lorenz, whom Blazé calls "one of the handsomest men of his generation," was evidently a 'bon viveur,' and a Byronic figure, reportedly "debonair, a little ahead of his time, seemingly irresponsible, and altogether attractive." He "smoked too hard... was fond of his beer [and] was popular with the opposite sex as with his own." It seems that his jokes did not always "bear repetition" to staid women "of that Victorian age" (ibid: 224). But Blazé adds that "it would be ungracious":

> to cavil at the time and energy he [Lorenz] sometimes dissipated in worldly enjoyment since it is impossible to forget the time and energy he constantly spent in service to others. (ibid: 223)

Prone to "worldly enjoyment" Lorenz like many Euro-Asians excelled in music and the arts. Johan Lorenz, his Prussian father, a gifted man interested in theatricals and a composer of poetry in German and English, taught young Charles music, dancing, poetry and painting. Charles Lorenz played the flute, and throughout his life drew cartoons and made drawings of events that interested him, including one of the family orchestra. He was "the social humorist, sketching light pictures of contemporary men and affairs" (ibid: 68), one of his cartoons appearing in *Punch* in 1854 (ibid: 100). He was bold enough to sketch, in jail, Gongalegoda Banda, the leader of the 1848 rebellion in Sri Lanka; and in the words of Blazé, while in England, Lorenz indulged in "his flair for sketching ... and one of his more famous caricatures was of the great Thackeray, drawn from life, sitting in a London omnibus" (ibid: 100).

Nascent Oppositional Politics

Although a local bourgeoisie had arisen by the mid-1860s and a considerable accumulation of capital had been made by locals in plantations, trade and the liquor business, political representation remained at the levels of 1833 – namely a Legislative Council composed of the principal officers of government, known as 'Officials' and "respectable inhabitants European or native," called 'Unofficials'; the latter consisted of three Europeans and one each for the Sinhalese, Tamil and Burgher ethnic groups. This so-called liberal policy of the 1830s was condemned by the British diehards of the time as utopian ideas of Levellers (Jayawardena 2000: 69). But by the 1860s, this system had become not only outmoded and out-of-step with the economic development of the colony, but also unrepresentative of the emerging bourgeoisie which included many highly qualified professionals. Although the Legislative Council was more or less frozen in terms of unofficial representation until the early 20th century, local government politics had been promoted. In 1865 when the Municipal Council of Colombo was inaugurated, Lorenz was one of the first members of the Council, representing the Cottanchina (Mutwal) ward and "doing strenuous pioneer work there" (Blazé 1948: 199).

But even a Governor such as Sir Henry Ward (who was earlier a Liberal, and member of parliament) was wary of political reforms, saying that the majority of people in Sri Lanka were not ready for such changes. He opposed increased representation for the Burghers, as they "were a small fraction of the community and a *class most dangerous to trust with large powers of legislation*" (Balasingham 1968: 131 emphasis added). "If you value the peace of Ceylon, you must never give these gentlemen a preponderance in the Legislative Council," Ward wrote of the Burghers, in a confidential despatch in 1859 (quoted in ibid: 131). It was indeed a repetition of the fear that Euro-Asians were potentially subversive.

There were, however, some tussles in the legislature, especially as distinguished lawyers and personalities – Richard Morgan, James de Alwis, Charles Lorenz, Muttu Coomaraswamy and George Wall – had made their presence felt as councillors, urging political reform including the increase of 'Unofficial' representation. One key issue that irritated the 'Unofficials' and resulted in a political crisis was the military expenditure of the island. They argued that the cost should be borne by the imperial and not the local government as in other British dominions. What Blazé called "the first great milestone in Ceylon's march to freedom," was the occasion when the 'Unofficials' finding there were only five 'Officials' present, passed a vote of censure on the government. When this was later reversed, the six 'Unofficials' walked out of the

Legislative Council. Lorenz never returned to the legislature, but his action made him "the leader of the movement for political emancipation" (Blazé 1948: 248-49) and inspired the formation of the Ceylon League.

The Ceylon League, begun in 1865 by Charles Lorenz, George Wall (a former planter), John Henry Eaton (a Euro-Asian lawyer), John Capper (a British journalist), William Thompson (a British resident) and James de Alwis (a lawyer), was the first such organization to criticize the authorities. On behalf of the Ceylon League the six founders issued a document stating that their resignation from the legislature was a "vehement protest against the serious encroachments which... have been made on [the] constitutional privileges" of British subjects (D'Alwis 1939: 118-19). The language used was fairly harsh, accusing the British government of being interested only in "what they can exact" from the colonies and asserting that justice would only be obtained "by reliance on ourselves":

> It must be evident to every one who considers the spirit in which the Home government has treated the representations from Ceylon, whether from individuals, public bodies or the Council itself, that it is useless to trust any longer to their sense of justice.

Urging that reliance on the good intentions of the Governor was not enough, the Ceylon League said "We must agitate for our rights ... the time has thus arrived, when the Colony must either defend its rights or become unworthy to enjoy them":

> If we endure in silence and supineness the treatment we have lately experienced from the authorities... we shall deserve the degradation to which we have been subjected, and such further humiliations as may be imposed upon us. (ibid: 120-21)

A call was made to "to everyone... to the importance of the present crisis... to agitate for a Council such as could not be compelled to reverse its own acts and pass measures repugnant to the opinions and principles of its members." The public were urged "to organise a *constitutional resistance* (in) ... *defence of their rights*" (ibid: 122, emphasis added).

In spite of his failing health, Lorenz devoted a lot of time and energy to the Ceylon League. This organization, although it did not continue into the 1870s, was according to Blazé, "not a complete failure, for it won the support of all classes, and succeeded in creating a general appreciation of the need for constitutional reform" (Blazé 1948: 221). It was an expression of the liberal tendencies of this era.

Lorenz's best-known writings, *Christmas Debates* (which he also illustrated) parodied the proceedings of the Legislative Council in the years 1860 to 1865. They were "plain burlesque, full of sly satire and mischievous allusions to persons and events" (Blazé 1948: 196). In one verse from the *Debates,* Lorenz expresses his own political stand:

> It is not with influence and Grandeur alone
> You can hope to succeed for an hour;
> But the love of the people can only be known
> When you share with the people your power. (ibid: 196)

While a liberal position was reflected in the walk-out by members of the legislature, this phase of politics was also based on an ideal of pluralism and a vision of future political self-determination. But it did not develop into a fully fledged anti-imperialist movement. Yet, as Blazé says, Lorenz "more than any one man… began the movement for the political emancipation of the Ceylonese" (ibid: 10). His death, aged 42 on 9th August 1871 from tuberculosis, was mourned by all classes, and on this occasion, 56 verses on Charles Lorenz in Sinhala were composed and published by Simon Silva.[2]

By the late 19th century, however, other movements based on specific ethnic and religious identities arose among Sinhala Buddhists, Hindu Tamils, and Muslims. This tendency even touched the Burghers, who in the early 20th century asserted a Dutch Burgher exclusiveness vis-à-vis other Burghers and Eurasians, and promoted a narrow patriarchal identity in the Dutch Burgher Union formed in 1908. Some have thought that Lorenz's untimely death marked the end of the phase of radicalism and a liberal worldview among Burghers. But there were other Burghers in the wake of Lorenz, who were inspired by the struggles he had pioneered. One such person was Leopold Ludovici.

Leopold Ludovici and the *Examiner*

A radical, unconventional Burgher of the Southern Province who was related to and influenced by Lorenz was Leopold Ludovici (1833-82), who in 1876 became the editor and owner of the *Examiner*. Born in Matara, his father Johan Hendrik Ludovici was the Secretary of the District Court at Tangalle, and his mother was Sophia Veenekam. Leopold was educated at the Tangalle Government School and at the age of 17 became the agent of *Young Ceylon* in Hambantota and Tangalle (Blazé 1948: 69-70). His early career was in the government Survey Department, which took him to all parts of the country. Ludovici wrote a pamphlet on rice cultivation, using "his experience as a surveyor to castigate the British administration's land policy" (*Journal of the Dutch Burgher Union [DBU]* Vol. XVIII, 1928: 80-83). He was an avid reader, a devotee of *Blackwood's Magazine,* and the author of a collection of monumental inscriptions from Dutch churches and churchyards of the island, entitled *Lapidarium Zeylanicum* (1876).

Ludovici, who in 1859 married Henrietta Ernst, a relative of Charles Lorenz, joined the staff of the *Examiner* and wrote on a variety of topics, often "taking up cudgels on behalf of the weak and oppressed." It was said that his "*penchant* for strong writing" brought him "within the meshes of the law of libel" – one defamatory article leading to a fine of Rs 1,000 (*Journal of the DBU,* op cit.). His outspoken comments led to some reaction from sections of the British community. On one occasion a planter took offence to Ludovici's writing, and armed with a riding whip, went to the *Examiner* office to punish him. Seeing that Ludovici was unusually tall and big-made, the planter left promptly (ibid: 82). This incident is reminiscent of similar threats to Lorenz and Derozio's encounter with a whip-wielding Britisher in Kolkata (see Chapter 5). It also reveals the tensions that could arise between Euro-Asians in South Asia and resident Britishers who behaved arrogantly. Such contradictions and clashes between foreign diehards and the local liberal intelligentsia were not uncommon.

Like Lorenz, Ludovici was enlightened in his attitudes on many social issues, including corporal punishment. He wrote a strong editorial in the *Examiner* against a school principal (J.B. Cull) who had caned a pupil for absence from school – the student, Donald de Zilwa, being known to Ludovici. A case for assault was taken, but the Magistrate named Penny threw it out. Ludovici's editorial entitled "Two-penny-half-penny Justice" deplored the magistrate's "pigheadedness and impudence" and referred to "numerous complaints which are made against the arrogance of bumptious boy magistrates." Ludovici's writings on such occasions reflected the hostility of educated, radical Burghers to certain British officials. In this connection Ludovici also satirized the recruitment procedures of the civil service:

> Any green-grocer's …son, who may happen to have been the head butler or steward of an aristocratic establishment… can get a nomination to the Ceylon Civil Service, and if he succeeds in passing the Examination… he comes out to Ceylon as a writer, and once amongst a lot of cringing natives the idea dawns upon him that in the midst of such a degenerate race he must be a demi-god. (*Journal of the DBU,* op cit.)

Ludovici, who kept in touch with events in India, criticized the seeming complacency of Indians and Sri Lankans when faced with white racist attitudes:

> This unfortunately is not the experience of Ceylon alone; it is exactly the same throughout India. But whatever may be the case in India, the natives of Ceylon are a tamer and milder race than even the proverbially mild Hindoo, and if they do not grow noisy and bluster over their grievances, it is not to be presumed they have none. (ibid)

It was obvious that long before the emergence of political nationalism in India and Sri Lanka, the Euro-Asian radicals were "to grow noisy and bluster," as seen in the outspoken, bold critiques by Leopold Ludovici and his group. Ludovici also edited a magazine called *Puck* and wrote for the journal of the Ceylon branch of the Royal Asiatic Society (Norah Roberts 1993: 93). Michael Roberts refers to him as a far-seeing man in proposing that the "Ceylonese" should "deplore ethnic designations" (Roberts et al.1989: 159). But ironically, as noted earlier, such opposition to ethnic categories came on the eve of those movements in the late 19th century that arose among Sinhalese, Tamil and Muslims to assert ethnic and religious identities.

J.L.K. van Dort – Artist of Social Satire

Linked to Lorenz and the Burgher liberals of the Young Ceylon group, and reflecting their attitudes in his art, was J.L.K. (John) van Dort (1831-98), one of the first locals to become a leading practitioner of western art in the island. Van Dort was from a leading Dutch Burgher family; his father Johannes had served in the Civil Engineers Department involved in road construction. John van Dort attended the Colombo Academy where his skills in drawing were appreciated. He may also have been influenced by the British artist Andrew Nicholl, who for a period taught at the Academy. Another possible inspiration was Hippolyte Silvaf (1801-79), a Euro-Asian of French-Indian origin from Pondicherry who lived near van Dort's home in Small Pass (San Sebastian). Silvaf was a medical draughtsman, free-lance portrait painter and watercolourist, who with his daughter ran an art school in the Pettah in the 1840s. Silvaf provided drawings for the *Illustrated London News,* for Emerson Tennent's *Ceylon* (1859) and A.M. Ferguson's *Souvenirs of Ceylon* (1868).

Van Dort married Cornelia Henrietta Spittel (a Dutch Burgher); their daughter Grace van Dort became one of the pioneer women artists of the country (see Chapter 10). Van Dort joined the Surveyor-General's office as a draughtsman and thus had the advantages of travel and critical observation of urban and rural life. He became known for his satirical sketches and line drawings of local life, covering all classes and communities. He was influenced by the humourous illustrations in Charles Dickens' books. By the 1850s, his drawings appeared in *Young Ceylon*, and his work on "law-court characters" was reproduced in A.M. Ferguson's *Souvenirs of Ceylon* (1868). He did illustrations for John Capper's *Old Ceylon* (1877), and also for the *London Graphic,* to which he contributed until his death (van Dort 1951). He drew upon "many incidents in the social life of his community" and was sensitive in his portrayals of the urban and rural poor (ibid: Introduction). Van Dort's more political sketches were for *Muniandi*, a fortnightly satirical journal which, as R.K. de Silva states: "provided a medium for publicising political, social and moral issues together with suggestions for remedying them" (1998: 6). His social criticism is reflected in illustrations of rapacious tax collectors and arrogant bureaucrats, expressing in art the radical inclinations of the intelligentsia of the Lorenz group.

Thus, like other Euro-Asian liberals of the time, van Dort had the advantage of being able to take a critical and satirical look at British official pomposity, as well as at the vagaries of local society. The Euro-Asians continued to be in the forefront of modern art in the 20th century, producing the country's leading artist, George Keyt (1901-96), whose themes were mainly drawn from Hindu and Buddhist culture. Other Euro-Asian artists – Geoffrey Beling, Aubrey Collette, Ivor Baptist, Richard Gabriel and George Classen of the '43 Group' of modernists were inspired by the famous aesthete Lionel Wendt, a relative of the Nells.[3]

While the 19th century Euro-Asian radicals influenced the political climate of the times, they also passed their legacy of critical social analysis and political dissent to the next generation of concerned intellectuals and activists. One such person was A.E. Buultjens, a radical and visionary in the tradition of Lorenz, who gave leadership to the earliest movement for workers' rights in Sri Lanka. He publicized the need for such a movement, and helped in 1893 to form the island's first trade union – the Ceylon Printers' Union – as discussed in the next chapter.

Note

1. C. Drieberg, (a relation of Charles Lorenz) was a student in Kolkata in the 1870s and had Anglo-Indian friends. He wrote of the meetings he attended, addressed by Indian "big men" including Surendranath Bannerji, "a thorn in the side of the government," and the reformist leader Keshab Chandra Sen, of the Brahmo Samaj (Drieberg 1933: 13).
2. The Sinhala verses on the death of Lorenz, kindly loaned by Ismeth Raheem, were republished (by the Social Scientists' Association in 2006) as a pamphlet, edited by Ananda Wakkumbura.
3. In later years modernism and avant garde trends by Euro-Asians in design, art, photography and architecture were expressed by Terry Jonklaas, Barbara Sansoni, Dominic Sansoni and Ashley de Vos respectively.

8

FROM RADICALISM TO WORKERS' RIGHTS

> [In London] the object lesson of nightly debaucheries, of hopeless drunkenness in the gin palaces, of the homeless and starving thousands, of the piteous cries to Government, and the *public demonstrations of dissatisfied socialists*, all this was a picture I shall never forget.
>
> A.E. Buultjens, "Why I became a Buddhist," 1899, p.8, emphasis added

The Tradition of Charles Lorenz

A new phase and a significant 'leap forward' in Sri Lanka's social history occurred in the 1890s with the early stirrings of the Colombo working class, resulting in two historic events – the first strike and the formation of the first trade union in the country. Prominent among the leaders of this movement were Alfred Ernst Buultjens (1865-1916), a relative of Charles Lorenz whose mantle he inherited, and Dr Pedro Manuel Lisboa Pinto, a Goanese who was part of several dissident movements. Lorenz, as noted earlier, was inspired by the events of 1848, the radical trend in British politics, the challenges to orthodox Christianity, and the liberal-democratic ideologies of the time. In the heyday of imperial expansion, Lorenz and his group laid the foundation for self-government, by confronting the authoritarianism and racist attitudes among the British rulers, by propagating liberal and proto-nationalist ideas, and championing the rights of the workers. Burghers and other "educated Ceylonese," said Digby, think the "thoughts of John Stuart Mill" (1879: 63), one of the eminent liberal political theorists of his time. Buultjens and other workers' leaders took the struggles further, to include the earliest attempts to organize the nascent working class of Colombo.

Charles Lorenz's influence and appeal had been based on his concern for the peoples' rights, as "the doughty champion of the weak and oppressed' (Weinman 1918: 12). One reason for Lorenz's charisma was his involvement with working people several decades before the rise of the trade unions and labour leaders. He was held in "extraordinary veneration" and people turned to him wherever there was "a good cause... as their champion and chief" (Blazé 1948: 183 & 186). In 1848 he had joined Dr Christopher Elliot in agitating against oppressive taxes and when there was a serious shortage of rice, crowds appeared at Lorenz's house asking him to intervene with the Governor. "Lorenz alone was their hero and leader." (Blazé 1948: 184). As a lawyer, he often appeared for poor litigants; and as a legislative councillor, he spoke out about the grievances of government clerks. Lorenz who was critical about the government's rejection of higher pay for clerks, described their specific problems: "House-rent and food are dearer than they ever were before; (and) ...the cost of clothing is such as to be beyond the reach of the poorer classes" (Blazé 1948: 186-87). He perceived the inflationary rise in prices, and in the *Examiner* wrote of its effects on the living standards of clerks, who had always been an educated, but economically dissatisfied element of society:

> We have seen the price of all commodities rise, while *their* wages have remained... the same. We have seen the 'high price of provisions' urged successfully as a ground for increasing the salaries of every other section of the service, Civil and Military; but the clerk's pay alone is supposed to possess an elasticity which can adapt itself to any conceivable rise in the market... If the position of the Government clerks was bad four years ago, it is far worse at present. (ibid: 186)

Lorenz was also one of the earliest to make an analysis of the class divisions of colonial society. In an indictment, contrasting the gains made by both foreign merchants and the local bourgeoisie with the poverty of the clerks, he noted that: "the elements that enrich our British merchants, our Coffee Planters, and our Native Traders, bring *them* (clerks) no succour, but combine to impoverish them still more" (ibid: 187). Lorenz was also concerned about workers' welfare on the coffee plantations. When Dr W.G. van Dort's report on the high mortality among these workers was criticized by the planters, Lorenz praised Dr van Dort's "single-handed combat" with the Planters' Association (Roberts et al. 1989: 63). In contrast to many educated Burghers, who showed more dislike than sympathy for the working-class mechanics of mixed Portuguese descent, Lorenz was sensitive to their plight. As he wrote in 1862: "There is perhaps no class in Ceylon more neglected or more ignorant, than the class conventionally termed 'mechanics' or more frequently 'Portuguese' ... artizans who minister to the most pressing needs of civilized society." They included "the Shoemakers, the Tailors, the Printers, the Tinkers and the Saddlers," who are "forgotten and left behind in the general progress of the island." Lorenz quoted a Christian clergyman's account of these workers who "live in wretched hovels, ... their mode of life, their meals, their dress, are generally of the most wretched description." Lorenz offered a gift of a house he owned in Slave Island, Colombo, as a refuge for some of this class, but the project failed since the government refused to make a grant for expenses (Blazé 1948: 77-78).

A.E. Buultjens Follows Lorenz

Charles Lorenz's radicalism and concern for the poor was shared by his relative, Alfred Ernst (A.E.) Buultjens. The Lorenz clan of Matara were friends and relatives of the Buultjens family. A.E's father John Buultjens (born in 1829, son of William Buultjens, a Galle schoolmaster), was a lawyer and his mother Emilia Ernst (1835-1904) was a second cousin of Lorenz (see Table 2; Blazé 1948: 27-28, & 70). John Buultjens was a contemporary and friend of Charles Lorenz, and John's son A.E. would have known Lorenz, who died when A.E. was six years old.[1] A.E. Buultjens was, no doubt, influenced by stories of the radicalism and exploits of this fabled family member who was a heroic figure among Sri Lankans, and a 'favourite son' of the Burgher community, many of whom were named for Lorenz over the following decades.

The history of dissent and rebellion against the established norms of colonial society was evident in theory and practice in the life of A.E. Buultjens (1865-1916). His first revolt was in the sphere of religion. Charles Lorenz, too, was not religious, as noted earlier, and "made no parade of his religion"; and moreover, in an age when Christian orthodoxy was questioned, he had doubts on "dogmatic Theology" (Blazé 1948: 62). Lorenz generally cared little for labels and, though born a Calvinist Presbyterian, switched to the Church of England (Episcopalian) on marriage (ibid: 89). He had also made caustic remarks on the setting up of the Good Shepherd Convent in Jaffna in 1861 (see Chapter 7). Alfred Buultjens has described the "Christian surroundings and influence" of his early years, and refers ironically to his baptism: "I was stamped with the hallmark or rather watermark of a Christian," surmising that he must have made his protest with "a continuous scream and howling." He had also as a boy listened to the conflicts among Christians of different denominations and to "the spectacle of a church divided against itself"– between High and Low Church tendencies (Buultjens 1899: 1-2).

Buultjens was greatly influenced by a famous teacher of the time, Robert (R.H.) Leembruggen, the headmaster of the Government Boys' School in Matara which he attended (Brohier 1994: 26). In Buultjens' words, Leembruggen was "not a churchgoer," and was known to be "an avowed freethinker and agnostic (who) had a great effect upon my mind" (Buultjens 1899: 2). At St Thomas' College, Colombo (from the age of 14 to 19), Buultjens came under Warden Rev. E.F. Miller's tutelage and received a good classical education. He recalled that: "besides… the subjects required for the Calcutta and Cambridge Local Examinations, we were carefully drilled in… the Book of Common Prayer… the Bible …and the original Greek of the Gospels" (1899: 2). Buultjens won the Bishop's Prize for Divinity and was also 'confirmed' as a member of the Church of England in 1881. He later questioned his baptismal rites:

> I do not acquiesce in the compulsory baptism performed on me by my 'pastors and masters' when I was a legal 'infant.' I denounce the practice and rebel against it as an *infringement of rights of children.*" (Buultjens 1899: 2-3, emphasis added)

While at St Thomas', he "entertained the first passing doubt about the truth of Christianity," inspired by a "materialistic work" (Dr Buchner's *Matter and Force*) that a fellow student, J.R. Molligoda, gave him. From that time he was "naturally *opposed to authority and disposed to rebel* against what people generally accept as gospel truth upon mere blind belief" (Buultjens 1899: 3, emphasis added).

Buultjens' brilliance as a student won him the scholarship of £150 annually for four years that the colonial government awarded for university studies in Britain. Between 1883 and 1887 he was at St John's College, Cambridge, where he graduated in history and political economy, one of his teachers being the eminent economist Alfred Marshall. His doubts about Christianity increased during the years in Cambridge, for there he "met all shades of opinion," including divinity students who were taught that "the Bible was not an inspired book literally, but a historic account of the Israelites." "The shades of opinion" also included Britishers who were "avowed agnostics" and admirers of Thomas Huxley and Charles Bradlaugh. Buultjens was disenchanted with Christianity. "Having once become convinced that God did not... make the world, I gave up, one by one, the fond and cherished beliefs of my childhood" (ibid: 4). What is more, as an undergraduate he was "determined to bring matters to a crisis," and he defied the College rules of compulsory attendance at chapel. He was granted permission to keep away (ibid: 6).

Buultjens was emboldened in his agnostic views by other rebellious Britishers, including distinguished academics, who were a source of strength to him. Buultjens, like the earlier Euro-Asian radicals, made a clear distinction between the diehards and the dissident elements of British society. Citing his religious rebellion, he wrote:

> Was I to say that I was no longer a Christian, or was I to remain silent? I preferred to speak out. I was not alone in my Agnostic views – several University men, Englishmen, especially those who were studying for the Moral Science and Natural Science triposes, and some...going in for the law thought as I did. (Buultjens1899: 6)

Secular and Socialist Influences

Buultjens was in Britain in the 1880s during a time of increasing political dissent and spread of heterodox social and political beliefs. There were Marxist, socialist and anarchist groups active in London (where Marx died in 1883). British socialists such as Bernard Shaw, Annie Besant, Sidney Webb and the Fabians not only questioned British institutions, but also the sexual puritanism of the Victorian era. There was, moreover, a crisis in Christianity, with Darwinians, freethinkers and theosophists denouncing orthodox theology. It was also a turbulent period in Britain when workers' agitation took the form of strikes and demonstrations, with militant trade unions emerging as a new force. Debates were held on women's franchise, and women made their voices heard on issues of their emancipation (Jayawardena 1972: 80-81).

If Darwin had provided the theory, atheists such as Charles Bradlaugh led the action and fuelled public debate with their opposition to Christianity. Buultjens was inspired by Bradlaugh (1833-91), a social reformer who was a close associate of Annie Besant in her atheist, socialist phase, and with whom he edited the *National Reformer*. When elected to parliament in 1880, Bradlaugh had refused to take the oath on the Bible and was unseated as a result. He was elected again several times and was unseated for the same reason – during the years when Buultjens was in Britain. When Bradlaugh was finally permitted to enter parliament in 1888 radicals and non-believers celebrated the event, and non-Christians and dissidents in India and Sri Lanka hailed it as an important victory.

Buultjens was perhaps the first Sri Lankan to have witnessed and been influenced by the meetings and demonstrations of socialists in Britain. His description of protests in London is the first written reference by a Sri Lankan to socialist agitation. The many mass demonstrations in London in the 1880s included marches of the unemployed in 1886; and in 1887, a huge meeting on the Irish issue as well as the historic 'Bloody Sunday' demonstration protesting against curbs on free speech, which ended in violence. Buultjens saw a class aspect in these events and expressed strong views on "the extreme wealth side by side with the grovelling debasement, poverty and misery of the East End of London" (Buultjens 1899: 8).

Buultjens claimed that Christians in Sri Lanka had no idea of these conditions: "Could such things be in Christian England?" he asked, strongly criticizing "the immense wealth" spent on the grand churches – Westminster Abbey and St Paul's – "while there was no money to feed the starving poor." Buultjens wrote of the hollowness of "practical Christianity." It was "a mockery, for with the export of missionaries and Bibles there was a far larger export of Bottles and Bullets, the one to kill the mind, the other the body" (ibid: 8). This became a popular theme of the 1890s. The Irish theosophist J. Bowes Daly, manager of Buddhist schools in 1889-90, wrote: "Men of Ceylon, don't be cowards... don't allow yourselves to be intimidated by proselytisers who... come among you preaching Beer and Bible" (Jayawardena 1972: 57).

From Agnosticism to Buddhism

A Burgher non-believer would not have aroused much attention in 19th century Sri Lanka, but when Buultjens while in Cambridge went as far as to proclaim himself a Buddhist, this caused quite a stir. The Anglican Church in Sri Lanka – as well as his Burgher relatives – were shocked by his public renunciation of Christianity. A Burgher Buddhist was an anomaly in colonial society, and as Dr W.A. de Silva, a Buddhist leader, remarked, Buultjens' conversion and break with family tradition was considered "a social offence" (Jayawardena 1972: 81). J. Bowes Daly, who had been in the Irish Home Rule movement, praised Buultjens as "a man who has disregarded the... prospects of an unusually brilliant academic training, sacrificing even family connection, to throw his lot in an unpopular cause." He told the Buddhists that Buultjens "establishes a claim on your confidence which no European can rival" (*The Buddhist*, 9 Sept. 1892). The gravity of Buultjens' change of religion was seen in the strong reactions to his conversion. St Thomas' College disowned him by removing his name off its panel honouring distinguished students; and the resentment he whipped up caused the Anglican Archbishop to engage him in a bitter exchange of letters about his apostasy, to which Buultjens (like Lorenz in his time) made spirited replies (Jayawardena 1972: 82).[2]

Buultjens was active in Buddhist education, which he regarded as a national cause, and clashed with the colonial government and missionaries on this issue. In 1889, aged 24, he had become the principal of the Pettah Buddhist Boy's School (later Ananda College), and from 1890 for the next ten years he was the General-Manager of Buddhist Schools. He openly challenged the educational policies of the colonial government, including the Quarter-Mile Clause of 1892, which disallowed government grants to new schools within a quarter-mile of another government-aided school. Buultjens also made the political point that the movement for Buddhist education was "*a national movement*" and that the Quarter-Mile clause was *directed against the nation* (ibid: 84, emphasis added). He organized a mass petition to the Secretary of State, claiming that "this clause is one of *those iniquities which can only be perpetrated with comparative safety in a distant colony.*" In 1893 Buultjens made a political point about the patriotic role of Buddhist schools in fostering among the young an ability "to better appreciate *free constitutions and councils*" (ibid: 83, emphasis added).

Like many educated Burghers, Buultjens travelled in Europe and visited Holland. He had a scholar's interest in history, wrote to learned journals and gave talks at the local Royal Asiatic Society. He also wrote on Buddhist texts and translated part of the *Visuddi Magga* into English. Buultjens was in Britain at a time when issues of women's rights were debated, and following in the tradition of Burghers who spoke out for women's education, he was prominent in the movement for Buddhist girls' secondary education. He was active in the Women's Education Society (*Nari Shiksha Dana Samagama*) and was manager of the Sangamitta School for Buddhist girls, started in 1890 in Colombo, which by 1893 had over 100 pupils studying in the English medium.

Striking at Capital

The most outstanding aspect of A.E. Buultjens' career was his pioneering work in organizing a section of skilled workers into a trade union and leading a historic strike. By the late 19th century the time was ripe for such a development. Mercantile capitalism had expanded, and urban factories, offices and transport facilities had increased significantly to create an embryonic working class of skilled and unskilled labour. The skilled workers included printers and book-binders, compositors and proofreaders in printing firms and newspaper offices. They were literate workers who had an earlier history of forming provident associations (like the British benefit societies) with contributions from members. The aim was to promote thrift, provide financial relief in times of need, and assist widows and orphans. One of the early provident funds, begun during the economic depression caused by the crash of the coffee industry, was that of government clerks, who formed the Public Services Mutual Provident Association in 1883. A year later, clerks in the private sector started the Mercantile Mutual Provident Association in Colombo, and several such organizations arose in other towns. In 1890 government and mercantile clerks jointly formed the Ceylon Family Benefit Association, for funeral benefits (Jayawardena 1972: 30).

Euro-Asians dominated these organizations. In 1893 the Public Service Mutual Provident Association had 9 Euro-Asians on its committee of 10, and the Mercantile Mutual Provident Association had 9 Euro-Asians on its committee of 17 members. The Ceylon Family Benefit Association in 1892 had Euro-Asians in key posts: the chairman was J. Weinman; the secretary E. Ondaatje, the treasurer C.W. Schumacher; W.S. Christoffelsz and M.D. Cockburn were on the committee (ibid: 31). Several clerks in benefit societies were linked to the earliest manifestations of trade unionism; and three members of the Mercantile Mutual Provident Association, J.G. Fernando, J.M. Perera and D.J. Caspersz were committee members of the Ceylon Printers' Union, formed in 1893 (ibid: 31). Caspersz, a Burgher born in 1887, who worked as a printer at the Examiner press, was the grandfather of the Jesuit priest Fr Paul Caspersz, a propagator of liberation theology, famed for championing the cause of plantation workers through his organization in Kandy, 'Satyodaya.'

Buultjens, who was in touch with the Colombo workers, raised the issue of trade unionism for the first time in the *Independent Catholic,* a small dissident journal of breakaway Catholics (see next section). Buultjens wrote about his travels "in industrial towns" of Britain, and the "public spirit shown by the working classes of other nations." He argued for a trade union, in Colombo, among printers, who were "a fairly strong body more enlightened than their fellow-workers of the other trades." Buultjens mentioned "the wrongs" faced by local printers and urged "energetic members of the trade" to communicate with him to draw up "a definite plan of action" (Jayawardena 1972: 84-85). When they responded, Buultjens acted swiftly. At a public meeting of printers, he spoke of their low wages and long hours, and found fault with local capitalists for keeping "their capital hoarded in strong chests thereby giving little employment for the labourers," and criticized foreign capitalists who "had ignored the rights of their workmen" (ibid: 95). The Ceylon Printers' Union was formed with Buultjens as secretary. He was also involved in the first strike of skilled workers in the country – the printers' strike in September 1893 at H.W. Cave & Co., a leading British-owned printing firm of Colombo.

If his 'apostasy' as an individual had caused a scandal among the Christian establishment, Buultjens' championing of the rights of workers as a class and organizing them in trade-union and strike activity was a profound challenge in the sphere of labour-capital relations. The printers' strike – the first flash of class-conscious action by Colombo workers – caused concern among employers, and led to much comment in the columns of the press and editorials of the time. Significantly it took place in September 1893 when Friedrich Engels, at a meeting in his honour in Vienna, said his reward for years in the labour movement was that the struggle had become global: "from the jails of Siberia and the gold mines of California to far-off places like Australia." The strike in Colombo of 60 printers over a delay in wage payments lasted five days, but was crushed by the refusal of the employers to give in; the five 'ring leaders' were dismissed, and one of them was imprisoned for a week for breach of the Labour Ordinance (Jayawardena 1972: 100). By 1894 the printers' trade union had fizzled out, but their example was cited with the resumption of working-class agitation in later years.

Disillusioned by quarrels among Buddhists, Buultjens subsequently practised as a lawyer after being enrolled in 1904. He also tended his coconut and citronella plantations, Silverdale and Batadela in Matara. A.E. Buultjens' unorthodoxy was reflected in his civil marriage in 1897 to Sylvia Keller, daughter of H.D. Andree, an accountant. The bride had been formerly married and had two daughters. Buultjens and Keller had three more daughters. His death in 1916 at the age of 51 cut short the career of one of the leading radicals of Sri Lanka; and his contribution remained 'erased' until recent years.

Lisboa Pinto and the Indo-Portuguese Connection

Linked with A.E. Buultjens in the printers' agitation was another Euro-Asian, a doctor from Goa, Pedro Manuel Lisboa Pinto (1857-98), a Catholic of Portuguese-Indian origin. Sections of the working class in Sri Lanka included Portuguese descendants, employed in small-scale occupations such as cobblers, tailors and mechanics, with only a few entering the clerical grades or the professions. The Goan migrants, however, were a recent addition to society. The Catholic Church in Sri Lanka up to 1886 came under the jurisdiction of the Archbishop of Goa, but a crisis occurred that year when the local Catholic Church was put under the authority of Rome, causing deep resentment among local Goans. A few families broke off to form the Independent Catholic Church, establishing their own journal – the *Independent Catholic* – and taking over a church – Our Lady of Good Death – in Hulftsdorf, Colombo. Leading this schism was Dr P.M. Lisboa Pinto, who had qualified in Mumbai and kept his links with Goa, even after moving to Sri Lanka. Dr Lisboa Pinto, described as "the special envoy of Christendom in the Orient," went to Lisbon to protest, and in an address to the Geographical Society there said: "as far as concerns the cessation of the Catholics in Ceylon [to Rome], it is my opinion that this cannot be justified by any principal at all" (Flores 2000: 114). Returning to Colombo, he began his campaign against the Catholic Church. Lisboa Pinto expressed himself forcefully on this issue, and like Buultjens, he challenged the Church, and referred to "the dark deeds of the Catholic Church in the East." This led to controversy and Lisboa Pinto was accused of "defaming the Church and the Papacy" and holding up local Catholics "to the contempt of other religionists" (Jayawardena 1972: 86).

Lisboa Pinto was clearly a man of strong beliefs, matched by a streak of activist courage, who joined several other causes with enthusiasm, including the temperance movement. He was outspoken against the prevalence of alcoholism, and advised temperance workers to "have no dread of being called singular," urging them to "put aside all false notions of social customs and politeness, despise the ridicule of fools" and to "remain faithful to your noble purpose." He added that temperance workers "would be laughed at," for refusing alcohol, but reminded them that "the world seldom receives any great reform or discovery without heaping ridicule or worse on its benefactors" (Jayawardena 1972: 87).

Lisboa Pinto, who had a flourishing medical practice in Dam Street – a busy commercial and working-class neighbourhood of Colombo – founded the *Independent Catholic* and wrote in it frequently on the conditions of the Colombo workers. The most important agitation he was involved with was the organization of the Colombo working class. He was President of the Ceylon Printers' Union, and opened up the columns of the *Independent Catholic* to articles by Buultjens on workers' grievances and trade unions. "No one is better qualified to speak on this subject than a physician or a clergyman," Lisboa Pinto wrote in 1893, referring to "the anguish of body and mind" of the workers, while elaborating on their low wages, indebtedness and living conditions (ibid: 94). He sharply criticized employers, commenting that the local capitalist was "as much exacting and relentless as the Englishman, perhaps more" (ibid: 88). At the first public meeting of printers, Lisboa Pinto boldly called himself an "agitator and great raiser of rebellion," and argued the need for trade unions (ibid: 95). But the failure of the printers' strike caused interest in trade unions to wane; and Lisboa Pinto, in 1894, expressed his "great grief" that "the Ceylon printer expects everyone to come to his help but is himself apathetic" (ibid: 97).

Lisboa Pinto died in 1898 at the age of 41, not living long enough to witness the working-class action of subsequent years. It was no coincidence that the leadership of the first trade union in 1893 came from Euro-Asian professionals – Buultjens and Lisboa Pinto. This was thirty years before a strong trade union of Colombo workers emerged in the 1920s under the full-time leadership of A.E. Goonesinha. The Euro-Asian reformers had clearly "caught the dawn." Their early expressions of consciousness on issues of national importance were remarkable, occurring many decades before fully fledged movements for nationalism, workers' rights and women's rights emerged.

Lorenz, Morgan, the Nells, Ludovici, Buultjens, Lisboa Pinto and many other radicals of mixed East-West origin had led the way as pioneer reformers and modernists with a utopian-like ability to visualize the future. Morgan and Lorenz, unencumbered by local conventions, imbued with radical and liberal ideas and inspired by dissenting movements elsewhere, were brave enough to support movements in rural and urban Sri Lanka against injustices of the colonial regime. They, along with others of the Young Ceylon group advocated free speech, representative government and ethnic pluralism. Buultjens and Lisboa Pinto went further and showed unusual courage, not only in facing scandal by challenging the powerful Church of England and the Catholic Church, respectively, but also in agitating against social oppression, colonial institutions and policies, and especially in defying foreign capitalists and the local bourgeoisie by giving leadership to the working class of Colombo.

Euro-Asian radicalism persisted and a year after A.E. Buultjens' death, a future leader of the Ceylon Communist Party, Pieter Keuneman was born in October 1917. He was related to Buultjens through his grandmother Alice Harriet Ernst (see Table 2). Keuneman was from a Matara Burgher family of lawyers and judges. His father Arthur Eric Keuneman, born in 1885, and educated at Pembroke College, Cambridge was a Supreme Court judge, described by Pieter Keuneman as "a liberal in the real sense" with "all the good points and weaknesses of genuine liberals" (Perera 1967: 3). Pieter's mother was Marjorie Schokman. He joined his father's college in Cambridge in 1937, graduating in English and becoming involved in the Cambridge Union Society debates. A Union Society history referred in 1939 to him as "one of our brightest and best who arrived from his Burgher family in Ceylon … to dazzle Cambridge with his sophistication and omniscience" (ibid: 18). He was active in Cambridge in the Communist movement, and visited Spain during the civil war. In 1941 he returned to Sri Lanka with his wife Hedi Simon, a fellow student, who was an Austrian refugee from fascism. In the years up to 1945 she was active in the Left politics of the period (see Jayawardena 1995).

Pieter Keuneman, a full-time politician throughout his life, became the General Secretary of the Ceylon Communist Party. He entered parliament in 1947 – the first elected Euro-Asian, although the community formed less than 1% of the voters in his working-class constituency of Colombo Central (Perera 1967: 54). In 1970 he became Minister of Housing and Construction in the coalition government led by Sirima Bandaranaike. But Keuneman was the last Euro-Asian to win an election or give leadership to political movements. It was the end of the era of Euro-Asian radical leadership, although many Burghers and Eurasians continued to join movements of protest.[3]

Notes

1. B.R. Blazé writes that John Buultjens was born a fortnight before Lorenz and was "probably one of his henchmen of the Mysterious Club," which was "a juvenile Secret Society" (1948: 26-28). John's father, William Cornelius Buultjens (1804-79), born in Galle, was a government schoolmaster in Galle and later salt storekeeper at Hambantota. His wife Agenita Petronella Gomez, born in Galle in 1823, was (judging from her name) of Portuguese descent. I am grateful to Andrew Buultjens for lending me the Buultjens' family tree.
2. The Bishop of Colombo denounced Buultjens and wrote: "your own career as one who has apostasized from Christianity makes it impossible for me to cultivate with you those relations which I could adopt even to one who has always been a Buddhist"; Buultjens replied by criticizing the Bishop for taking

"public Buddhist money" from the government, and said; "we did not know that the head of the Anglican Church draws a distinction in his relations towards a born Buddhist as against a Buddhist converted from Christianity" (Jayawardena 1972: 82-83).

3. One forgotten 'agitator' of the Burgher community was Julien Edema Ludowyk (Professor E.F.C. Ludowyk's uncle), a renowned teacher of mathematics in St Aloysius' College, Galle, and a pioneer of the Galle labour movement. He was active in politics, and was founder and Secretary of the Southern Province Teachers' Association from 1918 to 1927, fighting on the issue of teachers' low salaries and achieving some concessions in salary scales and pensions. It was reported that "at one stage no school would allow him the use of its premises" for meetings, and that the police were "alerted to watch his movements." J.E. Ludowyk was also president of the Galle Maha Jana Sabha and had ambitions to enter the legislature. (*St Aloysius' College Centenary Magazine,* p.173).

Among the pioneer skilled workers involved in the railway workers' agitation and strikes was a Burgher, William Henry Bocks, a fitter, who was on the committee of the Ceylon Workmens' Provident Association, formed after the Railway Strike of 1912. During the Buddhist-Muslim Riots of 1915, Bocks and others considered "ring leaders" and "agitators" were banished to Batticaloa. Bocks' grandson Clifton Bocks was active in Left politics.

Euro-Asian LSSP leaders of the 1930s, and activists of the Suriya Mal movement included Terence de Zylva and Robin Rutnam; and trade unionists in Colombo, Oscar Pereira and J. Mortimer, both leaders of mercantile clerical workers. There were also many Euro-Asian women secretaries and clerks who were members of the Ceylon Mercantile Union (CMU). They actively participated in the militant strikes for better wages and conditions in the late 1940s and 1950s. I am grateful to Clifton Bocks and Aurele Samuel (formerly of the CMU) for this information.

Table 1

The Nell Family Tree

Frederick Augustus Nell x Catherine Petronella de Fonseca
Married 1793

George Michael Nell x Maria Elizabeth Conderlag
Married 1823

Charles Lorenz x Eleanor Nell
(1829-1871) (b1825)

Louis Nell x Lucia Julia Andree
(1830-1922)

George Frederick Nell
(1828-1867)

Dr Winifred Nell
(1862-1943)

Dr Andreas Nell
(1864-1956)

Paul Nell x Ms Newman

Agnes Nell x George E de Silva
(1884-1961)

Anil de Silva
1909-1996

Minnette de Silva
1917-1998

The symbol x is used for marriage
Compiled from B.R. Blazé, The *Life of Lorenz*, 1948
and Deloraine Brohier *Alice de Boer and some pioneer Burgher Women doctors*, 1994

Table 2

The Lorenz— Nell — Buultjens — Ludovici — Keuneman Connection

George Nicolaas Ernst x Gertrude Podree
(b 1749)

Helena Ernst x Dr Johan Smith
(b 1775)

Johan Michael Ernst x Maria Ludovici
(b 1781) (b 1801)

John Harry Ludovici x Sophia Vennakam
(b 1802)

Anna Smith x Johan Friedrich Lorenz
(b 1792) (b 1772)

George Edward Ernst

Henrietta Ernst x Leopold Ludovici
(b1835) (b1833)

Charles Lorenz x Eleanor Nell (see table 1)
(1829-1871) (b 1825)

Emelia Ernst x John Buultjens
(b 1829)

John Henry (Harry) Ernst

A.E.Buultjens
1865-1916

Evelyn Beatrice Buultjens x Gerard Henry Keuneman

Alice Harriet Ernst x Gerard Edmond Keuneman

Arthur Eric Keuneman x Marjorie Eleanor Schokman
(b1885)

Pieter Keuneman
(1917-1997)

The symbol x is used for marriage

Compiled from B.R. Blaze The *Life of Lorenz*, 1948, pp.27-8, 70
& A.Wright, *Twentieth Century Impressions of Ceylon*, 1907.

The *Examiner*, editorial group, *1862;* left to right: seated Leopold Ludovici, Charles Lorenz, and Francis Beven, standing left to right Samuel Grenier and James Stewart Drieberg.
From B.R. Blazé, *The Life of Lorenz*.

"The Pretender of 1848, in his convict dress. Drawn at the Borella Criminal Gaol, March 8, 1849 Ch. A.L" (Charles Lorenz's sketch of Gongalegoda Banda) from: A.C. Dep, *A History of the Ceylon Police*, Vol 1.

Orchestra Conductor

Sketches by Lorenz 1853-1855. From B.R. Blazé, *The Life of Lorenz.*

Mrs. Lorenz, unwell, sewing in her cabin

At the Piano

"We heard Jenny Lind on Saturday last." — Letter from Amsterdam, dated March 10, 1855

Dr. Christopher Elliot

Charles Lorenz

Richard Morgan. From *Memoirs & Desultory Writings of the late James D' Alwis.*

Frederick Nell. From *The People Inbetween*. Courtesy Michael Roberts, Ismeth Raheem & Percy Colin-Thomé

Henry Derozio

John Ricketts

David Hare

The DEROZIANS of 'YOUNG BENGAL'

Pearychand Mitra

Tarachand Chakrabarti

Dhakshinaranjan Mukherji

A.E. Buultjens, his wife Sylvia and children. From A. Wright, *20th Century Impressions of Ceylon*.

Dr Pedro Manuel Lisboa Pinto.
Courtesy Bernard Lisboa Pinto

Part III

GENDER, PATRIARCHY AND NATION

Anil de Silva, circa 1955, photographed in Paris by Henri Cartier-Bresson

9

MYTHS of the 'ORIENTAL' and EURO-ASIAN WOMAN

In that perfumed land, fondled by the sun,
I knew – beneath a canopy of trees aglow with crimson,
And palms from which languor pours upon your eyes –
A créole lady whose charms are unknown to the world.[1]

Charles Baudelaire, the first verse of "*À une dame créole*," 1837, in Scarfe, *Baudelaire,* 1961, p.5

Europe was charmed by an Orient that shimmered with possibilities, that promised a sexual space, or voyage away from the self, an escape from the dictates of the bourgeois morality of the metropolis.

Rana Kabbani, *Europe's Myths of Orient*, 1986, p.67

Fantasizing the 'Orient' in Western Culture

Colonial rulers were perennially concerned about sedition and revolt, especially after the loss of Britain's American colonies, the revolutions in France and rebellions in the Caribbean (see Chapter 4). Linked to this was the recurrent spectre of disloyal Euro-Asians, admirers of Europe's political ideologies of liberty, equality and freedom of speech, but also closely tied to the local society into which they were born. As such, they were considered by the foreign rulers to be dangerous role models for the 'native' intelligentsia. But while Euro-Asian men were politically suspect as actual or potential subversive elements by the colonizers, the attitude towards Euro-Asian women differed significantly. They were part of the 'desire and denigration' syndrome of both Europeans and locals. The intellectual achievements of Euro-Asian women, however, and their pioneer contributions to women's emancipation, especially in the fields of education, employment and franchise rights, have only been recently recognized, with the increasing interest in women's hidden history.

Westerners were exposed to Orientalist fantasies through popular culture and fiction which promoted myths about the Euro-Asian woman. She was, to the European, partly 'one of us,' and at ease in male society, but also different and exotic, arousing both attraction and contempt. But ironically, the Euro-Asian woman also remained through the centuries an object of desire for the colonized Asians, who were not only attracted by her difference in appearance and culture, but also found her more accessible (as a 'daughter of the soil') than European women. The Euro-Asian woman in the 19th century was generally more literate and educated than other local women, but she was frequently demonized by nationalists on grounds of her non-traditional social practice. And by virtue of her European lifestyle, dress and customs she was considered to be 'one of them.'

Euro-Asians themselves were the creation of the West's intrusion into Asia and the resulting East/West confrontation and assimilation. These new communities of mixed European-Asian parentage, in all corners of the 'Orient,' arose because of the absence of European women, and the liaisons of European men with Asian women that took place over the centuries. This involved all classes of Europeans, awakened to the existence of another fascinating world of 'difference.' The writer Osbert Sitwell claimed that "a certain love of the exotic was, perhaps, innate in those of English blood," which was "a … counterpart indeed, of our proud insularity" (quoted in Buruma 2002b: 46); but the phenomenon was not only English, it was also European and included the whole 'western' world.

Interest in the 'difference' of the Orient arose from travellers' tales and historic dramas of medieval Europe, followed by colonial conquest, the expansion of trade, and subsequent curiosity about the lives and customs of peoples of the East, especially its women. Europe went through an 'Oriental Renaissance,' but, as Edward Said argued, the first Renaissance in Europe, based on a rediscovery of Greek culture, "was essentially assimilative in that it flattered Europe without disturbing Europe's self-affirming cultural centrality," whereas the 'Oriental Renaissance' was "a phenomenon of difference" (quoted in Schwab 1984: xviii). Buruma describes:

> a sensual, even erotic, element in encounters, imaginary or real – between East and West since the ancient Greeks. The European idea of the Orient as female, voluptuous, decadent, amoral – in short as dangerously seductive – long predates the European empires in India and South East Asia. (2002b: xiv)

Colonial conquest, however, meant going beyond romanticizing history and enjoying stories of the mythic 'Other' in the 'mysterious Orient.' It meant an actual physical presence of an imperial power, imposing its control on the land and inhabitants of the colonized territories. Along with the armies of conquest came the erudite Orientalist scholars, East India Company traders, colonial bureaucrats and Christian missionaries, as well as the archaeologists, writers, artists and poets, and all those who 'represented' the East to the West. They translated the old texts, mastered local languages and wrote about colonized societies (Said 1985). In the process, the West invented and constructed an 'Orient' of despots, 'noble savages' and exotic women – all being part of what V.G. Kiernan calls "Europe's collective day-dream of the Orient" (quoted in Kabbani 1986: 73). "Stick to the East... the public are orientalizing," said Lord Byron urging his friend Thomas Moore to write an 'Oriental' poem. Moore's *Lalla Rookh* (1817) made a fortune for the author, documenting, as Rana Kabbani critically notes, "the same Orient of the disordered imagination," namely "doe-eyed women... languishing with love... wicked men who kept them in captivity, rich banquets, gorgeous brocades... jewels, perfumes, music, dance and poetry" (1986: 33-34).

A great influence on the European public was Antoine Galland's translation in 1704 of *Les Mille et Une Nuits* (popularly known in English as *Arabian Nights),* which swept Europe in the succeeding centuries. By 1800 there were numerous translations, including many popular versions that fired the imagination of the general reader. The book "took Europe by storm," and became the chief inspiration for western romantic writing on the East, promoting racist and sexist stereotypes of the Orient, and "perpetuating the Victorian notion of promiscuous Eastern women" (Kabbani 1986: 22 & 51). Fatema Mernissi's challenging book, *Scheherazade Goes West,* discusses the impact of *Arabian Nights* on westerners, who were interested only in "adventure and sex," totally overlooking "the intellectual Scheherazade" and her political acumen (2001: 62-64). Claiming that in the Arab man's fantasy, a woman had to be intelligent, learned and skilled in using "The Mind as an Erotic Weapon" (as a chapter in her book is entitled), Mernissi deplores the West's depiction of Eastern women as compliant and silent, and argues that:

> Ironically, in the Orient – land of harems, polygamy, and veils – Muslim men have always fantasized, in both literature and painting about self-assertive, strong-minded, uncontrollable, and mobile women. (Mernissi 2001: 164)

European culture went through a phase that celebrated exoticism. Tzvetan Todorov, referring to the popular use of exoticism claims that "the best candidates for the role of exotic ideal are the peoples and cultures that are most remote from us." Exoticism thus involves "an act of self-criticism," and for the exoticist "the country with superior values is a country whose only relevant characteristic is that it is not my own" (Todorov 1993: 264-65). Similarly, 'primitivism' with its idealization of the 'Other' and "its obligatory counterpart, the critique of one's own society," was represented in many European narratives and political polemic writing between the 16th and 18th centuries (ibid: 270-1). Montesquieu's *Les Lettres Persanes* valorized Persian society in order to attack French political institutions; and for Diderot, the Tahitian 'savage' is 'innocent' 'mild' and 'happy' whereas 'civilized' people are 'corrupt' 'vile' and wretched' (ibid: 276). Ian Buruma also notes that, "Guiltless eroticism is associated with the noble savage, the beautiful, simple, human creature whose mind is uncluttered by moral and intellectual complexity" (Buruma 1996: xvi).

Catherine Stimpson has commented on race, gender and the "terrible romance with 'the primitive'," that "structured western culture

– its art, anthropology, literature and mythic narratives" (Torgovnick 1990: back cover). Numerous artists, poets, writers, composers of music and choreographers of dance were influenced by Orientalist romantic fantasies. Byron, for example, became the "poet of Oriental tales" (*The Giaour, The Death of Sardanapalus*) with their "outcasts and wanderers, pashas and potentates… kidnapped slave-girls and doomed lovers" (Eisler 1999: 756).* But this phenomenon was not without its detractors. The scholar Raymond Schwab, referring to the prevalent rage for things 'Oriental,' said:

> The strangeness it offered …produced an entire Orient of sofas and erotic and satanic masques that only too often encouraged literary history to frolic in shabby exoticism. (1984: 4)

Todorov describes such "shabby exoticism" that in 19th century France, "went by the name of Pierre Loti"; he invented the "novelist formula" of the adventures of a French naval officer with women in distant lands (Turkey, Tahiti and Japan) who were inevitably abandoned (Todorov 1993: 308-14). Political critics linked this exoticism to imperial conquest, and in a poem entitled "Pierre Loti" (1925), the Turkish poet, Nazim Hikmet sharply denounced Loti for promoting Orientalist mythologies of opium, submission and *kismet.*[2] Like Hikmet, Todorov dismisses one of Loti's books as "racist, imperialist, sexist, and sadistic," noting that this "did not prevent the Académie Française from honouring Loti" (ibid: 322). Significantly too, Loti deplored the political changes in

---

* Others who 'looked East' included Coleridge (*Kubla Khan*), Oscar Wilde (*Salome*), Racine (*Berenice*), Chateaubriand (*Description de l'Egypte*), Flaubert (*La Tentation de Saint Antoine*), Victor Hugo (*Les Orientales*), and Pierre Loti (*Madame Chrysanthème*). 'Oriental' themes in music and ballet ranged from Mozart (*The Abduction from the Seraglio*) and Haydn (*Armida*), Handel (*Queen of Sheba*) to Puccini (*Madame Butterfly*), Bizet (*Les Pêcheurs de Perles*), Verdi (*Aida*), Gilbert and Sullivan (*The Mikado*), and Sergei Diaghilev (*Scheherazade*). Stories and pantomimes such as *Aladdin* and *Alibaba and the Forty Thieves* also exposed western children to a make-believe Orient.

Turkey, which would ruin his fantasies. "From the point of the picturesque Turkey will lose much through the application of the new system ... Parliamentary Government will be the ruin of Turkey" (ibid: 336).

This genre of writing on the doomed love of a European man for a 'native' woman became popular. In these stories, such unequal relationships were short-term, inevitably ending in disaster, since the man's race, class, social status, education, and power allegedly made a long-term relationship impossible with a woman of 'colour' of a different social class, possessing neither education, power nor influence in society. In Kipling's stories, where liaisons occur across boundaries of class and race, the Indian woman belongs "to the lower social orders," and the end is tragic, the victim "callously abandoned" (Sen 2002: 178-80).

In Leonard Woolf's short story, "A Tale Told by Moonlight" (1924), remniscent of Pierre Loti, a British writer falls in love with Celestinahamy, a woman from a Colombo brothel: "He was a civilized cultivated intelligent nervous little man and she was an animal, dumb and stupid and beautiful." They live together, but his ardour palls and she commits suicide. He compares her love to that of "a slave, ... the love of dogs and... big-eyed women of the East" (Woolf 1962: 263). Similarly in Loti's novel *The Romance of a Spahi,* the woman is looked upon as "an inferior creature" manifesting "the devotion of a dog for its master" (Todorov 1993: 320). And in *Madame Chrysanthème*, Loti says that "it is a hundred to one she has no thoughts whatever" and she is "extremely decorative" while asleep "and like this, at least, she does not bore me" (ibid: 316). Mervyn de Silva, writing on Woolf's story, notes its "curious ambivalence" and "emotional disequilibrium," implying that Woolf is "uncertain of his attitude to the material he is handling" (de Silva, in Woolf 1961b: liv). Todorov comments that the local woman and the foreign country are both "desired, governed and abandoned":

> at no moment do we see the world through their eyes. The relation is one of domination, not reciprocity. The Other is desirable because it is feminine; but if the Other is objectified, this is woman's destiny. The man ... enjoys the same superiority with respect to women that the European enjoys with respect to other peoples. (Todorov 1993: 315)

The gaze on the Oriental woman, however, was not restricted to males. In 1763 Lady Mary Montagu in her *Letters* from Turkey gave vivid descriptions of women in a harem – a place not accessible to men travellers – and claimed more sexual liberation for harem women than was available to women in Europe. Writing on the power of the female gaze, Indira Ghosh discusses two feminist views about this issue. Some claim that Lady Montagu and other women travellers were "implicated in Orientalism as they too constitute the other into an object of knowledge," thereby contributing to the "unequal power/knowledge nexus." Others see a "cross-cultural women's solidarity at work... subverting patriarchal ... representations of the harem" (Ghosh 1998: 56). Ghosh argues that a "more ambivalent reading of female spectatorship in the harem is necessary." She cites the mid-19th century British traveller and writer Fanny Parks in *Wanderings of a Pilgrim* (1850) and notes her erotic and "voyeuristic pleasure in gazing at other women" in the *zenana*.[3]

Gayatri Spivak, however, has reminded us that one cannot read 19th century British literature "without remembering that imperialism, understood as England's social mission, was a crucial part of cultural representation of England to the English" (1999: 113). Edward Said also exposed European attitudes to Empire, to which "everyone, from the ordinary lower-middle-class jingoist to the highest of philosophers, seems to have subscribed" (2000: 30). One such notable example, Rudyard Kipling, according to Said, was:

> Supported by... the authorized monuments of nineteenth-century European culture, for whom the inferiority of non-white races, the necessity for them to be ruled by a superior civilization, and the absolute unchanging essence of Orientals, blacks, primitives, women were ...undebatable, unquestioned axioms... (Said 2000: 30)

Moreover, in the race theories of the period, as Said argues, it was held to be "scientifically proven that the white man stood at the pinnacle of development and civilization" – views evident in the works of Macaulay, Carlyle, Arnold, Ruskin and John Stuart Mill, "plus every major novelist, essayist, philosopher, and historian of note" who accepted, in Gobineau's phrase, "the inequality of the races" (ibid: 30). Robert Young has also observed that many novelists were "almost obsessive" about "the uncertain crossing and invasion of identities" of class, gender, culture and race, citing Emily Brontë, Graham Greene, Jean Rhys, and D.H. Lawrence. Claiming that such issues were "*the* dominant motif of much English fiction," he remarks that many 'colonial' novels and travel-writings were "concerned with …cross-cultural contact, interaction, an active desire, frequently sexual, for the other." But rather than this being a celebration of the 'Other,' he alleges that the attractions and fantasies of "colonial desire" were undoubtedly "complicit with colonialism itself" (Young 1995: 2-3). According to Thorburn, the colonial project also activated the public taste for "the exotic and adventurous," and Rudyard Kipling, Rider Haggard, Robert L. Stevenson and Joseph Conrad catered to this trend. Conrad's "romanticism, escapist tendencies, search for exoticism and indulgence in neo-primitivism" are seen in his novels set in Asia, notably *Almayer's Folly* (1895) and *An Outcaste of the Islands* (1896) (Thorburn 1974: xii & 24).

The visual impact of the Orient, with scenes of the sublime as well as portrayals of the 'exotic,' was recorded by 19th century artists. Eugene Delacroix's 1827 painting "*La mort de Sardanapale*" (an Assyrian king), influenced by Byron's poem, was Orientalist in content – with jewelled women, slaves and violent killings. After a visit to North Africa he did a series of paintings including the famous "*Femmes d'Alger*" in 1834 (Kabbani 1986: 75-76). Many modern artists of the early 20th century challenged orthodoxy and were inspired by Japanese, Chinese, and African art, but continued to represent the 'Orient' as a site of exoticism. They included, notably, Renoir, Gauguin and Matisse. As Mernissi critically comments, Matisse's Turkish harem "*Odalisque à la Culotte Rouge*" (1921) was painted in an era of modernization in the 1920s, when Turkish women were "throwing away their veils and flying planes." It seems strange, she says, that "an Oriental military man like Ataturk was dreaming of liberated women, while… Matisse, bred in a democracy, was dreaming of odalisques and an Islamic civilization that he confused with women's passivity" (Mernissi 2001: 199-200).

Kabbani also describes the eroticism of "*Le Bain Turc*"– a painting by Ingres consisting of 26 women in a Turkish bath – as "a collage of hackneyed themes of Eastern sensuality," which was "a parody of itself," more descriptive of Europe than the East. She argues that all this reflected the repressiveness of European bourgeois society, and that: "the gaze into the Orient had turned, as in a convex mirror, to reflect the Occident that had produced it" (Kabbani 1986: 84-85). Gauguin, who despised European bourgeois society, felt the 'lure of the exotic' and fled abroad to Tahiti and the Marquesa islands. Referring to his "duality of character," art critic Kunio Motoe quotes Gauguin (1888): "There are two people inside me, an Indian and a sensitive man. The sensitive man has disappeared. The Indian is marching ahead with bold strides" – a reference to Gauguin's own Peruvian ancestry:

> I am going soon to Tahiti... where the material necessities of life can be had without money... [In Europe] everything is putrefied... There under an eternal summer sky, ...the Tahitian has only to lift his hands to gather his food; and... he never works. ...happy inhabitants of the unknown paradise... To live, for them, is to sing and to love. (Motoe 1987 : 20 - 24)

This vision of a primitive "unrealistic view of paradise," Motoe notes, resulted from Gauguin's alienation from Europe (ibid: 24). The West was effete, Gauguin claimed: "The entire East ... is worth studying, and I feel I can revitalize myself out there ... even a Hercules can ... gain new vigor by touching the ground [of the Orient]" (Ives & Stein 2002:73). The escape was from bourgeois morality with its class and race biases.

"I will to Egypt... In the East my pleasure lies," says Anthony in Shakespeare's *Anthony and Cleopatra.* Subsequently this became a standard cliché of the literary and artistic world. "The invented Orient of the Western imagination," claimed Kabbani, provided a respite "from Victorian sexual repressiveness" (1986: 36). The woman of the 'Other,' from the North African harem to the Japanese geisha, also cut across class. Cleopatra, the Queen of Sheba, Salome and Scheherazade were all linked to palaces, while the fantasies also included 'noble savage women' and other Euro - Asian poor women who became part of an exploitative master-servant relationship. But as Buruma argues, the "sexual attraction of the East" was complex, because it included "guilt-free" eroticism available to those "burdened by Christian guilt," as well as the "power and domination" of the colonial encounter, which the French painters of Orientalist themes of harems and slave markets depicted. He notes that the image of the 'geisha girl' who is "submissive, pliable, … ready to indulge any fancy" dovetailed with the view of the East as a "passive, feminine receptacle of masculine Occidental vigour" (Buruma 2002b: xvi).

What is more, the repressive patriarchal society of the European bourgeoisie mirrored the accounts of harsh Arab patriarchy. Kabbani describes the role of Richard Burton, the 19th century British traveller and writer, in perpetuating the "fiction of an erotic East." For Burton, the Orient was: "An illicit space and its women convenient chattels who offered sexual gratification." But such sexism was part of "the articulation of racism"; women were considered inferior in patriarchal European society "just as other races were sub-groups within the colonial enterprise" (Kabbani 1986: 7).

Orientalist fantasies were also in evidence in films and songs. Elvis Presley in 1965 sang: "You'll feel like a Sheik, so rich and grand, with dancing girls at your command" (Mernissi 2001: 17). A persistent popular component of western films, Buruma notes, was the "erotic encounter of a young western man, …with a beautiful woman of a different culture or race" (*New York Review of Books*, August 2002a). Escapist Orientalist films included *Kismet* (1920), *The Sheik* (1921), versions of *The Thief of Baghdad* (1924 and 1940) and *Arabian Nights* (1942). Mernissi notes that in subsequent decades "the formula was reproduced" (2001: 72). Such films included *Cleopatra, Solomon and Sheba, South Pacific* and *Lost in a Harem,* and the popular 'Road' movies – *Road to Morocco, Road to Bali,* and roads to many other so-called exotic places of the world, where Bob Hope and Bing Crosby chase Dorothy Lamour, the 'native' beauty. Even today the film *Memoirs of a Geisha* (2005) perpetuates orientalist fantasies. In films such as *South Pacific* (1958) there was no question of the 'native' girl marrying the white soldier, but in *The Sleeping Dictionary* (2003) one sees a change–the white bureaucrat in Sarawak leaves his wife to run away with the tribal woman of mixed origin (played by a Mexican American, Jessica Alba) whom he had lived with in order to learn the language – hence "the sleeping dictionary."

The 'Half-Caste' Woman

All such fantasizing included Euro-Asian women. In addition to the 'dancing girls' and attractions of the imaginary 'Other,' a popular theme and an essential component of the Orientalist vision of the East was the attraction of the woman of mixed black/white origin. She became the western man's object of fantasy in European literature and poetry, while also being, in reality, a more accessible object of exploitation. During Portuguese, Dutch and British rule, when there were few European women in the colonies, the choice of partner or wife often extended to 'native' and 'mixed origin' women. John Comaroff has described the 'savage' as a fabrication of the 'Other,' a phantom conjured upon and "a product of European bricolage" (Torgovnik 1990: back cover). Similarly, the 'savage' woman was "conjured up" as an object of domination and desire. But if the 'savage' woman had European ancestry, turning her from '*café noir*' to '*café au lait*' ('black coffee' to 'coffee with milk'), she became an even greater attraction; and as Ronald Hyam claims, in colonial times "mixed-blood women were preferred from Montreal to Madras" (1990: 206).

Of particular relevance, in this context, is Charles Baudelaire (1821-67), whose interest in 'exotic' subjects arose from his journey to Mauritius in 1841. "Is it not pleasant," he wrote, "to sometimes look towards the distant Orient to see if we can yet discern the red glow of morning?" (in Scarfe 1961: 3).[4] Returning to Paris he met Jeanne Duval, a Caribbean woman of mixed origin – a '*mûlatresse*' (as the French called her), with whom he had an open liaison for a long period, and whom he taught to read. His attraction for the "dark enchantress" was expressed in his famous poems, "*A une dame créole*," "*A une malabaraise,*" and in the "*Jeanne Duval Cycle*" of poems – evoking sun-drenched, perfumed lands, palm trees and sultry evenings, and "*la splendeur orientale*" (ibid

1961: 107). Buruma says that climate was a part of the lure of the Orient, and for centuries the East "represented the sunny, pagan, hedonistic alternative to the cold, pinched and dreary climate of the Christian, especially Protestant, West" (Buruma 2002b: xv). He adds:

> It is easy to imagine the giddy sense of freedom felt by Englishmen from rainy Northern towns, or Americans from god-fearing Midwestern plains, when they came to Japan, or Thailand, or Ceylon, or wherever their idea of Arcadia happened to be. (ibid: xiv-v)

Kabbani also makes the distinction between Baudelaire's desire for the dark woman, Jeanne Duval, and his platonic love for the more erudite white woman, Madame Sabatier, who "reminded him of his mother":

> Duval was recreated in hot images; in her hair lurked 'la langoureuse Asie et la brulante Afrique'... Her dark body... disturbed as it attracted; it was a flower of evil, to be sampled away from the blooms of the bourgeois conservatory. (Kabbani 1986: 71)

What is more ironical is that the colonial bourgeoisie itself, exposed through education to European literature, poetry and art, often absorbed Europe's 'collective day-dream' of the 'Other' without critically questioning its political implications. Baudelaire's poems on '*dames créoles*' are celebrated without consideration of their somewhat dubious content. Thus, European racism vis-à-vis the colonies was internalized by the colonized themselves in the guise of 'high culture.'

The woman of mixed origin, however, was not always seen as the sexually available woman on the beach, or in the harem or Turkish bath, favoured by European painters and poets. There were also cases where Euro-Asian women were sought after as wives by high officials of the British East India Company; in 1825 a Kolkata English-language newspaper commented that "many elegant and accomplished half-Indian girls have been respectably married, whose blood may soon mingle with that of the proud nobility of England" (quoted in Stark 1934: 23). The same applied to the French. Apart from the famous cases of Josephine Beauharnais, Napoleon's 'quadroon' (quarter black) wife from Martinique who became the Empress, and Alexandre Dumas' grandmother of African origin, there was the earlier example of Joseph-Francois Dupleix, Governor-General of the French possessions in India. In 1741 he married Jeanne Albert who was born in 1706 in Pondicherry, south India, the daughter of Jacques Albert, surgeon of the French East India Company, and Rose de Castro, of Portuguese-Tamil origin. On her marriage Jeanne moved to Chandenagar, where she had a salon devoted to drama, music and literature. In 1741, when Dupleix was given a local title by the Moghul ruler of Delhi, his wife became 'Begum Jeanne,' "receiving equal honours with her illustrious husband" (Stark 1934: 21-22).

The myth of the Oriental princess also persisted. If a Euro-Asian woman had upper-class origins and the aura of a princess, she could be identified with the fairy-tale romances of the East that had so attracted the European public. One such interesting example is that of Katherine (Kitty) Aurora Kirkpatrick (1802-89), daughter of James Kirkpatrick (1764-1805), the British Resident to the Nizam's Court in Hyderabad, and Khair un-Nissa of a Hyderabadi noble family. The couple, says Dalrymple, "inhabited a world that was far more hybrid, and with far less clearly defined ethnic, national and religious borders" (2002: ix). Their daughter, was known as Noor un-Nisa (Sahib Begum) in India, and later as Kitty Kirkpatrick in Britain where she was educated as a child; she was "absorbed into the upper echelons of Victorian literary society, fascinating her cousin's tutor, the young Thomas Carlyle" (ibid: xxxix).

Kitty Kirkpatrick personified the acceptable, rich Euro-Asian woman on two counts – her "quite remarkable beauty (and)... her father's generous legacy"; Carlyle in his *Reminiscences* described Kitty as "strangely complexioned... with soft brown eyes and floods of bronze-red hair" and refers to her "foreign bit of magnificence and kindly splendour" (quoted in Dalrymple 2002: 475). He calls her mother, a "Hindoo Princess" whom her "father fought... and scaled walls for" (ibid: 477); "...an Indian *romance*, mother a sublime *Begum*, father... [an] English official, ...withdrawn in their own private paradise, a romance famous in the East" (ibid: 475). But as Dalrymple comments, Kitty's mother was neither 'Hindoo' nor a princess, but the British, being often impressed by Indian titles, were awed by Kitty's reputed royal connection, which "seems to have done as much as her relations, beauty and fortune to ease her passage in English society" (ibid: 478 n).

Thomas Carlyle had met Kitty when he was poor – an "unknown and struggling Scottish writer" – and ironically, despite Kitty's Indian origins, "marriage to Carlyle was regarded as inappropriate for Kitty, due to the perceived disparity in class and status between the two" (ibid: 475 & 478). But nevertheless, she came into "dazzling focus" in Thomas Carlyle's novel *Sartor Resartus* as the heroine Blumine, described as having "a many tinted radiant aurora... the fairest of the Orient light-bringers" (ibid: xxxix). This novel, popular in Sri Lanka among the Euro-Asians of the Young Ceylon group, was referred to as one of Charles Lorenz's "treasured possessions" (Roberts et al. 1989: 71). Kitty Kirkpatrick married Captain James Winslowe Phillips in 1829, had four children, and lived in Torquay until her death in 1889. Her English relations belonged to prominent families, and included her cousins – Julia Kirkpatrick who married Edward Strachey, grandfather of Lytton Strachey, the writer; and Isabella Kirkpatrick, who married Charles Buller, a Member of Parliament (Dalrymple 2000).

The Euro-Asian Image

But upper-class social attitudes hardened; racist theories flourished, and strict divisions between colonizer and colonized became official policy. Buruma describes the withering away of "the hedonism of British libertines in 18th century India." Even the images changed: "the West was virile, dynamic, expansive, disciplined, and the East was indolent, decadent, pleasure-loving, passive" (Buruma 2002: xix). Official disapproval of mixed liaisons and marriages affected only government servants, but among other Europeans such alliances continued to prevail.

By the late 19th century, with the growth of racism and identity consciousness among the British, the person of mixed origin was persistently portrayed in a negative way in the media and literature: Euro-Asian men as being unreliable, subversive and politically dangerous; and the women as having no culture or tradition, and certainly no morality.

There was often a difference between the portrayal of Euro-Asian men and women. One prejudice against Euro-Asian men was the fear that they might marry European women. As Hawes wrote: "The Eurasian daughter of a military officer might well marry back into her 'class' [but] ...young educated Eurasian men were not welcome at the public dances where many of their sisters met British husbands." And these sisters, it was said, "conscious of their superior prospects, look down upon their male relatives with an undisguised disdain" (Hawes 1996: 19).

In patriarchal and patrilineal society where men carry the family line and name, they may more safely marry 'out,' of class, caste and race. But women, as carriers of culture but not the family name, were seen as needing protection from being 'stolen' by other males. And of course, extramarital liaisons might be tolerated in men but were taboo for women. Thus, although white men might have liaisons with mixed-race women, the same freedom was certainly not applicable to white women and Euro-Asian men. The comments of British lawyer H.C. Sirr in 1850 also made the invidious distinction: the male "half castes" of Sri Lanka had features that were "ill formed... being as deficient in corporeal attractions as they are destitute of moral rectitude and probity," while the "females... in early life are remarkable for their beauty" (quoted in Roberts et al. 1989: 148). In literature, too, while the Euro-Asian woman is usually portrayed as attractive, Euro-Asian men were often described as lacking charm. In E.M. Forster's *A Passage to India* (1924), Harris, the Euro-Asian driver of the Nawab of Bahadur, tries "to look and feel like a European," and is "inclined to be flustered":

> He still wore a topi, despite the darkness, and his face, to which the Ruling Race had contributed little beyond bad teeth, peered out pathetically, and seemed to say, '... Don't worry me so, you blacks and whites. Here I am, stuck in damn India same as you.' (Forster 1979: 88-89)

Forster also speculates on the dilemma of the Anglo-Indian, as portrayed by Harris:

> When English and Indians were both present, he grew self-conscious, because he did not know to whom he belonged. For a little he was vexed by opposite currents in his blood, then they blended, and he belonged to no one but himself. (ibid: 88-89)

Other writers have also stereotyped the Euro-Asian male as unattractive. A Romanian historian of comparative religion, Mircea Eliade, who lived in India in the late 1920s, had a brief affair with his Indian guru's daughter Maitreyi, and fictionalized the episode in a novel, – *Bengal Nights*. He also wrote an autobiography, in which the Indian and Euro-Asian males, in Buruma's words, "behave according to type." Euro-Asians are depicted "living in their seedy boarding houses, are all oversexed, vulgar and racist... idiots and fanatics" (Buruma 2002b: 102).

The idea also persisted that the mixing of races was conducive to women's immorality. As a result, the term 'Eurasian' fell out of favour with Indians of mixed origin since it was used negatively. For example, Noel Coward's song "Half-Caste Woman" (written in 1931) led to a protest by the Anglo-Indian writer Cedric Dover (1937: 14) about its "seductive half-caste harlots," who sang:

> Drink a bit, laugh a bit, love a bit more,
> I can supply your need,
> Drink a bit, chaff a bit, what's it all for?
> That's my Eurasian creed.
> (Coward 1983: 107)

The stereotypes have not changed much seventy years later. In John Le Carré's *The Constant Gardener,* Ghita Pearson, a Euro-Asian officer at the British Embassy in Kenya, is portrayed as devious and unpredictable. "Ghita's enigmatic eyes fixed on him... admiring or hating... were her oblique glances flirtatious or disdainful? With Eurasian beauties how did you tell?" (Le Carré 2001: 341). The uncertainty was compounded by the representation that Ghita as one of the "English-educated Brahmin's daughters who talk like us and dress like dervishes." Le Carré also speculates about Ghita:

> She had agonized about injuries, real and imagined, that she had endured every day for being Anglo-Indian. She saw herself as... a half black girl in search of God, half white woman superior to lesser breeds without the law. Waking and sleeping, she had demanded to know where she belonged in a white man's world. (ibid: 338)

In the English-language 'Indian' novels of the colonial period, the depiction of the Euro-Asian woman inevitably conformed to racist stereotypes. Flora Annie Steel, in *Miss Stuart's Legacy* (1893), contrasts the English 'heroine' to her stepsisters who are Euro-Asian: "Inscribing the myth of the Euro-Asian's inheriting the worst qualities of both races, the text shows the racially mixed girls displaying 'Anglo-Indian' idleness, frivolity and love of pleasure" (Sen 2000: 87). The Euro-Asian woman in such novels, who is "deceptively European in her appearance," really represents "the black 'face' behind a near-white 'mask' whose marriage to a white man is seen as a threat to... imperial and ethnic identity." As Indrani Sen writes, the fictional Euro-Asian is a "disturbing figure" who draws the white man into a sensuous ambiance:

> Clearly, anxieties about her subversive sexuality underlie the fictional stereotype of the sensuous/beautiful Eurasian, who is passionate and shiftless beneath the white 'mask.' (Sen 2002: 88)

Mimi Chan, in her book *Through Western Eyes: Images of Chinese Women* (1989), has stated that Euro-Asian themes abound in many of the novels and stories written in English but situated in China and especially in Hong Kong. The mixed marriages and love affairs of Chinese women and European men became a part of this genre of literature with its star-crossed lovers and 'white man – Chinese whore' theme, such as *The World of Suzy Wong* by Richard Mason (1959) and in some of Somerset Maugham's stories set in the Far East. But there were other stereotypes in the "Hong Kong novels" where Euro-Asian women figure, "as secretaries, mostly girl-Fridays, competent and capable." But even in such instances, we see a reference in *The World of Suzy Wong* to Miss Ruggeroni, the assistant to the British Consul in Macau, who has "the dreamy yearning voice of a Eurasian who belongs nowhere." In

James Clavell's *Noble House* (1981), the Portuguese-Chinese Olanda Ramos is "the Oriental sulky siren stereotype" (Chan 1989: 226-27).

The portrayal of the Euro-Asian woman in films has also been biased and problematic. White actresses often acted the part of Euro-Asians, while some Euro-Asian actresses ('passing' for white) became 'stars' in their roles as British or American white women. The Euro-Asian woman was mostly portrayed as a temptress or victim who could never marry the white hero, and whose liaison inevitably came to a sad end through separation or death. In the Hollywood racist code of ethics of the time, 'miscegenation' was taboo, biracial liaisons never had a happy ending, and stories with women of mixed origin became merely excuses for exoticism. John Masters' novel *Bhowani Junction* (1956) was filmed with Ava Gardner as an Anglo-Indian, who moves from a romance with a Sikh, to a fling with a British soldier, only to end up with an Anglo-Indian of her own class and railway background. The film was denounced by "responsible" Anglo-Indians as "little more than pornography" (Gaikwad 1967: 7-8).

There were two world-renowned actors – Merle Oberon and Vivien Leigh – who never revealed their Indian connection. Merle Oberon (1911-79), wife of Sir Alexander Korda, claimed to be from Tasmania. Fearing stigma, she never spoke of her origins, and during her lifetime few knew that she was an Anglo-Indian of Irish origin from Kolkata named Estelle Merle O' Brien Thompson, who had worked as a film extra in London calling herself Queenie O'Brien. Changing her name to Merle Oberon, she shot to fame for her portrayals of British women – Anne Boleyn in *The Private Life of Henry VIII* (1933), Catherine in Emily Brontë's *Wuthering Heights* (1939), and an upper-class socialite woman (Lesley) in *The Divorce of Lady X* (1938). Vivien Leigh (1913-67) was born in Darjeeling, India, and educated in England. Her father Ernest Hartley was from Yorkshire, and her mother Gertrude Yackjee, born in 1888 in Darjeeling, was of Indian or Anglo-Indian origin. Vivien Leigh also acted as a typically English woman in film roles such as Emma in *Lady Hamilton* (1941). She achieved world-fame and Oscars for her roles as white American Southern women in *Gone with the Wind* (1939) and *A Streetcar Named Desire* (1951). Her mixed origin was appropriate, however, for her portrayals of Cleopatra in the film of Bernard Shaw's *Caesar and Cleopatra* (1945) and in 1951 in the London theatre productions of both Shaw's *Caesar and* Cleopatra and Shakespeare's *Anthony and Cleopatra,* on alternate days.

But there were also some rare cases of denial by Anglo-Indians who preferred to be known as Indian. An interesting example was the worldwide publicity that surrounded Marlon Brando's short-lived first marriage to Anna Kashfi, who portrayed 'exotic' women in films. She 'passed' as 'pure' Indian, but her original name was Joan O'Callaghan, of an Anglo-Indian family that had left India to settle in Cardiff, Wales. She did not reveal her family history but asserted an Indian identity and wore a sari at her marriage.

Leonard Woolf and Pablo Neruda among Euro-Asians

Casual sexual encounters between Euro-Asian or other local women and foreign men temporarily resident in Sri Lanka were frequent, including, notably, Leonard Woolf and Pablo Neruda. Both achieved fame in later years, Woolf as a political writer, publisher and husband of Virginia Woolf, and Neruda as a left-wing poet who won the Nobel prize in 1971. Woolf, a government servant in Jaffna in 1905, in his autobiography refers to a young Burgher woman as "a notorious Jaffna character – a loose liver as they said... being kept by a Tamil lawyer." Woolf, who "spent the night" with the woman, was later amused to hear that the Tamil lawyer had brought a case against her for abuse and indecent language, alleging that "she had come to his house, where he lived respectably with his wife and family, and... shouted 'come out, you son of a whore!'" The judge (Woolf's colleague Dutton) fined her Rs 10, but "regretting to have to convict a pure young girl," paid the fine himself. The story, says Woolf, gave the people of Jaffna, "immense pleasure and amusement," but no doubt also amused Woolf, who regarded the Burgher woman as "notorious" (1961: 68). And in his private correspondence with his university friend, Lytton Strachey, Woolf refers to spending time with a "half-caste whore" (in Spott 1989: 102), providing an interesting example of an enlightened bureaucrat in a colonial context indulging in 'desire and denigration.'

Woolf was also a judge in a paternity cases involving a local woman in Hambantota and a Boer from South Africa named Henry Engelbrecht. He had been interned in Sri Lanka during the Boer War, and choosing to stay on in the island, was given the post of Game Sanctuary Ranger in Hambantota. As the Assistant Government Agent and Police Magistrate in this district, Woolf had learnt his "shooting and tracking" from Engelbrecht; the latter (according to Woolf) "behaved to the Sinhalese as the Boers behave to the Negroes in Africa" (1961: 202). Woolf had to adjudicate in a case brought by "a good-looking" Sinhalese woman who had been living with Engelbrecht. The woman held up a baby in court to prove that it was "a white baby." Woolf made a maintenance order, and the tension subsided among the large crowd of locals who had packed the court (ibid: 203). Such "white babies" were absorbed into the local community and enumerated in the Census as belonging to their mothers' ethnic group. Engelbrecht, who died in 1928, had eight children by the Sinhalese woman (C. Ondaatje 2005: 222-25) Two of their grandchildren, who still live in Hambantota, have been photographed by Christopher Ondaatje. (See page 280a).

The memoirs of Chile's most celebrated poet, Pablo Neruda (1904-73), who in the late 1920s and early 1930s was the consul for his country in Myanmar, Sri Lanka and Java, describes his isolated life in a suburb of Colombo and his encounters with 'native' women. He discusses the desire and ambivalence felt by westerners for women of a different class and race. In Myanmar in 1928, he claims that he "lost his heart" to a woman who led a 'double' life. She was:

> a native girl a kind of Burmese panther [who] in the street dressed like an Englishwoman and used the name Josie Bliss, but in the privacy of her home, which I soon shared, shed those clothes and that name to wear her dazzling sarong and her secret Burmese name. (Neruda 1978: 86-87)

When Neruda left, the abandoned Josie Bliss followed him to Colombo, "pitched camp" in front of his house in Wellawatte, bringing with her a sack of rice, "our favourite Paul Robeson records and a long rolled-up mat, threatening to burn down the house, and attacking a sweet Eurasian girl who had come to pay a call." All this attracted the attention of the police, and "the love-smitten terrorist," as Neruda called her, decided to leave (ibid: 96).

Neruda recalls other encounters with "girls of various colorings" in Colombo. One of them, named Patsy, showed up frequently with some of her friends – "dusky and golden, girls of Boer, English, Dravidian blood. They went to bed with me sportingly, asking for nothing in return." One of these women related her visits to "chummeries," which were "the bungalows where young Englishmen, clerks in shops or firms, lived together to save money." Neruda asserts that she was "not a prostitute" but "just another product of colonialism, a candid and generous fruit off its tree" (ibid: 99). His 'encounters' were not only with Euro-Asians, but also included a Tamil woman cleaner (in his house), whom he compares to "one of the thousand-year-old sculptures" from South India. "It was the coming together of a man and a statue," Neruda writes, adding that "she was completely unresponsive" and was "right to despise me" (ibid: 100). Neruda does not refer to any other women in Sri Lanka in his memoirs, although by the early 1930s women had achieved franchise rights and there were many women professionals.

Euro-Asian Self-portrayals

One of the first widely popular cases of Euro-Asian women writing of their own experiences was Han Suyin, a medical doctor, whose father was Chinese, and mother Belgian. She fictionalized her own story of the 1950s in *Love is a Many-Splendoured Thing*, (1955) which was also filmed with Jennifer Jones in the lead role. The story concerned a woman of Chinese-European origin in Hong Kong, who has an affair with a European journalist who dies in the Korean War. As a controversial writer, Han Suyin brought issues concerning Euro-Asian women from their own marginalized point of view, into the mainstream. She was often preoccupied with the 'dilemma' of mixed parentage and wrote of her return from Europe to China. "Maybe you cannot live *in* China," she ruminates, "maybe you are only a Eurasian, a dirty half-caste, as some people say, but you cannot live *without* China for without China you die" (Han 1972: 360).

Hari Kunzru, a writer of Indian and British parentage, in his first novel *The Impressionist* (2002), portrays Pran Nath Razdan, the son of Ronald Forrester, a British official, and Amita, a Kashmiri Brahmin. Pran Nath muses on the confusion of his origins, but distances himself from Anglo-Indians:

> What is the feeling of not being who you think you are?... If his father was the strange Englishman ... then logically he is half-and-half, a blackie-white. But he feels nothing in common with those people. They hate Indians. They hate him, that is for certain. He does not think of England as his home. Home is here. (Kunzru 2002: 41-42)

According to Ranjana Kaul, recent books by Anglo-Indians have contested the stereotypes. These writers include Hugh and Colleen Gantzer, whose novel *The Year Before Sunset* (2005) focuses on class and 'caste' in the community and "portrays a section of Anglo-Indian society rarely encountered in works written by outsiders" (Kaul 2005: 37). Kaul argues that earlier books by outsiders, from the colonial period onwards, have led to "the proliferation of stereotypical images" of Anglo-Indians often based "on the lowest socio-economic strata" of the community, thereby adding to their negative stereotype (ibid). In fact Penny, the Anglo-Indian in the Gantzers' novel, parodies 'railway' life:

> I have to be a railway girl, living in a railway colony, bringing up my brood of railway kids. And the bright boys might become officers, the less bright will start by firing shunters. The bright girls will become nurses in railway hospitals or stenos in railway offices and our conversation [about trains] will be full of 9- up and 10- down. (Gantzer & Gantzer 2005: 178)

A Sri Lankan Burgher, Carl Muller, in *The Jam Fruit* Tree (1993), has a highly entertaining account of the lives of a Burgher 'railway' family. On the cover of his book, the Burghers are called "a handsome and guileless people, (who) have always lived it up, forever willing to 'put a party.'" Neluka Silva, however, has critiqued Muller's "essentialist presuppositions about the Burghers" and the ideological assumption that Burghers, "particularly the women, are preoccupied with sex"(2002: 119). Muller, however, has dismissed this criticism.

The Asian Gaze on Euro-Asians

The Indonesian writer Pramoedya Ananta Toer, in his political novel *This Earth of Mankind*, sympathetically uses the story of a Euro-Asian woman, Annelies Meleema, to highlight the complexities of the East-West confrontation in colonial times. Annelies symbolizes both the Dutch world of her father and the Javanese society of her powerful mother, and enables her westernized Javanese lover Minke to come to terms with the reality of these double influences, giving him the strength to relate to the reality of Indonesia.

In popular novels in Sri Lanka in the past, and in Sinhala films and television dramas of recent years, women of mixed ancestry were inevitably portrayed as fun-loving and promiscuous, lacking 'purity' in origin and being 'impure' in behaviour. As Neluka Silva (2002: 104) writes, their "Westernized lifestyle" was constructed as a "sign of sexual permissiveness," and "the mantle of immorality" was unfairly placed on the Burgher woman, who was "conspicuously positioned as the 'siren' who exploited her sexuality for social gain."

The Sinhala novelist Piyadasa Sirisena (1875-1946), notes Michael Roberts, claimed to protect "the boundaries of the Sinhala race" from pollution and wrote "moralistic melodramas" emphasizing 'Aryan' virtues and the dangers of Sinhala Buddhists mixing with people of other races and religions. Sirisena extended the critique to Sinhala Christians and westernized Sinhala-Buddhists, and emphasized "the greatness and purity of Sinhala civilization in the past." Harsh diatribes on "the corrupting influence" of the 'hybrid' Burghers, "especially Burgher women was standard fare in Sirisena's novels" (Roberts et al. 1989: 11). It corresponded to what Mary Douglas calls certain peoples' "belief in horrible disasters which overtake those who inadvertently cross some forbidden line or develop some impure condition" (1989: 1). For example, in Sirisena's *Apata Veçça Dé* (What Befell Us), written in 1909, the son of a village family goes to the city, becomes westernized and marries a Burgher, which results in the mother's illness and death. The father castigates his son and threatens to disinherit him, denouncing his marriage as an "act of buffoonery," adding significanatly that he might have even accepted a marriage with a Sinhala girl of 'low' caste, to the "despicable... act... of abandoning religion and race by marrying a Burgher" (Roberts et al. 1989: 15).

Such attitudes (which still prevail) are also reflected in Sinhala films. Analysing "the good woman/bad woman" dichotomy of some Sinhala films of the 1990s, Malathi de Alwis shows how rural women are portrayed "in heroic terms" – in contrast to the "urban, 'westernized' woman... positioned as her degenerate other." The latter includes "the 'half-breed' Sinhalese, or the Burgher Christian woman," who is cast as a *'femme fatale'* (*Pravada* 1992, Vol. 1, No. 4).

In India, negative stereotypes of Anglo-Indians were reinforced by the film industry, where Anglo-Indian actresses were confined to the role of performers in night clubs and bars. They included the dancers Cuckoo, and Mary Evans, called Nadia Wadia after her marriage to the film-maker Homi Wadia. But the most captivating and famous was 'Helen' who appeared in around 700 films as the night-club dancer and gangster's girl friend. She was Helen Richardson, born in 1938 in Burma, who claimed French, Burmese and Spanish ancestry, but was considered to be an Anglo-Indian Christian. "If you wanted a vamp, it would be best to draw her from that degenerate community and to also portray her ... as belonging to that community," writes her biographer Jerry Pinto. It would then be "natural" for her:

> To sing and dance for men, to be part of a gang, to wave a gun, to show a bit of body, to coquette and pirouette without... endangering the patriarchal notions of virginity as an attribute of the Indian woman. (Pinto 2006: 53-54)

Helen was thus "the perfect outsider for whom the rules did not have to apply"; and in films was 'Miss Kitty,' 'Lilly,' 'Rosie' or 'Dolly' (ibid: 49). The vamp, asserts Pinto, could not be a Hindu:

> we needed an other around which to build fantasies and Helen was available, a white woman in a brown world, a woman who could produce sensuality out of golden cages, flamingos, an excess of blue eye shadow and oversize orange earrings. (ibid: 46 & 10)

Another example is given by a contemporary writer from Singapore, Catherine Lim, who in a short story called "Kenneth Jerome Rozario" stereotypes Singapore Eurasians. The young man Rozario is a dropout from high school, from a troubled background, living with his aunt: "his father is... in Brunei and his mother ran off with an European." His teachers are unsympathetic and disparage Eurasians; one teacher, Mrs Chee, has a "favourite theory" that Eurasians are not only immoral but also "extravagant and pleasure loving and lazy"; and another observed that "the Eurasian girls in her class were bold and cheap in their behaviour" (Lim 1980: 64). When a proposal was made to use Lim's book as a text in schools, Singapore Eurasians protested on the ground that this story maligned the community (Braga-Blake 1992: 20).

Recent writings in India have portrayed the tensions in Euro-Asian society in a more sympathetic light, highlighting certain specific aspects of class and 'caste.' A new novel on Anglo-Indians, *Chinnery's Hotel* (2004) by Jayasinh Birejepatil, deals with the "dilemma of inhabiting two disparate worlds." The chief character Grace Chinnery, a British woman who had lived in India, dislikes Anglo-Indians, for having absorbed "the unconscious elitism of the British ruling class" along with "arcane notions of caste purity" also prevalent in the Indian attitude to persons of mixed origin (Kaul 2005: 36). Ranjana Kaul, reviewing this book, remarks that, "while upper-class Anglos... are acceptable... the vast majority are seen to be tainted and unworthy because of their economic debility" and "the low- caste blood on the Indian side of the family" (ibid: 36).

Salman Rushdie also tries to capture the 'dilemma' of hybridity in his novel *The Ground Beneath Her Feet*, which is concerned with "the blurring of every frontier: colour, death, East and West, imagination and reality" (Ruth Padel in *The Independent*, quoted in Rushdie 2000). This protagonist Vina Apsara is of mixed origin – born in Virginia to a Greek American named Helen and an Indian lawyer, Shetty. Her childhood was in the USA and Mumbai, and her fame as a rock singer was achieved in London and New York. Perhaps Rushdie, too, conforms to the stereotype of the Euro-Asian when he writes:

> For Vina Apsara, the right place was always the one she wasn't in. Always in the wrong place, in a condition of perpetual loss, she could unaccountably take flight and disappear; and then discover that the new place she'd reached was just as wrong as the place she'd left. (Rushdie 2000: 163)

To conclude, Euro-Asian women, often demonized in nationalist and popular Asian writing and in films, were fantasized about in European literature as desirable because of their exotic 'difference' and their imagined subservience. The reality, however, was for a long time 'erased' from history. Among Euro-Asian women of India and Sri Lanka was also the 'New Woman' of the epoch – the pioneer of women's emancipation, leading the vanguard on women's issues, ranging from education and employment to political rights – and with her own utopian vision of a better future for women. Her very 'hybridity,' regarded as 'polluting,' was on the contrary her best asset, as discussed in the next chapter.

Notes

1. *Au pays parfumé que le soleil caresse,*
   J'ai connu, sous un dais d'arbres tout empourprés
   Et de palmiers d'où il pleut sur les yeux la paresse,
   Une dame créole aux charmes ignorés (Scarfe 1961:5)
2. Opium!
   Submission!
   Kismet! ...
   This is the Orient the French poet sees.
   the Orient of those books
   that come out from the press
   at the rate of a million a minute
   But yesterday,
   today or tomorrow
   an Orient like this
   never existed
   and never will
   Orient has had enough!...
   We're sick of it, sick!
   But you, as a French officer, Loti...
   you are no better than a charlatan...
   (translated excerpts of Nazim Hikmet from Baybar 1967: 19-20)
3. Parks writes with emotion on such an Indian woman, named Mulka:
   How beautiful she looked! Her animated countenance was constantly varying, and her dark eyes struck fire... I felt no surprise when I remembered the wondrous tales told by the men of the beauty of an Eastern woman... I had heard of Mulka's beauty... as the loveliest creature in existence.
   (quoted in Ghosh 1998: 58)
4. *N'est-ce pas qu'il est doux...*
   De chercher quelque fois à l'Orient lointain
   Si nous voyons encor les rougeurs du matin...
   (Scarfe 1961: 3)

10

THE EURO-ASIAN 'NEW WOMAN'

> Middle class Burghers were conscious, by virtue of their European origin… of liberalism. …Local traditions, customs and feudal social structures were not restraints on their lives… This liberal tradition … extended to the Burgher women who found it easier to break with accepted practice and emerge as the 'new women' of their time…
>
> Deloraine Brohier, *Dr Alice de Boer and some Pioneer Burgher Women Doctors,* 1994 p.19

Feminist Consciousness among Euro-Asians

The emergence of the 'New Woman' both in the West and East, including parts of the colonial world, was one of the startling challenges to patriarchy of the late 19th and early 20th centuries. In Asia, she was the educated, bourgeois woman who was in the process of liberating herself from patriarchal domination, not only by joining women's associations, publishing feminist journals and demanding gender equality in terms of social and political rights, but also by asserting her personal independence and sexuality (Jayawardena 1986: 12-13).

Already by the late 18th century, a group of women intellectuals – known as 'Blue Stockings' – had made their mark in Britain; and one of the thinkers of the 'Enlightenment,' Mary Wollstonecraft challenged prevailing patriarchal beliefs with her pathbreaking work *The Vindication of the Rights of Women* (1792), in response to the famous French "Declaration of the Rights of Man" (1791). Not surprisingly, she was denounced by many male contemporaries, including the writer Horace

Walpole, who called her a "hyena in petticoats." To add to the scandal, Wollstonecraft's husband William Godwin, a political radical, had denounced marriage as "the most odious of all monopolies" (Jayawardena 1981: 23). In France, a debate on women ('*querelle des femmes*') had existed from the 15th century onwards. Christine de Pisan (1363-1431), a learned woman at the French court, wrote *Le Livre de la Cité de Dames* advocating equal education for women. Molière ridiculed the phenomenon of women intellectuals in his play *Les Femmes Savantes* (1672). By 1791 the issue of equal rights had arisen, and Olympe de Gouge caused a stir with her *Declaration of the Rights of Women* (ibid: 1-20).

With the spread of liberalism and movements for democratic rights in the 19th century, the demands of western women for education, employment, franchise rights and birth control increased. This contrast between ideas of bourgeois respectability and feminism was expressed by the French painter Paul Gauguin (who, as noted previously, was the epitome of South Sea escapism). His grandmother, ironically, was Flora Tristan, the famous socialist and feminist of the 1830s and 1840s. "She was a strange woman," Gauguin wrote, "a socialist, a blue-stocking, an anarchist," adding that "perhaps she could not even cook" (quoted in Mies 1981: 60). In this context one can speculate whether, in Europe, where women's emancipation was a topic of debate and a site of agitation, some male reaction and backlash against these trends was reinforced by the fantasy of other 'Oriental' cultures – where women were allegedly not concerned about equality, and the 'noble savage' woman's mind was "*uncluttered by moral and intellectual complexity*" (Buruma 2002b: xvi, emphasis added).

The Sri Lankan Debate on Women

In the late 19th and early 20th centuries, when ideas about women's rights were debated, the concept of the 'New Woman' was discussed in Asia and the Middle East (Jayawardena 1986: 13). In South Asia, Euro-Asian women were at the forefront of these movements. Far from being merely the '*dames créoles*' of dubious morality, as represented in European culture, they were among the first women to make a historic breakthrough, confronting traditional attitudes and patriarchal practices. The crucial advance, as in many countries, was first in education, and subsequently employment outside the home.

Many Euro-Asian women and men in Asia expressed modernist and liberal views on key issues of female emancipation and liberation. In Europe and the USA, questions of women's status had been raised frequently in the mid-19th century, and Indian and Sri Lankan readers of British journals and the local press were aware of such debates. The important controversies in Britain relating to women's higher education and political rights, resulted in the establishment of two women's colleges in Cambridge – Girton (1869) and Newnham (1873) – and the London School of Medicine for Women in 1874. The National Women's Suffrage Society in Britain, by 1868, had launched the long, militant struggle for female franchise.

In India and Sri Lanka the initial challenge to patriarchal structures came from the pioneer women teachers, nurses and doctors who were Euro-Asians (Anglo-Indians, Burghers and Eurasians). They paved the way for women of other communities to excel in education and obtain employment. In Sri Lanka, Euro-Asian men, the most Anglicized and educated section of the local bourgeoisie, expressed their views on women's social status in the columns of *Young Ceylon* in the 1850s. While some articles, in the romantic tradition, praised women for their warmth and beauty, Frederick Nell took a remarkably more advanced attitude, contrasting the 'angel in the home' syndrome, to women's "intellectual qualities":

> It is not the mere *graces physiques,* which constitutes the chief charm of woman; it is the intelligence with which she is gifted that ennobles the mind, which lends such an additional attraction to personal charms and which survives in pristine excellence when all else perishes. (Roberts et al. 1989: 73)

Nell argued that, in addition, the "perfect woman" required "the proper and judicious cultivation" of *moral* powers. In short, the "cultured

Gentleman" needed a "perfect woman" by his side, for woman epitomized "moral feelings" (ibid: 73-74). It was, perhaps, the beginning of a consciousness in Sri Lanka of a woman's capacity to play an important role in society. In 1867, as Queen's Advocate, Frederick Nell, stressing the importance of women's education, welcomed the appointment of a school mistress in the provincial town of Kurunegala, resulting in a number of girls being educated "to read and write English." This, he claimed, would also be "of very great help in the education of the male population" (*Sessional Paper VIII of 1867*: 118).

By the mid-19th century, the status of women was frequently debated. A member of the local intelligentsia (writing as Henry Candidus), in a dialogue, revealed this preoccupation, and remarked critically on foreign influences on local domestic life:

> Is it not a fact that the more we strive to *imitate these foreigners*, the more we are *dissatisfied with Our Domesticoe res*?...Has not our English education detached our thoughts and feelings from the *sacred Altar of home*?...Has it not, by destroying all sympathy with our own and attaching us to recent importations placed us in a false position? (Roberts et al. 1989: 73, emphasis in the original)

While Candidus reflected the familiar conservative view on women, there were also signs of early feminist consciousness among Euro-Asian males, one remarkable example being young Alfred Drieberg, son of John Drieberg and Harriet Lorenz, the sister of Charles Lorenz. While at school in Britain in 1856 (before going to Cambridge), Alfred, hearing that his father might also send his sisters Fanny and Agnes abroad for education, eagerly supported the idea, referring to "the good which would result from the foreign education they would get there and various other benefits." He boldly stated: "I don't think it right that *boys alone should be sent here from Ceylon – Why not girls*?" – making him, as Roberts comments, "ahead of his parents and ahead of his time" (ibid: 62, emphasis added). Perhaps his views were also influenced by his uncle and aunt Charles and Eleanor Lorenz, and her brother Fredrick Nell.

The journal *Young Ceylon,* started by Lorenz and others, frequently wrote on women's role in society. In 1850 an article on

European "Female Writers" stressed the need for "the cultivation of the intellect" in local young women as "expedient" and "a matter of obvious duty." The "duty" being one owed to educated men. "We hope," said the writer:

> The thirst for knowledge and the desire for improvement, happily so active in the breasts of our young men, may be communicated to our young women; and that a cultivated mind may at no very distant period prove to be an ordinary and distinguished feature... of the ladies of Ceylon. (*Young Ceylon,* Vol. 1, No. 8: 169-70)

A *Young Ceylon* editorial in 1850 also raised the issue of early marriage, which was then the norm among all groups including Euro-Asians. Commenting on the practice where the bride is "led to the altar a child in feeling (who) remains the same even after," the editor expressed strong opinions on the gap in intellect between "a man of education, feeling and taste" and the wife who "may be quite incapable of joining him in mental recreation of any kind":

> her tastes, if she has any are totally opposed to his and this want of congeniality in likings and dislikes must naturally prove a bar to domestic harmony and tranquility. (*Young Ceylon,* Vol. 1. No. 4: 74)

Euro-Asian families valued girls' education, and the Cambridge Junior and Senior examinations, introduced in 1880, attracted young Burgher and Eurasian girls who were also the first to go in for higher education. Concern about women's education had been expressed among intellectual families such as the Driebergs, and Hetty Drieberg led the way. In 1881 she obtained second-class honours at the Cambridge Junior examination – referred to as "a remarkable success for a girl," in a contemporary newspaper (quoted in Brohier 1994: 26). Hetty Drieberg had attended the Female Seminary whose headmaster in 1879 was the renowned teacher Robert Leembruggen, whose wife Henrietta Koch was the 'first assistant.' This school achieved "striking successes" at the Cambridge Junior examinations (ibid: 26). The Female Seminary was an important forerunner of women's secondary education, started before the other prestigious girls' high schools appeared from the 1890s onwards. Educated women also had access to the reputed Pettah Library and Reading Room, begun in 1829, and administered and patronized mainly by the Euro-Asian intelligentsia, who thereby had access to foreign books and journals (ibid: 27).

Charles Lorenz, the most outspoken radical of his time, was fully supportive of girls' education and in 1867 responded to a government inquiry on education, stating: "Female education among the Natives is the great desideratum of the day." Arguing that "the education of the girls of a family is... really more important than that of the boys," he highlighted the role of the mother:

> An educated... mother is a more powerful instrument of good than the best of fathers... no system of education will be complete, which does not include the instruction of females, and a very much stricter system of instruction than that of the males. (*Sessional Paper VIII of 1867*: 163)

Education was, however, often seen as a means of improving a girl's marriage prospects, since in a colonial situation educated women were more publicly 'presentable' and might command a good dowry. The Principal of the Weslyan Mission Girls' School, Pettah, Ms E.M. Shire, in 1912 expressed the view that:

> Apart from the practical value for those who want to go in for teaching, it improves a girl's position socially to have passed a Cambridge examination, and this helps towards a better marriage settlement. (*Sessional Paper XIX of 1912,* p.22, quoted in Denham 1912: 427 n)

But many educated Sri Lankan men, who had been impressed by the learning displayed by some women in England, regarded local women as "silly creatures" (Roberts et al. 1989: 73). Interestingly, in William Thackeray's *Vanity Fair* (1848), the character Amelia is described as a "foolish creature" and a "silly thing" compared to the feisty Becky Sharp who famously threw Johnson's Dictionary out of the carriage window on leaving school. Lorenz and his circle admired Thackeray, and Blazé notes that in London, Lorenz sketched "the great Thackeray" (1948: 100). But some local women were far from being "silly creatures" – as seen from the life of Eleanor Lorenz, and the careers of the pioneer women nurses and doctors in Sri Lanka who were Burghers and Eurasians. Moreover, as Brohier notes: "Burgher women were a spirited group, being among the earliest Sri Lankan women to ride bicycles and drive cars"; and they excelled in sports – in 1899, a Burgher women's cricket team played a men's team on the Batticaloa esplanade (1994: 24).

A landmark event occurred in 1909 inspired by Dr Mary Rutnam, a Canadian woman doctor (married to a Sri Lankan) who had founded the Ceylon Women's Union. At a meeting of the Union five Burgher women (Ms Beling, Ms W. Greve, Ms de Kretser, Ms C. de Zilwa, and Ms E. de Zilva) performed a "Dialogue on Women's Rights." Dr Rutnam described it as "splendid." This event, an early public expression of women's rights in Sri Lanka, was no doubt influenced by suffragist movements in Europe and North America, frequently referred to in local newspapers (Jayawardena 1993: 18).

The Euro-Asian Headstart in Education

An important trend of the 19th and 20th centuries in Sri Lanka in terms of caste and class mobility was the rush for both male and female education. Euro-Asian women made dramatic strides in education; and the great gap between the literacy and educational levels of Burgher and Eurasian women on the one hand, and Sinhala, Tamil and Muslim women on the other, was evident in the 19th century. But very significantly, *Burgher and Eurasian women's literacy was even higher than that of men of the Sinhala, Tamil and Muslim communities*. The gender-aggregated census data for the period 1881 to 1911 also reveals the progress made in education in the thirty year period by some communities, and the pockets of near illiteracy among others.

In 1881, 25% of Sinhalese males were literate, rising to over 30% in 1891; whereas Burgher and Eurasian *women* were already nearly

Table 3

Percentage of Literates of each Sex and Race, 1881, 1891, 1901, and 1911.

Race.	Males.				Females.			
	1881.	1891.	1901.	1911.	1881.	1891.	1901.	1911.
All Races	**24·6**	**29·9**	**34·7**	**40·4**	**2·5**	**4·4**	**6·9**	**10·6**
Europeans ..	84·8	89·5	89·9	93·2	74·2	85·0	85·2	86·3
Burghers and Eurasians	59·5	63·7	70·2	70·0	49·6	58·0	65·7	67·3
Sinhalese { Low-country	25·1	31·0	40·8	47·9	2·2	4·0	11·1	17·4
Sinhalese { Kandyan ..			30·7	36·4			1·6	2·8
Tamils { Ceylon ..	21·4	25·5	28·2	46·0	2·0	3·0	4·1	10·9
Tamils { Indian ..				20·4				1·5
Moors { Ceylon ..	26·3	29·7	33·2	31·4	1·4	1·0	2·5	2·6
Moors { Indian ..				51·8				1·9
Malays	40·2	46·1	53·4	53·3	3·3	6·0	16·1	14·3
Veddas	2·9	2·6	3·6	8·0	0·3	—	0·02	0·7
Others	25·1	31·9	44·5	42·2	3·1	6·0	16·4	12·3

From E.B. Denham, *Ceylon at the Census of 1911,* p.401

50% literate in 1881, and 58% by 1891. Sinhala women's literacy, however, was only 2.2% in 1881, rising to 4% in 1891, and in 1911 – when the statistics for Sinhala were divided – low-country Sinhalese women were 17.4% literate and Kandyan women only 2.8% (Table 3). In 1911 low-country Sinhalese men were 48% literate, whereas the figure for Burgher and Eurasian women was 67% (Denham 1912: 401).

The literacy rates for the City of Colombo and Western Province were, however, higher, although the gap between Burghers and Eurasians and the others remained. In the Colombo Municipality in 1911, there was almost 27% literacy among low-country Sinhalese women, and 20.2% among Kandyan Sinhalese women (Denham 1912: 412).

As a result of the advances that Burgher and Eurasian women had made in literacy, as well as in secondary and higher education, they made inroads into professions open to women. This was especially true of the teaching profession, where for many decades up to the mid-20th century, Burgher and Eurasian women teachers were very prominent in the English educational scene. Many locals, aspiring to achieve social mobility and advance their opportunities, were taught by Euro-Asians. Anagarika Dharmapala (1865-1933), the Buddhist ideologue, recalls that as a child he attended a "girls School in the Pettah where Dutch Burgher girls were taught English… and the teachers were Dutch Burgher ladies" (Guruge 1965: 697-98).

Another school, known as 'Miss Marshall's School' (later St Clare's) in Kollupitiya, was run by Ruth Marshall who was Eurasian. She encouraged several of her students to become doctors – among them Sri Lanka's first Sinhala woman doctor, Verona Wirasekera, and Augusta Abeyratne, née Pinto of Goan origin. Marshall also helped an impoverished student, Constance Blacker, née Jansen, who went on to start her own school. Ruth Marshall's sister Priscilla Marshall, a graduate of Madras University, was also a legendary principal, heading the Princess of Wales' College, Moratuwa, from 1909 to 1938. She too inspired her pupils to go in for higher studies and employment; many became doctors, nurses, teachers, school principals and university lecturers (*Princess of Wales' Centenary Magazine*, 1976: 20).

Deloraine Brohier has emphasized that middle-class Burghers – men and women – were "the great modernizers" of the time who believed in liberal values, especially equality of opportunity and democracy. By the 1890s, Burgher and Eurasian women had definitely set the pace as modernizers of Sri Lanka; they were westernized in their lifestyles, socializing freely in public with men, and also pioneering women's entry into education and employment, not being restrained by "local… customs and the hierarchies of the caste system" (Brohier 1994: 19). Brohier also comments on the aspects of Burgher society conducive to women's advance:

> education and study created an intellectual climate that favoured liberal attitudes, a wide range of interests as well as the recognition that women also had the right to education and to professional work. (ibid: 24)

In both India and Sri Lanka, the Euro-Asian woman teacher was a well-accepted phenomenon – the field extending to the teaching of music, dressmaking, art, nursing, as well as typing, secretarial and clerical work, linked with the needs of an expanding colonial economy. Visits to homes to teach secluded girls who did not attend school was another pioneering venture. In Galle, Burgher teachers taught Muslim girls at home, and Norah Jansz a retired teacher, was active in "itinerary work," from 1928 to1938 visiting 14 homes in the Fort to teach Muslim girls (Norah Roberts, 1993: 120 & 123).

Given the significant headstart in education, Euro-Asian women were among the first in Sri Lanka to publish English poetry, fiction and articles in journals and newspapers, and to exhibit their paintings. But many wrote under assumed names and remain unknown. Among the known writers was Ina Trimmer (1890-1982), daughter of A.C. de Zilwa, a proctor of Matara. Her husband was a tea planter, and "the isolation of a tea estate in Madulkalle" gave her the milieu for creative writing – mainly short stories and contributions to several newspapers (de Mel & Samarakkody 2002: 44-45). There were also some Burgher, Goan and Eurasian women art teachers in schools. The daughter of Hippolyte Silvaf, a Eurasian from Pondicherry, taught at the school they ran in the 1840s in Colombo. A century later, an art teacher at Ladies' College Colombo in the 1940s was Patricia Lobo, daughter of the Goan pioneer of the trade-union movement in Sri Lanka – Dr Lisboa Pinto. But few women gained recognition as painters. One who succeeded was Grace van Dort (born in 1861), daughter of J.L.K. van Dort, one of the country's leading artists of the 19th century (see Chapter 7). Influenced by her father, she painted landscapes in oils and watercolours, and became the secretary of the Ceylon Society of Arts (Brohier 2003). Another Burgher, Sybil Keyt was a modern artist of the 20th century.

Among pioneer Eurasian women was entrepreneur, Emily van der Poorten (1889-1975), the owner of the Hotel Metropole in Colombo. Her mother was R.M. Menika, a Kandyan Sinhalese who had married Belgian planter, landowner and businessman A.J. van der Poorten (see Chapter 3). Emily helped run her father's large estate. She was presented at court to the King of Belgium, and returning to Sri Lanka, married a Jewish trader from India named Horowitz, a business associate of her father. They moved to Kolkota, but after the marriage failed she returned to Colombo with her daughter Julia (born in 1913). Julia married a planter, William Outram Hermon, from a well-known Kandyan Eurasian family; their daughter Dr. Patricia Alailima, an economist, was formerly Director-

General of the National Planning Department, Colombo. Emily's second husband Guillain started the Hotel Metropole with her money, but she took over control of the hotel after her husband ran into financial difficulties. The hotel became famous for good cuisine and did well during the Second World War, when it was popular with foreign service personnel stationed in Sri Lanka. The success did not last beyond the 1960s, when Emily sold the enterprise.

Breaking into the Medical Patriarchy

Many of these Euro-Asian women in South Asia thus challenged the usual stereotypes about their domesticity or frivolity. They were also to achieve intellectual recognition and achievement, often promoting modern ideas in their work. The most spectacular success of Burgher and Eurasian women in Sri Lanka was their entry into the Medical College. Many of them had links to the medical field through relatives and others of the community who dominated the profession. As noted earlier, men of the community had attained eminence in the medical and legal professions in the 19th century; the first principals of the Ceylon Medical College started in 1870 were Euro-Asians (the doctors Loos, Koch and van der Straaten), as were 16 out of 33 medical students in 1875 (Brohier 1994: 18). Deloraine Brohier – whose great aunt Alice de Boer was the first woman doctor in Sri Lanka – has argued that the liberal tradition that prevailed among sections of educated Burgher men in 19th century Sri Lanka was also found among Burgher women who were, in many ways, the 'new women' of the time (ibid: 19).

The breakthrough of women into the patriarchal structures and male-dominated medical profession took place in stages. Women were first recruited as vaccinators, midwives, nurses and apothecaries. In 1877 women were admitted to a special 'secondary class' in the Medical College to fill the need for trained apothecaries, and by 1904 there were three women apothecaries in hospitals, of whom two were Burgher (Moriera and Siebel), the third (Canagasabey) being Tamil. While women had always functioned as midwives, a training school for midwives was begun in 1880 at the de Soysa Lying-in-Home which attracted Euro-

Asian women; there also existed a fee-charging group of European and Euro-Asian women known as 'Ladies' Nurses' who visited homes. A Nursing School at the General Hospital was established in 1877, which had many Euro-Asian pupils. In 1881 the head nurse of the school was a Burgher, Ms Mothau (ibid: 4). In 1886, when vaccination against smallpox was made compulsory, female vaccinators were appointed for Muslim women (Uragoda 1987: 210-11).

While women in Britain had a bitter struggle to enter the medical faculties, in India and Sri Lanka the colonial governments actually promoted the training of women doctors, as some local women refused to be treated by males. The Ceylon Medical College was opened to women in 1892, when Evelyn Davidson (Eurasian) and Henrietta Keyt (Burgher) broke the male monopoly of medical studies. They were followed by other Euro-Asians – Alice de Boer, Winifred Nell, Claribel van Dort, Rachel Christoffelsz, Ursula van Rooyen, Helen Kiddle, and Sylvia Ebert – all of whom qualified in the 1890s and the early 20th century. The first woman to qualify (in 1898) was Alice de Boer (1872-1955), who won the government scholarship for studies abroad in 1899 and obtained higher qualifications from Edinburgh and Glasgow. She worked at the Lady Havelock Hospital for Women, before leaving for Britain in 1925; there she practised in Hemel Hempstead for many years in order to help support grand-nephews in their studies in Britain (Brohier 1994: 27-30).

Another doctor of Goan ancestry, was Maria Augusta Pinto, whose father and brother ran a pharmacy in Colombo. Dr Pinto, who married Dr L.O. Abeyratne, worked at the Lady Havelock Women's Hospital, Lady Ridgeway Hospital for Children, and the VD Clinic. She was also a pioneer in family planning. Among the other eminent doctors of mixed origin who worked at the Lady Havelock Hospital was May Ratnaike, daughter of Dr John de Livera and Rose Gibbons of London. Dr Ratnaike did further studies in Britain and was one of the earliest local women surgeons.

One important aspect of this advance by Euro-Asian women was the support they received from liberal Burgher doctors, most notably Dr James Loos (born in 1822), who after qualifying in Kolkata and

Scotland became the first principal of the Ceylon Medical College. He had been in Britain at the opening of the London School of Medicine for Women in 1874, and was aware of the campaign for women's rights in Britain, greatly admiring the work of Florence Nightingale. Returning to Sri Lanka, he sponsored the campaign for women apothecaries, nurses and doctors. In 1877 he urged educated women to choose a vocation, to be strong and active, to detest idleness, and "to have too much self-respect to live a life of dependence" (Brohier 1994:6). Dr Loos' advocacy of women's independence, including education and employment, was quite radical for the time when most middle-class males strongly believed that women should be dependent, and that their only place was in the home. He was influenced by the advances in India, where women had entered the medical faculties, and by the support in India for this policy from the Viceroy, Lord Dufferin, and the establishment of the Lady Dufferin Fund for raising money for women's hospitals. Dr Loos, who visited Kolkata in 1890, met Indian women medical students, and subsequently campaigned for the entry of women into the Ceylon Medical College (*Ceylon Independent*, 4 March 1893, quoted in Brohier 1994: 11). Brohier describes Loos as:

> a typical liberal of his day; well-versed in events abroad and willing to enter into controversial debates, which other more conservative doctors might have shunned... Before and after retirement, he took up his pen on the debate on women in medicine. (1994: 6)

Also entering the debate on vocations for women was a Burgher, Ms Cuylenburg, who was studying medicine in Britain. She gave a talk to the Mothers Union in Galle in 1896, criticizing "the usual upbringing of girls in Burgher families" where marriage was the "end and aim of feminine existence and female education." She spoke of women's destitution if the male bread-winner died. "Why not fit girls to earn their own living as you fit boys?" she asked, also making the suggestion, unusual for the time, that for girls, marriage should only be "a happy accident in their lives" (*The Ceylon Mirror*, 28 Nov. 1896, quoted in Brohier 1994: 21). The educated modern woman's opinions were often sought on matters of public interest. For example, Dr Alice de Boer, who strongly believed in women's education and employment, was asked in 1912 for her views on the content of women's high-school education. She said it should be for:

> The development of character; the training of the intellect so as to enable them to take an active interest in the questions of the day; ... the acquirement of special knowledge which will be of direct service in earning a livelihood. (quoted in Brohier 1994: 29)

Anglo-Indian Pioneers

In India, the earliest teachers included many from the Euro-Asian community. By the early 19th century, many of the educated military 'orphans' of mixed origin – both men and women – became teachers "pioneering what was later to become an important source of employment and contribution to society of many Anglo or Euro-Indians" (Hawes 1996: 32). The Baptists, who had started schools in their missions from the late 18th century, educated numerous Anglo-Indian women, some of whom formed a society for the education of other Indian women; by 1822, this society had 6 schools with 160 pupils (Jayawardena 1995: 27). The early headstart of Anglo-Indian women resulted in their presence in large numbers as teachers in 19th century India. The Loretto Convents, established in India from the 1840s onwards, attracted Anglo-Indian girls from middle-class families as students; these schools gave a high-school education in English, and produced many generations of lay teachers and some nuns. The first superior at the Loretto Convent in Entally, India, for example, was Mother Christine Finch, an Anglo-Indian, as were many of the other Catholic nuns (ibid: 45-46). Anglo-Indian and Goan women were successful in the medical profession too, some of the earliest being Goans – Dr D'Abreu and Dr Emmeline da Costa née da Cunha (1873-1973). The latter did the LMS degree in 1894 at the Bombay Medical College.

Under British rule, there were also cases of Anglo-Indian women who were recruited for posts in Sri Lanka or who married Sri Lankans. Once such notable case was Bertha Irene Rodgers (1911-99), born in Kolkata of an English father and Bengali mother. She studied in a Catholic school and graduated from Kolkata University in 1927 in Mathematics, French and English, qualifying in education at the London University in 1934. Rodgers, like others of mixed origin who could internalize both the East and West, was able to 'breach the divide' and combine modernism with support for local religion and culture. In London she was recruited by D.B. Jayatilake, a Buddhist politician who was looking for a principal for Mahamaya Girls' College, a Buddhist school started in Kandy in 1932, run by an organization (Kulangana Samithiya) of Buddhist women. She assumed duties in 1937, combining "a modern English education with Buddhist and Sri Lankan traditions," and introduced new creative methods of teaching in a "relaxed liberal atmosphere," so that the children "loved attending school." Bertha Rodgers also encouraged higher education, sports activities and Girl Guides, while following the Buddhist "religious and national ideals" of the Kulangana Samithiya (Meegama 2003: 117-19). Closely linked to the school was the prominent Kandyan family of Ratwatte – especially Sir Cuda Ratwatte. But the school was fraught with factionalism. Bertha, who in 1943 had married Stanley Ratwatte, a son of Cuda Ratwatte, was caught up in the imbroglio about tradition and modernity in the school. She resigned in 1949, and from 1952 to 1959 was the principal of another Buddhist girls' school, Musaeus College, Colombo (ibid: 117-19).

Modernism in Education

An innovative teacher was Constance Blacker, who in 1924, started the Girton School in Nugegoda on the outskirts of Colombo. Constance Blacker, born in 1894, was the daughter of William Daniel Jansen, an auctioneer of Dutch Burgher origin, and Gertrude Maud Dias, a dressmaker of Portuguese descent. Constance studied at St Clare's School, Kollupitiya, run by Ruth Marshall, and later taught at this school. In 1920 she married a Eurasian, Shelton Blacker, who worked at the Colombo Commercial Company. His grandfather William Blacker was one of the early English officials of the Madras government, sent from India to govern the island after Dutch capitulation. In naming her school after Girton – the first College for girls in Cambridge – she was in a sense "hitching her school to a star" (Alfreda de Silva, manuscript).

The aura of local Cambridge examinations and the ideals of Girton College Cambridge had inspired many ambitious women in Sri Lanka. Blacker specialized in the liberal arts and concentrated on drama, music, dancing and art and used modern techniques of non-competitive education. Girton School, considered the first 'progressive' school in the country, became known for its successful public drama performances – a mixture of Western and Eastern plays in English, which included *Alice in Wonderland*, *Sakuntala*, *Hiawatha*, Tagore's *Post Office*, and Gilbert and Sullivan's *HMS Pinafore*. The students and staff were mainly Euro-Asians. Alfreda de Silva, who attended the school, described Constance Blacker's efforts at a new type of teaching, transforming the education department syllabus, "with an exciting syllabus of her own, which gave freedom to the individual learner and took her away from the boredom of too great a dependence on the text books" (ibid).

Linked to the school as a teacher was a Eurasian, Cora Abraham née Blacker, Constance Blacker's sister-in-law. She, like Constance, had no formal higher education, but was an inspiring teacher, later blossoming out to start the Melbourne Art Classes for children in 1949. Her much-celebrated school abandoned old-style methods of teaching art, using modern ways of encouraging freedom of artistic expression and boldness in the use of colour. Cora Abraham inspired many budding artists of the time and is remembered for her contribution in the teaching of art to children and organizing the Young Artists Group. She was also politically active on the Left, being in 1948 a member of the Eksath Kantha Peramuna (EKP) – an autonomous women's organization that brought together women of the various Marxist parties and their sympathizers.

Other pioneering ventures in education by Euro-Asians included the Fröebel School, started in Bandarawela in the 1940s by a Burgher couple, Dorothy and Brian Beven. It was based on the educational principles of Friedrich Fröebel, the 19th century German founder of the kindergarten system, who emphasized children's play and self-activity, including music, singing, and rambles in the countryside. This school, which attracted the children of British officials and planters in Sri Lanka, also had a few local children whose parents were keen on 'progressive' education. It was co-educational with none of the usual school traditions of uniforms, strict discipline or grading by marks. There were several Burgher women teachers (Modder, Colin-Thomé, van Dort) and a European Jewish refugee known as Madame Kodischek who taught French. The school's successful operatic production of Ibsen's *Peer Gynt,* with music by Grieg, is remembered by former pupils, who also speak of the walks in the hills and the relaxed atmosphere of the school.[1]

Pioneers of the Nell Clan

Eleanor Lorenz

An outstanding example of Euro-Asians who took the lead on women's issues were members of the Nell clan. For several generations, this enlightened family produced many talented 'New Women' – Eleanor (Nell) Lorenz, Dr Winifred Nell, Agnes (Nell) de Silva and her daughters Anil Marcia and Minnette de Silva (See Table 1). Their intellectual contributions, professional successes, political commitment, courage and dynamism were remarkable.

The founder of the Sri Lanka branch of the Nell family was Frederick August Nell who had come to the island during Dutch rule and had married a Sinhalese, Catherina Petronella de Fonseka (Brohier 1994: 40). Their grandson George Michael Nell, an auctioneer, and his wife Maria Elizabeth Conderlag were the parents of Eleanor, Frederick and Louis Nell. The Nell brothers were part of the Young Ceylon group led by Charles Lorenz; and Eleanor (born in 1825) was also associated closely with these radicals. In 1850 Eleanor married Lorenz, then aged 21, and as part of the marriage settlement she received a valuable house in York Street and a house in Sea Street, in which they resided (Blazé 1948: 97) Eleanor Lorenz was among the earliest local women to travel to Europe, accompanying her husband there in 1853-54.

Ludovici praised Eleanor Lorenz as having "a cultivated mind" and called her "perhaps the most accomplished of Ceylon's daughters ...learned and clever" (Blazé 1948: 40). She wrote articles and stories for *Young Ceylon* and no doubt helped in its publication. Blazé also claims that, "for a woman of those times she was something of a scholar," who translated (from French to English) two historical documents – one on the British takeover of the island from the Dutch and another on the account by Admiral Spilbergen of his travels to the Dutch East Indies. Deloraine Brohier (1994: 41) notes that this revealed:

> Eleanor's interest in history and archival records which her nephew Dr Andreas Nell later cultivated. In this way medicine and history, the arts and culture, archives and books, study and learning were very much nurtured and developed in the Nell family over several generations.

Blazé (1948: 40) also speculates that Eleanor Lorenz owed her "intellectual superiority and attainments" to the "circles in which she moved" and also to the "cultured family to which she belonged." It was common in the 19th century, in the West and Sri Lanka, for girls to benefit from the family ambience, to participate in discussions and studies with their brothers, and receive encouragement from their fathers and other learned persons or professionals who supported women's education.

Winifred Nell

Eleanor Lorenz's brother's daughter was Dr Winifred Nell (1862-1943), one of the country's earliest women doctors, who entered Medical College in 1893, qualified in 1898, and studied in Scotland in 1899 obtaining the LRC & P (Edinburgh) and LRCF & S (Glasgow). She and Alice de Boer were among the first two women doctors to do higher studies in their field. Brought up in an intellectual milieu, Winifred Nell was the daughter of Louis Nell, lawyer and writer (part of the Young Ceylon group, and later Queen's Advocate), and Julia Andree, a relative of Lorenz. Winifred was a niece of Frederick Nell who supported women's education. It was a family of professionals including several doctors who would have encouraged Winifred. Her brother Dr Andreas Nell, an eminent opthalmologist and historian, achieved fame in the early 20th century; her older sister Ruth was married to a Burgher doctor, W.E. Leembruggen, Assistant Colonial Surgeon (ibid: 41). By 1900 Winifred

Nell was assistant to the Port Surgeon and later became the house surgeon at the Lady Havelock Hospital for Women. Subsequently she also worked at the Leper Hospital in Hendala and was the Registrar of Births and Deaths (in Kotahena) – a post often given to women doctors. Her grand-niece Anil de Silva described her as very tall, with "a commanding personality" (ibid: 41).

Agnes de Silva

A worthy successor to the Lorenz-Nell tradition of non-conformity and courageous radicalism in politics was Winifred Nell's niece Agnes, the daughter of Paul Nell and his wife Alice Newman. Agnes was born in 1884 and spent her early years on a tea plantation in Pussellawa with her sisters Grace (later Wright) and Elsie (later Grenier). Paul Nell has been described by his granddaughter Minnette de Silva as a "very broad-minded Burgher… who detested all ideas of social superiority," and her mother Agnes as someone who "equally abhorred injustices of any kind" (de Silva 1998: 25). Like her radical Burghers relatives, Agnes had no qualms or fears about defying convention and going against notions of middle-class respectability. As a Burgher from a distinguished family she made an enormous break with tradition to marry George E. de Silva, a Sinhalese lawyer of humble social origins. She married in 1908 and started a family, but often expressed regret at her lack of opportunity to study further – her greatest dream had been to go to university in Cambridge. And according to her daughter, she remained, all her life, "an inveterate reader" (personal communication, Minnette de Silva 1996).

Agnes de Silva involved herself in her husband's politics, and was an executive committee member of the Ceylon Labour Party and the All-Ceylon Trade Union Congress led by A. E. Goonesinha (Jayawardena 1972: 277-78n). She was also active in the Kandy Arts and Crafts Society, aimed at encouraging local artisans. Agnes de Silva attended the sessions of the Ceylon National Congress in 1925, and along with Aseline Thomas proposed a resolution that "a limited suffrage be immediately extended to the women of this country" (*Handbook of the Ceylon National Congress*, 1928: 714; and Russell 1981: 51). Agnes was a leader of the women's franchise movement of the late 1920s and among the boldest of the middle-class women making claims to political equality. The Ceylon Labour Party and its leaders A.E. Goonesinha and George E. de Silva were supportive of universal suffrage and the female suffrage movement, whereas many in the Ceylon National Congress opposed these demands.

Agnes moved closely with local and foreign politicians. With her husband, she was not only prominent at the receptions in Kandy in 1924 for Ramsay McDonald, the British Labour Party leader, but also hosted the visits to Kandy of the Indian National Congress leaders – Mahatma Gandhi (and his wife Kasturba) in 1927, and in 1931 Jawaharlal Nehru (with his wife Kamala and young daughter Indira), along with the two most outstanding Congress women leaders, Kamaladevi Chattopadyaya and her sister-in-law Sarojini Naidu. All this occurred in an era when the British Labour Party was not favoured by colonial officialdom, and the Indian National Congress and its leaders were anathema to the authorities. It took courage to publicly associate with personalities such as Gandhi.

Agnes de Silva's link with Sarojini Naidu was close, as the latter had stayed for a time in Agnes' hill-top home in Kandy where they discussed a wide range of issues affecting women. As Jane Russell has written of that important encounter, "Sarojini's ideas rubbed off on Agnes who had long nurtured suffragette ambitions" (1981: 43). The subjects they discussed included:

> the women's movement in Britain and India, and its implications for Ceylon; the iniquities of the dowry system and arranged marriages, the question of inter-caste, inter-communal marriages; the need for widespread education for women; the right to vote, and to have a profession outside motherhood. (Russell 1981: 43)

Burgher and Eurasian women had shown interest in suffragist movements elsewhere, and in 1927, when the Women's Franchise Union was formed in Sri Lanka, several of them were at the forefront of the agitation. The most active was Agnes de Silva, one of the joint-secretaries of the Union and a spirited campaigner. In reply to Sir Ponnambalam Ramanathan's diatribe – that giving women franchise rights was "casting pearls before swine" – she retorted that prejudiced men were the swine. The press gave full coverage to her provocative speech:

> Why should Ceylon be one of the few countries in the world which insulted its womanhood by denying the privilege which every civilized country had accorded to its women? Women had proved that they were the equals of men. Why should they be silent while some narrow minded and selfish men said that they were illiterates? The Tamil knight had referred to 'throwing pearls before swine' but he seemed to forget that in that instance the swine were men. Good pearls could not be crushed even by men who regarded them as their household goods and chattels. They were not so ignorant of the political life of the country as people seemed to think. (de Alwis & Jayawardena 2001: 22)

In this speech Agnes, replied to the usual criticisms of women's suffrage. She quoted Charles Dickens, and said women were not like the famous comic character Mrs Jellyby in *Bleak House*, who neglected her own children in her enthusiasm for the natives of Borrio-boola Gha in Nigeria (ibid: 28).

When the Donoughmore Commission on constitutional reforms took evidence in 1927, Agnes de Silva was part of the delegation of the Women's Franchise Union; she was ready to reply to any line of questioning, even on the controversial issue of voting rights for plantation workers of Indian origin – on which the Ceylon National Congress was split. Including working-class women in her agenda, Agnes' views were the most radical among the women's delegation:

> We went in the spirit of Crusaders and answered questions in an inspired manner. I held a watching brief for any questions that we had not prepared. I remember one now. Lord Donoughmore asked if we wanted Indian Tamil women labourers on the estates to have the vote, I replied: 'Certainly, they are women too. We want all women to have the vote.' (Russell 1981: 57-58)

The announcement of reforms and male and female franchise rights to all over 21 in 1928 was, in Agnes de Silva's words, "a victory beyond our wildest dreams" (ibid). That same year she travelled to Britain with her husband and the Ceylon Labour Party leader A.E. Goonesinha – all of whom canvassed British MPs in favour of the proposed constitutional reforms for the island.

But after women's franchise was won, there were no women candidates in the general election of 1931. A Burgher woman, Dora Godlieb, née Nathanielsz, who had in her own words "organized movements concerning the health and welfare of the people," tried to contest, but was not given permission by the authorities as her husband Dr E.S. Godlieb was in government service. In an indignant letter to the Secretary of State for the Colonies, Dora Godlieb protested against the infringement of her political rights, inquiring pertinently, and somewhat boldly, whether such a prohibition applied to the father and other relatives of a government servant (de Alwis & Jayawardena 2001: 61). The prohibition remained. By 1932, however, two women, Adeleine Molamure and Neysum Saravanamuttu entered the Legislature in by-elections.

In 1933 Agnes de Silva, as a Ceylon Labour Party candidate, unsuccessfully contested the Galagedera seat in a by-election. In this constituency (next to the Kandy electorate George E. de Silva had won in 1931), semi-feudal relations and oppressive caste structures prevailed. It was a plantation and smallholders' economy producing tea, paddy and spices. Agnes de Silva's opponent in the election was P.R. Ranaraja, from a family of 'feudals' with influence in the area. He polled 6,764 votes to Agnes de Silva's 4,565 – her voters including poor farmers (from 'depressed' castes), plantation workers, and women. Sections of the press singled out Agnes for attack, alleging that women like her were "consumed… [by] wild ambition" to enter politics (ibid: 68). Agnes de Silva's failure to win the Galagedera seat in 1933 ended her political ambitions; and in future decades there were few Burgher men or women in electoral politics. Agnes de Silva dropped out of politics for health reasons, and supported her husband's political career. She also absorbed herself in family matters, and in popularizing simple recipes especially geared to the food shortages during the Second World War. In the years before her death in 1961, she led a sedentary life, continuing, however, to read widely.

Anil de Silva

The pioneering spirit of Agnes de Silva was continued through her rebellious daughters: Anil de Silva, an early woman journalist, art critic and political activist; and Minnette de Silva, Sri Lanka's first woman architect (see, de Mel 2001; de Silva 1998). Both daughters were inspired by their mother's activities in politics, social issues and local arts. Jane Russell, referring to the line of inspiration and "pioneering blood" from Dr Winifred Nell to Agnes de Silva, commented that "an adventurous spirit always characterized the women of this family" (1981: 48.)

Anil Marcia de Silva (1909-96) was influenced by her parents, who had defied 'establishment' conventions by participating in political and suffrage movements, and associating with Indian Congress leaders, Sri Lankan politicians and social reformers. Given this background, Anil had no difficulty from a young age in being unconventional and outspoken. In the 1920s she had lived through the local labour upsurges and political debates; and visiting Britain with her parents in 1928, she was exposed to British politics and all the excitement of London of the epoch. She stayed on in London and became a journalist – a pioneering venture for a Sri Lankan woman.

Neloufer de Mel has analysed the prevailing puritanism and nationalist rhetoric, which were "important rubrics of respectability [and] the very boundaries that Anil de Silva defied through the choices she made in her life" (2001: 107 & 152). Being of Sinhala-Burgher origin, Anil was in the anomalous position of being outside the high-caste Sinhala elite (because of her father's origins), yet linked to the high class and intellectual status of her mother's Burgher family. She was viciously attacked in some nationalist journals of the early 1930s for refusing "to conform to [nationalist] paradigms," and making "criticism of the motherland" in her articles in the British press (ibid: 108). Anil was also attacked for her critique of Sri Lankan culture and social practice as well as her cosmopolitanism and lifestyle.

Except for short visits to Sri Lanka, Anil chose to live abroad the rest of her life – in Britain, India and France. In London in the early 1930s, she was married for a few years to an Irishman, Robert Nichol-Cadell. Although it was a time when Sri Lankan men were marrying

Europeans, it was still unusual for a local middle-class woman to marry a foreigner. A Sri Lankan journal the *Searchlight* mocked Anil: "One should not be surprised, if in her next insane ramblings... she advocated ardently the principle of fusion of races, and herself delivers an object lesson, by precept and example" (quoted in de Mel 2001: 102.)

After Anil de Silva left Britain in the 1940s, the next phase of her life was in India where she lived with the writer Mulk Raj Anand, and together edited *Marg,* a new journal of the arts recognizing "excellence in India's myriad aesthetic forms" (Raj Thapar 1991: 12). She organized the first exhibition in India of the work of George Keyt, the leading modern artist of Sri Lanka – also of Burgher origin. Anil was close to the Indian Communist Party, and became the secretary of the Indian Peoples' Theatre Association – a vibrant leftist theatre group which had great success in the 1940s (see de Mel 2001). Anil's wide circle of friends and admirers included the Communist leader S.A. Dange and other party stalwarts, as well as the editors of *Seminar*, Ramesh and Raj Thapar, the journalist Ramesh Sanghvi, the scientist Dr Homi Bhabha, and members of the noted Tata, Masani, Wadia, Sarabai, Swaminathan and Hajibullah families. Raj Thapar in her memoirs, describes her as "remarkable and attractive" (1991: 12), and also records that Anil "reflected the intellectual excitement of those times in the initiatives she took over a wide range of activities" (ibid: 58). From the 1930s onwards, Anil de Silva's love life had been the topic of criticism from nationalist journals in Sri Lanka, and in the 1940s she was denounced for the same reasons by sections of the Indian Communist Party. As Romila Thapar commented, there was "a strong streak of puritanism" in revolutionary parties, including the Indian Left (quoted in de Mel 2001: 123.)

Leaving Mulk Raj Anand, Anil moved to France in 1950, and married a French doctor Philippe Vigier, an activist in the Communist Party. They had a wide circle of French Communist and other leftist friends including many artists, politicians, American 'refugees' from McCarthyism who were living in Paris, and Indians living or studying in France. Anil followed a course in Asian art and wrote *The Life of the Buddha* (1955), as seen through Asian sculpture and paintings, published by the prestigious Phaidon Press. Anil was to move again, divorcing Dr Vigier and settling in Cambridge, England, where she spent the rest of her life. She produced art books, including one on the Dunhuang caves in China which she had visited, and historical biographies of Christine de Pisan and John of Gaunt (see de Mel 2001).

It is interesting to speculate whether Anil's characteristic *joie de vivre* came from the Euro-Asian tradition of 'high spirits' which Charles Lorenz also had in abundance. Anil de Silva, of course, was several generations after Lorenz, but she had also been part of the Burgher social life of the late 1920s. Her school friend Doris Gratiaen, also from Bishop's College, was the mother of the writer Michael Ondaatje, who (reminiscent of Fitzgerald's *Gatsby*) describes the parties, dances, drinking, swimming and fast driving, of a set of high-living Burghers of the period (Ondaatje 1984). But Anil had an intellectual and political side. She was not only keenly aware of her Sri Lankan and Asian identity – reinforced by her association with Sri Lankan politics and Indian nationalism – but was also a product of the Indian left movement. Until her death in Cambridge in 1996, she continued to be absorbed in writing and keeping in touch with her wide network of friends, which included many younger Sri Lankans whom she influenced.

Minnette de Silva

Anil de Silva's younger sister Minnette (1917-98) was also an adventurous and creative pioneer in many ways. As a child in the 1920s, she was exposed to her parents' world of politics, and to their political friends who included (in her words) "eminent Ceylonese and the great Indian leaders who visited Ceylon":

> I remember my family entertaining visitors from abroad … a world of notables and I grew up without the usual inhibitions of race, religion or class. (de Silva 1998: 48)

The visitors she and her sister (mentioned earlier) met included young Indira Gandhi who befriended Minnette. Accompanying her family to Britain in 1928, Minnette attended school there and spent time with her sister in London. Returning home she decided to venture into the male world of architecture. In spite of financial problems and parental disapproval, Minnette moved to India where she studied architecture in Mumbai, supported financially by her great uncle Dr Andreas Nell. Mumbai was, as she wrote, "a mixed cosmopolitan world of the political Left and Right: industrialists, army generals, executives, struggling artists, writers, film-makers, dancers, actors" (ibid: 65.) Apart from her sister's political and artistic friends, Minnette had numerous colleagues among Indian architects, notably Jhabvala and Minoo Mistry. It was a far cry from the limited and rather confined world of Sri Lanka of the period.

Minnette completed her architectural studies (ARIBA) in London after the Second World War. She became not only the first local (and possibly Asian) woman architect, but also the first in Sri Lanka (in the 1950s) to pioneer a synthesis of modernism and tradition in architecture. She was inspired by her friend Le Corbusier and other modernist architects, and using traditional design and local materials, she developed a distinct style of her own. She continued until her death to practice and write on architecture from her parents' home on a hill in Kandy. While later avant-garde architects received success and publicity, Minnette felt these had eluded her, because she was a single woman, living somewhat reclusively in Kandy, away from opportunities provided by the capital city. However, her pioneering role was widely acknowledged in Sri Lanka and abroad, and her book *The Life and Work of an Asian Woman Architect* (1998) has given us a vivid glimpse into the achievements of a woman who, in the Lorenz family tradition, went 'against the grain.'

While Sri Lankan women of mixed Asian and European descent thus played an important role in promoting modernism, pioneering women's education, employment and political rights, they have until recently remained unrecognized. Cultural myths of the 'exotic' and 'promiscuous' Euro-Asian woman have persisted and continue to be propagated in both western and eastern cultures. In this way the reality is still overshadowed by racist Orientalist fantasies of colonial times.

Note

1. At the Fröbel School in 1943-44 were Suriya Wickremasinghe and Goolbai Gunasekara, whose foreign mothers – Doreen Wickremasinghe and Clara Motwani, respectively – were interested in modern education.

Agnes Nell driving an early Ford car, with her cousin.
Courtesy Minnette de Silva.

11

RACISM, REVIVALISM AND GENDER

> I want to...write a book called *The Importance of Being Thuppahi.*[1] It'll be my answer to the exclusivism and purity-obsession of Sinhalese and Tamils that have brought this country to the edge of destruction. And in it I'll flaunt proudly the badge of thuppahi-ness that others have pinned on us as an object of scorn. Yes, we are hybrid... and in that hybridity we are truly Sri Lankan, authentic members of one of the most hybrid nations on God's earth.
>
> Regi Siriwardena, *The Lost Lenore*, 1996, p.44

Euro-Asians as '*Mischmaschvolk*'

Colonial rule in South Asia had created a mixed population of Euro-Asians – namely Anglo-Indians in India, and Burghers and Eurasians in Sri Lanka. As discussed earlier, the Burghers in Sri Lanka were divided into those of Dutch origin (including some of German and French ancestry whose forebears had worked for the Dutch East India Company), and those of Portuguese origin, who were generally poor descendants of Portuguese *casados* who had married locals. The group called 'Eurasians' were of British origin – divided into two classes: the wealthy descendants who had been endowed with plantations and other property by their British fathers, and poor Eurasians who were frequently abandoned children brought up at the Kandy Convent or the Paynter Homes in Nuwara Eliya. While wealthy Burghers and Eurasians kept a social distance from the poor of their own communities, members of the Burgher and Eurasian privileged families often intermarried. A kind of 'caste system' operated among the mixed community based on class and skin colour. But to the other ethnic groups, these distinctions were not important, since all Euro-Asians were 'hybrid' and therefore 'outsiders.'

Anagarika Dharmapala, who in 1892 argued that the Sinhalese belonged "to a superior race" (Guruge 1965: 515), not surprisingly, agreed with Europeans who held that those of mixed origin were the 'lesser breeds.' Dharmapala frequently denounced "hybrids and bastards of Sinhalese" as traitors to the country (ibid: 524), and also criticized the adoption of foreign names and alien dress by Sinhala men and women. In 1891 he remarked that "it was absolutely impossible… to distinguish a Sinhalese from a Goanese; for in name and dress he is no more than a Eurasian" (ibid: 640). Dharmapala again warned in 1912 that if the Buddhists did not wake up, Christian missionaries would convert the population, and an ancient race, which had "kept up the traditions of Aryan learning for 2000 years," would vanish and be replaced by a "hybrid race of Eurasians" (ibid: 766).

The concept of racial purity/impurity, already established by the colonial rulers, as well as the local caste-based concepts of 'high' and 'low,' 'pure' and 'polluted,' defined attitudes to those locals with European antecedents. With the growth of nationalism and politics of identity in the late 19th century, a consciousness of racial 'purity' and religious superiority increased among South Asians. The image was of communities of high-standing, ancient lineage, noble traditions and religions, in contrast to the racial impurity and religious inferiority of the colonial masters, and the lack of 'authenticity' of local Christians and 'bastard mongrelized' mixed communities. The Euro-Asian thus became a subverter of the 'purity' of both races, challenging racial essentialism, and creating a new mixed category, which questioned both the European and South Asian ideals of 'the chosen race.'

The purity and chastity of women was also in question, and there was guilt and shame on both sides at the presence of Euro-Asians in society. It meant that European men had sexual liaisons with native women and had created 'impure,' illegitimate children. From the point of view of local men, some of their women (usually considered to be 'whores') had shamefully consorted with white men, thereby inducing guilt at their inability to 'control their own women.'

In a society also stratified on caste lines, 'out-castes' and 'half-castes' were terms used for those who did not 'belong' and were thus 'beyond the pale.' Significantly, in colonial times when racial lines were closely drawn, the products of mixed unions were referred to as half-breeds, mulattos, créoles, *métis* (French), *mestizos* (Spanish), or *mestiços* (Portuguese). In this sense, if one half was 'pure/good,' the other half was 'polluting.' To the Europeans any tinge of 'blackness' was always polluting, and in US slave society one-eighth black ancestry was enough for the classification 'octroon.' As Major Forbes, a British engineer in Sri Lanka in the 1840s, noted: "The slightest mixture of native blood with European can never be eradicated" (Roberts et al. 1989: 48). To Asians, it was the western half that was polluting, and the terms popularly used by locals for those of mixed origin were inevitably demeaning and insulting, ranging from lower forms of animal life, *karapoththa* (cockroach), to expressions like *mico* (mechanic) and *thuppahi* (mixed) (ibid: 6-7). To South Asians who put a high value on 'purity,' the mixed population was *sankara* – namely 'impure' (ibid: 11). And to the West, they were 'a mongrel race' (ibid: 48). In contrast, enlightened bureaucrats like Sir Alexander Johnston (Chief Justice of the island, 1811-18) and William Digby, the liberal writer, viewed "mixed-bloods as mediators and catalysts in the transmission of European skills to Eastern peoples" (Roberts et al. 1989: 48).

Colonialism had produced new communities of Euro-Asians, but one of the unresolved issues remained that of the mixed community. For many locals, their main contact with western civilization was through Burgher and Eurasian school teachers and professionals – especially lawyers and doctors – of these communities. As Alexander Johnston noted, Burghers were "thoroughly acquainted with the language, habits, manners, and usages and prejudices of the natives," while at the same time, because of their descent, features, names, religion, laws, education and language, "feel bound by every tie of affection and interest to the British government" (ibid: 47). Digby had remarked on the way Burghers had helped in the "ingraft of Western civilization" on Sri Lanka (ibid: 49). This double contact, which included an understanding of the language and customs of both rulers and ruled, gave the Euro-Asians an indisputable mediatory position. In Sri Lanka some Sinhalese, Tamils and Muslims, anxious to modernize, copied the lifestyle of the Euro-Asians. And the British rulers often got an understanding of 'native opinion' from Euro-Asian interlocutors and informants. This close contact with those of mixed origin resulted in the 'Burgherization' of Sinhala middle-class urban dwellers, leading to cries of alarm expressed by Sinhala-Buddhist ideologues and novelists.

In India, however, while there were similar expressions of concern at western influences, there arose, especially in Bengal, a strong critique of Hindu society and an expression of more liberal views – on the lines of the Derozians and the Young Bengal movement. One outstanding example is Rabindranath Tagore's famous novel *Gora* written in 1909, on the unusual theme of a local nationalist who turns out to be a white man. Ashis Nandy describes the novel as "an allegory to problematize the political complexities and personal issues of 'Self' and 'Other' in the East-West confrontation." The hero, an ultra-nationalist, who strictly observes orthodox Hindu practices was nicknamed 'Gora' (whitey) because of his fair skin, is told later in life that he is an adopted child whose father and mother were Irish. This "reduces him overnight" as Nandy writes, from his life as an Indian Brahmin, "to an untouchable and a non-Indian." The story sympathetically portrayed is "one of loss and recovery of self," and includes a critique of nationalism and tradition in the context of a westernized Bengal (Nandy 1994: 34-39). Gora, on hearing of his ancestry, breaks the caste taboo, and in the last line of the book, asks the "Christian outcaste servant … from whose hands the earlier Gora, orthodox Brahman could not accept drinking water" to bring him a glass of water (Spivak 2002: 49). Thus in one moment Gora's ethnic origin, caste, and religion dissolved into thin air. He comes to terms with both his 'whiteness' and 'Indianness,' and although he had an Indian upbringing, retains sensitive "elements of his western self" (Nandy 1994: 45). As Gora exclaims:

> No I'm not a Hindu… I have been told I was a foundling… my father was an Irishman! …the doors of every temple are today closed against me… I, having got absolute freedom find myself standing

> in the midst of a vast truth! ...Now I have truly the right to serve her [India] for the real field of labour is spread out before me it is the actual field of welfare for the three hundred millions of India's children. (Tagore 2002: 566-67)[2]

It was a moment in South Asian history when a clash as well as a fusion of cultures was taking place and when issues of hybridity, modernity and pluralism came to the fore. Gora states: "what I wanted to be day and night but couldn't be, I am today. I am Indian today. *In me today there is no conflict among Hindu, Muslim, and Christian society*" (quoted in Spivak 2002: 59, emphasis added). This daring and progressive current of thinking as reflected in Tagore's *Gora* was perhaps another indicator of the saying that Bengal was politically decades ahead of other parts of India.

While such advanced views – as expressed by Gora – were rare in literature in India, they were almost non-existent in Sri Lanka where the common and popular themes of Sinhala novels were the economic threat from the minorities and the dangers of 'miscegenation.' Women, according to many Sinhala and Hindu nationalists, had to be protected from 'the evils of westernization,' but modernization was necessary for men to advance in colonial society. Hence the task of preserving religious, ethnic and caste identities fell on the women, and the dichotomy between the traditional home (*ghar*) and the outside modern world (*bahir*) became marked (Chatterjee 1989).

The 'Pure' and the 'Hybrid'

By the late 19th and early 20th centuries, when Sri Lankan merchant capitalism was in full swing, the revival of Buddhism and concern about Sinhala identity led to discussions centred on national awareness and the concept of the Sinhala-Buddhist nation. The Buddhist bourgeoisie gave leadership to such trends. It was a class living off monopoly advantages in arrack renting, traders' profits, rentier wealth from absentee landownership, income from plantation produce, as well as money from professional services and assets from dowries. Ideologically, sections of the class were preoccupied with hierarchy and status, also focusing on distinctions of caste, ethnic origin, religious practice, and gender. The type of merchant capitalism that arose, rather than obliterating concerns about ethnic and religious divisions, led to a greater involvement in promoting such identities (Jayawardena 2000). Based on an exclusivist, majoritarian vision of a Sinhala-Buddhist nation, campaigns were launched to mobilize Buddhists at many levels – especially to urge them, through the temperance movement, to sober up. As Kanishka Jayasuriya (2000) remarked:

> Having made their fortunes in the liquor trade, a significant part of the Sri Lanka elite got off the booze wagon... to hitch a political ride on the growing temperance train which played a key role in shaping a Sinhalese Buddhist national consciousness.

The Sinhala-Buddhist campaign demarcating 'the internal frontiers' between Sinhala Buddhists, and the religious and ethnic minorities, focused initially on confronting Christianity and the missionaries. The Christian religion was vilified as foreign superstition, which had a polluting influence. Christian society, Dharmapala insisted, was characterized by "killing animals, stealing, prostitution, licentiousness, lying and drunkenness" (Guruge 1965: 482), and also by "cruelty...and wife-beating" (ibid: 479). Underlying all this was the accusation that Christianity was the religion imposed by the imperialists. In order to counteract harmful foreign influences, Christianity had to be challenged – a process started earlier in the 19th century, which took the form of public debates and written polemics between Buddhists and Christians. While early Buddhist resistance was directed against missionary education and Christianity, care was taken, however, not to sound too political or 'seditious'; the attacks made were on missionary education rather than directly against imperialism.

The Buddhist revival in the latter half of the 19th century was also a response to the privileged position of Christianity as the (established) religion of the colonial rulers. At a time when the superiority of the white race and the universality of Christianity were being forcefully asserted, the response took the form of diatribes invoking science and rationalism. Thus the claims of 'rational' Buddhism over Christian 'superstition' were asserted, 'unscientific' Biblical accounts of 'Creation' were ridiculed, and Buddhism was upheld as being compatible with the findings of modern science.

The emphasis in Sri Lanka on 'correctness' in 'blood and belief' was influenced by similar trends in Europe. Myths of 'purity' of race and of religious 'truth' were particularly heightened in Europe after the imperial conquest of Asia and Africa from the 16th century onwards. Claims of racial superiority and inferiority became a rationalization for colonialism, since the 'white man's burden' was to bring both 'civilization' and Christianity to the 'heathens,' who were in Kipling's words, the "lesser breeds without the law." There was thus a two-fold emphasis on 'purity' and 'truth', which encompassed white (racial) and Christian (religious) categories. In Europe, as Caplan writes, there was "much theorizing centred on the dangers of miscegenation and the infertility, degradation and moral weakness of racial hybrids" (2001: 4). 'Scientific' explanations abounded, and 19th century pioneers of race theory claimed that hybridity was not a viable option and that racial "separation and purity were the sole alternatives to extinction" (ibid: 4, quoting Biddiss). By the late 19th century, the ideologues of racism included the anti-Semitic lobby, which denounced Jews as 'Christ-killers' and as 'polluters' of the race through their marriages with non-Christians. Subsequent extreme right-wing ideology in Europe was characterized by beliefs in 'Aryan' mythology, white supremacy and anti-Semitism (Poliakov 1977).

A wave of irrationalism, romanticism, and rejection of liberalism and the Enlightenment, led to a growth of interest in ancient rituals, spiritualism, occult practices and theosophy – such movements in Germany even becoming part of the ideological basis of fascism. Rohan Butler writes of the inability of the Nazis to distinguish "the heroic from the trumpery." He argues that their beliefs in the Nordic pagan cult and "primitive myths," as well as the denunciation of some peoples as "*untermensch*" (subhumans), were to become the foundation for Nazi anti-Semitism and racism (in Goodrick-Clarke 1992: x, Introduction).

Nicholas Goodrick-Clarke traces the occult and 'Aryan cult' roots of Nazism, which not only included dangerous beliefs in a race of "Aryan god-men," and the need to exterminate "inferiors," but also promoted a vision of a "wonderful millennial future of German world-domination" (ibid: x). He notes that Ariosophy, defined as occult wisdom linked to the Aryans, became a cult in Germany and Austria, combining "German *volkisch* nationalism and racism with occult notions borrowed from the theosophy of Helena Blavatsky." Such cults alluded to: "a prehistoric golden age, when wise Gnostic priesthoods had expounded occult-racist doctrines and ruled over a superior and racially pure society." But they believed that an "evil conspiracy of anti-German interests," namely non-Aryans, Jews and Catholics, had promoted "spurious egalitarianism," resulting in racial confusion, denounced as the cause of the problems of the modern world (ibid: 2). Ariosophy, with its anti-rational roots, rejection of modernism, and resort to occult practices and secret societies, filtered down to those anti-Semitic groups and ultra-nationalist organizations that were the forerunners of the early Nazi movement.

In this way, racism against non-whites, the assertion of white racial 'purity' and the hatred of racial mixing, propagated by some of Europe's eminent philosophers, entered the popular mainstream in the 19th century. But such views had earlier roots – Immanuel Kant, for example, in 1798 wrote:

> The Spaniard [is] born of a mixture of European and Arab (Moorish) blood... as shown by bull-fights, his character is cruel which is proved by the auto-da-fé of former times and this taste shows that his origin lies in part outside Europe. (quoted in Poliakov 1977: 172)

Racial prejudices against non-Europeans were categorized as 'scientific' even among some philosophers of the Enlightenment in France (ibid: 169). And in Germany, the philosopher J.G. Fichte "galvanized" the youth with his "Talks to the German Nation," referring to Germans as an original race (*urvolk*) and lauding their superiority and 'destiny': "There is no way out: if you collapse the whole of humanity will collapse with you and there will be no hope of recuperation" (ibid: 99-100). In Britain, Thomas Arnold, the headmaster of Rugby, referred in 1842 to Germany as:

> The land of our Saxon and Teutonic forefathers; the land uncorrupted by any Roman or other mixture; the birthplace of the most moral races of men that the world has yet seen – of the soundest laws – the least violent passions and the fairest domestic and other virtues. (quoted in Poliakov 1977: 231)

Arnold's "moral races of men" did not include women, whose only task was to uphold "domestic virtues." In fact, exclusion of middle-class European women from the public sphere in the 19th century had led to attempts to further control their sexuality. Deviations that were deplored included cross-links whether political or sexual between white and black, Christian and non-Christian, or in racist terms, between 'Aryan' and 'non-Aryan.' White women, the guardians of 'racial purity,' were thought to be particularly susceptible to racist and religious betrayal; and in Asia, European women who renounced Christianity, married Asians or joined struggles against colonial rule were considered by the foreign rulers to have 'gone *jungli,'* and were branded as traitors to the white race, the Christian religion, and to the colonial state (Jayawardena: 1995).

The Aryan Myth in Asia

Theosophy had a strong South Asian connection, and the founders, Colonel Henry Olcott and Helena Blavatsky, travelled and worked in India and Sri Lanka, the Theosophical Society finally making its headquarters in Adyar, Chennai. Theophists popularized Aryan supremacist mythology, which had found a ready audience among some Hindus and Buddhists. Moreover, the work of Orientalists, especially Max Müller, who had written on the links between European languages and Sanskrit was wrongly interpreted, in historian Leslie Gunawardana's words, to mean, that "the affinity between languages" was indicative of a "common racial stock," and that "the same blood flowed in the veins of both the Englishmen and the Bengalis" (1985: 88). As Romila Thapar writes, "The notion of an Aryan race has now been generally discarded in scholarship and what we are left with is essentially a linguistic category: the Indo-Aryan speaking people" (1989: 226). Müller himself latterly dissociated himself with his own theory, but as Thapar commented, although "the identification of language and race was seen to be a fallacy," it was too late, and "the idea had taken root" (quoted in Bandaranayake 1985: 6). Poliakov also deplored "the confusion between language and blood" that had become "a permanent feature of German history" (1977: 77).

Another source of anti-Semitism was the Pan-German League (a forerunner of Fascism) started by Alfred Hugenberg, to promote heroic, expansionist ideas in support of German colonialism. He was succeeded by the lawyer Heinrich Class, who in 1908 published an ambitious political programme ("If I were Emperor"), which included a struggle against the Social Democrats and a vicious campaign against Jews, whom he termed *mischmaschvolk* (bastard people). Poliakov comments on the meeting in 1920 between the young Hitler and his mentor Heinrich Class and noted that the Pan-German League "was strengthened by Class and Hugenberg's ties with heavy industry," which gave the "financial support for the propaganda machinery of anti-semitism" (ibid: 303-4).

Obsession with racial 'purity' grew among South Asians. Nationalist ideologues of the 19th century were well versed in Orientalist writings from Europe that glorified and romanticized Asian civilizations and religions. They were also exposed to Aryan race theories from Europe with their beliefs in racial superiority and racial purity. Some Indians and Sri Lankans not only included themselves as part of the Aryan 'race,' but also absorbed, paradoxically, the arguments of European ideologues against non-white peoples. Using the language of racial supremacy, local ultra-nationalists marginalized minority ethnic and religious groups and drew internal boundaries between such groups and the majority. Thus the language and diatribes of racism – including preoccupation with mythic origin, 'purity,' and consequently a hatred of the 'hybrid' – were also inspired by European sources, and used extensively in South Asia in polemic debates on identity.

But South Asians were not without their own concepts of 'purity.' In caste society, those at the top of the hierarchical caste system valorized purity and condemned *varna sankara* (mixture of castes) as an unnatural phenomenon. In an era when European racists were projecting themselves as 'Aryans' of superior heritage, Sinhala Buddhists also constructed an identity based on imagined Aryan ancestry, claiming a mythic origin from a Bengali prince Vijaya who, according to legend, landed in Sri Lanka on the day of the Buddha's death.

Some South-Asian nationalists of the late 19th and early 20th centuries were cognisant of German philosophers, especially Kant, Fichte, Müller and Hegel. Even the tone, language and content of some South-Asian writings sounded like European ultra-nationalist polemics. The Aryan myths of both Europe and Asia posited an antithesis of the non-Aryan (Semitic/Dravidian). In Europe the Jew, as Poliakov notes, became the devil incarnate, while the Aryans were "the most noble species in nature" (1977: 311); the Aryans once lived as vegetarians "in primitive innocence," and Christ tried to show the way back but his message was not only perverted but also "polluted by animal flesh and the poison of Jewish blood" (ibid: 312). Diatribes against Jews in European racist literature found an echo in South-Asian writing of the early 20th century, when Muslim traders were compared to the stereotyped Jew. Interestingly, one of the favourite Shakespearean texts and plays in English-medium schools in colonial Sri Lanka was *The Merchant of Venice*, with many a student hamming it up as Shylock.[3] Thus in colonial times, anti-Semitism also came into the local vocabulary through British education, and the word 'Jew' was used derogatorily.

The claims of the Sinhalese to be Aryans, and therefore highly cultured, were constantly asserted, and over the decades, entered Sinhala consciousness through the media and textbooks. The emphasis was not only on purity and superiority in race and religion, respectively, but also on the historic destiny of the Sinhalese to protect Buddhism. Anagarika Dharmapala wrote in 1902: "the glorious inheritance of Aryan ancestors, uncontaminated by Semitic and savage ideas... has been preserved by the Aryan Sinhalese" (Guruge 1965: 487). The contrast was with the British, who 2,400 years earlier were "in a state of absolute savagery and barbarism." Although they were powerful today, Dharmapala claimed, the British had hereditary tendencies of "cruelty, drunkenness and other vices," in contrast to the valour, purity, culture and 'Aryanness' of the Sinhalese (ibid: 479-80). "There exists no race on this earth today that has had a more glorious triumphant record of victory than the Sinhalese" (ibid: 481). But Sri Lanka, which was the repository of the pure religion of the Buddha, he said, had been besieged: "Brahmans and Christianity were the two forces that came like avalanches and buried the pure, refined, kind-hearted children of Lanka" (ibid: 482). Imperialism, too, played its part, and commenting on the 'disorder' and havoc of Portuguese rule, Dharmapala denounced: "these demons in human form who destroyed temples, ... outraged womanhood [and] threw... infants to crocodiles" (ibid: 482).

Both the Portuguese and their mixed descendants were demonized. Michael Roberts has analysed the strong feelings of certain Sinhala ideologues regarding the disastrous impact of foreign rule, which had resulted in many kinds of 'disorder' and dangers to the 'race.' He refers to the novels of Piyadasa Sirisena, which "postulated the following equation":

> Mixed blood = unstable and fickle = disordered. Contrawise to be Arya Sinhala was to be pure (*pirisidu*) and to be the epitome of Virtue, Stability and Order. (1989: 17)

Anthropologists have recalled that in many societies, disorder is thought to be caused by impurities and contagion often attributed to demonic forces (Douglas 1966). Bruce Kapferer has described the belief that demons are "the result of mismarriages between those of highborn and lowly castes" (quoted in Roberts et al. 1989: 19). Roberts links this to the emergence of the mixed community, and says (ibid: 19):

> The ideas of impurity embedded in caste ideology linked up with a longstanding opposition to foreigners (*paradesakkarayo*) in Sinhala thinking and with the Aryan mythology imported by Europeans.

Creating Tradition

Through newspapers, journals, novels and poetry, Buddhist ideologues depicted the Sinhalese as the 'chosen people' of superior race whose destiny was to protect the pure form of Buddhism. This necessitated not only an all-out critique of Christian influences, but also an attempt to return to traditional practices and social rituals – what Gombrich and Obeyesekere call the 'creation of tradition' in keeping with the needs of the bourgeoisie and petty bourgeoisie of Sinhala Buddhists:

> The embourgoisement of Sinhala society came from a variety of sources, but it was Dharmapala's reform that gave Buddhist legitimation to these new values and permitted later generations of the Sinhala Buddhist elite to introject them as quintessential Buddhist ethics. (1988: 256)

While there were rules of conduct for monks, there were no detailed rules for the laity. In Sri Lanka an attempt to fill this gap was made by Dharmapala in a pamphlet published in 1898 on a "Daily Code for the Laity" (*Gihi Vinaya).* This advice was on behaviour in private and public, and rules about cleanliness, eating habits and domestic ceremonies. To combat western influences, 'correct' conduct pertaining to women, children and servants was advocated. Dharmapala's 'Protestant Buddhism' (a name coined by Gananath Obeyesekere) reflected the needs of the time, and provided "a value system to a new class, an emerging bourgeoisie" (Gombrich & Obeyesekere: 214-15). For women, the message included the (somewhat Calvinist) duties of a wife, based on thrift, protecting property, and entertaining kith and kin 'correctly.'

At the turn of the 20th century, Buddhist ideologues were preoccupied with promoting change through a return to Sinhala names and forms of dress, as well as Buddhist ceremonies and rituals. Specific rites of passage were given publicity, especially practices involving marriages, funerals, auspicious times and Sinhala New Year rituals. Since the English-educated bourgeoisie followed a more 'Christianized' way of life, attention was paid to wedding rituals since these were occasions linked to producing the next generation, or in other words, 'reproducing the nation.' What is more, in traditional Sinhala Buddhist society, where marriage was "not a sacrament and often divorce was by mutual consent," the marriage ceremony (*poruwa*) needed to be "sacramentalized" to bring it "closer to the Christian ideal and thereby make the event more respectable" (Gombrich & Obeyesekere 1988: 256). The existing, simple traditional marriage ceremony, with no religious connotations, was reinvented as a 'Sinhala Buddhist' ritual, with "reversals of traditional symbolism" and "Buddhist *sacralia* introduced into the ceremony" (ibid: 264). All this was intended to satisfy English-educated Buddhists, who felt the need for 'traditional' ceremonies and 'ancient' ritual.

Gender and Nation

Several feminist writings on Sri Lanka have analysed the question of gender and nation, and the traditional role of women as the guardians of ethno-religious and cultural identity (de Mel 2001; Jayawardena 1992; Jayawardena & de Alwis 1996.) Women, seen as the symbolic 'Mothers of the Nation,' were its actual biological reproducers, also playing a key part in socializing children into their traditional ethnic and religious roles. Women were, moreover, cultural carriers in terms of dress, adornment, behaviour and ritual. Drawing distinctions between 'purity' and 'pollution,' women's responsibilities were to ensure the unblemished continuity of ethnic, religious and caste identities.

These trends gained ground with the advance of capitalist development in the 19th century when identity assumed importance, and nationalists warned of the dangers of 'ethnic contamination' through women 'going astray.' In order to project appropriate norms for local women, there had to be ideological constructs, not only about how women should conduct themselves, but also more specifically about inappropriate behaviour, which was defined as 'Western' as opposed to correct 'Eastern' practices.

The Sinhala-Buddhist revival sought to exclude certain 'alien' practices and customs, and to reactivate what was believed to be tradition, and in doing so, promote Sinhala patriotism. But keeping up with the times was also crucial, and a modern education in English for the children of the local Buddhist bourgeoisie was simultaneously promoted. There were, however, some immediate tasks which included preserving the 'purity' of the 'Aryan Sinhala' nation, combating Christianity and missionary education, and discouraging 'hybridization' and mixed marriages of Sinhala Buddhists to Christians, Euro-Asians and foreigners. Central to these issues was the question of gender and nation and the responsibility of Sinhala-Buddhist women towards the nation. The imagined Aryan wife was essentially 'respectable,' conforming to the prevalent patriarchal attitudes in bourgeois society (Jayawardena 1992). Caste moved from the public to the private sphere of the family; and in arranging 'correct' marriages and negotiating dowries within the relevant caste and class, women played a crucial part.

At the turn of the 20th century, Sinhala-Buddhist revivalists became active on gender issues. In contrast, however, to many nationalists of neighbouring countries, who projected ideas of the 'New Woman' and spoke of women's emancipation, the conservative Buddhists argued that what was needed was a return to tradition and the old values, imposing a restraint on unacceptable types of 'modernity.' This was to counteract the 'corrupting' influences on local women of Christianity, missionary education and western values. Since Christianity was denounced as the religion of the imperialists, combating harmful foreign influences began with confronting Christianity.

In this campaign for 'national purity,' gender came to the fore. One manifestation of the Buddhist nationalists' critique of Christianity was a vilification of women of the Bible. In the 1890s, there was the publication of a racy pamphlet "*Kanni Mariyage Hati*" (What the Virgin Mary Is Really Like) by the well-known *bhikku* Battaramulle Sri Subuti. The colonial government banned the publication as obscene, but it circulated furtively and even reappeared in anti-Christian polemics of the 1950s. In the late 19th century, a British anti-Christian journal, the *Freethinker*, which was popular in Sri Lanka, gained some notoriety with its ribald stories about women biblical figures, leading to protests by missionaries about its local circulation (Jayawardena 1972: 52).

For Sinhala-Buddhist women and men, 'reproducing the nation' meant guarding the heritage by marrying within their given ethnic and religious group, subject to boundaries of caste and class. As mentioned earlier, a parallel preoccupation was reviving or creating Buddhist marriage rituals and customs, and adopting Sinhala names instead of fashionable Western ones. The rules of the game were clearly set out by Buddhist leaders, and much debate ensued on 'purity' of ethnic origin and 'correctness' in religion.

Sinhala-Buddhist womanhood thus became a key focus of the Buddhist revival. This involved two strategies: preservation of the 'purity' of local women and glorifying their beauty, while insisting on the immorality and unattractiveness of European and Euro-Asian women, whose looks and clothes became popular targets of vituperative comment. One line of attack was their 'ugliness' – defined as brown hair, and light eyes which in popular parlance were called 'cat's eyes' (*balal as*), and a reddish fair skin which was likened to lobsters. In contrast was the traditional concept of beauty – long black hair, black eyes and golden-hued skin as celebrated in the Sinhala classics. Local cultures thus valorized fair skin, but in Sri Lanka as in India, fairness was presumed to be from 'Aryan' origin and not from any racial admixture with Europeans.

'Peculiarities' of dress were also seized upon; clothes and hats worn by European and local westernized women were scorned and made the subject of cartoons by nationalists. The large hats of the Victorian era, adorned with fruits and feathers, were also worn by local bourgeois women, who were compared to *vatti ammas* (women vendors) (Guruge 1965: lxxv). Dresses revealing women's legs were held to be provocative and indecent. Women who socialized with men in public, drank, smoked or danced, were seen as immoral or lacking in refinement. Dharmapala denounced Europeans for the "promiscuous dancing of men and women regardless of the laws of decency," which, while revealing their absence of culture, were also vestiges of their "primitive customs when they lived half-naked and painted their bodies" (Guruge 1965: 479-80). Since Euro-Asian women led a westernized lifestyle, socializing, dancing and moving freely in public, they were frequently condemned for 'immoral behaviour.' This was reflected in the newspaper diatribes and critical novels of the Sinhala writer and journalist Piyadasa Sirisena.

Even in the 1920s and early 1930s, the same arguments were used against women's franchise. For instance, the campaigns by the Women's Franchise Union, along with the granting of women's suffrage in 1931 and women's political participation in the legislature, were subjected to much criticism in the Sinhala and Tamil press (de Alwis & Jayawardena 2001). Piyadasa Sirisena, blamed the westernized Sinhalese, for the "decline of the race.' A polemical diatribe he wrote in 1934, *Parivarthanaya* (Transition), took the form of a debate where proponents of women's franchise were vilified as immoral, westernized women who neglected their families and ended up in the divorce courts.

"They be all Whores"

In both colonial and post-colonial South Asian societies, white women have been demeaned by nationalists. The white man (*suddha*) had been the enemy, coming in many forms, as ruler, trader, soldier, exploiter – who through superior arms, higher levels of technology and access to capital, dominated the colonized people directly and indirectly. But the white man's woman, derogatorily referred to as *suddhi*, although having no power in her own right, was often reviled in terms of her sexuality as shameless, if not promiscuous. The imagined 'immoral white woman' was frequently targeted in nationalist, anti-imperialist discourse. However, there were also the 'White Goddesses' – namely those European women working for Buddhist or Hindu causes, who were inevitably placed on a pedestal. One example was a German, Marie Musaeus Higgins, who in 1894 started Musaeus College for Buddhist girls and was affectionately known as *sudu amma* (white mother) by her students. Others in India included Sister Nivedita and Annie Besant (Jayawardena 1995).

In this ideological contest, the foreign colonizers projected themselves as the defenders of chaste white womanhood against the rapacious dark-skinned man. 'Native' women were portrayed by

Europeans as uninhibited, wild and promiscuous, in contrast to "the white, civilized lady of temperate climates" who was the opposite of "that dark primitive woman of the torrid zones" (Tiffany & Adams 1985: 30; Jayawardena 1995: 3). There was also an implied critique of the morally corrupt 'native' men who tolerated this licentiousness. The British seafarer Robert Knox in 1681, referring to customs in the Kandyan regions, said: "Indeed the Publik Trade would be bad, and hardly maintain them that exercised it, the private one being so great. And I think they be all whores, yet they abhor the name of Vesou, which is Whore" (Knox 1989: 262).

To Buddhist ideologues, female 'devils' were of three distinct groups – the European, the Euro-Asian and the local Christian – who became the permanent 'Others,' subverting and undermining Sinhala-Buddhist society and culture. The European community in Sri Lanka included missionary women teachers, who (Buddhists alleged) not only denounced Buddhism but also promoted Western values, thereby deculturizing the young. Other foreign women were the European wives of all classes of British residents – bureaucrats, planters, businessmen, engine drivers, soldiers, and shop assistants – whose dress, behaviour and social habits were considered to be a bad influence. The second category of 'evil' woman was the Euro-Asian, whose lifestyle, attitudes and greater proximity to 'native' society, made her a greater and more immediate danger and a corrupting influence. As a result, much effort was spent (as noted earlier) in books, dramas and propaganda to demonize the 'hybrid' woman. The third group was composed of those Sinhala-Christian women educated in English, who from the late 19th century onwards had assimilated Christian and European culture and values, and were therefore perceived as subverters of the traditional inheritance. They were castigated for not being 'authentic' Sinhalese and often called 'half-Sinhalese.'

Neloufer de Mel has analysed the reactions of nationalist playwright John de Silva to the English-educated, westernized local woman whom he lampoons in his social satire *Sinhala Parabhava Natakaya* (1920), calling her the hybrid (Sinhala-English) *Singili Nona.* One of his popular songs on this theme included the lines:

> Now, the Singili lady, rice and curry, she cannot eat
> But she's got accustomed to drinking claret and whisky neat
> The science of the saucepan into a corner they throw
> They take to the quill pen instead and long epistles flow.

Also in words reminiscent of Molière's 17th-century satire *Les Femmes Savantes,* the song ridicules learned women:

> More and more the ladies grow so languid and so slack,
> From the weight of French and Latin that's loaded on each back.
> (de Mel 2001: 68-69)

A common feature of all the demonized women was that they were Christian, and therefore purveyors of false beliefs. Such prejudices and perceptions originated in the late 19th century, and have continued to pervade Sinhala-Buddhist consciousness, as reflected sometimes in current social practice and media representation (see, de Mel 2001, Jayawardena 1991, Silva 2002). Thus, in a period of heightened awareness of identity associated with the Buddhist revival, an attempt was made to return to the past, to reinvent ritual, adding some Christian practices in a setting of change caused by economic development and modernization. The dilemma continued right throughout the 20th century and exists today. One issue that became contentious was that of mixed marriages with 'outsiders' as discussed in the next chapter.

Notes

1. See Chapter 1, p.26, for a discussion of the word *thuppahi.*
2. Bimanbehari Majumdar has suggested that *Gora* was based on Sister Nivedita, the Irish disciple of Swami Vivekananda. She was a devotee of the Goddess Kali, and supporter of Vivekananda's brand of 'muscular' Hindu nationalism (Nandy 1994: 36, n54). She was a complex blend of East and West – simultaneously a revolutionary supporting the Bengali 'extremists' of the time, and a 'Holy Mother' (Jayawardena 1995: Chapter 13).
3. *The Merchant of Venice* was staged in 1915 at St Aloysius' College, Galle, a Jesuit-run school (St Aloysius' College, *Centenary Magazine*). Also around this time, at a Buddhist school, Ananda College, the author's father A.P. de Zoysa (a teacher) played the role of Shylock in a school production.

12

'CORRECTLY' REPRODUCING THE NATION

> Partly because of empire, all cultures are involved in one another; none is single and pure, all are hybrid, heterogenous, extraordinarily differentiated, and unmonolithic... As an Arab with a Western education... I have felt that I belonged to both worlds, without being completely *of* either one or the other... when I say 'exile' I do not mean something sad or deprived. On the contrary, *belonging... to both sides of the imperial divide enables you to understand them more easily.*
>
> Edward Said, *Culture and Imperialism*, 1994, p.XXV-VI (emphasis added)

> That spirit of pure devotion to religion and country... has become extinct in the modern, hybrid, superficially educated, half-anglicised Sinhalese... Hybrids and bastards of Sinhalese... have become traitors to the country...
>
> Anagarika Dharmapala, in Ananda Guruge (ed.), *Return to Righteousness,* 1965, p.524

Laissez-faire and Mixed Marriages

One issue the colonial authorities had to tackle was that of mixed marriages or liaisons. By the late 19th century, the race lines were firmly drawn, and marriages and alliances of European men to local women and of local men to European women – considered to be inappropriate crossings of race and class barriers – were socially and even officially deplored. The extreme cases, such as marriages of Indian royalty to British working-class women, were especially traumatic to race - and class-conscious British officials in India. One such occurrence was the marriage in 1893 of the Maharajah of Patalia to Florrie Bryan of London, an event which, Strobel says, confused "the racial, sexual and class hierarchies of Empire" (1991: 4). Another case was that of the Maharajah of Kapurthala, who in 1910 married a Spanish dancer, Anita Delgado (*The Island*, 11 Sept. 2006). Anton Gill writes that in 1910, Maud Allan, an erotic dancer was prohibited from performing in India as this would "undermine the image" of British women, and what was worse "young Indians would be allowed to buy tickets" (1995: 91). The presence of white prostitutes and barmaids in India was also officially deplored "on the usual grounds that they threatened the prestige of the ruling nation" (ibid: 128).

Moreover, the continuance of liaisons between British government servants in the colonies and local women resulted in a circular from London in 1909, warning new recruits to the colonial service of the "disgrace and official ruin" that would result from "concubinage with girls or women belonging to the native populations" (quoted in Hyam 1990: 157). The colonial governments reacted in different ways to this circular. In Sri Lanka, Governor McCallum argued that such occurrences were no longer prevalent, and that there would be a scandal if the circular was leaked to the press. An outspoken civil servant in Colombo, R.E. Stubbs made cynical observations on a British engineer who was:

> considered 'socially impossible' because he used to play cricket with his bastards – the objection taken being not that they were bastards or... that he played cricket with them, but that he did so on ground adjoining the Lawn Tennis Club's courts. (quoted in Bell & Bell 1993: 202)

But if men with local partners were tolerated as long as they observed certain proprieties, the same did not apply to white women. Mrinalini Sinha has analysed the upsurge of feeling on gender and race in India in the 1880s involving white women and 'native' men. The unsuccessful Ilbert Bill of 1883, giving 'native' civil servants jurisdiction over Europeans in criminal cases outside the main towns, provoked a "white mutiny" over the prospect of the "pure and defenceless white woman in India" being tried by an Indian judge (Sinha 1992: 98-99). A 'cause célèbre' occurred a few months later, with a 'scandalous' crossing of race and class boundaries. Alice Hume, wife of the public prosecutor of Kolkata James Hume, had an affair with their Indian servant, Hurroo Mehter. The latter was tried for assault and jailed for eight years. White society became hysterical over the perils faced by white women in India, but it was later revealed not only that the *memsahib* and the worker had been "romantically involved for some six months before the episode," but also that the accused had been framed [1] (Sinha 1992: 102-3). A similar trumped-up case occurred in Sri Lanka around this period (see Chapter 3). These cases raised issues of individual freedom, class and race.

The impact of revolutionary ideas from Europe was felt in radical and reformist circles in 19th century Sri Lanka. At the forefront were the Euro-Asian intelligentsia of professionals who, inspired by the events of 1848 in Europe, wrote frequently of liberty and equality. Their articles and poetry were published in the newspapers of the 1840s. Some of them, notably Charles Lorenz and Richard Morgan, had joined with British radicals of Colombo such as Dr Christopher Elliot who were part of the 1848 ferment and agitation in Sri Lanka (see Chapter 6). Politically, the move was away from slavery and aristocratic privilege; and socially, it sought to do away with the excesses of caste discrimination and feudal social practice which were questioned by sections of the local bourgeoisie. While much was debated about political and social freedom, also popular was the concept of economic freedom in line with Adam Smith's ideas. Mercantilist restrictions on private trade by the East India Company, compulsory labour (*rajakariya*) and archaic taxes were opposed, and instead, policies of a laissez-faire economy (free trade, free enterprise and free labour) were promoted.

The freedoms advocated also extended to the social and personal spheres. They included the individual's freedom to choose a marriage partner. Under colonial laws, one could (within a stipulated age and consanguinity) marry a person of any class, caste, ethnicity or religion. The rhetoric, reinforced by romantic literature, was that marriage should not be forced or arranged, but based on love, companionship and mutual respect. Theoretically, there was thus freedom of choice in marriage. In colonial times, when marriages were often registered in churches, the pithy saying in Sinhala was that 'anyone's mother can marry anyone, as long as the church warden (*palliye appu*) was paid the marriage fee'. In traditional society, however, the crucial determinant in marriage was caste, a breach of which was rare. While marrying out of one's caste was never socially condoned, from the time the Portuguese conquered the maritime regions, mixed marriages had taken place with foreigners or those of Portuguese descent and Christian religion. The Dutch rulers, while not officially encouraging mixed marriages, themselves married into the existing *mestico* community or had liaisons with local women. In Sri Lanka during colonial rule, marriages also took place between local men of wealth and high social status and women of British, Dutch and Portuguese origin.

Mudaliyars, Capitalists and Professionals Marrying 'out'

In the 18th and early 19th centuries, there had been a few marriages between foreigners and locals belonging to prominent *mudaliyar* and other bourgeois families, including the Bandaranaike clan. In June 1820, a Sinhala-English marriage took place in London between Rev. Hendrick (Henricus) de Saram (1795-1858) and Frances Treherne of Middlesex, England. De Saram and his cousin Balthazar de Saram had been sponsored by the colonial government to study in Britain in 1811 and, according to Paul Pieris, Hendrick's "selection of an English woman for his wife was... not surprising," as he himself was the descendant of a Sinhala-German marriage (Pieris n.d.: 75). When, after their stay in Britain, the return passages of the de Saram cousins were booked, Balthazar absconded on the excuse that he had such strong feelings about Hendrick's marriage that he wanted "to avoid being forced into their company during the long voyage" (ibid: 79). Balthazar, in explanation, described his problems in adjusting to British life, and said he had grown up "in all the peculiarities of a Native," unlike Hendrick who had been from his infancy reared in a family "whose only deviation from the manners, language and costume of the Dutch was his Father's native dress" (ibid: 72-73). The reference here was to Hendrick de Saram's half-German grandmother Cornelia Scharff, the daughter of Jan Christoffel Scharff, a German who worked in the Dutch East India Company in Sri Lanka, and in 1734, had married Elizabeth de Saram, a Sinhalese (Roberts et al. 1989: 365-66). Of their ten children, three married into the de Saram-Bandaranaike *mudaliyar* clan.[2] Others of the Philipsz-Scharff group married Burghers belonging to the van Dort, Heyman and Spittel families (ibid: 53 & 365-66).

Just as the Portuguese *casados* who had married local women branched out in two directions – some becoming Sinhala, others Burgher, the de Saram family provides (as Michael Roberts' research shows) that their "linkages with leading Burgher families were paralleled by a network of marriages… with the 'first class Goigama' families" (Roberts et al. 1989: 53-54). Some of the de Sarams married into the famous endogamous *mudaliyar* clan composed of the Illangakoon, de Livera, Obeyesekere, Dias Bandaranaike, Perera, Pieris Siriwardena, Deraniyagala and de Alwis families (ibid: 53). Others of the de Saram family continued the Burgher, Eurasian and foreign connections for generations, marrying into the families of Maartensz, Stewart, van Cuylenberg, Prins, van Langenberg, Morgan, Dickman, Nell and Cooke (ibid: 53). The 'Sinhalese de Sarams,' however, called themselves Sinhalese in spite of being married to non-Sinhalese for several generations, and the Bandaranaike extended family has regarded the de Sarams as part of the 'community' (ibid: 54, quoting Gooneratne 1986). Of the Bandaranaike-Obeyesekere family some continued to marry Europeans, including Christoffel Obeyesekere's son Forrester who married Isabel Sykes of Britain. Their daughter Ezlynne Deraniyagala was the first Sri Lankan woman barrister and Oxford graduate, and a champion of women's rights in the 1950s, both in Sri Lanka and internationally.

Apart from these *mudaliya*r families, among the new rich – whose fortunes were made in trade, the liquor business, graphite and plantation produce – there were several mixed marriages. In the family of Charles de Soysa, the wealthiest of the new class, and his wife, the heiress Catherine de Silva, there were some marriages to foreigners. Their younger son J.S. Walter de Soysa's first marriage in 1904 was to Maria

Micada Albo of Spain (Wright 1907: 546); Victor de Soysa Sr, the grandson of Charles de Soysa, married Mary Knight of Britain; and E.L.F. de Soysa Jr (another grandson) also married a British woman. Similarly, the Vidanalage de Mels, a leading business family, had several mixed marriages. Two of Sir Henry de Mel's sons had British wives – Bishop Lakdasa de Mel married Joan Keyser, and Eksath de Mel's wife was Joan Hill. Sir Henry's grandson Maitripala Goonewardena married Doreen Wills of Britain. (see Edith Fernando 1989).

Mixed marriages also occurred among the Sinhala business community of rural origin. There were several such marriages in the family of W.D. Carolis a Buddhist from Ranne in the Hambantota district, who in 1879 had a prosperous tannery and leather export business. Carolis, converted to Christianity on his marriage to Madelena Fonseka. In 1916 their son Charles Don Carolis, during an extended stay in Britain, met Lillian Gregory (1893-1980) of Newcastle and married her in Colombo. His brother Edward, a barrister, had a British wife, Marion, and his other brother, Dr M. D. Carolis, married a Burgher, Ethel Cotterling.[3] The mixed marriages in this family continued and Charles Don Carolis' son, C. Godwin Don Carolis married Christobel Rowlands. Her father was A.P. Rowlands (of British origin), the founder of the well-known motor engineering firm of Rowlands and her mother Dr Rachel Christoffelsz (from a leading Dutch-Burgher family) was a pioneer woman doctor in Sri Lanka (Brohier 1994: 45).

Another case of several mixed marriages in one family is that of Gate Mudaliyar Douglas Samarasinghe of Kurunegala who married a Burgher, Mabel Hepponstall. (The family joke was 'it happens to all"). Their son was Maxwell Samarasinghe, grandfather of politician Mahinda Samarasinghe (whose wife is Swiss). The Gate Mudaliyar's daughter Sylvia Dorothy (known as Birdie) married Brigadier Christopher Jayawardena. Their daughter Sita marrried Saliya Parakrama, son of J.S. (Perera) Parakrama and his wife Elizabeth Craig Cowe of Scots-Irish descent from Berwick-on-Tweed in Northumberland.[4]

There were also notable mixed marriages among Muslims. A gem merchant from Galle, Mohamed Yusuf Salie, popularly known as 'Prince

Salie,' who travelled widely on business, in 1889 married an Australian, Elsie Goldsbrough of Melbourne. Their descendants married into several elite Muslim families of Sri Lanka. Other such cases included the family of Sri Lanka's world-renowned architect Geoffrey Bawa, whose immediate ancestors had married Europeans and Burghers; his grandfather Ahmadu (Arthur) H. Bawa, a lawyer, while in Britain married Georgina Matilda Ablett. Their elder son Benjamin W. Bawa, a leading lawyer, married a Burgher, Marion Schrader, in 1908. Thus their son Geoffrey Bawa, while bearing a Muslim last name, was only one quarter of Muslim origin. One of Arthur Bawa's other sons, Alfred, also married a Burgher, Martha Van Twest, while another Dr Harry Bawa, married an Anglo-Indian (Roberts et al: 282-83; and Wright 1907: 690 & 565). Other Muslims who married 'out' included the businessman Onally Gulamhussein to a Burgher, Yvonne Toussaint in the 1940s; H.S. Moosajee to Doris North of London – known as Zarina; and Alavi Macan Markar, in 1941, to Joan Fromant from Britain, called Farida.

From the late 19th century onwards, mixed marriages became more common, and several marriages of Sinhala and Tamil professionals and businessmen with Europeans and Euro-Asians were recorded in *20th Century Impressions of Ceylon* (1907).[5] Such marriages among doctors included that of Dr Simon de Melho Aserappa (1832-1906) to Julia Wake, the daughter of an Anglican vicar from Wells, England (Paul 2001: 19); and Dr John de Livera to Rose Gibbons, from London. Their daughter, Dr May Ratnaike, became a pioneer woman surgeon of the 1920s.

While the foreign wives were from all classes, many of them were dissidents in their own societies including theosophists, freethinkers, socialists, feminists and artists. There were some such marriages in the Ponnambalam-Coomaraswamy family. The Legislative Councillor and barrister, Muttu Coomaraswamy in 1877 married an English theosophist, Elizabeth Beeby. Their son, the savant Ananda Coomaraswamy, was married four times, in each case to a talented Western woman interested in both Western and Eastern culture: Ethel Partridge, who lived in Sri Lanka for some years and wrote on art and music; Alice Richardson, who gave recitals of Indian song and music in Europe; the painter Stella Bloch; and Dona Luisa Runstein, a photographer from Argentina. Among Ananda Coomaraswamy's cousins, were the three brothers of the Ponnambalam family; the eldest, P. Coomaraswamy, married a British woman, while the more famous brother Sir P. Ramanathan – a political personality – made a second marriage in 1906 to Australian theosophist R.L. Harrison, who took the name Lilavati (Jayawardena 1995). The third brother was the national figure Sir P. Arunachalam, whose son A. Padmanabha had a British wife. Their son was the writer Jayanta Padmanabha. Another grandson of Sir Arunachalam, was Ramanathan Arunachalam (Aru) who in 1966 married Tula Tuominen of Finland.

A unique and early case of a foreign professional woman marrying a local was the marriage, in New York in 1896, of Mary Irvin of Canada, a pioneer Canadian woman doctor (who had been chosen by a Christian mission for work in Jaffna), to S.C.K. Rutnam, a Sri Lankan who had been sent by Christian missionaries to the USA for studies. The marriage provoked much controversy and displeasure among the missionaries, who argued that if their recruits were allowed to marry 'natives,' families would not permit their daughters join the missions abroad. The Rutnams, after their expulsion by the missionaries, moved to Colombo, where S.C.K. Rutnam wrote a pamphlet on "Racism among the Missionaries." Dr Mary Rutnam apart from a successful career as a doctor, was a pioneer of many women's organizations which promoted gender equity, franchise rights and rural women's development. The Rutnams' five children made further marriages with Europeans and Euro-Asians (Jayawardena 1993).

Some foreign wives, however, were not from bourgeois or professional backgrounds, giving rise to the popular stereotype that they were barmaids' or landladies' daughters. Leonard Woolf, Assistant Government Agent in Hambantota, writing in 1909 to his Cambridge friend Lytton Strachey, gave voice to such prejudices:

> There are no Europeans in Hambantota... except a white woman who was I believe a lodging house keeper's daughter and has married a rather low-caste Sinhalese engineer who went to the Isle of Man

and met her there and she thought he was an Indian prince and so married him. (Spott 1989: 38)

The number of marriages to westerners among professionals, politicians and other middle-class persons in public life also increased over the years, adding to the pluralistic social life of Sri Lanka. The list is long, but a few can be highlighted. They include Sir Oliver Goonetilleke – the former Governor General whose second marrriage was to Joan Miller of Britain in 1948, and the artist Ivan Peries who married Veronica Perry of Britain. Among the many doctors who married British women were Dr V. Gabriel to Mary McCulloch, Dr S. Somasunderam to Martha Stella Davis and Dr I. A. Senanayake to Maude Smith. Several university professors married foreigners, including I.D.S. Weerawardena whose wife Joan was British; and S.J. Tambiah, who married an American, Mary Wynne Huber. Many women from France, Russia and Germany and several of Jewish origin married Sri Lankans.[6]

More numerous, however, were the marriages of prominent Sinhalese and Tamils to Euro-Asians, namely Burghers and Eurasians. They include the marriages of the famous Saravanamuttu brothers –T. Saravanamuttu to Ruth Arndt, and Manickam Saravanamuttu to Mona Kingston; as well as Professor Gerald Cooray to Joan Loos; C.R. Hensman to Pauline Swan; Pinsiripal 'Pin' Fernando to Pam de Vos; S.A. ('Jingle') Dissanayake to Phyllis Dickman; Cyril Gardiner to Mavis Henry; Jayanta Dhanapala to Maureen Elhart; Ben Fonseka to Daphne Muller; Dr R.O.B. Wijesekera to Marina Joachim; Senake Senanayake to Jennifer Hamer; Dr Peter Jayawardena to Beryl de Rosairo; Ratna Deshapriya Senanayake to Gloria Schokman; Sidney de Zoysa to Dr Corinne Jackson; and T. Arasanayagam to Jean Solomons.

Local Bourgeois Women Defying Tradition

Less frequent, more non-conformist and therefore more daring were the marriages of educated local women from well-known families who defied tradition to marry foreigners or Euro-Asians. In 1793 a prosperous Sinhalese woman, Catherina Petronella de Fonseca married Frederick August Nell; and many Burghers had maternal links with well-to-do

Sinhala and Tamil families. Another case of a local woman marrying a foreigner was that of Magdalene (Maria) Aserappa, a Colombo Chetty from a family of notables, who in 1866 married Arthur Kurt von Possner (1836-1900), a German who had started the New Colombo Ice Company. After his death she ran the Company (Paul 2001: 4). In 1893 Agnes Weerasooriya, from a leading Dodanduva family, married Arthur Paynter, an unorthodox British missionary (see Chapter 3). There was also a mixed marriage in the family of Methodist clergyman Rev. D.J. Gogerly (1792-1862) who was in Sri Lanka for many years; his son Daniel Gogerly became head of the Colombo Academy. The latter's son married a Sinhalese, Ms Gunawardena, and their descendants are the Gogerly-Moragoda family (Harris 2006: 229n3).

In the rare matrimonial unions of local upper-class women and foreigners, the Dias Bandaranaikes set the pace, as seen in the case of Amy Dias Bandaranaike, the third daughter of Udugaha Mudaliyar Don Christoffel Henricus Dias Bandaranaike (grandson of Cornelia Scharff) and Anna Philipsz Pandithuratna. Amy's sisters had married within the endogamous family, as did her only brother Sir Solomon Dias Bandaranaike, who married Daisy Ezline, the daughter of S. Christoffel Obeyesekere. Amy Dias Bandaranaike, reputed for her beauty, was described by her brother Solomon as "a strong and extraordinary personality …at times wilful" (Gooneratne 1986: 53). She was certainly more than wilful. After the Grand Tour of Europe and presentation at the British Court in 1897, she met "a handsome Italian, Signor Eduardo Roversi in Rome" and married him in 1898. This shocked the family, and the usual scornful jokes were made about Roversi's social origins. Yasmine Gooneratne, a family member, notes that the rumour was that, "having been encountered in a hotel [he] was most probably a waiter or a gigolo" (ibid: 56-57). The marriage ended in 1905, and Amy and their three children first settled in Britain, returning to Sri Lanka in the 1920s.

Several other 'rebellious' women from bourgeois families also married foreigners – one notable case in the early 1930s was Anil Marcia de Silva (1909-96), daughter of the nationalist politician George E. de Silva and his politically active wife Agnes Nell. Anil de Silva was married twice, to Europeans (see Chapter 10). Another spirited woman who rebelled against tradition was Helena de Mel. Born in 1906, she was the daughter of Sir Henry de Mel, of the famous Vidanalage de Mel family of merchants, liquor renters and plantation owners. She caused a stir by divorcing her husband Watson Peiris (son of the wealthy Hennadige Joseph Peiris) in the 1940s to marry Major J.B. Crosthwaite, and lived the rest of her life in Britain. In the Warusahennedige de Soysa family, Charles de Soysa's granddaughter Daisy (his son A.J.R. de Soysa's daughter) married Hulme King, a British businessman working in Colombo. Another de Soysa granddaughter, Varuni (Veronica) Pieris (1910-2001), the daughter of Louis Pieris and Selina de Soysa, married British sculptor Atri Brown, and later married another Britisher, John Hunt, a concert pianist. Varuni, an artist and sculptor, had been taught both by her artistic mother, and also by local artist David Paynter.

Buddhists Against Mixed Marriages

By the 1920s, marriages of Sinhalese-Buddhist males to foreigners and Euro-Asians attracted some attention from Buddhists. Concern was aroused especially because there had been marriages of Buddhists from prominent families to foreign, Burgher or Eurasian women. An interesting case is the family of a wealthy plantation owner William de Abrew Rajapakse, reputed for philanthropy to Buddhist causes, whose son Peter de Abrew donated land for a Buddhist girls' school, Musaeus College. William's other son, Richard de Abrew married Beatrice Perkins, a Eurasian; and their son Bertie de Abrew married a Eurasian, Mig Ralph. Peter de Abrew's nephew Walter de Silva married Laura Flanagan, who was Irish.[7]

Marriages of other Sinhala Buddhists to British women also took place including: Dr D.E. Wijewardene of the Tudugalle Wijewardene family to Corinne Jennings in 1919; Patrick de S. Kularatne to Hilda Westbrook in 1920 and her first cousin Margaret Russell to Dr G.P. Malalasekera in 1927[8]; Dr A. P. de Zoysa to Eleanor Hutton in 1929; Dr H.O. Gunewardene to Dorothy East in 1929; Lionel Weerasinghe to Margaret Harper in the early 1930s; Dr S.A. Wickremasinghe to Doreen Young in 1933; and J.V. Fonseka to Lily Margaret Walker in the 1940s. Several prominent Sinhala-Buddhists married Burghers, including

George E. de Silva to Agnes Nell in 1909, D.T. Devendra to Clarice Ruth Felsianes in 1928, H. Sri Nissanka to Muriel Spaling Christoffelsz in 1929, and Ediriweera Sarachchandra to Eileen Belleth in the 1940s.Two grandnephews of Anagarika Dharmapala had foreign first wives – Anil Moonesinghe in 1948 married Jeanne Hoban who was of Irish origin, and Mangala Moonesinghe's wife Jocelynne, was French. In the families of Philip and Kusuma Gunawardena (both Left MPs) there were mixed marriages. Kusuma's eldest brother Dr C.D. Amarasingha's second wife was Ena van Geyzel, a Burgher; and two of the Gunawardena children married foreigners – Prasanna Gunawardena to Darinka Rudan, a Croatian; and Lakmali Gunawardena to Stanley Sporney of the USA. Philip Gunewardena's nephew Gamini (Kuru) Gunawardena's second wife was Paula Gregory of Britain.

Mixed marriages had led to continuous public comment in the late 19th century when the increasing number of marriages of Buddhists to Christians and Burghers was frequently discussed. In the period 1891-1900, while there had been many Buddhist-Christian marriages between Sinhalese, there were also 270 marriages of Sinhalese to Burghers and 23 of Sinhalese to Europeans. Sections of the bourgeoisie, who financed Buddhist education, were conscious of the need for Buddhist girls' schools, as was the articulate group among the petty-bourgeois Buddhists, composed of clerks, journalists, teachers, traders, and small landowners. Many of these families, whose daughters were educated at village-level Sinhala schools, or in Catholic and Protestant girls' schools run by foreign nuns and missionaries, felt the need for English-medium schools for Buddhist girls that would produce educated, modernized wives for upwardly mobile Buddhist men.

The debates in Buddhist journals reflected these concerns. Deploring the lack of educated Sinhala women, one article in *The Buddhist* (3 Oct. 1890) complained: "we cannot marry these ignorant women… we want companions who shall stand shoulder to shoulder with ourselves." The next year the same journal continued to carry articles and letters expressing dismay at the frequent marriages of Buddhists to Christians, as young Buddhist men "imbued with European customs and manners" had difficulty finding "girls among Buddhists to suit their tastes" (*The Buddhist*, 13 March 1891). With the demand for Buddhist girls' schools giving a modern education in English, the Sanghamitta School was started in 1890, followed by Musaeus College (1894), and later Visakha Vidyalaya (1917). But even in 1924, after several more schools had been added, Dharmapala deplored the paucity of schools for Buddhist girls and lamented that "Kandy is no more a Buddhist town... Kandyan girls attending Hillwood College became either Christians or indifferent Buddhists" (Guruge 1965: 773).

The Sinhala press in the 1920s launched a campaign against mixed marriages (*misra vivaha*), with the public joining the debate and writing letters to newspapers. The outcry was led by Piyadasa Sirisena, editor of *Sinhala Jathiya,* who campaigned for the prohibition of marriages to foreigners and Euro-Asians. The argument was that such marriages resulted in the hybridization of the Sinhala race; those who made such marriages were 'retarded' persons who had rejected local traditions (*kula charithra*) and should be ostracized (*jatiyen pitaman kirima*) (15 March 1927). Another such letter condemned those who had rejected both their village roots and their country, lured by the pursuit of white women. They were 'hybrid traitors' (*sankara brashtayan*) who 'betrayed the race' (*Sinhala Jathiya*, 22 March 1927).

In March 1927 a public meeting to denounce mixed marriages was held at the Tower Hall in Colombo, presided over by C. Batuwantudawe, a well-known political figure and Buddhist activist. The main speaker was Piyadasa Sirisena, whose popular novels reflected concern that 'pure' Sinhala Buddhists, instead of being guardians of the nation, were diluting and thereby 'polluting' it through mixed marriages. With the increase in the numbers of local students going to Britain for study, there had been several mixed marriages in the 1920s, including those of Buddhist students. It was, most likely, Patrick de S. Kularatne's marriage that particularly irked local Buddhists. At the meeting, Piyadasa Sirisena moved a resolution that:

> This meeting deplores the inter-marriages between Sinhalese and European races, recommends a complete boycott of such Sinhalese

> Buddhists and asks all Buddhist associations in which such people hold office, to take appropriate action. (*Ceylon Daily News*, Weekly edition, 28 March 1927)

The speeches referred to harmful consequences of mixed marriages, such as the 'weakening' of the race, as the children of such marriages "always thought and acted according to Western ideas as a result of the influence of the mother." Moreover such children "did no good to the Sinhalese nation." Another problem discussed at the meeting was that, if educated Sinhalese men married Europeans, "Sinhalese women of the educated classes would find no husbands" (ibid). In the same month, a debate on mixed ethnic and caste marriages was held among senior students of the Buddhist girls' school Ananda Balika; it was organized by Hilda Kularatne, the British wife of Patrick Kularatne, herself the founder and principal of this school and several other Buddhist girls' schools including Mahamaya (Kandy), Maliyadeva Balika (Kurunegala) and Sri Sumangala (Panadura). At the debate, 16 voted against and 8 voted in favour of such marriages (*Sinhala Jathiya*, 27 March 1927). Clearly the concern of the critics was to keep the debate alive, based on the need to 'correctly reproduce the nation.' A leap from opposition to mixed marriages, to admiration for German racism occurred in the mid-1930s, when those who opposed the marriages of Sinhala women to Malayalis cited with approval Hitler's laws against "Aryans marrying non-Aryans" – namely Jews (*Viraya*, 17 April 1936).

In spite of the occurence in high places of mixed marriages, and the resulting 'hybridization' that took place, phobias about racial mixing persisted among sections of society. While the reality was that many Sinhala-Buddhist bourgeois men were marrying Euro-Asians, foreigners and Christians, the nationalist rhetoric continued to be one of abhorring such alliances. E.F.C. Ludowyk, speaking of his experience before the 1950s, said most Sinhalese parents would have had "an apopletic fit if the son and heir wanted to marry a Burgher" (quoted in Roberts et al. 1989: 9). Such views die hard in some circles. Roberts quotes a nationalist Buddhist monk's comment in 1985, which "placed *jati sankara* (ethnic mixing) in the same list as traitors (*jati drohi*) leading to the decline of the nation" (ibid 1989: 10, quoting *Divaina,* 18 Aug. 1985).

The disapproval was on the other side too. In *The Jam Fruit Tree,* Carl Muller gives a fictional portrayal of the reactions of a Burgher named von Bloss when a Sinhalese clerk, who wants to marry his daughter Anna, boasts of his ownership of paddy fields and buffaloes. Using all the Burgher stereotypes about rural Sinhalese-Buddhists, von Bloss says:

> How to face if I gave our Anna to a Sinhalese? Funny thing, no? Walking in sarong all over house, and putting wooden clogs and... my God, going to temple! ...and she put housecoat and cooking country rice and dry fish. Have Sinhalese girls, no? They know how to drive buffaloes ...and pound rice ... and go to temple with you. (1993: 36)

It was remarkably similar in India. In John Masters' novel of railway life, *Bhowani Junction,* an Anglo-Indian engine driver says that, although his grandfather had married an Indian, "he didn't... put on a dhoti, my God! He raised her to *his* level, he did not sink down into all the Indian ways... and go crawling on his stomach in front of the idols in the temples" (Masters 1960: 192).

Statistics of Admixture

Each Census from 1891 recorded an increasing number of marriages, registered locally, of Sinhalese and Tamils to Burghers, Eurasians and Europeans. Between 1891 and 1920 there were 1,411 mixed marriages made by Sinhalese (1,163) and Tamils (248) to Burghers, Eurasians or Europeans. The Censuses do not give a gender breakdown of these statistics, but we can assume that they were generally marriages – registered locally – by Sinhala and Tamil men; only a few women defied family opinion and tradition to marry outsiders.

Table 4 Mixed Marriages

	1891-1900	1901-10	1911-20	1921-35	1936-45
Sinhalese and Europeans —	23	22	24	not available	47
Sinhalese and Burghers —	270	315	509	---	1,221
Tamils and Europeans —	5	10	5	---	15
Tamils and Burghers —	53	66	109	---	243
Total	**351**	**413**	**647**	**---**	**1,526**

(Extracted from E.B. Denham, 1912, *Ceylon at the Census* of 1911, p.343; A. G. Ranasinghe, 1950, *Census of Ceylon, 1946, General Report*, p.201)

Due to the economic depression of 1931, the Census was not fully taken that year, but given the earlier figures and the rising trend of such marriages, there were probably around 1,500 in the 17-year period 1920-35. Fortunately the figures for 1936-45 are available; with 1,268 Sinhalese and 258 Tamils making such marriages (Ranasinghe 1946: 201). Thus, for a 55-year period (1891-1945) the total number of locally registered mixed marriages was approximately 4,500. The 1946 Superintendent of the Census commented that although the numbers were "relatively small," the trend "towards intermarriage seems to have advanced in recent decades," adding that intermarriage between Sinhalese and Burghers "is seen to be the greatest" (Ranasinghe 1950: 201). Not reflected in Census statistics, however, were marriages registered abroad of Sri Lankans to foreigners, as well as the numbers of liaisons between European men and local women, whose children were often absorbed into and categorized for Census purposes with the mothers' community.

Given the patriarchal structure of society and the emphasis placed on descent in the paternal line, foreign women who married locals lost their names and identity upon marriage, and their children (who were actually Euro-Asian) were recognized as Sinhalese, Tamil or Muslim.

Thus many such locals who had foreign, Burgher or Eurasian mothers, took on not only their fathers' family name, but also the paternal ethnic and (often) religious identity.* While there were, and still are, many such Sri Lankans, some prominent in national life, those with Burgher, Eurasian or foreign grandmothers are even more numerous.** In all these cases, the mothers and grandmothers were 'erased,' and the following generations became Sinhalese or Tamils – their Euro-Asian identity often being forgotten or passed over.

Earlier waves of racial mixing had occurred when white males – over the centuries of colonial rule – produced children by local women. These women were also erased from memory, and their existence often denied. In that era, white women having liaisons with local men was the big taboo. But the tide changed and the number of local men marrying foreigners increased. In the earlier colonial phase, the 'white man-local woman' phenomenon had a class dimension, the women being mainly from the poorer sections of society – from working class, plantation and peasant families. A major change occurred with bourgeois local women marrying white men, a practice that has also increased among the Sri Lanka diaspora in the post-independence era. Among the younger generation the trend continues.

* They include Geoffrey Bawa, Dr Sriani Basnayake, Shirani Captain, Ananda Coomaraswamy, June (Somasunderam) Chanmugam, Valentine Daniel, Anil de Silva, Minnette de Silva, Ezlynne Deraniyagala, Tissa Devendra, Manel Fonseka, Dr Tony Gabriel, Goolbai Gunasekera, C.I. and Dallas Gunasekara, Nelun and Lakshman Gunasekera, Norman Gunewardene, Rohini Hensman, Kumari Jayawardena, Parakrama Kularatne, Vinod Moonesinghe, Saliya Parakrama, Christopher Pinto, Jayantha Padmanaba, Roland Sri Pathmanathan, Rohan Pethiyagoda, Chitra (Malalasekera) Ranawake, Dr May Ratnaike, Nasreen Sansoni, Dr. Manorani Saravanamuttu, Ranjit Sri Nissanka, Maya (Kularatne) Senanayake, Krisantha Sri Bhaggiyadatta, Connie Welikala, Bradman Weerakoon, Ray Wijewardene, Lyn Wirasekera, Suriya and Suren Wickremasinghe.

** The list includes Otara Gunewardene, Ajit Gunewardene, Ramani Gunatilake, Arjuna Parakrama, Luxman Nadarajah, Neluka Silva, Rumesh Ratnayake, Athula Senanayake, Rosy Senanayake, Nihal Welikala, Anoma Wijewardene, Richard de Zoysa, and many others.

Mixed Marriages in India, Pakistan and Bangladesh

In colonial India, mixed marriages and liaisons between European men and Indian women dating back to the 18th century, have been described in earlier sections of this book. By the 19th century foreign women were also marrying Indians, one early example being a British woman who wrote under her married name as 'Mrs Meer Hassan Ali,' whose husband was from an upper-class family of Lucknow. She is known for her two-volume book on Indian Muslim society written in 1832 (MacMillan 1988: 215). By the 20th century several Indians prominent in national life made inter-racial marriages, the most famous being that of Rajiv Gandhi to Sonia Maino of Italy in 1968.

Earlier, in the 1920s and 1930s many Indian nationalists and leftists had western wives who were active in politics. Several revolutionaries in M.N. Roy's communist group married foreigners; Roy himself was married from 1917 to 1925 to Evelyn Trent, an American leftist, active in revolutionary politics with him in the USA and Europe. His second wife Ellen Gottschalk, a German whom he married in 1937, had been in the German Communist Party, but she and Roy abandoned communism and returned to India to promote radical humanism. Others in the Roy group in Europe who married Europeans included: Abani Mukherjee to Rosa Filingoff (of Russian-Jewish origin); Dr Anadi Bhaduri whose Jewish wife Imgaard was from Berlin and Saiyid Abdul Wahid Abai who married Kaethe Hulda Wolf – also of German-Jewish origin. Brajesh Singh, one of Roy's associates, was the partner for some years of Stalin's daughter, Svetlana. The rival Indian communist group in the early 1920s, based in Berlin was led by Virendranath Chattopadyaya whose partner was Agnes Smedley of the USA (later famed for her political writings on China); and among this group was Pandurang Khankhoje who in 1936 married a Belgian, Jeanne Sindic. (Jayawardena 1995: 226 & 230-6.)

In undivided India of the 1930s, several other men associated with the Left movement had British wives, among them the writer Mulk Raj Anand and B.P. Bedi, who with his British wife Freda was active in the

Communist Party of India. They were the parents of the actor and director Kabir Bedi. The famed leftist poet Faiz Ahmad Faiz, of Lahore, married Alys George of Britain who had worked in the 1930s with Krishna Menon's India League in London (ibid: 226-27). Among the Indian Congress Party nationalists with foreign wives were J.M. Sen Gupta, who in 1909 while studying in Cambridge married Nellie Grey, a Britisher. On their return to India they were both involved in politics and trade union activity, and were jailed in 1930 for their role in Gandhi's civil-disobedience movement in Bengal. In 1933, when the Congress sessions were to be held in Kolkata, Sen Gupta was arrested and Nellie Sen Gupta took over and presided at the meeting and was later sentenced to jail. After Sen Gupta's death, she continued to live in Bengal, and in Bangladesh after 1971 where she was a member of the legislature (ibid: 154-55).

An interesting case of a secret mixed marriage was that of the Congress leader Subhas Chandra Bose, who married a German, Emilie Schenkel, in the 1940s while he was in Berlin, planning with the Nazis to overthrow the British in India. The marriage was kept a secret for political reasons and only revealed after his death in 1945 (ibid: 226). However, many eminent Indians, such as Gandhi, Vivekananda, Aurobindo and Tagore had educated, politically committed foreign women, not as wives, but disciples cum soul-mates, some of whom were publicly recognized and honoured (ibid: 175-207).

Several local members of the Theosophist Society had foreign wives, and even the 'charismatic' J. Krishnamurti, promoted by the theosophists as the coming "World Teacher," had many foreign women partners. Theosophist women involved in women's rights included; Dorothy Graham, the British wife of C. Jinarajadasa of Sri Lankan origin (who lived in India), was the secretary in 1917 of the Women's Indian Association, started by theosophist Margaret Cousins (Jayawardena 1995: 150). Another such marriage in 1930 was that of an Indian theosophist, Kewal Motwani, to Clara Heath of the USA who became the principal and founder of several Buddhist girls' schools in Sri Lanka (Gunasekara 2007). Many prominent western theosophists had Indian wives; they included George Arundale who married Rukmani, the daughter of a judge, and F. Gordon Pearce, the Principal of Mahinda College (Galle) in the 1920s, whose wife Anu was also from India.

In the Indian film and business world there have been numerous marriages to westerners. Shashi Kapoor of the famous film dynasty married Jennifer Kendall, daughter of James Kendall of a noted English theatre family. Well-known foreigners in the film world married Indian women – notably Roberto Rosselini to Sonali Das Gupta, Michael Caine to Shakira, and David Lean to Lila Matkar. Ruth Prawer a novelist and Oscar-winning scriptwriter for Merchant Ivory films was married to architect Jhabvala. The most famous of India's pioneer businessmen, had J.R.D. Tata, (1904-1993) a strong French connection. His mother Suzanne Brière was French; he was born and educated partly in Paris and his wife Thelma was French. Another leading businessman, Naval Tata's French wife Simone founded the Lakmé India cosmetics company.

Biracial marriages of eminent South Asians have included those of Amartya Sen to Eva Colorni of Italy, and later to Emma Rothschild; Professor Partha Das Gupta to Carol Meade; N.Ram to Susan Hacker; Imran Khan to Jemima Goldsmith; and the famous artists S.H. Raza and Akbar Padamse whose wives are French. Such marriages continue in South Asia and in the West.

Details of many mixed marriages remain unrecorded – one exception being the marriage of Dr Shanti Behari Seth to Henny Gerde Caro, a German-Jewish refugee. The story of their life in London has been made famous by Vikram Seth (Dr Seth's nephew) in his book *Two Lives* (2005). He generalizes that:

> There was ... something in common between the bourgeois middle-class Indian ethos and that of middle-class Germany; perhaps more particularly middle-class Jewish Germany, in its respect for the professions, for education, for savings, for house and home. (Seth 2005: 401)

Some Indians, Pakistanis and Bangladeshis prominent in politics, business, culture and intellectual activity had western mothers. The Communist leader, Rajani Palme Dutt's mother was Swedish – a relative of Olaf Palme, the former Prime Minister. Sara Sulieri, a Professor of English at Yale, had a Pakistani father and Welsh mother – Mair Glenys Jones – known as Surraya; the Indian writer Anita Desai had a German mother and novelist Monica Ali's mother was British and father Bangladeshi. Amrita Shergil, one of India's highly acclaimed artists, was the daughter of Umrao Singh Shergil, a Punjabi, and his wife Marie Antoinette Gottesman, a Hungarian. Born in Budapest in 1913, Amrita studied art in Paris and spent her life between India and Hungary, returning to India in 1934. She married her Hungarian cousin Victor Egan, but died in 1941 in Lahore (Sundaram 2001). Other interesting cases of persons of mixed origin include Rahul and Priyanka Gandhi who are half-Italian and Priyanka's husband Robert Vadra whose mother Maureen is of European origin. The famous daughters of Ravi Shankar – Anoushka Shankar (the sitar player) and Nora Jones (the jazz singer) – have foreign mothers. In the case of the Professor of Sociology, André Béteille, however, his father was French, and mother Bengali.

The examples cited above document the mixing of races that occurred at the top levels of society in South Asia. But unrecorded East-West partnerships occurred among all classes. While tradition was firm about keeping the race 'pure,' the reality was different, and a 'laissez-faire' attitude in choice of marriage partner became increasingly prevalent over the decades. But with mixed marriages, the woman of the 'Other' was 'erased,' and the 'hybrid' children – rather than joining an existing Euro-Asian community – generally kept within the ethnic boundaries of the male ancestor. Thus over the centuries, from Portuguese colonialism onwards, racial mixing has continued with each generation, making South Asia an example of hybridization, which is a continuing process today. The concern with gender and nation, which preoccupied both foreigners and locals in colonial times, continues on occasion to be problematized on both sides. Losing 'our women' is an issue of permanent concern in patriarchal society, and the concept of 'correctly' reproducing the nation has dominated the thinking in the identity politics of the region.

Notes

1. This event was made into a TV film in 2001 by Sonali Fernando entitled *Affairs of Empire*, for the BBC Channel 4 series *Victorians Uncovered.*
2. The eldest, Susanna Scharff (1743-81), in 1759 married Rev. Henricus Philipsz, son of Liyanage Philip Philipsz Wijekoon Panditharatna (grandfather of James de Alwis). Another daughter, Cornelia Henrietta Scharff (1765-1824) married Christoffel de Saram Wanigasekera Ekanayake (4th Maha Mudaliyar). Their daughter Cornelia de Saram married Don Solomon Dias Bandaranaike, the 1st Udugaha Mudaliyar, whose son Don Christoffel Henricus Dias Bandaranaike married Anna Florentina Philipsz Panditharatne. They were the parents of Solomon Dias Bandaranaike, Maha Mudaliyar and grandparents of S.W.R.D. Bandaranaike (Roberts et al. 1989: 365-66).
3. I am grateful to Christopher Don Carolis for this information and for the photograph of his grandparents Lilian Gregory and Charles Don Carolis.
4.I thank Shehara de Silva, Arjuna Parakrama and Neville Weereratne for these details.
5.These included Daniel John Fernando to Maria Felsinger in 1882; Samson Abeysooria, a planter and writer, to Hannah Lewis in 1904; Dr Edwin de Livera, from a family of *mohandirams* of Hewagama Korale, to Eliza Maartenz in 1897; and Dr Leo Ekanayake to Frances Pompeus.
6. Among those with French wives were G.G. Ponnambalam Sr whose first wife was Violette, and T. Sri Pathmanathan whose second wife was Yvonne Coulet of Paris. Lakshman Kadirgamar's first wife Angela Malik was of French-Indian origin. A.B. Perera, an ambassador and influential political figure, had a Swiss wife; and Professor Shanta de Alwis' wife is Swiss. Eminent Jewish wives of Sri Lankans include the writer and poet Anne Ranasinghe, née Katz, from Germany, who married Dr D.A. Ranasinghe; and an American left-wing journalist Rhoda Miller of Lithuanian origin – cousin of the writer Howard Fast – who married Sri Lankan political activist Joseph de Silva in 1951; she became a victim of McCarthyism, and was deported from Sri Lanka in 1954 (but later returned) (Pasqualge, 2007). The Russian wives of Sri Lankans include Tanya Iousova, an architect, wife of architect Suren Wickremasinghe; and among the numerous German wives are the lawyer Sepala Munasinghe's wife Dorothea and lawyer V. Krishnadasan's wife Doris.

Several Jewish refugees from fascism married Burghers – among them, a distinguished Hungarian psychiatrist of the 1930s, Edith Gymroi who in 1941 married E.F.C. Ludowyk, a Professor of English at the University of Ceylon. Another marriage was that of Hedi Simon of Vienna, who in 1939, after graduating from Cambridge, married Pieter Keuneman – a leader of the

Communist Party of Ceylon. They divorced and in 1952 Keuneman married a Britisher, Maud Rogerson, an assistant to Rajani Palme Dutt, one of the leaders of the British Communist Party.

7. I thank Chandima de Silva and the late Neville Kanakaratne for lending me the de Abrew-Rajapakse family tree.

8. Hilda Westbrook, a Cambridge graduate, was the daughter of theosophist Francis Westbrook and Jessie Duncan, an orientalist scholar, suffragist and translator of Sufi poetry into English. The latter's sister Elizabeth Duncan and George Russell of the Foreign Office were the parents of Margaret Russell who had been a student of the London Academy of Music. After her marriage to Malalasekera, Margaret taught music at Ananda Balika, a Buddhist girls' school founded by her cousin Hilda. Both were active in the local Women's Franchise Union (started in 1927) but Margaret died young in 1930. (I am grateful to her daughter Chitra Malalasekera Ranawake for these details.)

Anglo-Indians

Vivien Leigh as Cleopatra

Merle Oberon

Anna Kashfi and Marlon Brando

Sri Lanka medical students 1911. The four women students from left to right are Rachel Christoffelsz, Claribel van Dort, Sylvia Ebert and Verona Wirasekera. Courtesy Christobel Don Carolis

Dr Alice de Boer.
Courtesy Deloraine Brohier.

Dr James Loos.
Courtesy Deloraine Brohier.

Constance Blacker
Courtesy Alfreda de Silva

Cora Abraham

Bertha Rodgers
Courtesy Indrani Meegama

Emily van der Poorten and daughter Julia Hermon in the early 1930s. Courtesy Patricia Alailima

Paul and Alice Nell's Family - 1909. Back row, standing from left, daughter Elsie, sister Dr Winifred Nell, daughter Agnes (Nell) de Silva, her husband George E. de Silva, and daughter Grace. Seated Paul Nell and wife Alice; front row, Melville and Marc Nell (nephews), and granddaughter Anil Marcia de Silva on the nanny's lap. Courtesy Minnette de Silva

Jawaharlal Nehru, Agnes de Silva, and George E. de Silva, at a reception in Kandy, 1939. Courtesy Minnette de Silva, *The Life & Work of an Asian Woman Architect.*

Minnette de Silva (centre) with Pablo Piccaso (left) and Mulk Raj Anand (right corner) at a Peace Conference in Poland, 1948. Courtesy Minnette de Silva, *The Life & Work of an Asian Woman Architect.*

Clara and Kewal Motwani with daughter Goolbai. Courtesy Goolbai Gunasekara.

J.S. Walter de Soysa and first wife Maria Micada Albo of Spain, in 1904. From A.Wright, *20th Century Impressions of Ceylon.*

Charles Don Carolis and his bride Lillian Gregory in 1916. Courtesy Christopher Don Carolis.

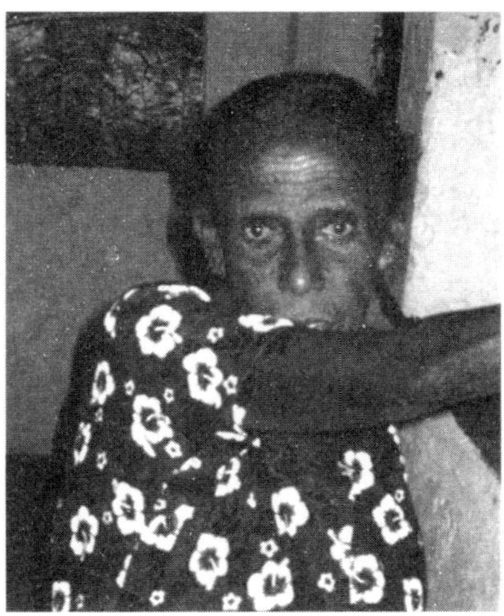

Henry Engelbrecht's granddaughter "Sudu Amma" Lilynona. From *Woolf in Ceylon*. Courtesy Christopher Ondaatje.

Patrick Kularatne and his wife
Hilda Westbrook in the early 1920s.
Courtesy Maya Senanayake

Dr G.P. Malalasekera's marriage to
Margaret Russell in 1927.
Courtesy Chitra Ranawake

Dr S.A. Wickremasinghe and Doreen Young with their children Suriya and Suren and dog Rajah.

The author with her parents Eleanor Hutton and Dr A.P. de Zoysa

13

CONCLUSION

EURO-ASIANS AS PUBLIC INTELLECTUALS

> It celebrates hybridity, impurity, intermingling, the transformation that comes of new and unexpected combinations of human beings, culture, ideas, politics... It rejoices in mongrelization and fears the absolutism of the Pure. Mélange, hotch-potch... is how newness enters the world... It is for change-by-fusion, change-by-conjoining. It is a love-song to our mongrel selves.
>
> Salman Rushdie, 1991, "In Good Faith," in *Imaginary Homelands,* p.394, describing his book *The Satanic Verses.*

This book on the Euro-Asians in its time frame extends from the Portuguese colonial invasions and occupation of parts of Asia in the late 15th and early 16th centuries, to the conquests of the Dutch and British in later centuries. The main focus has been the Euro-Asian communities of Sri Lanka, with some case studies from India, Singapore and other colonies. But this is not a history of South Asian Euro-Asians – aspects of which have been documented among others by Gaikwad (1967), Fernando (1972), McGilvray (1982), Roberts et al. (1989), Hawes (1996), Caplan (2001), and Roychowdhury (2003). The discussion has been more on the background and politics of the radical Euro-Asians who were a minority of men and women of the community, as well as on related issues of gender and nation. Although Euro-Asians have been considered by many writers as a 'marginal community,' this study has emphasized their ideological and activist contributions as pioneers for peoples' rights and political and social change. It suggests that it was not their *marginality*

– namely the pursuit only of Euro-Asian sectarian issues – but their *centrality*, emphasizing questions concerning the *whole of society,* that characterized their utopian vision of a better world.

During the past decades, South Asia has been ridden with many divisive movements – religious fundamentalism, communalism, ethno-nationalism and exclusivist identity-politics – that have resulted in violent conflicts and even wars. In India and Sri Lanka, the 'past' has dominated the 'present,' often involving a denial of a pluralist, multiethnic society. This book, while discussing the emergence of Euro-Asian communities, has brought to the surface their role in movements linked to anti-colonialism, democracy, feminism and labour agitation, as well as secularism, pluralism, modernity and avant-garde trends in South Asia. The radical Euro-Asian consciousness – with its early vision of a future democratic society – was reminiscent of elements of Utopian thinking of 19th century Europe, which influenced Marxism and other movements of social change.

Many forget that South Asia was 'hybrid' from its early history and that no community could claim 'purity.' In Sri Lanka waves of settlers from India, other parts of Asia and the Arab and African world had over the centuries created a mixed population. With colonialism further admixtures in the population came to include a European component. From the 16th century onwards, while the Euro-Asian community prided itself openly on its European descent, other local communities – Sinhala, Tamil and Muslim – also had inputs of European 'mixture.' This phenomenon, usually unacknowledged, was prevalent at all levels in society – in the urban, rural and plantation sectors of the island, and among all classes.

This inquiry into aspects of hybridity and multibridity in South Asia since Portuguese rule found that there were stereotypes, prejudices and discrimination by both Europeans and Asians against Euro-Asians linked to deep-seated concerns about purity, pollution and contamination. Both groups, even while benefiting from the talent, skills and scholarship of Euro-Asians, tended to reject them politically, socially and culturally for a variety of reasons discussed in earlier chapters. South Asians, as this research has shown, are in many ways more 'Euro-Asian' than they care to acknowledge; and while often opting for a western way of life, they disclaim foreign ancestry as 'contaminating' and a 'stain' on the family. In Michelle de Kretser's words:

> Pater says there's not a Ceylonese without mongrel blood in his veins… We've all got at least one skeleton in the family closet – a Tamil, a Moor, a Swiss mercenary, someone we'd rather keep quiet about. (2003: 19)

But why was admixture in the past considered to be such a dark secret, a "skeleton in the closet" to "keep quiet about" – and not celebrated à la Rushdie? In discussing the question, this study describes the way Euro-Asians, although born and living in South Asia, were yet not part of the caste or other traditional systems with their rules, restrictions, taboos and rituals. Euro-Asians who had strong patriotic feelings about the land of their birth, did not become defenders of its oppressive social structures and cultural orthodoxy. Simultaneously, as victims who had experienced the racial arrogance and hauteur of Europeans, the Euro-Asians were made conscious of their rights – or lack of them. They strongly opposed any denial of democratic rights, especially opposing inequality under the law, cruel punishments, discrimination and refusal of full citizenship. A big shake-up of colonial society thus took place with the emergence of a 'two language' group of Euro-Asians who were subversive of both their European and Asian lineages, while not fully belonging to either. They had to deal with the British class system and its prejudices as well as the local caste system and its hierarchies.

Two outstanding aspects of the Euro-Asian presence in South Asia have been highlighted in this work. First, the Euro-Asian intellectuals and professionals were "children of the Enlightenment" supportive of the liberal agenda of 18th and 19th century Europe, whose impact was felt in the colonial world. Radical pioneers from the Euro-Asian communities were involved in social reform, gender equity, concern for the rights of the rural and urban poor, the furtherance of democracy, opposition to dogmatic Christianity and the promotion of secularism. They played the role of 'public intellectuals' by taking on important causes concerning peoples' rights. But as recent scholarship by Jonathan Israel has shown, the Enlightenment had both radical and moderate components; the radical tendency influenced by Spinoza was materialist, egalitarian and secular while the moderates were more hierachical and even religious (Israel 2002). The Euro-Asians also were similarly divided. While the radicals dealt with in this book took on many controversial causes, the moderate Euro-Asians were cautious and conventional while being champions of individual rights. The second aspect, also influenced by Enlightenment ideology and democratic movements, was the promotion of gender equity by Euro-Asian males and by the women of the community. The latter attained high levels of education and pioneered women's employment in the modern sector in Sri Lanka and India.

Thus in crucial moments in history, dissenters of mixed European and Asian origin pioneered social and political reform, and in later decades were involved in anti-colonial, trade union and feminist movements. In the earlier phase, after the revolts in the Caribbean, the colonial powers had feared the 'mulattos' or 'half-castes' because they were an aspiring group, with strong grievances, revolutionary ideology and a presence in the military that gave them access to arms, and therefore with possibilities of conducting armed struggle. Apart from events in the Caribbean, the revolutions in France also led to alarm amongst the British in India and Sri Lanka about the potential for subversion by Euro-Asians in their midst.

Unease about Euro-Asians was also prevalent among the local population. For example, the Young Bengal movement attracted the hostility of the Hindu conservatives of Kolkata, and Henry Derozio was condemned as a 'vagabond *firingi*'(foreigner). The contribution of the Euro-Asians was not highlighted by later nationalist ideologues and their role was hidden in the footnotes of South Asian history. It is not difficult to see why this was so. In India Henry Derozio, a Euro-Asian, never became a 'national hero' (although he pre-dated the Hindu and Muslim nationalists and social reformers by many decades); in Sri Lanka too, it was the mixed origins of Charles Lorenz and other pioneers of social and political rights of the colonized, that precluded their recognition at a national level.

The discussion in this book has also rejected the stereotypes and myths concerning men and women of Euro-Asian origin, which have erased their contribution to social and political movements and kept them out of the mainstream of history. It also discusses the issue of why hybridity was demonized as 'impure,' and why claims were made for the 'purity' of 'chosen peoples.' These developments were linked to myths about purity and to the political ideologies on race prevalent in Europe, and picked up and popularized by Asian nationalists. Another strongly held myth about Euro-Asians was that they were only concerned about Western philosophy, literature and history, and were ignorant of local culture, societies and religions. The reality, however, is that many among the Euro-Asian intelligentsia were involved in analysing and writing about all aspects of Sri Lankan society and culture. Their intellectual contribution is reflected in writings on history, studies of the flora and fauna of the island, translations of Buddhist texts, research on legal issues, and articles in academic journals.

This book has focused on the class, race and gender components of communities of Euro-Asians. It has highlighted the class differentiation within the mixed communities, which was linked to status consciousness and status anxiety. The concern with class, however, was found both in Europe and in the colonial societies of South Asia – the latter, however, being further stratified by caste. The mixed communities were victims of the race ideology of the 19th and 20th centuries, and in both Asia and Europe, the *mischmaschvolk* or 'hybrids' were distrusted as being politically disloyal, and despised as 'impure' and 'tainted.' Ironically, therefore, Euro-Asians were at the receiving end of diatribes by both the colonial rulers and by local nationalists; the former regarded them as potentially subversive if not seditious, and the latter felt they were loyal to the colonial rulers, and therefore disloyal to local political causes.

Gender is a key factor in understanding hybridity and the emergence of mixed communities. Each colonial power faced problems arising from the paucity of western women in the colonies and the vexing question of Europeans making alliances with local women – these women themselves often being dismissed as lowly beings by the both Europeans and locals. As noted earlier, the 'founder' of Kolkata, Job Charnock, had a liaison with a Hindu woman in 1682, that led to censure by his superiors (Hawes 1996: 2-3). And Robert Knox, a seaman captive in Sri Lanka in the 17th century (whose crew took Kandyan wives), had a dim view of local women, saying "they be all Whores." In turn, not only did many South Asians have similar views of western women, but they looked down on the Euro-Asian community because of the alleged 'low caste' status of the local maternal ancestor. Similarly some westerners regarded 'white' women who married 'natives' as low in class – landladies' daughters or barmaids.

The political distrust of Euro-Asians extended to the personal sphere where they were regarded as 'undesirable' marriage partners by both colonial rulers and the local population, in spite of which there was still much racial intermingling. Hence the taboo as well as the campaign against mixed marriages and liaisons occurred on both sides of the colonial divide. The British colonizers, having for a period tolerated alliances of British men of all classes with local women, later condemned them. The nationalists in turn publicly denounced mixed marriages as 'dangerous contamination' posing a threat to the 'nation.'

In terms of the sexuality of the Euro-Asian, it is paradoxical that the politically subversive Euro-Asian man is generally depicted in western culture not as a strong fearful threat to white womanhood, but as a person who is unattractive and weak. In contrast, the Euro-Asian woman at all levels of western culture is seen as the 'exotic' object of desire. But the western view of the Euro-Asian woman as an Orientalist fantasy, contrasts with the reality that in India and Sri Lanka, the first women to breach the patriarchal barriers in education and employment were Euro-Asians. They were proto-feminists and had many advantages, including their exposure to education and modernization, to the latest trends in the West, and to liberal attitudes towards women's rights.

The book therefore highlights the unrecognized contributions of Euro-Asian women and men to reforming colonial society, and their pioneering role as catalysts of change, and visionaries of a better world. They were, indeed, the first to 'catch and reflect the dawn.' Further, the book upholds the multi-ethnic identity of South Asia, in contrast to purity myths and the refusal by nationalists to accept the reality of racial admixture. There have been other South Asians such as Salman Rushdie who celebrate "hybridity, impurity, intermingling," and recognize the potential for transformation contained in "new and unexpected combinations of human beings, culture, ideas, politics" (1991: 394). There are others, however, who persist in prejudice against those of mixed origin – usually in the cultural sphere. Such attitudes, according to the writer Sunanda Datta-Ray, are generational. Writing on the wearing of the sari in India, he says his mother's and grandmother's generation "would not be seen dead in skirts"; the reason being neither "aesthetic nor nationalistic" but that they "dreaded being mistaken for Christian converts or Eurasians, both implying social diminution in those days" (Datta-Ray, 2005).

But times are changing. In today's context, the new generation celebrates mélange and multi-racialism. For example, a trendy Indian-owned restaurant in London is playfully named 'Chutney Mary' – a term used for Anglo-Indian women 'passing' for white. The diaspora from the 'Third World' living in the 'First World' has given rise to Euro-Asians of various types. Several writers of South Asian/European origin living abroad – Hanif Kureishi, Hari Kunzru, Michael Ondaatje, Anita Desai, Sara Sulieri, Monica Ali and Michelle de Kretser, to name only a few, have made their mark internationally as creative writers, often tackling issues of 'hybridity' and pluralism, as have some Sri Lankans of Euro-Asian origin who did not migrate – notably Carl Muller and Jean Arasanayagam.

The Euro-Asian utopian vision reflected hope for a democratic society where inequalities based on class, caste, ethnicity and gender would be challenged – where there would be social justice, pluralism and, in a colonial situation, a move towards political self-determination. Those utopians of the mixed communities of South Asia did not have manifestos or blueprints for a future Golden Age, but they spoke out in public – raising crucial issues – although with no immediate prospect of achievement and based on long-term goals. It was a liberal and radical agenda which formed part of the process towards greater democracy.

The revolution in transport and communications has made it easy for different cultures to flourish, and for people to celebrate multiple identities. Rather than hiding Euro-Asian origins, or confining the achievements of mixed-race persons to footnotes in small print, the Euro-Asian can now be given a new and acceptable face in the main text. The 'half-caste' has been 're-cast'. And the time has come to appreciate the utopian vision projected by our Euro-Asian compatriots of the past, to recognize their contributions towards achieving a more democratic and humane society, and to acknowledge their role during British rule as some of the earliest public intellectuals in the region.

Portrait of Agnes de Silva by David Paynter.
Courtesy Minnette de Silva.

Bibliography

Addy, Premen, and Azad, Ibne, 1973, "Politics and Culture in Bengal," in *New Left Review*, May-June, London, New Left Review Ltd.

Anderson, Benedict, 1983, *Imagined Communities – Reflections on the Origins and Spread of Nationalism*, London, Verso.

Arasanayagam, Jean, 2001, *Inheritance*, Colombo, S. Godage.

——— 2006, *A Nice Burgher Girl*, Colombo, Social Scientists' Association.

——— Forthcoming, *Dragons in the Wilderness*.

Arunachalam, Ponnambalam, 1902, *Report on the Census of Ceylon, 1901,* Colombo, Government Printer.

Azvedo, Carmo, 1993, "The Casados," in (ed.) B.S. Shastry, *Goan Society through the Ages*, New Delhi, Asian Publication Services.

Balasingham, S.V., 1968, *The Administration of Sir Henry Ward, Governor of Ceylon 1855-60,* Dehiwala, The Ceylon Historical Journal.

Ballhatchet, K. 1980, *Race, Sex and Class under the Raj – Imperial Attitudes and Their Critics*, 1793-1905, Weidenfeld & Nicholson.

Bandaranayake, Senake, 1985 [1984], "The Peopling of Sri Lanka; the National Question and Some Problems of History and Ethnicity," in *Ethnicity and Social Change*, Colombo, SSA.

Baudelaire, Charles, see Scarfe, Francis

Baybars, Taner, 1967, *Selected Poems, Nazim Hikmet,* London, Jonathan Cape.

Bell, Bethia N., and Heather, K., 1993, *H.C.P. Bell, Archaeologist of Ceylon and the Maldives*, Clwyd, Wales, Archetype Publications.

Bhabha, Homi, 1997, "Of Mimicry and Man: The Ambivalence of Colonial Discourse," in (eds) F. Cooper & A. Stoler, *Tensions of Empire, Colonial Cultures in a Bourgeois World,* Berkeley, UC Press.

Bhattacharji, Shobana, 1999, "Byron and India," unpublished article.

Bhattacharya, Bijoy, 1968, *Derozio the Maker of Young Bengal*, New Delhi, Well-Print Publications.

Blazé, B.R., 1934, [A. Ohnimesz], *The Lees of Lanka*, Colombo, published by the author.

———1948, *The Life of Lorenz*, Colombo, Associated Newspapers of Ceylon.

Boxer, C.R. 1954, "An Introduction to Joao Ribeiro's Historical Tragedy of the Island of Ceylon," *Ceylon Historical Journal*, Vol. 3, No. 3 & 4.

——— 1973a [1969], *The Portuguese Seaborne Empire* (1415-1825), Middlesex, Pelican Books.

——— 1973b [1965], *The Dutch Seaborne Empire 1600-1800*, Middlesex, Pelican Books.

Boyd, William, 1889, *Autobiography of a Peria Durai*, Colombo, A & J. Ferguson.

Bradley-Birt, F.B. 1980 [1923], *Poems of Henry Louis Vivian Derozio – A Forgotten Anglo-Indian Poet*, Calcutta, Oxford University Press.

Braga-Blake, Myrna (ed.), 1992, *Singapore Eurasians - Memories and Hopes*, Singapore, The Eurasian Association.

——— & Ebert- Oehlers, Ann, 1992 "Where the Twain Met" in Braga Blake (ed) 1992.

Brohier, Deloraine, 1994, *Alice de Boer and some Pioneer Burgher Women Doctors*, Colombo, Social Scientists' Association.

——— 2002, "The History of the Burgher Community in Sri Lanka," in (eds) S. Kelegama and S. Madawela, *Four Hundred Years of Dutch - Sri Lanka Relations*.

——— 2003, "Running in the Family with brush and palette," *Sunday Island,* 11 May.

Brohier, R.L., 2000 [1984], *Changing Face of Colombo* (1505-1972), Colombo, Lake House Investments.

Buultjens, A.E., 1899, *Why I became a Buddhist,"* reprinted in 1984, Colombo, C.A. Wijesekera.

Buruma, Ian, 2002a, "Making a Fetish of Mystery," *New York Review of Books*, August.

——— 2002b, [1996], *The Missionary and the Libertine, Love and War in East and West*, London, Faber and Faber Ltd.

Butler, Marilyn, 1981, *Romantics, Rebels & Reactionaries - English Literature and Its Background, 1760-1830,* Oxford University Press.

Calder, Jenni, 1977, *Heroes: from Byron to Guevara*, London, Hamish Hamilton.

Cameron, David, 1973, "Derozio – the Poet," in (ed.) Mary Ann Das Gupta, *Henry Derozio, A Memorial Volume.*

Caplan, Lionel, 2001, *Children of Colonialism. Anglo - Indians in a Postcolonial World*, Oxford & New York, Berg.

Chan, Mimi, 1989, *Through Western Eyes: Images of Chinese Women in Anglo-American Literature*, Hong Kong, Joint Publishing (HK) Co.

Chatterjee, Indrani, 1999, "Colouring Subalternity: Slaves, Concubines and Social Orphans in Early Colonial India". In *Subaltern Studies*, Vol 10, (eds.) Gautam Bhadra, Gyan Prakash and Susie Tharu, New Delhi, Oxford University Press.

Chatterjee, Partha, 1989, "The Nationalist Resolution of the Women's Question," in *Recasting Women, Essays in Colonial History,* (eds) K. Sangari and S. Vaid, New Delhi, Kali for Women.

Chaudhuri, Nupur, and Margaret Strobel, 1992, *Western Women and Imperialism, Complicity and Resistance*, Indiana University Press.

Chaudhuri, Rosinka, 2000, "Young India: A Bengal Eclogue or Meat-eating, Race, and Reform in a Colonial Poem," *Interventions, International Journal of Post-Colonial Studies*, Vol. 2, No. 3.

Coward, Noel, 1983, *Lyrics of Noel Coward*, London, Methuen.

Cox, Oliver Cromwell, 1948, *Caste, Class and Race, A Study in Social Dynamics*, New York, Monthly Review.

Dalrymple, William, 2002, *White Mughals – Love and Betrayal in Eighteenth-century India*, New Delhi, Viking Penguin Books.

Darling, Evangeline (ed.), 1991, *Story of a Christian Mission*, Colombo, published by the editor.

Das Gupta, Mary Ann (ed.), 1973, *Henry Louis Vivian Derozio* (1808-1831), *Anglo-Indian Patriot and Poet – a Memorial Volume,* Calcutta, Derozio Commemorative Committee.

Das Gupta, R.K, 1980, [1923], Foreword to F.B. Bradley-Birt (ed.), *Poems of Henry Louis Vivian Derozio, a Forgotten Anglo-Indian Poet,* Calcutta, Oxford University Press.

Datta-Ray, Sunanda K., 2005, "Unravelling the Sari," *International Herald Tribune*, 28 April.

Dekker, Rudolph M. and Lotte C. van der Pol, 1989, *The Tradition of Female Transvestitism in Early Modern Europe,* New York, St. Martins Press.

de Alwis, (D'Alwis) James, 1939 [1878], *Memoirs and Desultory Writings of the Late James D'Alwis,* edited/published by A.C. Seneviratne, Colombo.

——— *The Rebellion of 1848*, unpublished copy owned by James Rutnam; typescript in the Sri Lanka National Archives.

de Alwis, Malathi, 1992, "Of Rural Heroines and Urbanized *Femmes Fatales,*" *Pravada,* Vol. 1 No. 4, Colombo.

——— and Kumari Jayawardena, 2001, *Casting Pearls – The Women's Franchise Movement in Sri Lanka*, Colombo, SSA.

de Kretser, Michelle, 2003,*The Hamilton Case*, New York, Little, Brown & Co.

de Mel, Neloufer, 2001, *Women and the Nation's Narrative – Gender and Nationalism in Twentieth Century Sri Lanka*, Colombo, Social Scientists' Association, and New Delhi, Kali for Women.

——— and Minoli Samarakkody (eds), 2002, *Writing an Inheritance, Women's Writing in Sri Lanka 1860-1948*, Colombo, Women's Education and Research Centre.

Denby, David, 2004, "Northern Lights," *The New Yorker*, 11 October.

Desai, A.R., 1966, *Social Background of Indian Nationalism*, Bombay, Popular Prakashan.

de Silva, Alfreda, "Constance Blacker," manuscript, Social Scientists' Association.

de Silva, C.R., 1971, "A Portuguese *casado* in a Sinhalese Village," *Modern Ceylon Studies,* January, Vol. 2, No. 1.

———1972, *The Portuguese in Ceylon*, 1617-38, Colombo, H.W. Cave.

de Silva, K.M., 1965, (ed.) *Letters on Ceylon 1846-50, The Administration of Viscount Torrington and the 'Rebellion' of 1848*, Kandy/Colombo, K.V.G. de Silva & Sons.

de Silva, Mervyn, 1961, "Introduction," (ed) S. Saparamadu, *Leonard Woolf, Diaries in Ceylon* 1908-1916, Colombo, *The Ceylon Historical Journal.*

de Silva, Minnette, 1998, *The Life and Work of an Asian Woman Architect*, Kandy, George E. de Silva and Agnes Nell de Silva Trust.

de Silva, R.K. & Beumer, W.G.M. 1988, *Illustrations and Views of Dutch Ceylon, 1602-1796*, London & Leiden, Serendib Publications.

——— 1998, *19th Century Newspaper Engravings of Ceylon - Sri Lanka*, London, Serendib Publications.

Denham, E.B., 1912, *Ceylon at the Census of 1911*, Government Printer, Colombo.

de Zilwa, Dr Lucien, 1967, *Scenes of a Lifetime – The Autobiography of Dr Lucien de Zilwa*, Colombo, H.W. Cave & Co.

Digby, William, 1879, *Forty Years of Official and Unofficial Life in a Crown Colony: The Life of Sir Richard Morgan. Vol. 1,* Madras, Higginbotham & Co.

Douglas, Mary, 1989 [1966], *Purity and Danger – An Analysis of the Concepts of Pollution and Taboo,* London and New York, Ark Paperback, Routledge.

Dover, Cedric, 1937, *Half-Caste,* London, Martin Secker & Warburg.

Drieberg, C, 1933, *Looking Back*, Colombo, Platé Ltd.

Duncker, Patricia, 2000 [1999], *James Miranda Barry*, London, Picador.

Edwards, Thomas, 1980 [1884], *Henry Derozio*, Introduction by Dr R.K. Das Gupta, Calcutta, Riddhi – India.

Eisler, Benita, 1991, *Byron – Child of Passion, Fool of Fame*, London, Hamish Hamilton.

Engels, Friedrich, 1969 [1880], "Socialism, Utopian and Scientific," in *Marx and Engels – Basic Writings on Politics and Philosophy*, Lewis S. Feuer (ed.), Great Britain, Collins, Fontana Library.

Fernando, Edith M.G., 1989, *Journey of a Family – Mahavidanelage de Mel*, Colombo, published by the author.

——— 1998, *Journal of a Family, a Portrait in Words and Pictures from the Fernando Album*, Colombo, published by the author.

Fernando, Tissa, 1972, "The Burghers of Ceylon," in *The Blending of the Races*, (eds) N. Gist and A. Dworkin, New York, John Wiley.

Ferrar, Major M.L. (ed.), 1922, *The Diary of George Callandine (1793-1837)*, London, Eden Fisher & Co.

Flores, Jorge Manuel, 2000, *Hum Curto Historica de Ceylan: 500 Years of Relations between Portugal & Sri Lanka*, Lisbon, Fundaco Orient.

Fonseka, Manel, 2001, *Great Days – Memoirs of a Ceylon Government Medical Officer of 1918 – P.R.C. Peterson,* Colombo, Social Scientists' Association.

Foot, Michael, 1988, *The Politics of Paradise*, Boston, HarperCollins.
Ford, Boris, 1962, *From Blake to Byron*, Middlesex, Penguin Books.
Forrest, D.M., 1967, *A Hundred Years of Ceylon Tea 1867-1967,* London, Chatto & Windus.
Forster, E.M., 1970 [1924], *A Passage to India*, Middlesex, Penguin Books.
Freud, Sigmund, 1986 [1915], "The Unconscious," in *The Essentials of Psychoanalysis: the Definitive Collection of Sigmund Freud's Writing*, selected by Anna Freud, Middlesex, Pelican Books.
Gaikwad, V.R. 1967, *The Anglo-Indians, a Study in the Problems and Processes Involved in Emotional and Cultural Integration*, Bombay, Asia Publishing House.
Gantzer, Hugh & Colleen, 2005, *The Year Before Sunset*, New Delhi, Penguin.
Ghose, Indira, 1998, *Women Travellers in Colonial India -The Power of the Female Gaze*, New Delhi, Oxford University Press.
Gill, Anton, 1995, *Ruling Passions*, Sex Race and Empire, London, BBC Books.
Gist, Noel, and Dworkin, Anthony, 1972, *The Blending of the Races*, New York, John Wiley.
Gist, Noel. and Wright, R.D., 1973, *Marginality and Identity – Anglo-Indians as a racially mixed minority in India,* Leiden, E.J. Brill.
Gombrich, Richard, and Obeyesekere, Gananath, 1988, *Buddhism Transformed, Religious Change in Sri Lanka*, NJ, Princeton University Press.
Goodrick, Clarke, 1992, *The Occult Roots of Nazism*, London, I.B. Tauris.
Gooneratne, Yasmine, 1968, *English Literature in Ceylon,* 1815-1878, Dehiwala, Tisara Prakasakayo.
——— 1986, *Relative Merits: a Personal Memoir of the Bandaranaike Family of Sri Lanka*, London, New York, St. Martin's Press.
Goonewardena, Karl, 1958, *The Foundation of Dutch Power in Ceylon* [1638-1658], Amsterdam, Djambatan.
Gunasekara, Goolbai, 2007, *Chosen Ground, The Clara Motwani Saga*, Colombo, Vijitha Yapa Publications.
Gunawardana, R.A.L.H., 1985, "The People of the Lion: Sinhala Consciousness in History and Historiography," in *Ethnicity and Social Change,* Colombo, Social Scientists' Association.
Gunder Frank, André, 1998, *ReOrient – Global Economy in the Asian Age*, New Delhi, Vistar Publications.

Guruge, Ananda (ed.). 1965, *Anagarika Dharmapala, Return to Righteousness: A Collection of Speeches, Essays and Letters,* Colombo, Ministry of Education and Cultural Affairs.

Han Suyin, 1972, *A Mortal Flower*, London, Panther Books Ltd.

Harris, Elizabeth, 1994, *The Gaze of the Colonizer*, Colombo, Social Scientists' Association.

——— 2006, *Theravada Buddhism and the British Encounter – Missionary and Colonial Experience in 19th century Sri Lanka*, London, Routlege.

Hawes, C. J. 1996, *Poor Relations – the Eurasian Community in India,* Richmond, Sussex, Curzon Press.

Hikmet, Nazim: see Taner Baybars.

Hobsbawm, Eric, 1987 [1962], *The Age of Revolution 1789-1848*, London, Abacus.

——— 1985 [1975], *The Age of Capital 1848-1875,* London, Abacus.

Hulugalle, H. A. J, 1960, *The Life & Times of D. R. Wijewardene*, Colombo, Associated Newspapers of Ceylon.

Hyam, Ronald, 1990, *Empire and Sexuality – the British Experience*, Manchester, Manchester University Press.

Israel, Jonathan, 2002, *Radical Enlightenment: Philosophy and the Making of Modernity 1650-1750.* Oxford, Oxford University Press.

Ives, Colta & Stein, Susan Alyson, *The Lure of the Exotic, Gauguin in New York Collections.* New Haven, Yale University Press.

James, C.L.R., 1980 [1938], *The Black Jacobins – Toussaint l'Ouverture and the San Domingo Revolution,* London, Alison and Busby.

Jayasuriya, Kanishka, 2000 "The Making of the Sri Lankan Bourgeoisie," a review of *Nobodies to Somebodies,* by Kumari Jayawardena, *Sri Lanka Economic Journal,* Vol. 2, No. 1, June, 2000.

Jayawardena, Kumari, 1972, *The Rise of the Labor Movement in Ceylon*, NC, Duke University Press.

——— 1986, *Feminism & Nationalism in the Third World*, London, Zed Books.

——— 1992, "Aspects of Religious and Cultural Identity and the Construction of Sinhala Buddhist Womanhood," in *Religion and Politics in South Asia,* Douglas Allen (ed.), Connecticut, Greenwood Press.

——— 1993, *Dr Mary Rutnam – A Canadian Pioneer for Women's Rights in Sri Lanka*, Colombo, Social Scientists' Association.

——— 1995, *The White Woman's Other Burden: Western Women in South Asia during Colonial Rule*, London and New York, Routledge.

——— 2000, *Nobodies to Somebodies, The Rise of the Colonial Bourgeoisie in Sri Lanka*, Colombo, SSA and Sanjiva Books.

——— forthcoming, "Popular Revolts in 18th & 19th century Sri Lanka."

Jayawickrama, Sarojini, 2004, *Writing That Conquers: Re-reading Knox's An Historical Relation of the Island Ceylon*, Colombo, Social Scientists' Association.

Kabbani, Rana, 1986, *Europe's Myths of Orient,* Bloomington, Indiana University Press.

Kaul, Ranjana, 2005, "A Crack that Hyphenates," *The Book Review*, Vol. XXIX, No.8, August, New Delhi.

Keble, W.T., 2001 [1940], *Ceylon Beaten Track*, Colombo, Sooriya Publishers.

Kelegama, Saman, and Madawela, Roshan (eds), 2002, *400 Years of Dutch-Sri Lanka Relations:1602-2002*, Colombo, Institute of Policy Studies.

Kiernan, V.G, 1969, *The Lords of Humankind: European attitudes to the outside world in the imperial age*, Middlesex, Pelican Books.

Knighton, William, 1854, *Forest Life in Ceylon*, 2 volumes, London, Hurst and Blackett.

Knox, Robert, 1989 [1681], *An Historical Relation of the Island Ceilon,* (ed.) J.H.O. Paulusz, reprinted S.D. Saparamadu, Dehiwela, Tisara Press.

Kunzru, Hari, 2002, *The Illusionist*, New York, Dutton, Penguin Pulman Inc.

Lamming, George, 1984 [1959], *The Pleasures of Exile*, London and New York, Allison Busby.

Le Carré, John, 2001, *The Constant Gardener*, London, Hodder and Stoughton, Coronet Books.

Lewis, Frederick, 1926, *Sixty Four Years in Ceylon,* Colombo Apothecaries.

Lim, Catherine, 1980, *Or Else, the Lightning God and Other Stories*, Oxford, Heinemann.

Ludowyk, E.F.C., 1989, *Those Long Afternoons – Childhood in Colonial Ceylon*, Colombo, Lake House.

Madge, Elliot Walter, 1980 [1905], *Henry Derozio, The Eurasian Poet and Reformer*, (ed.) Subir Ray Choudhuri, Calcutta, Naya Prokash.

Masters, John, 1960, [1956] *Bhowani Junction*, Middlesex, Penguin Books.

Maurois, André, 1984, *Byron*, London, Constable and Constable.

McGilvray, Dennis, 1982, "Dutch Burghers and Portuguese Mechanics: Eurasian Ethnicity in Sri Lanka," in *Comparative Studies in Society and History*, Vol. 24, Cambridge University Press.

Motoe, Kunio, 1987, "Introduction." In *Catalogue of Paul Gauguin Exhibition* at the National Museum of Modern Art, Tokyo.

Meegama, Indrani, 2003, *With a Fistful of Rice: Buddhist Women and the Making of Mahamaya Girls' College,* Colombo, Mahamaya Old Girls Association.

Mendis, G.C. (ed.), 1956, *The Colebrooke-Cameron Papers, Documents on British Colonial Policy in Ceylon*, 1796-1833, Vols I & II, London, Oxford University Press.

Menon, K.P.S. 1981, *Many Worlds Revisited – An Autobiography*, Bombay, Bharatiya Vidya Bhavan.

Mernissi, Fatema, 2001, *Scheherazade Goes West, Different Cultures, Different Harems,* New York, Washington Square Press.

Mies, Maria, 1981, "Utopian Socialism and Womens' Emancipation," in Maria Mies and Kumari Jayawardena, *Feminism in Europe, Liberal and Socialist Strategies*, The Hague, Institute of Social Studies.

Millie, P.D., 1878, *Thirty Years Ago, or Reminiscences of the Early Years of Coffee Planting in Ceylon,* Colombo, A.M. and J. Ferguson.

Moldrich, Donovan, no date, *The Eurasian Community*, unpublished.

Muller, Carl, 1993, *The Jam Fruit Tree*, New Delhi, Penguin Books India.

——— 1994, *Yakada Yaka, The Continuing Saga of Sonnaboy von Bloss and the Burgher Railwaymen,* New Delhi, Penguin Books India.

Müller, J.B, 2006, *The Burghers,* Battaramulla, The European Heritage Project.

Neruda, Pablo, 1978, *Memoirs*, translated by Hardie St Martin, London, Penguin.

Nandy, Ashis, 1994, *The Illegitimacy of Nationalism: Rabindranath Tagore and The Politics of Self,* New Delhi, Oxford University Press.

Ondaatje, Christopher, 2005, *Woolf in Ceylon – an Imperial Journey in the Shadow of Leonard Woolf, 1904-1911*, Toronto, Harper Collins.

Ondaatje, Michael, 1984, *Running in the Family*, London, Picador.

Pasqualge, Judith Waters, 2007, *International McCarthyism: the case of Rhoda Miller de Silva,* Colombo, Social Scientists' Association.

Pathak, S.M., 1967, *American Missionaries and Hinduism: a Study of Their Contacts from 1873-1910*, Delhi, Munshi Ram Manoharlal.

Paul, A.T.S., 2001, *The Colombo Chetty Community*, published by the author.

——— 2002, *My Trek to the Heart: a Cardiac Surgeon's Story of Adventure and Endeavour 1920-80*, Colombo, published by the author.

Perera, Basil, 1967, *Pieter Keuneman – a Profile,* Colombo, Ceylon Communist Party.

Pereira, Alexius A., 1995, *Singapore Eurasians: Their Management of Ethnic Identity*, unpublished thesis, National University of Singapore.

Perniola, V., 1991, *The Catholic Church in Sri Lanka, The Portuguese Period, 1620-1658*, Vol. III, Dehiwala, Tisara Press.

Philips, Amali, 2004, "Gendering Colour: Identity, Feminity and Marriage in Kerala," *Anthropologica 46.*

Pieris, Paul E, 1983 [1914], *Ceylon in the Portuguese Era, Being a History of the Island for the Period 1505-1658,* Vols. I & II, Dehiwala, Tisara Press.

——— no date, *Notes on Some Sinhalese families, Part V: The De Sarams in England 1811-1821*, Colombo, Colombo Apothecaries.

Pinto, Jerry, 2006, *Helen – the Life & Times of an H. Bomb,* New Delhi, Penguin Books India.

Poliakov, Leon, 1977, *The Aryan Myth: A History of Racist and Nationalist Ideas in Europe*, New York, Meridian Books.

Post, Ken, 1978, *Arise Ye Starvelings – The Jamaican Labour Rebellion and its Aftermath*, The Hague, Martinus Nijhoff.

Potts, E. Daniel, 1967, *British Baptist Missionaries in India, 1793-1837,* Cambridge, Cambridge University Press.

Powell, Geoffrey, 1973, *The Kandyan Wars 1803-1818*, London, Leo Cooper.

Ranasinghe, A.G., 1950, *Census of Ceylon 1946*, Vol. 1, Part I, General Report, Colombo, Ceylon Government Press.

Reimers, E., 1932, (translation) *Memoir of Ryckloff Van Goens, Governor of Ceylon, 1663-1675, delivered to his successor*, Colombo, Ceylon Government Press.

Reynolds, Henry, 2005, *Nowhere People – How International Race Theory Shaped Australia's Identity*, Penguin, Australia.

Roberts, Michael, 1975, *Facets of Modern Ceylon History through the letters of Jeronis Pieris*, Colombo, Hansa Publishers.

Roberts, Michael, Raheem, I., and Colin-Thomé, P., 1989, *People Inbetween: The Burghers and the Middle Class in the Transformation within SriLanka*, Moratuwa, Sarvodaya Books.

Roberts, Norah, 1993, *Galle as Quiet as Asleep*, published by the author.

Rowbotham, Sheila, 1977 [1973], *Hidden From History - 300 years of women's oppression and the fight against it,* London, Pluto Press.

Roychowdhury, Laura, 2002, *The Jadu House – Travels in Anglo-India*, London, Black Swan.

Rudé, George, 1964, *Revolutionary Europe 1783-1815*, London, Fontana/Collins.

Rushdie, Salman, 1991, *Imaginary Homelands, Essays and Criticism*, 1981-1991, London, Granta Books and Penguin Books India.

——— 2000, *The Ground Beneath Her Feet*, London, Vintage.

Russell, Jane, 1981, *Our George – a Biography of George Edmund de Silva*, Colombo, Times of Ceylon.

Said, Edward W., 1985, *Orientalism*, Middlesex, Peregrine Books.

——— (ed.) 2000 [1987], Introduction, R. Kipling's *Kim*, London, Penguin.

——— 1994 [1993], *Culture and Imperialism*, New York, Vintage Books.

Sarkar, Sumit, 1985, "The Complexities of Young Bengal," in Sumit Sarkar (ed.) *A Critique of Colonial India*, Calcutta, Papyrus.

Sarkar, Susobhan, 1979, "Derozio and Young Bengal," in Susobhan Sarkar (ed.) *On the Bengal Renaissance*, Calcutta, Papyrus.

Sastri, Sivanath, 1907, *Ramtanu Lahiri Brahman,* translated and edited by Sir Roper Lethbridge, Calcutta, Swan Sonnenschein & Co.

Scarfe, Francis (ed.), 1961, *Baudelaire, Selected Verse,* Penguin Books.

Schwab, Raymond, 1984, *The Oriental Renaissance: Europe's Discovery of India and the East, 1680-1880,* New York, Colombia University Press.

Sen, Indrani, 2002, *Woman and Empire: Representations in the Writings of British India (1858-1900)*, New Delhi, Orient Longman.

Seth, Vikram 2005, *Two Lives,* New Delhi, Penguin Books India.

Sengupta, Pallab, 2000, *Derozio*, Delhi and Calcutta, Sahitya Akademi.

Silva, Neluka, 1996, "Hybridity and Nationalism: The Image of the Burgher in Contemporary Sri Lankan Writing in English," *Nethra,* Oct-Dec.

———(ed.), 2002, *The Hybrid Island: Culture Crossings and the Invention of Identity in Sri Lanka*, Colombo, Social Scientists' Association.

——— 2003, "The Politics of Intermarriage in Sri Lanka in an Era of Conflict," in *Feminists Under Fire: exchanges across war zones*, (eds) Wenona Giles et al., Toronto, Between the Lines.

Sinha, Mrinalini, 1992, "Chathams, Pitts, and Gladstones in Petticoats," in (eds) N. Chaudhuri & M. Strobel, *Western Women and Imperialism: Complicity and Resistance*, Indiana University Press.

Siriwardena, Regi, 1996, *The Lost Lenore*, Colombo, ICES.

Spivak, Gayatri Chakravarty, 1999, *A Critique of Postcolonial Reason: Towards a History of the Vanishing Present,* Cambridge & London, Harvard University Press.

——— 2002, "Resident Alien," in *Relocating Postcolonialism*, (eds) David Theo Goldberg and Ato Quayson, Blackwell Publishers.

Spott, Frederic (ed.), 1989, *Letters of Leonard Woolf*, San Diego, New York, London, Harcourt Brace Jovanovic.

Stark, Herbert A., 1934, *John Ricketts and his Times*, Calcutta, Wilson & Sons.

——— 1936, *Hostages to India,* Calcutta, Star Press.

Stoler, Ann Laura, 1991, "Carnal Knowledge and Imperial Power: Gender, Race and Morality in Colonial Asia," in *Gender at the Crossroads of Knowledge,* (ed) M. di Leonardo University of California Press.

——— 1995 *Race and the Education of Desire*: *Foucault's History of Sexuality and the Colonial Order of Things*, NC, Duke University Press.

——— 1997, "Sexual Affronts and Racial Frontiers: European Identities and the Cultural Politics of Exclusion in Colonial Southeast Asia," in *Tensions of Empire,* (eds) F. Cooper & A. Stoler, Berkeley, University of California Press.

——— 2004, "Affective States," in *A Companion to the Anthropology of Politics*, (eds) D. Nugent and J. Vincent, Oxford, Blackwell.

Strobel, Margaret, 1991, *European Women and the Second British Empire*, Bloomington, Indiana University Press.

Sundaram, Vivan, 2001, *Retake of Amrita*, New Dellhi, Tulika.

Tagore, Rabindranath, 2002 [1910], *Gora,* translated by W.W. Pearson, New Delhi, Rupa and Co.

Tiffany, Sharon, and Adams, Kathleen, 1985, *The Wild Woman: an Inquiry into the Anthropology of an Idea,* Cambridge, Mass. Schenkman Books.

Thapar, Raj, 1991, *All These Years – a Memoir*, New Delhi, Seminar Publications.

Thapar, Romila, 1989, "Imagined Religious Communities? Ancient History and the Modern Search for a Hindu Identity," *Modern Asian Studies* Vol. 23, No. 2.

Thorburn, D., 1974, *Conrad's Romanticism*, New Haven and London, Yale University Press.

Todorov, Tzvetan, 1993, *On Human Diversity – Nationalism, Racism and Exoticism in French Thought*, translated by Catherine Porter, Cambridge, Harvard University Press.

Toer, Pramoedya Ananta, 1996, *The Earth of Mankind*, New York, Penguin.

Torgovnick, Marianna, 1990, *Gone Primitive, Savage Intellects, Modern Lives*, Chicago, University of Chicago Press.

Turner, L.J.B., 1923, *Report on the Census of Ceylon 1921*, Colombo, Ceylon Government Press.

Uragoda, G.G. 1987, *A History of Medicine in Sri Lanka*, Colombo, Sri Lanka Medical Association.

van Dort, John L.K., 1951, *Ceylon – The Near Past*, printed privately by Hilda Obeyesekere Pieris.

van Schagen, Linda, 1997, "Where have all the Nice Clubs Gone?,"*Daily News*, 4 October.

Wallerstein, Emmanuel, 1974, *The Modern World-System: Capitalist Agriculture and the Origins of the European World-Economy in the Sixteenth Century*, New York, Academic Press.

Weinman, J.R., 1947, *Our Legislature – Interesting and racy reminiscences of persons and incidents connected with the old Legislative Council*, Colombo, Associated Newspapers of Ceylon Ltd.

Woolf, Leonard, 1961a, *Growing:an Autobiography of the years 1904-1911*, London, Hogarth Press.

———1961b, *Leonard Woolf Diaries,* (ed.) S. Saparamadu, Ceylon Historical Journal.

——— 1989, *Letters of Leonard Woolf*, see (ed.) Frederic Spott.

Wright, Arnold (ed.), 1907, *Twentieth Century Impressions of Ceylon*, London, Lloyd's Greater Britain Publishing Co.

Wright, Lorna, 1976, *Just Another Shade of Brown*, New South Wales, E.J. Dwyer Ltd and Freedom from Hunger Campaign.

Young, Robert, J.C. 1995, *Colonial Desire – Hybridity in Theory, Culture and Race,* London and New York, Routledge.

Yule, Henry, and Burnell, A.C., 1986 [1886], *Hobson-Jobson: A Glossary of Anglo-Indian Words*, (ed.) William Crooke, New Delhi, Rupa.

Documents, Journals and Reports

1849 *Second Report of the Select Committee on Ceylon*, London.

1850-52 *Young Ceylon*, Colombo.

1855 *Ceylon Almanac and Annual Register*, 1855, Colombo, William Skeen, Government Printer.

1867 Sessional Paper No. VIII on Education, Report of a Sub-Committee of the Legislative Council, Colombo, Ceylon Government Press.

1912 Sessional Paper XIX, Report of the Educational Committee, Colombo, Ceylon Government Press.

1928 *Journal of the Dutch Burgher Union*, XVII October, Colombo.

1934 *The Searchlight*, Colombo.

1976 *Souvenir of the Princess of Wales' College*, Moratuwa.

1992 Paynter Homes, *Annual Report.*

1992 *Pravada* (now *Polity*), Colombo, Social Scientists' Association (SSA).

1995 *St. Aloysius' College Centenary Magazine 1895-1995*, St Aloysius' College, Galle.

1997 Daily News, Colombo.

2006 The *Island*, Colombo.

Index

A

Abeyratne, Augusta (Pinto,) 220, 223
Abraham, Cora, 227
Academic Association, 107, 111, 116
Addison, Thomas, 122
Addy, Premen, 100, 111, -15120-21
Age of Reason, The, 94, 106, 110
Alailima, Patricia, 221
Alba, Jessica, 195
Albuquerque, Viceroy Alfonso, 23
Alexander, Bombardier, 74, 76
Ali, Monica, 278, 287
All Ceylon Trade Union Congress, 230
American War of Independence, 88
Anand, Mulk Raj, 235, 275
Ananda Balika, 271
Anderson, Benedict, 28, 98-99
André Maurois, 114
Anthony and Cleopatra, 193, 203
anti-Semitism, 245, 248-9
Arasanayagam, Jean, 54, 63-64, 72, 266, 287
Arasanayagam, T. 266
Ariosophy, 246
Arnold, David, 68,
Arnold, Thomas, 247
Arunachalam, Sir Ponnambalam, 44
Arundale, George & Rukmani, 277
Aryan, 4, 247-50, 254,
Aserappa, Dr Simon, 264
Aserappa, Magdalene, 267
Aurobindo, Sri,120
Azad, Ibne, 100, 111, 120-21

B

'Blue Stockings', 212-13
Ballhatchet, K. 39-40
Banda, Gongalegoda, 134, 159
Bandaranayake, Senake, 248
Bannerji, Krishnamohan, 111
Baptists, 86, 91-94, 123, 225
Barnes, Sir Edward, 96
Baudelaire, Charles, 185, 195-96, 211
Bawa, Benjamin W, 264
Bawa, Geoffrey, 264
Beauharnais, Josephine, 196
Bedi, B.P. 275
Bell, H.C.P, 56-57, 66
Bell, Heather & Bethia, 56-57
Belleth, Eileen, 269
Bengal British India Society, 111-12
Bengal Spectator, 111
Besant, Annie, 95, 172, 255
Beven, Dorothy & Brian, 227
Beven, Francis, 156
Bhabha, Homi, 98
Bhattacharji, Shobana, 116-17
Bhattacharya, Bijoy, 104-105, 109, 117
Birejepatil, Jayasinh, 209,
Bishop's College, 236
Blacker, Constance, 220, 226-27
Blackwood's Magazine, 147, 163
Blavatsky, Helena, 246-47
Blazé, B.R, 58, 147, 160-62
Bleak House, 232
Bloch, Stella, 265
Blunt, Wilfrid Scawen, 115
Bocks, Clifton, 82, 181
Bocks, William Henry, 181
Boer War, 77, 204
Bonjean, Archbishop, 157
Bose, Subhas Chandra, 276
Boswell, James, 104
Boxer, C.R. 20, 27, 36
Boyd, William, 62
Bradlaugh, Charles, 95, 171-72
Bradley-Birt, F.B. 105-106
Braga-Blake, Myrna, 35, 45-46, 51-53
Brahmo Samaj, 101
Brando, Marlon, 203
Bright, John, 129-30, 132, 144
British Labour Party, 231
Brohier, Deloraine, 212, 220, 222, 229
Brohier, R.L. 32, 42
Bryan, Florrie, 259
Buckingham, James Silk, 97, 123
Burgher Recreation Club, 81
Burke, Edmund, 94
Burns, Robert, 107, 118-19
Burton, Richard, 194
Buruma, Ian, 35-6, 187-88, 194, 196, 198, 200

Butler, Marilyn, 114-15
Butler, Rohan, 245
Buultjens, A.E. 12, 15, 166, 167-180 (Chapter 8)
Buultjens, John, 169, 180
Buultjens, William Cornelius, 169, 180
Byron, Lord, 9, 88, 115-17, 126, 159, 187, 189

C

Caesar and Cleopatra, 203
Calcutta Journal, 97
Calcutta Literary Gazette, 105
Calder, Jenni, 115
Calladine, Colour Sergeant, 76-77
Calvinist, 29-30, 32, 34, 40, 50, 158, 251
Cameron, Charles Hay, 66, 96
Cameron, Evan Wellesley, 67
Cameron, Julia Margaret, 66
Caplan, Lionel, 47, 245
Capper, John, 161
Carey, Jabez, 123
Carey, William, 93, 123
Caribbean, 88- 90, 92, 185, 195, 284
Carlyle, Thomas, 147-48, 152, 191, 197-98
Carolis, W.D. see Don Carolis
casado, 23-25, 31, 239, 262
Caspersz, Fr. Paul, 175
caste, 7, 101, 107-8, 112, 151, 153, 209, 220, 244, 250, 254, 271
Ceylon Communist Party, 180
Ceylon Family Benefit Association, 175
Ceylon Labour Party, 230
Ceylon League, 155, 161-62
Ceylon Medical College, 222-24
Ceylon National Congress, 230, 232
Ceylon Printers' Union, 166, 175-76, 178
Ceylon Women's Union, 218
Chakrabarti, Tarachand, 111
Chan, Mimi, 201
Charnock, Job, 102, 286
Chartists, 130, 138, 148
Chatterjee, Partha, 243
Chatterjee, Indrani, 74-75,
Chattopadyaya, Kamaladevi, 231
Chattopadyaya, Virendranath, 275
Chaudhuri, Rosinka, 108-109
'Chutney Mary', 287
Christmas Debates, 162
Christoffelsz, Dr Rachel, 223, 263
Christoffelsz, Muriel Spaling, 269
Class, Heinrich, 248
Clavell, James, 202
Cleopatra, 193-94, 203
Clive, Robert, 37
Cobden, Richard, 129-30
Colebrooke-Cameron Commission, 96
Colenso, Bishop, 95
Colin-Thomé, Percy, 33-34
Colombo Academy, 135, 140, 145-47, 149,165
Comaroff, John, 195
Conrad, Joseph, 192
Cooke, Fanny, 67
Coomaraswamy, Ananda, 264-65
Coomaraswamy, Muttu, 146, 160, 264
Coomaraswamy, P, 265
Cooray, Gerald, 266
Corbusier, Le, 237
Corn Laws, 129, 144
Cornwallis, Lord, 91
Couperus, Louis, 35
Cousins, Margaret, 276
Coward, Noel, 200

D

D'Abreu, Dr 225
D'Oyly, John, 76
da Costa, Dr Emmeline, 225
Dalrymple, William, 38, 40, 91, 102, 197-99
Daly, J. Bowes, 173
Dange, S.A. 235
Darwin, Charles, 86, 95, 146, 155, 172
Das Gupta, R. K. 100, 120
Das Gupta, Partha, 277
Das Gupta, Mary Ann, 113, 120
Datta-Ray, Sunanda, 287
Davie, Major Adam, 76
de Abrew, William, 268
de Almeida, Lourenco, 21
de Alwis, James, 128, 146, 155, 160-61
de Alwis, Malathi, 208, 252, 255
de Boer, Dr Alice, 223-25
de Fonseca, Catherina Petronella, 152, 266
de Kretser, Michelle, 51, 81, 283, 287
de la Nerolle, Laisne de Nanclair, 34
de Livera, Dr John, 264

de Mel, Bishop Lakdasa, 263
de Mel, Helena, 268
de Mel, Henry, 268
de Mel, Neloufer, 234, 252, 256-57
de Meuron, Colonel Charles Daniel, 32-3
de Pisan, Christine, 213, 236
de Rosairo, Beryl, 266
de Roze, G.A.W. 120
de Saram Balthazar, 261
de Saram, Elizabeth, 262
de Saram, Rev. Hendrick , 261
de Seixas, Lancarote, 24
de Serpa, Gaspar Figueira, 25
de Silva, Agnes Nell, 15, 230-34, 267, 269
de Silva, Alfreda, 227
de Silva, Anil, 230-34, 267
de Silva, C.R. 24, 36
de Silva, Catherine, 262
de Silva, George E. 230, 233, 267, 269
de Silva, John, 256-57
de Silva, Mervyn, 190
de Silva, Minnette, 230, 234, 236-37
de Silva, Dr R.K. 166
de Soysa, Charles, 262
de Soysa, J.S. Walter, 262
de Soysa, Jr, E.L.F. 263
de Soysa, Victor, 263
de Vos, Pam, 266
de Vos, F.H. 59
de Zilwa, Dr Lucien, 64
de Zoysa, A.P. 257, 268
de Zoysa, Sidney, 266
Dekker, Eduard Douwes, 88
Delacroix, Eugene, 192
Delft, 77-78
Denham, E.B. 44, 86, 219
Deraniyagala, Ezlynne, 262,
Derozians, 115, 152, 242
Derozio, Francis, 103
Derozio, Henry, 8, 14, 93, 100-126 (Chapter 5), 149, 163, 284
Derozio, Michael, 93, 103
Desai, A.R. 120
Descent of Man, The 95
Devendra, D.T. 269
Dhanapala, Jayanta, 266
Dharmapala, Anagarika, 219, 240, 244, 249-51, 258, 269, 270
Dharrumtollah Academy, 118-19
Dias Bandaranaike, Amy, 267
Dias Bandaranaike, Sir Solomon, 267
Dickens, Charles, 147, 165, 232
Dickman, Phyllis, 266
Diderot, Denis, 188
Digby, William, 30, 33, 62, 69, 79, 135, 145, 149, 241
Dissanayake, S.A. (Jingle), 266
Don Carolis, Charles, 263
Don Carolis, C.Godwin, 263
Don Carolis, W, 263
Douglas, Mary, 4, 207-208, 250
Dover, Cedric, 50, 200
Drieberg, Alfred, 152, 215
Drieberg, C, 166
Drieberg, Hetty, 216
Drummond, David, 103
Drummond's, Academy, 104
Duff, Alexander, 110
Dufferin, Lord , 224
Dufferin, Lady Dufferin Fund, 224
Dumas, Alexandre, 196-97
Dupleix, Joseph-Francois, 197
Dutch Burgher Union, 52, 59-60, 162
Dutch East India Company, 29-34, 41, 52, 239, 262
Dutt, Rajani Palme, 277, 280
Duval, Jeanne, 195-96

E

East India Company (British), 37-38, 47, 90, 93, 132, 260
East Indian, The 117-118
East Indians' Petition to Parliament, 124
East, Dorothy, 268
Eaton, John Henry, 161
Eden, Fanny, 75
Edwards, Thomas, 103, 117-21
Eisler, Benita, 114, 126, 189
Elgin, Lord, 114
Elhart, Maureen, 266
Eliade, Mircea, 200
Elliot, Dr Christopher, 93, 132-36, 138-39, 141-42, 147-48, 168
Engelbrecht, Henry, 204
Engels, Friedrich, 87, 96, 126, 130, 176
Enlightenment, The 87, 95, 101, 106, 146, 151, 212, 245-46, 283-84
Episcopalian, 156-57, 170

Ernst, Alice Harriet, 179
Ernst, Emilia, 169
Ernst, Henrietta, 163
Examiner, 154-55, 158, 164, 168

F

Fabians, 172
Faiz, Ahmad Faiz, 276
Falkland, Viscountess Amelia, 68
Felsianes, Clarice Ruth, 269
Female Seminary, 216
Ferdinands, Charles, 94, 149-50
Fernando, Pinsiripal 'Pin', 266
Ferrar, Major M.L. 76-77
Fichte, J.G. 3, 246-47
Fonseka, Ben, 266
Fonseka, J.V. 268
Foot, Michael, 115, 126
Foote, G.W., 95
Forbes, Major, 241
Forster, E.M. 199-200
Fortescue, Sir John, 90
Fourier, Charles, 96, 99
free press, 127, 132, 134, 154
free speech, 172
free trade, 129-30, 132, 260
freethought, 86, 146, 172
French Revolution of 1789, 8-9, 14, 98, 101, 104, 106, 114, 146
French Revolution of 1830, 108,129, 146
French Revolution of 1848, 130-31, 136-37, 146
Freud, Sigmund, 19
Friends of Ceylon 141
Fröebel School, 227-28, 238

G

Gaikwad, V.R. 22, 46, 48, 50-51, 78-9, 102
Galland, Antoine, 187
Gandhi, Indira, 231, 236
Gandhi, Mahatma, 231
Gandhi, Priyanka, 278
Gandhi, Rahul, 278
Gantzer, Colleen & Hugh, 81-82, 206
Gardiner, Cyril, 266
Gardner, Ava, 202
Gauguin, Paul, 192-93, 213
geisha, 193-94
General Cemeteries Bill, 157
Gerlitz, Edward Theodosius, 67
Ghose, Ramgopal, 111
Ghosh, Indira, 68-69, 191
Ghosh, Kasiprasad, 108
Gill, Anton, 259
Girton College, Cambridge, 214, 227
Gladstone, William, 143-44
Glenie, O.S. Rev 158
Goans, 4, 27, 177, 220-1, 225, 240
Gobineau, J.A. 192
Godlieb, Dora, 233
Godlieb, Dr E.S. 233
Godwin, William, 213
Gogerly-Moragoda family, 267
Gogerly, Rev. D.J. 267
Goldsbrough, Elsie, 264
Goldsmith, Jemima, 277
Gombrich, Richard, 251-52
Good Shepherd Convent, Jaffna, 156-57, 170
Good Shepherd Convent, Kandy, 57, 67, 239
Goodrick-Clarke, Nicholas, 245-6
Gooneratne, Dandiris, 150
Gooneratne, Yasmine, 146, 267
Goonesinha, A.E. 95, 179, 233
Goonetilleke, Sir Oliver, 266
Goonewardena, Karl, 22
Gottschalk, Ellen, 275
Government Gazette, 124
Graham, Dorothy, 276
Gratiaen, Doris, 236
Greece, 114-16
Gregory, Lillian, 263
Grenier, Samuel, 154
Gulamhussein, Onally, 264
Gunasekara, Goolbai, 238, 276
Gunawardana, R.A.L.H. (Leslie), 247
Gunawardena, Gamini (Kuru), 269
Gunawardena, Kusuma, 269
Gunawardena, Lakmali, 269
Gunawardena, Philip, 269
Gunawardena, Prasanna, 269
Gunewardene, Dr H.O. 268
Gymroi, Edith, 279

H

Hamer, Jennifer, 266
H.W. Cave & Co., 176
Hare, David, 104
Harper, Margaret, 268
Harris, Elizabeth, 76, 267
Harrison, R.L. 265
Hassan Ali, Mrs Meer, 275
Hastings, Warren, 37
Hawes, C.J. 21-22, 39, 73-75, 91, 102-103,
Heath, Clara, see Motwani
Heber, Bishop, 91, 99
Helen, (Richardson), 208
Hensman, C.R. 266
Hepponstall, Mabel, 263
Hermon, William Outram, 221
Hesperus, 105, 117
Higgins, Marie Musaeus, 255
Hikmet, Nazim, 189, 211
Hindu College, 105, 107, 110-111, 117
Hindu Pioneer, 111
Hitler, Adolf, 248, 271
Hoban, Jeanne, 269,
Hobbes, Thomas, 87
Hobsbawm, Eric, 87, 131
Hobson Jobson, 26
Hotel Metropole, 222
Hubbard, William, 41
Hume, David, 87, 94, 104, 106, 126
Hume, Joseph, 130, 132, 139, 141-42, 144
Hutton, Eleanor, 268
Huxley, Thomas, 171
Hyam, Ronald, 65

I

Independent Catholic, 176-78
India Gazette, 105, 113
Indian Communist Party, 235
Indian Enlightenment, 104
Indian National Congress, 231
Indian Peoples' Theatre Association, 235
Ireland, 86, 97, 114, 134, 138-39, 172-73
Israel, Jonathan, 284
Italy, 114-115,129
Ives, Colta & Stein, Susan Alyson, 193

J

Jackson, Dr Corinne, 266
Jamaica, 86, 93
James, C.L.R. 28, 89-90
Jansz, Norah 221
Jayasuriya, Kanishka, 244
Jayawardena, Dr Peter, 266
Jayawickrama, Sarojini, 5, 34
Jesuits, 27
Jews, 21, 31, 36, 221, 228, 246, 249, 271, 279
Jinarajadasa, C, 276
Joachim, Marina, 266
John Bull, 118
Johnson, Arthur, 104, 112
Johnston, Sir Alexander, 124, 140, 149, 241
Jones, Nora, 278
Jump, J.D. 114

K

Kabbani, Rana, 77, 185, 187-88, 192-94, 196
Kandy Arts and Crafts Society, the, 230
Kant, Immanuel, 106, 246
Kapferer, Bruce, 250
Kapoor, Shashi, 277
Kashfi, Anna, 203
Kaul, Ranjana, 82, 206, 209
Keats, John, 9, 110
Keble, W.T, 78
Kendall, Jennifer, 277
Keuneman, Arthur Eric, 179
Keuneman, Pieter, 179-80, 279-80
Keyt, George, 166, 235
Khair un-Nissa, 197
Khan, Imran, 277
Kiernan, V.G. 187
Kipling, Rudyard, 1, 48, 192, 245,
Kirkpatrick, James, 197
Kirkpatrick, Katherine, (Kitty) 197-98
Knighton, William, 65-6
Knox, Captain Robert, 25, 40-41, 256, 286
Koch, Henrietta, 216
Kousbroek, Rudy, 55
Krishnamurti, J, 276
Kularatne, Hilda, 268, 271, 280

Kularatne, Patrick de S. 268, 270, 271
Kunzru, Hari, 38-40, 51, 78, 206, 287
Kureishi, Hanif, 287
Kyd, James, 124

L

L'Ouverture, Toussaint, 89
Lady Havelock Women's Hospital, 223
Lahiri, Ramtanu 108, 111
Lakminipahana, 155
Lanka Sama Samaja Party, (LSSP), 61
Lawrence, William McClean, 54
Le Carré, John, 200-201
Lee, Lionel, 43
Lee, Mother Ann, 92
Leembruggen, Dr W.E. 229
Leembruggen, Robert, 170, 216
Leigh, Vivien, 8, 202-203
Leitch, George E. 67
Levellers, 96, 160
Lim, Catherine, 209
'Little England,' 67- 68, 77
Liverpool, Lord, 39
Lobo, Patricia, 221
Locke, John, 87, 106
London School of Medicine for Women, 214, 224
Loos, Dr James, 223-24
Lorenz, Charles, 12, 14, 33, 88, 115, 143, 145-170 (Chapter 6), 179, 215, 217-18, 228, 237, 284
Lorenz, Eleanor, 12, 152, 215, 218, 228-29
Lorenz, Harriet, 215
Lorenz, Johan Friedrich Wilhelm, 33, 147, 159
Loretto Convents, 225
Loti, Pierre, 189-90, 211
Ludovici, Leopold, 12, 150, 155, 162-64, 179, 228
Ludowyk, E.F.C. 34, 42, 181, 271, 279
Ludowyk, Julien Edema, 181

M

Macan Markar, Alavi & Farida, 264
Madge, E.W. 121
Madras Mail, 69
Maetsuyker, Governor Johan, 31
Mahamaya Girls' College, 226
Maino, Sonia, 275
Malalasekera, G.P. 268, 280
Malcolm, Sir John, 97, 123
Mallik, Madhab Chandra, 107
Mallik, Rasikkrishna, 107, 111
Marg, 235
Marshall, Alfred, 171
Marshall, Priscilla, 220
Marshall, Ruth, 220, 226
Marx, Karl, 86, 95-96, 99, 130
Mason, Richard, 201
Masters, John, 48, 51, 202, 272
Matisse, Henri, 192
Maugham, Somerset, 201
Mazzini, Joseph, 115, 129, 135
McCallum, Governor, 259
McCarthyism, 235, 279
McChristie,T.Y. 132
McDonald, Ramsay, 231
McGilvray, Dennis, 26, 31, 33, 42, 59
Meade, Carol, 277
Meedeniya, Kamini, 62
Meegama, Indrani, 226
Melbourne Art Classes, 227
Mendis, G.C. 97
Menon, K.P.S. 67
Mercantile Mutual Provident Association, 175
Mernissi, Fatema, 188, 192, 194
Methodists, 92
Mies, Maria, 1, 99
Mill, John Stuart, 167,191
Miller, Rhoda, 279
mischmaschvolk, 4, 239, 248, 285
Mitra, Kishorichand, 109
Mitra, Pearychand, 104-105, 111
Moldrich, Donovan, 43, 49, 54, 60,62
Molière, 213, 257
Molligoda, J.R. 171
Montagu, Lady Mary, 191
Montesquieu, Charles de 87, 188
Moonesinghe, Anil, 269
Moonesinghe, Mangala, 269
Moosajee, H.S. & Zarina, 264
Morgan, Richard, 8, 54, 140-144
Morley, John, 114
Motoe, Kunio, 193
Motwani, Clara, 238, 276
Motwani, Kewal, 238, 276

Mukherji, Dhakshinaranjan, 111
Muller, Carl, 7, 10, 79-81, 206-207, 272, 287
Muller, Daphne, 266
Müller, J.B. 36, 82
Müller, Max, 247-48
Musaeus College, 255, 268, 270

N

Naidu, Sarojini, 231
Nandy, Ashis, 242, 257
Napoleon, Bonaparte, 90, 114, 196
National Women's Suffrage Society, 214
Nazism, 245-46
Nederburgh, J.A. 6
Nehru Jawaharlal, 231
Nell, Dr Andreas, 12, 229, 237
Nell, Dr Winifred, 223, 229-30
Nell, Frederick, 8, 115, 149-55, 214, 229
Nell, Louis, 115, 149, 154-45, 229
Nell, Paul, 230
Neruda, Pablo, 203-205
Newnham College, Cambridge, 214
'*New Woman*,' 210, 212, 222, 228, 253
Nivedita, Sister, 255, 257
Nolan, Lieutenant, 78
Nursing School, 223

O

O'Brien, Bronterre, 139
O'Connor, Fergus, 139
Oberon, Merle, 8, 202
Obeyesekere, Christoffel, 262, 267
Obeyesekere, Forrester, 262
Obeyesekere, Gananath, 251-52
Ochterlony, Sir David, 38
Olcott, Colonel Henry, 247
Oliphant, Lawrence, 132, 142
Ondaatje, Christopher, 204
Ondaatje, Michael, 55, 236
Orabi Pasha, Ahmed, 115
Orientalists, 4, 186, 189, 191-95, 237, 286
Origin of Species, On the 95, 155
Orphanages, Military, 74-75, 102, 122
Owen, Robert, 96, 99, 114

P

Padamse, Akbar, 277
Padmanabha, A. 265
Padmanabha, Jayanta, 265
Paine, Thomas, 87, 94-95, 106, 150-51
Palmer, General William, 38
Palmer, Mary, 38
Pan-German League, 248
Parker, Henry Meredith, 108
Parks, Fanny, 191, 211
Partridge, Ethel, 264
Patalia, Maharajah of, 259
Paynter, Arnold, 70-71
Paynter, Arthur, 68, 70, 72, 267
Paynter, David, 71, 268
Paynter, Evangeline, 71
Paynter Homes, 70-72, 239
Pearce, F.Gordon, 277
Pegg, Rev. James, 93
Peiris, Watson, 268
Pembroke College, Cambridge, 179-80
Pereira, Alexius, 7-8, 23, 33
Peterson, Dr. P.R.C. 60
Pettah Buddhist Boy's School, 174
Pettah Library, 217
Philips, Amali, 49-50
Pieris, Jeronis, 69
Pieris, Paul, 24-25, 261
Pieris, Varuni , 268
Pinto, Dr P.M. Lisboa, 177-79, 221
Pinto, Jerry, 208
Pitt, William, 37
Plumb, John H. 20, 36
Poddar, Arabinda, 116-17
Poliakov, Léon, 27, 246-49
Post, Ken, 93
Powell, Geoffrey, 73-74, 76
Prawer, Ruth, 277
Presbyterian, 155-57, 170
Presidency College, 104
Prestage, Edgar, 27
public intellectuals, 12, 129, 281, 283
Public Services Mutual Provident Association, 175
Puran Appu, 134

Q

Quakers, 92, 129, 144
Quarter-Mile Clause, 174
Quill, The, 111

R

Rajasinha II, King, 29
Ram, N. 277
Ramanathan, Sir Ponnambalam, 231, 265
Ranaraja, P.R. 233
Ranasinghe, A.G. 45, 273
Ranasinghe, Anne, 279
Ratnaike, Dr May, 223, 264
Raza, S.H. 277
Rebellion of 1848, (Sri Lanka), 148
Reform Bill, 113, 129
Revolutions of 1848 in Europe, 131, 136, 138
Reynst, Governor-General, 31
Richardson, Alice, 264-65
Ricketts, John, 14, 47, 93, 97, 118, 121-25, 149
Rights of Man, 94-95, 151
Risorgimento, 115, 129
Rizal, José, 88
Road Ordinance, 133, 140
Roberts, Emma, 108
Roberts, Michael, 2, 22, 26, 45, 58, 69, 145, 151-53, 164, 207-208, 250, 262
Roberts, Norah, 221
Rodgers, Bertha Irene,54, 225-26
Roosmalecocq, Andrew, 158
Rothschild, Emma, 277
Rousseau, 87, 106
Roversi, Signor Eduardo, 267
Rowbotham, Sheila, 3
Rowlands, A.P. 263
Rowlands, Christobel, 263
Roy M.N. 275
Roy, Rammohun, 101, 112, 120,
Royal Asiatic Society, 12, 164, 174
Roychowdhury, Laura, 46, 67-8, 78
Runstein, Dona Luisa, 265
Rushdie, Salman, 210, 281, 283, 287
Russell, Jane, 232, 234
Russell, Margaret, 268, 280
Rutnam, Dr Mary, 218, 265
Rutnam, S.C.K, 265

S

Said, Edward, 186-87, 191, 258
Salie, Mohamed Yusuf, 263
Salvation Army, 70
Samarasinghe, Gate Mudaliyar Douglas, 263
Samarasinghe, Mahinda, 263
San Domingo, St Domingo (Haiti and the Dominican Republic), 86, 89-90
Sangamitta School, 174
Sarachchandra, Ediriweera, 269
Saravanamuttu, Manickam, 266
Saravanamuttu, Neysum, 233
Saravanamuttu, T, 266
Sarkar, Sumit, 107, 109-10, 112-13
Sarkar, Susobhan, 104-5, 107-8, 110-111, 120, 125
Sastri, Sivanath, 108
sati, 101, 112-13
Scharff, Cornelia, 262
Scharff, Susanna, 279
Scheherazade, 188-89, 193
Schenkel, Emilie, 276
Schwab, Raymond, 189
Scottish Enlightenment, 103
Searchlight, The 235
secularism, 86, 94-95, 125, 146, 155-58, 172
Selby, John, 132, 135, 154
Sen, Amartya, 277
Sen, Dinesh Chandra, 109
Sen, Indrani, 5-6, 201
Senanayake, Dr I.A. 266
Senanayake, Ratna Deshapriya, 266
Senanayake, Senake, 266
Sengupta, Pallab, 101, 106, 121
Seth, Dr Shanti Behari, 277
Seth, Vikram, 277
Shakers, 92
Sharpe, Sam, 93
Shaw, Bernard, 172
Shelley, Percy Bysshe 9, 107, 126
Shergil, Amrita, 278
Sikh revolts, 136
Silva, Neluka, 207
Silva, Simon, 162
Silvaf, Hippolyte, 165
Simon, Hedi, 279
Singapore, 26, 45-46, 51-53, 209
Singili Nona, 256-7
Sinha, Mrinalini, 259-60

Sirisena, Piyadasa, 10, 207-208, 250, 255, 270
Siriwardena, Regi, 126, 239
Sirr, H.C. 199
Sitwell, Osbert, 186
slavery, abolition of, 92, 111, 124, 126, 140
Smedley, Agnes, 275
Smith, Adam, 36, 104
Socialist Labour League, 61
Somasunderam, Dr S. 266
Specx, Governor General Jaques, 30
Spinola, Fr Ardizone, 28
Spivak, Gayatri, 191, 242-43
Sri Nissanka, H. 269
St Aloysius' College, Galle, 181, 257
St John's College, Cambridge, 171
St Thomas' College, 65, 170-71, 173
St. Simon, Count Henri, 96, 99
Stark, H.A. 85, 90-91, 97, 121-25
Steel, Flora Annie, 201
Stimpson, Catherine, 188
Stoler, Ann Laura, 3, 6, 68, 131
Strachey, Lytton, 198, 203, 265
Stubbs, R.E. 259
Sulieri, Sara, 278, 287
Sunderam, Vivan, 278
Suyin, Han, 205-206
Swan, Pauline, 266

T

Tagore, Rabindranath, 117, 120, 242-43
Tahiti, 193
Tambiah, S.J. 266
Tata, J.R.D. 277
Tata, Naval, 27
Taylor, James, 62
Tennant, James, Emerson, 135, 139-40, 42
Thackeray, William, 147, 159, 217
Thapar, Raj, 235
Thapar, Ramesh, 235
Thapar, Romila, 235, 248
Theosophy, 86, 172, 245-47
Thomas, Aseline, 230
Thompson, George, 111
Thompson, William, 161
Thuppahi, Topass, 26, 32, 42, 58, 85, 239, 241
Todorov, Tzvetan, 188, 190
Toer, Pramoedya Ananta, 207
Torgovnik, Marianna, 189
Tories, 111, 130, 135, 143
Torrington, Lord, 65, 93, 97-98, 127, 130, 133,135-37, 139-40, 143
Toussaint, Yvonne, 264
Trent, Evelyn, 275
Treyne, Gilberto, 27
Trimmer, Ina, 221
Tristan, Flora, 213
Tuominen, Tula, 265
Turner, L.J.B. 37, 44

U

untermensch, 3, 245
Utopian Socialists, 86, 96-97, 99, 101, 99, 112-14, 126

V

Valentia, Viscount, 5, 90-91
Valignano, Fr Alexandre, 27
van den Vondel, Joost, 29
van der Poorten, A.J. 61-62, 221
van der Poorten, Emily 221
van der Poorten, Antoine (Tony), 61
van der Poorten, Michael, 61-62
van Dort, Dr Claribel, 223
van Dort, Dr W.G. 59, 169
van Dort, Grace, 165, 221
van Dort, J.L.K.(John), 164-65, 221
van Goens,Governor Rijkloff, 31, 34
van Schagen, Linda, 81
'Verandah Question', 141
Vidyasagar, 120
Vigier, Dr Philippe, 235
Villiers, Sir Thomas, 72
Visakha Vidyalaya, 270
Visuddi Magga, 174
Vivekananda, Swami, 120
Voltaire, 87, 94, 106
von Possner, Arthur Kurt, 267
vrij burgher, 31, 41

W

Walker, Lily Margaret, 268
Wall, George, 160-61
Wallace, Edgar, 48
Wallace, Kenneth E. 9

Wallerstein, Emmanuel, 19, 23, 32
Ward, Sir Henry, 160
Webb, Sidney, 172
Weber, Max, 32
Weerasinghe, Lionel, 268
Weerasooriya, Agnes, 70, 267
Weerasooriya, Arnolis, 70
Weerawardena, I.D.S. 266
Weinman, J.R. 145
Wendt, Lionel,166
Weslyan Mission Girls' School, 217
Westbrook, Hilda, see Kularatne
Whig, 110, 113-14, 130
Wickremasinghe, Doreen, 238, 268
Wickremasinghe, Dr S.A. 268
Wijesekera, Dr. R.O.B. 266
Williamson, Thomas, 40
Wirasekera, Dr Verona, 220
Wollstonecraft, Mary,87, 212
Women's Education Society, 174
Women's Franchise Union, 231-32, 255
women's rights, 112, 172, 214-18
Woolf, Leonard, 56-57, 190, 203-204, 265
Wordsworth, William, 89, 107, 152
Wright Lorna, 64, 71
Wright, E.B. 57-58

Y

Young Bengal, 88, 93, 100-101, 109-10, 112-13, 115, 149, 152, 242
Young Ceylon, 88, 94, 98, 140, 144-45, 148-49, 150-53, 155, 163,165, 179, 198, 214-17, 229
Young Ireland, 98, 138
Young Java, 98
Young, Doreen, see Wickremasinghe
Young, Robert, 4, 192

Portuguese Kaffiringha dancers. Design for a Christmas card, (1870s), by John L.K. van Dort. From *The Near Past*.